Hamlet Clark

Monograph of Halticidae in the Collection of the British Museum

Physapodes and Oedipodes Part I

Hamlet Clark

Monograph of Halticidae in the Collection of the British Museum
Physapodes and Oedipodes Part I

ISBN/EAN: 9783337218348

Printed in Europe, USA, Canada, Australia, Japan

Cover: Foto ©ninafisch / pixelio.de

More available books at **www.hansebooks.com**

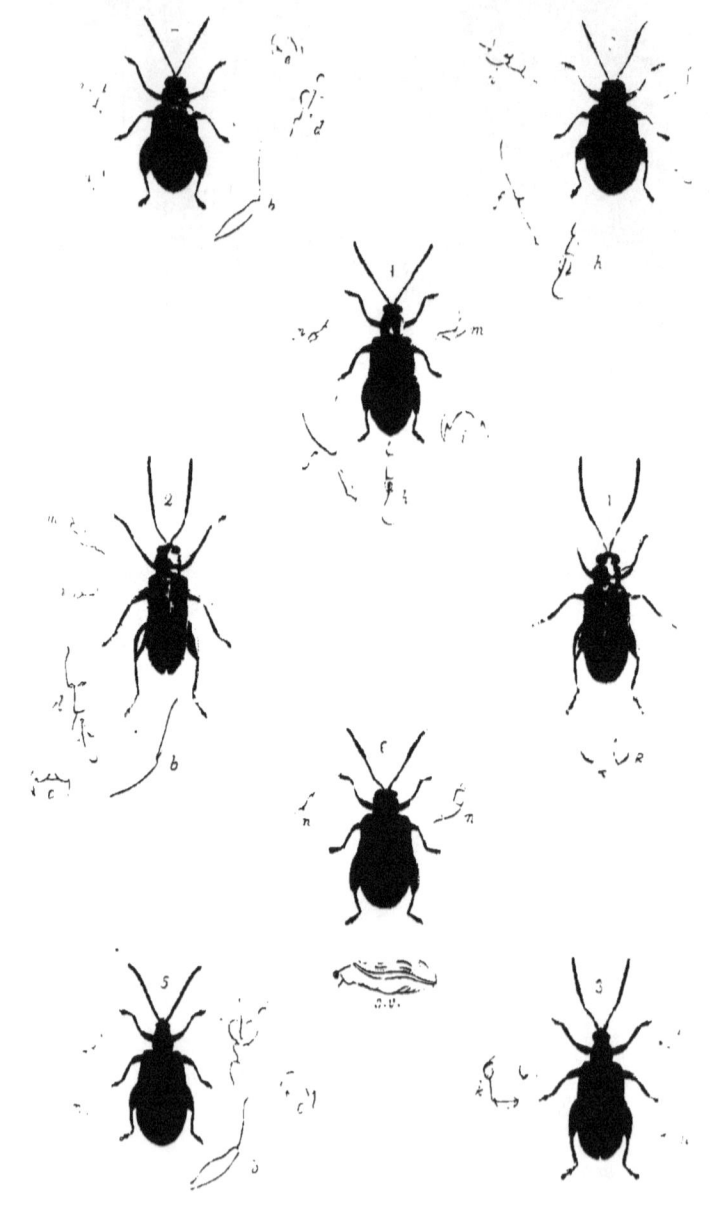

MONOGRAPH

OF

HALTICIDÆ

IN THE

COLLECTION

OF THE

BRITISH MUSEUM.

BY

THE REV. HAMLET CLARK, M.A., F.L.S.

PHYSAPODES AND ŒDIPODES.

PART I.

LONDON:
PRINTED BY ORDER OF THE TRUSTEES.
1860.

PREFACE.

This Catalogue contains descriptions of the species of Physapodous and Œdipodous HALTICIDÆ in the British Museum Collection, and of the species of the group which are contained in other Collections, showing the desiderata.

In the "Introductory Remarks" the Rev. Hamlet Clark has given an account of the group, and the object of the Catalogue.

JOHN EDWARD GRAY.

August 15, 1860.

INTRODUCTORY REMARKS.

During the winter of 1856 it was my fortunate lot to visit, in company with my friend John Gray, Esq., the country of Brazil. Several months were spent by us in travelling through parts of the province of Rio Janeiro. Our journey was undertaken with the simple object of seeing with our own eyes those glories of Nature, of which Mansfield and Kingsley, and especially Humboldt, have so graphically written, and of investigating (so far as such a brief visit would permit us) the insect life of the tropics; and, truly, the reality far surpassed even our sanguine expectations. Everything that we saw was to us not only new, but of surpassing beauty; forest and sea-shore, bare rock and grassy glade, all seemed as fairy-land, and this fairy-land marvellously teemed with life. At the present moment, the recollections of that visit, even amidst the comforts of an English home, and the great interest that attaches to the daily work of a Clergyman, leave only the sincere regret that it was necessarily so brief, and therefore so unproductive, comparatively, of practical results. For any one who has time and opportunity at his disposal, and who has in any degree an appreciation of the beauties of the works of the Great Creator, I know of no expedition that would be more full of interest or more profitable than a visit to this, or some similar subtropical or tropical region: the influence of such a visit must be healthy; it is intensely humbling, and at the same time, and for the same reason, invigorating.

To our short visit to Brazil this Monograph owes its origin. When, on our return to England, we endeavoured to ascertain what had been already done by former travellers in systematizing the Insect Fauna of that continent, it was very soon apparent that nearly every group of the Coleoptera of those regions (to which Order we confined our attention, as far as collecting went) was almost entirely unexplored ground. The public museums and private cabinets of Europe, however rich many of them are in species, possess the examples of most of those species unnamed, and often unarranged, and are in consequence of but (comparatively) little practical use in assisting the student; hence I resolved, at the suggestion of Dr. Gray, of the British Museum, to seek to reduce into systematic order some one of the groups that during our journey had especially attracted our attention. I selected, as one of the most interesting in beauty and variety of forms, as well as from being hitherto almost entirely neglected (but without any apprehension of the serious difficulties that such a subject would involve), a division of the HALTICIDÆ (a subgroup of the section of PHYTOPHAGA).

The present volume is the commencement of the work that I thus proposed to myself; it contains part of the first two divisions of that group, proposed by Illiger (Mag. für Insekt., Sechster Band, 1807), and consists of a classification and descriptions not only of the species of the section that are contained in the British Museum, but also of those existing in the cabinets of MM. Chevrolat, Deyrolle, Dohrn, and Lacordaire, as well as of Messrs. Baly, Bates, Fry, J. Gray, Miers, Murray, Waterhouse, and my own. The great kindness and liberality of these gentlemen has enabled me to describe in the present volume forty-two genera, consisting of 245 species.

With regard to the geographical stations of these species, one only is known from the kingdom of Chili; 136 are found in the regions of Brazil south of the Amazon (6 of these are insular, one being from the Island of St. Catherine, and 5 from the Island of St. Paul); 65 are found in the basin of the River Amazon (between the Delta and Peru), while the part of the continent north of the Amazon Basin furnishes 27 (of which the district round Cayenne supplies 11, Venezuela 6, New Granada 4, and Columbia 6). Six species are found in Mexico and the south of North America, one insular species (*Ædmon sericellum*) being indigenous to Porto Rico. In addition to these, 3 species are found in other countries of North America—one in Pennsylvania, and 2 in Philadelphia. Three species only are found in Africa—one (*Eutornus Africanus*) at Sierra Leone, one (*Physonychis smaragdina*) in Senegal, and a third (*Lithonoma Africana*) near Tangiers; two only are found in Europe (*Lithonoma cincta*,

Fab., and *L. Andalusiaca*, Rosenh.); and three others are, as to their localities, doubtful.

It thus appears that of the species contained in this volume,

South America produces	228
North America	9
Africa	3
Europe	2
Doubtful	3
	245

and Asia and Australia none.

Owing to the comparative rarity of all the species here described, and consequently the paucity of them in collections, it is not easy to assign to each its distinct geographical range; very few appear to be widely distributed; each seems to have but the basin of a single river, or one single island on the coast, or one range of mountains as its sole locality; and it is interesting to observe that the range of the *genera* as well as that of the individual species appear to be (as a rule) equally circumscribed. For example, the beautiful genus *Monoplatus* has as yet been found only on the Organ Mountains and in the neighbourhood of Rio Janeiro*; the very distinct form of *Cerichrestus* is met with only in the north of that continent, the Amazon, and Cayenne; the two European species of the genus *Lithonoma*, found in Spain and Portugal, are closely allied to each other; and although a third species of this genus has been discovered in Africa, it was taken near Tangiers, on the immediately opposite coast of the Straits of Gibraltar.

On the other hand, however, instances are to be found where a single genus appears to have a *widely extended* range. The genus *Loxoprosopus* is represented in the province of Rio by *L. ceramboides*, while, in the far-distant region of the Amazon, other species that evidently belong to this same genus have been taken by Mr. Bates. In a case like this, we may reasonably infer that other species of the genus still have to be discovered in the vast central district of Brazil, which will unite together these species geographically.

* *M. semiviolaceus* is stated to be from Cayenne; but this, in my opinion, seems to require to be substantiated.

So far as we know, the southern and colder regions of the continent of South America, Patagonia, and the south of La Plata supply no representatives of the groups described in this volume*,— the limits of their distribution throughout the world being apparently, in the south, 32° or 34°, and in the north, 40°. The European species are found, as has been noticed, in the south of Portugal and Spain (that is, between the degrees of 36 and 38); although on one occasion I took examples of *Lithonoma cincta*, Fab., at Barquero, on the Asturian shores of the Bay of Biscay, in latitude 43° nearly†.

But between these limits the group would appear to be *generally distributed*; we have no reason to suppose the existence of any special numerical centre or centres; wherever the district has been examined, there species have been found to be indigenous, and the number of species discovered always bears a fair proportion to the amount of labour and patience that has been expended in research. Thus (and thus solely) we have more species from the neighbourhood of Rio Janeiro than from any other three or four localities united; not because the province of Rio is a focus where examples of this group especially abound, but because in other provinces we have not had the advantages of the residence of such zealous and able naturalists as Mr. Fry and Mr. Miers.

Thus, also, the district of the Amazon supplies to us, in this and other groups, more new genera and species than the districts of Bahia and Pernambuco; but only because we still have to find some one who, impelled by an earnest love of nature, will devote himself to the exploration of the basin of the San Francisco River with the same patient energy that has been manifested by Mr. Bates in his researches during many years in the district of the Amazon.

In considering, with reference to this group, the interesting question as to the probable amount of influence exercised by *tropical latitudes* on the size and the brilliancy of species, as contrasted with subtropical latitudes, our present very imperfect knowledge of the fauna of the Continent as a whole will not permit more than the

* In Chili, which ranges from 40° to 34°, a single species has been detected, *Hypolampsis melanotus*.

† The *isothermal line* of 43° in Spain, however, is the same as that of 36° N. in the United States.

adoption of general conclusions; the knowledge, however, that we possess, scant as it is with regard to many vast districts, completely bears out the rule that has been established in other groups of insects,—that while in tropical and in subtropical countries equally, small and dull-coloured species are found, it is for the most part in the tropics, properly so called, that (over and above these) large and splendidly marked species are to be met with. The genus of this group that of all others is distinguishable for brilliancy of clothing and coloration is *Octogonotes*; the species of this genus have been discovered only in the tropical north of S. America. The same rule applies (so far as we are able to fix the distinct regions of the species) with regard to the genus *Thrasygœus*; while, in Africa, the splendid *Physonychis smaragdina* is found only in Senegambia and Old Calabar (both within the tropics).

To this general rule, however, the genera before us supply two important exceptions: *Loxoprosopus ceramboides*, the largest species not only of the genus but of the whole group, has been found only on the southern limits of the tropics, and the handsome genus *Monoplatus* also is only to be met with in the same latitude, that of Rio Janeiro; these two examples (one of which is the example of a single specific form) are distinct exceptions to what appears to obtain as a very general law. With regard to the geographical range of the species of the vast genus *Œdionychis* (the subject of the second part), it may be urged that, in their case also, there is no inferiority of stature or coloration among the subtropical as contrasted with the tropical species. This may perhaps for the most part hold good; but in several instances at least, I believe that it may be shown that this, however *primâ facie* an apparent, is not a real exception; and that it will be seen, when that portion of the group is specially considered, that some (and probably many) of the brilliant species composing it, which certainly abound in subtropical latitudes, are merely local varieties of (if not almost identical with) species that are met with in tropical districts,—that is, that some species at least of the genus have, in their several local modifications, a range almost as extensive as the continent itself; a fact that we should, *à priori*, be led to expect from the *abundance* numerically of *individuals* of these species. Thus, there is a certain *parallelism of contrast* between this latter genus and the portion of the group now under consideration; for while, on the one hand, we have an actual paucity of examples (combined with comparative paucity of species) and a *limited* geographical range to each species,—on the other hand, we have abundance of examples (combined with abundance of so-called species) which occupy a very *extended* geographical range; that is, that there is in the latter case an all-pervading and powerful influence in favour of increase, which in the former seems to be wholly or almost entirely wanting. What may be the conditions and what the limits of this influence, why it affects the one and not the other group, we cannot now discuss; doubtless the question is as interesting as it is difficult: it is interesting because it is the investigation of a principle affecting all life; and it is difficult because our present means of knowledge are so scanty, and because it is so easy to fruitlessly dogmatize, and so *hard* to examine and in patience wait.

No travellers or collectors have given us any detailed information respecting the *habits* of these insects, either in their earlier stages or in their mature existence; it is probable that they pass the larva and pupa stages under conditions closely similar to those of the same group in Europe. Perty says of them (Delectus Anim. Artic. 1830, p. xvii), "*quoad mores, parum inter se differunt, pleraque plantas frequentant......*(p. xviii) *Halticæ in Brasilia copiosissime totum per annum æquali numero adsunt; magnitudine Europæas valde superant, moribus conveniunt. Pleræque in agmina congregantur, et copulationes hybridæ sæpissime observantur.*"

Lacordaire, in his valuable work on Subpentamerous Coleoptera (vol. i. p. xl), describes the general form of the larvæ of this group as, "iii. *Larves mineuses. Larves allongées, subcylindriques, atténuées à leurs deux extrémités, non mamelonées. Nymphes subissant leur métamorphose dans l'intérieur des feuilles où a vécu la larve, ou dans la terre.*—Altica."

In their perfect state, the insects of the group (as represented by the genus *Œdionychis*) are most abundant throughout the whole of Brazil. The traveller sees them flying across his path, or sunning themselves upon some leaf or flower; they may be taken readily by a sweeping-net, or an umbrella inverted, over which the branches of shrubs are beaten: this, as far as my experience goes, is the most effective method of securing specimens. There is, however (when once they are under the inspection of the collector), a manifest difference in the modes which they adopt to escape from danger. Some species seek for safety in flight, and use their wings as nimbly and aptly as a *Longicorn* or *Cicindela*; these are generally the brightly coloured species, such as those of the genera *Monoplatus* and *Œdionychis*, and doubtless *Octogonotes*; to these nature has given no protection but flight. Others seek protection by adopting a very different habit—they simulate death, and for some moments may be rolled over and over in the net or umbrella, to all appearance a mere dead bud, or atom of clay; they correspond, in their feigned lifelessness when captured, to the habits of *Chlamys*, *Lamprosoma*, and many genera of *Curculionidæ*: such are the habits of *Omototus* and *Homotyphus*.

In order that we may be able to examine the relationships and the different affinities of the members of this group *inter se*, it is necessary that we should first of all satisfy ourselves that its natural limits are clearly defined, and seek also to comprehend something of its position among, and connexion with, the other forms of the PHYTOPHAGA. What are its affinities? what are the forms that naturally compose it? and where ought they (with reference to others) to be placed? It is the more necessary to inquire into this, because, at the first contemplation of the forms comprising the proposed group, the species are anything but apparently cognate the one to the other. Such is the diversity of character, and want of similarity in external appearance, that we should be disposed, *primâ facie*, to intersperse them among other groups of the *Halticidæ*, or even, in some instances, to intercalate them among the *Eumolpidæ*. It is perhaps, however, hardly necessary to enter at length into the consideration of the question as to whether we should adopt the views of Fabricius, who broke up and separated the *Halticidæ* into other sections of PHYTOPHAGA (as *Galeruca* and *Chrysomela*), thus refusing to attach any value whatever to their saltatorial power; or whether the views adopted by Latreille and Illiger, and (to a great degree) by Lacordaire, are not the more sound, which, recognizing the saltatorial power as of some (though not of the highest degree of) importance, group together the species possessing it, as comprehending of themselves one distinct subsection of the PHYTOPHAGA.

This, the general question, we need hardly here consider, inasmuch as we have another and a more valuable character, which is common to all that portion of the *Halticidæ* that is the subject of this Monograph, *the globular and bladder-like inflation of the postical claw*. This, so far as we know, is a specialty affecting only this group of insects; it is unique, and seems not only to have (it may be) a greater value, as the basis of arrangement, than the incrassated posterior femora, but to possess sufficient importance to permit us, by means of it, to unite together forms of those saltatorial Halticidæ that in external facies are not otherwise than dissimilar the one to the other.

The thought at once suggests itself (if we have satisfied ourselves as to the soundness of this basis of arrangement), that if among these saltatorial Halticidæ we can discover a character (this globular inflation of the postical claw) which is sufficiently striking and permanent to bring together many different forms, included in the group, and which at the same time *does not introduce any single species* (from among the other sections of PHYTOPHAGA) *that does not possess this saltatorial power*, whether some *other* character may not be discovered among the *remaining* forms of Halticidæ *which is common to them, and to them alone*; and whether it does not, to some extent, supply an argument in favour of our seeking to unite together, as one subsection of the PHYTOPHAGA, all species, however dissimilar in form, that possess this saltatorial power. .

But to return to the more immediate subject before us: we believe that this globular inflation of the postical claw so far holds good as the basis of arrangement, that genera and species which possess it (although they may differ considerably *inter se* in general external form) are really, by means of it, more closely related to each other than they are to others which (with a greater appearance of resemblance) are deficient in this peculiar structure. When, however (having *satisfied* ourselves as to the questions, what are the *natural limits* of the group?, what forms ought to be included, and what excluded?), we begin to investigate *seriatim* the species from different countries that thus compose it, and seek to discover among them natural affinities and a natural sequence of arrangement, we find ourselves involved in some difficulty. A little examination, however, teaches us (as we should expect would be the case) that we can find important distinguishing characters in the length and dilatation of the antennæ, in the facies of the thorax, and especially in the form of the joints of the anterior tarsi and the form of the posterior tibia; these, when based upon, and considered in conjunction with another character (which is of more value even than they are), *the form of the palpi* (*especially the maxillary*), afford, we believe, characters amply sufficient for the establishment of well-defined genera. In the consideration of the different forms included in this Monograph, the only genus that has in its definition presented serious difficulties is the genus *Hypolampsis*; it contains within it at least three slightly but distinctly different forms—that of the first species (*H. melanotus*), from Chili, that of the first section of the genus, and that of the second section. Inasmuch, however, as the species of these latter groups* are not, in general form, absolutely constant *inter se*, I have, after much careful study and microscopic comparison, thought it better to unite (for the present at least) all together under one single genus, leaving the task of suggesting subdivisions to future students who shall have the advantage of a larger amount of materials. It is probable that other genera, as *Eupeges* and *Homamınatus*, will (when we know more of the insect life of the New World) also require subdivision.

I cannot conclude these preliminary remarks without expressing my sincere thanks to those of my friends who have supplied me, by the loan of examples from their cabinets, with materials for this work, and who have so patiently waited during what might have appeared to some of them an unnecessarily protracted interval for its completion, and the return of the examples which they entrusted to my care. I can only urge, in extenuation of any apparent delay, that the professional labours of a Clergyman in London are almost incessant, and that the subject itself has presented many formidable and unexpected difficulties. But, above all, my thanks are especially due to my valued friend John Gray, Esq., of Bolton-le-Moors:—to him,

* *Hypolampsis pilosa*, Ill., also represents another (North American) modification of form.

indeed, the merit of this Monograph (if any) is entirely owing; it was with him that I undertook the journey that originally suggested the work; he has, in furtherance of it, placed at my disposal all that I required of his valuable entomological library; and the least of his kindnesses has been the contribution of the Frontispiece to the volume, which contains figures of those species that were captured by ourselves during our excursion in Brazil.

It may be well perhaps to state (lest any one should suppose that time has been devoted to this work that might have been devoted to more important subjects) that the following pages have been entirely written during the early hours of the morning, before the serious business of the day has begun. I can testify to the fact that such studies are not merely not an impediment, but a congenial recreation and valuable aid: indeed that this is the case—that the study of Nature is not incompatible with graver pursuits—we have the high testimony of the illustrious Bacon; even he could find no wiser counsel than the following, to offer, as his parting words, to the students of his day:—

"Quamobrem et vos hortor, ut salvâ animi modestiâ, et erga veteres reverentiâ, ipsi quoque scientiarum augmentis non desitis; verum ut post volumina Sacra Verbi Dei, et Scripturarum, secundo loco volumen illud magnum operum Dei et creaturarum, strenuè, et præ omnibus libris (qui pro commentariis tantum haberi debent) evolvatis: Valete."

Ordo COLEOPTERA.

Sectio PHYTOPHAGA.

Fam. GALERUCIDÆ.

Subfam. HALTICARUM (femoribus posticis valde incrassatis) pars, continens *Illigeri* divisiones duas (*Mag. für Insektenkunde*, 1807, Sechster Band, p. 82).

"I. Familie, PHYSAPODES. Unguis posticus apice sursum globoso-inflatus; elytra temere punctata aut lævigata.
"II. Familie, ŒDIPODES. Unguis posticus apice sursum globoso-inflatus; elytra punctato-striata."

EUPODES, *Latreille*, *Règne Anim.* ed. 2. (1830) vol. v. p. 132 (English edition, p. xix and p. 134).
CHRYSOMÉLINES, *Dej. Cat. Col.* ed. 3. (1837) pp. 407–410.
 Genus *Octogonotes*, Drap., usque ad *Œdionychis*, Latr.
PHYTOPHAGES, *Lacordaire, Monogr. des Phytophages*, (1845) vol. i. pp. li, lii.

Corpus parvum, plerumque parallelo-oblongum, interdum etiam robustum aut globosum. Caput prominulum, aliquando porrectum. Palpi breves, aut filiformes aut incrassati; maxillaribus quadri- et labialibus tri-articulatis, ad basin sæpius occultatis. Oculi rotundati. Antennæ 11-articulatæ, art. 2° minuto, filiformes, aut ad apicem sive ad medium dilatatæ. Thorax plerumque inclinatus, ad latera marginatus et depressus. Scutellum triangulare, mediocre vel minutum. Elytra oblonga aut oblongo-ovata, interdum etiam rotundata aut gibbosa, plerumque læte colorata. Pedes validi, femoribus posticis valde incrassatis, tibiis rectis aut aliquando modice incurvatis; tarsis quadriarticulatis, art. ultimo ad apicem inflato, globoso; unguiculis bifidis, sæpius dente infra ad basin armatis.

Habitant in regionibus tropicis et subtropicis, præsertim in America meridionali; in foliis plantarum et arborum diversorum apricantes, et per vias sæpenumero volitantes.

TRIBUS I. *Palpi maxillares filiformes, articulo 3° haud dilatato, plus minus cylindrico, nunquam globoso, rarius quadrato.*

TRIBUS II. *Palpi maxillares ad apicem incrassati (articulo ultimo interdum minuto), art. 3° subgloboso aut transverso, nunquam elongato, rarius quadrato.*

TRIBUS I.

Genus 1. **MONOPLATUS***. (Front. figs. 1 & 2. Tab. I. figs. 1-4.)
Dej. Cat. ed. 3. 1837, p. 407.

Mandibulæ *robustæ, ad marginem inferiorem dentatæ.*
Palpi maxillares *subelongati ;* labiales *robusti.*
Antennæ *filiformes, art.* 1mo *et* 2^{ndo} *subdilatatis.*
Oculi *exstantes, globosi.*
Caput *leviter productum, antice subattenuatum, in* ♀ *transversum, latum, in* ♂ *constrictum.*
Thorax *transversus, angulis anticis subdepressis, lateribus marginatis, rectilinearibus, ad basin transverse foveolatus, impunctatus fere, et glaber.*
Elytra *sat lata, subcylindrica, ante medium plus minusve oblique depressa, punctato-striata plerumque, vel punctata ; sæpe colorata.*
Pedes *robusti ; tarsi anteriores breves, dilatati ; femora posteriora incrassata, oblique truncata ; tibiæ robustæ, longitudinaliter marginatæ, et apicem juxta dentatæ.*

Mas habet antennas longiores, caput brevius, oculos globosos et prominentes, elytra parallela subattenuata, tarsosque ad basin dilatatos.

Labrum transversely subrotundate.

Mandibles robust, deflected at the apex into a sharp, acute, double point; at the inner margin (immediately below the apex) is a single well-defined tooth, formed by a double depression in the surface.

Maxillary palpi (Front. figs. 1 *m* & 2 *m*) subelongate ; the second joint long, narrow, obliquely truncate; the third short, ovate; the apical joint longer than the second, and nearly as long as the third, subacute at its extremity.

Labial palpi (Front. figs. 1 *n* & 2 *n*): the first joint rounded at the apex; the second broad and short; the apical considerably narrower than the second, equal to it in length, and subacute.

Antennæ approximate, situated immediately below the inner margin of the eyes, tolerably robust, filiform ; in the males equal in length to that of the elytra, in the females shorter by one-third than the elytra ; the first joint broad, gradually dilated, and reflected outwards; the second short, ovate ; the third as long as the first, more attenuated than the second ; the fourth very slightly longer

---

* μόνος, solus ; πλατὺς, latus.

than, and similar in form to, the third; the rest somewhat shorter, subequal, oblong, the last (the terminal joint) being more elongate and subacute.

Eyes round, globular, prominent, not extending in either sex, laterally, so far as the anterior angles of the thorax; in the males situated at some little distance in front of, in the females immediately in front of, the base of the head.

Head (Front. fig. 1 a) slightly produced (not so distinctly as in *Rhinotmetus*) and subattenuate in front; in the males narrower and rather more elongate than in the females (in which it is broad and transverse).

Thorax broader than the head, transverse, rectangular; the anterior angles depressed, the sides rectilinear and marginate; at the base (apparent in every species) is a narrow transverse regular groove (running exactly parallel to the line of the margin), which terminates abruptly (before it reaches the posterior angles) by being deflected at right angles towards the basal line; the surface generally almost impunctate and glabrous.

Scutellum triangular, impunctate.

Elytra broader than the thorax, parallel, subcylindrical; in the females broader and much more robust than in the males; more or less transversely depressed from the antemedial suture towards the shoulders (by which an appearance of prominence is given to the part near the scutellum), punctate-striate or punctate, more or less distinctly; impubescent and brightly coloured.

Legs, in the males, longer and more robust than in the females. The *anterior femora* robust, subdilated medially, impubescent. The *tibiæ* straight, at the immediate apex incurved downwards, slightly thickened towards the base, truncate at their termination. The *tarsi* (Front. fig. 2 d) short; the basal joint broad and produced, broader than the apex of the tibiæ, ovate at the base and abruptly truncate at the apex; the second is minute, triangular and subelongate, in length not more than one-third of the basal joint, and in greatest breadth not one-half the breadth of the basal joint; the third joint is distinctly and broadly bilobed, in length not equal to the second joint, but transversely broader; the terminal joint is elongate, slender, slightly incurved, and gradually increasing in thickness towards its apex. The terminal claw (Front. fig. 2 e) is bifid and minute; the three basal joints are completely and densely fringed with thick pubescence. The *posterior femora* (Tab. I. fig. 1 f) are incrassated, extending in the males nearly to the apex of the abdomen; at the apex (at the insertion of the tibiæ) they are obliquely truncate. The *tibiæ* (Tab. I. fig. 3 g) are robust, straight, in length nearly equal to that of the femora; at the immediate base incurved downwards, and *gradually* more robust towards the apex: when seen obliquely, the surface throughout posteriorly is flattened, and raised on either side into two distinct marginations; on the *outer* margin near the apex are several spur-like prominences, giving the appearance of a coarsely-toothed saw; these projections (seen best when viewed obliquely from behind) are six or seven in number, becoming more distinct and frequent as they approach the base: immediately behind the last (the apical) in the margination, between this and the terminal incurved claw, is a short but abrupt ridge, which is armed with several closely disposed minute teeth; these are not only much more minute, but also more prominent, and acute, and closely arranged, than the projections in the margination. It is remarkable that this serrated emargination is only apparent in the *females*; in the males it is entirely wanting, or else represented merely by a little irregularity of outline. The insertion of the *tarsus* is at the apex of the tibia; immediately below the insertion are two incurved teeth, situated at the extreme apex of each of the lateral margins of the tibia: the *tarsus* (Tab. I. fig. 2*h*) is short; the basal joint is dilated, its breadth being greater even than that of the apex of the tibia, slightly carinated medially in its upper surface, and flat (in the females this joint is much narrower and more contracted, though of the same length as in the males); the second joint is elongate and narrower than the first, attenuated at the base and slightly tapering towards the apex; in both sexes this joint is of similar form; the third joint is shorter and somewhat broader, almost bilobed, and covered with a very fine and thick pubescence; the terminal joint (which is not so elongate as that of the anterior tarsi) is inflated at its extremity into a globular projection, which entirely covers, from above, the apical claw; the apical claw is minute, bifid, and armed at its inner surface with an almost obsolete tooth.

The sexual distinctions of this genus are striking and very interesting. I premise, however, that they are sexual (and not specific or generic) from the fact that, although during our collecting in Brazil we never succeeded in taking them *in copula*, both forms were taken together under the same circumstances, at the same times, and at the same different localities in the Organ Mountains. The antennæ in the *males* are longer, the head slightly smaller; the eyes are distinctly more prominent and globose; the body is much more narrow, cylindrical, and less robust; the legs are comparatively longer and more robust, and the basal joint of the tibiæ is very broadly dilated: these are sexual distinctions which we should expect to find in the male; but there is this peculiar characteristic in the female, that its posterior tibiæ are armed with series of tooth-like prominences, which are not only not so clearly developed, but are hardly traceable at all in the males.

To a greater or less extent in most of the *Halticæ* proper and *Longitarsi*, the enlargement of the basal joint of the tarsus (Front. fig. 2 a) holds good as a sexual characteristic. Sometimes this is only *faintly* expressed; thus in the European *Longitarsi* it may be traced distinctly, although *comparatively* obsolete. Mr. Wollaston finds the same sexual contrast in a Canarian species (*Longitarsus Kleiniiperda*, Woll.). In examples which I have received from him, the antical tibiæ (as well as the anterior tarsi) are dilated in the males; but the basal joint of the tarsi, although much *more prominent* than in European species, is considerably *less* developed than in the group before us—*Monoplatus*. Thus we find that in this instance at least, the sexual distinctions which obtain in a part of the same subfamily of insects, and which are *apparent* in the temperate zones, become more pronounced in the subtropical, and attain their *maximum* of difference in the representative group which is found in the regions nearer to the equator.

1. Monoplatus nigripes. (Tab. I. fig. 1.)

M. (♀) *oblongo-ovalis, subcylindricus, glaber, niger; capite brevi, depresso, antice inter oculos subtiliter foveolato, impunctato, flavo-ferrugineo; thorace quadrato, antice emarginato, ad basin transverse canaliculato, impunctato, flavo, nitido; elytris robustis, punctato-striatis, ad apicem subattenuatis, nigris, nitidis; antennis filiformibus, nigro-fuscis; pedibus nigris, femoribus anticis fusco suffusis.*

♀ Long. corp. 3 lin., lat. 1½ lin.

Oblong-ovate, robust, subcylindrical, impubescent, shining, black. *Head* short, depressed, not produced in front; the eyes are large, prominent, and black, situated at the base of the head, the distance between them being not greater than the diameter of either; above the base of the antennæ is an irregular medial depression; the surface is impunctate, shining, and rufo-ferruginous. *Thorax* broader than the head, transverse, and rectangular; the anterior margin is distinctly and circularly emarginate; the anterior angles are subacute and depressed; the sides marginate, especially anteriorly; the basal angles are *slightly* truncate: parallel to the margin of the base is a well-defined thread-like fovea, which does not extend to the sides, but is abruptly and at right angles deflected to the base; this fovea is in its course slightly subsinuate; the surface is impunctate, rufo-ferruginous, and glabrous. *Scutellum* triangular, impunctate, black. *Elytra* broader than the thorax, subcylindrical, and subattenuated towards the apex; an antemedial transverse obsolete depression gives prominence to the surface near the scutellary angles; punctate-striate, black, shining. *Antennæ* filiform, fuscous. *Legs* black, the anterior femora being at their base suffused with rufous.

Examples of the females of the species were taken by my friend Mr. Gray and myself at Petropolis (Organ Mountains, Province of Rio Janeiro), February 1859. A slight tendency to variation may be traced among them in the colour of the thorax.

2. Monoplatus Presidenciæ.

M. (♀) *oblongo-ovalis, subcylindricus, glaber, niger; capite brevi, impunctato, rufo, inter oculos (magnos, nigros) transverse subtiliter foveolato ; thorace transverso, antice emarginato, ad latera marginato, ad basin transverse canaliculato, impunctato, rufo ; elytris robustis, punctato-striatis, ad apicem subattenuatis, nigris, nitidis ; antennis filiformibus, fuscis ; pedibus rufis, tarsis tibiisque anterioribus fusco-nigris.*

♀ Long. corp. 3½ lin., lat. 1½ lin.

Oblong-ovate, robust, subcylindrical, impubescent, black, glabrous. *Head* short, transverse, not produced in front; the eyes are large, occupying a considerable portion of the head, prominent, and black; between the eyes is a minute transverse fovea; the surface is impunctate, glabrous, rufous. *Thorax* broader than the head, transverse, rectangular; the anterior margin is medially emarginate (but not so deeply as in *M. nigripes*); the anterior angles are subacute, slightly prominent and depressed ; the sides marginate: at the base is a transverse fovea (which runs parallel to the line of the base), but which is deflected (before it reaches the lateral margins) at right angles to the basal line; this fovea is not, as in *nigripes*, subsinuate, but accurately parallel to the line of the base: the surface is impunctate, shining, rufous. *Scutellum* triangular (somewhat longer and more distinct than in *nigripes*), glabrous, black. *Elytra* broader than the thorax, robust, subcylindrical, slightly attenuate at the apex, punctate-striate; near the scutellary angles the surface is somewhat gibbous (the striæ and punctures being more obsolete); at the fifth and sixth striæ near the shoulders is a slight longitudinal depression. *Antennæ* filiform, fuscous, the three basal joints being rufous. *Legs* rufous, the anterior tibiæ and tarsi being fuscous.

The only example of this species (a female) was taken at Presidencia (the English boarding-house kept by the late Mr. Land, Organ Mountains), during the visit of Mr. Gray and myself in February 1857. The species differs from *nigripes* and *distinguendus* (to both of which it is closely allied) by the coloration of its head and legs: from *nigripes* it is structurally separated by its transverse and linear fovea between the eyes, by its rectilinear (and not subsinuate) transverse canaliculation at the base of the thorax, and by the less deep emargination of the anterior margin of the thorax; from *distinguendus* it differs by its *concolorous* elytra, and by the absence of any spot on the crown of the head. The three species, although unquestionably closely allied, appear to me to have ample marks of difference which separate them each from the others.

3. Monoplatus distinguendus. (Tab. I. fig. 2.)

M. *oblongus, subparallelus, niger, nitidus; capite brevi, impunctato, ferrugineo; thorace transverso, rectangulari, antice subemarginato, angulis anterioribus prominulis depressis, apud basin fovea lineari transversa ornato, impunctato, flavo; elytris parallelis, subdepressis, punctato-striatis, ad basin paulum elevatis, nigris, ad humeros flavo-marginatis; antennis filiformibus, art. 1–4 ferrugineis, reliquis nigris; pedibus flavis, tarsis tibiisque apicalibus nigris.*

♂ Long. corp. 3 lin., lat. 1¼ lin.

Oblong, subparallel, subdepressed, black, shining. *Head* short, transverse, hardly produced; eyes *large*, prominent, black, occupying a considerable portion of the head; between the eyes is an obsolete longitudinal impression; ferruginous. *Thorax* broader than the head, transverse, in front slightly emarginate (not so distinctly as in the former species); the anterior angles are *slightly* prominent and depressed; the sides marginate and parallel; at the base is a narrow and well-defined channel, terminated (by being deflected at right angles to the line of the base) before it reaches the lateral margination; the surface impunctate and flavous. *Scutellum* tolerably large, triangular, impunctate, black. *Elytra* somewhat broader than the thorax, parallel, slightly depressed, rounded at the apex; punctate-striate, the punctures being distinct and frequent, the striæ shallow; near the scutellary angles the surface is impunctate, and slightly raised, in a subcircular form: black, *with the anterior (antemedial) margins flavous. Antennæ* tolerably long, filiform, fuscous, with the four basal joints ferruginous. *Legs* flavous throughout, the tarsi and the apical part of the tibiæ being fuscous-black.

Several males of this species (I have never seen the female) were taken by Mr. Gray and myself at Petropolis in February 1857.

Although of the preceding species (*M. nigripes* and *Presidenciæ*) I have only been able to examine females, and of this species only males, I have, after much examination, no doubt that they are abundantly distinct the one from the other. *M. distinguendus* may be known (irrespective of its different coloration, *especially the flavous margination of the elytra*) by its manifestly *less deep* striation on the elytra; sometimes this is almost imperceptible, except under a high power. There is also abundant distinguishing character in the markings on the head.

4. Monoplatus Grayii. (FRONT. fig. 1.)

M. oblongo-ovalis, subdepressus, parallelus, niger, nitidus; capite brevi, subdepresso, haud elongato, inter oculos longitudinaliter foveolato, fusco-bimaculato ad basin, inter oculos; thorace transverso, rectangulari, angulis anticis subacutis prominulis, ad latera marginato, ad basin fovea transversa haud latera attingit, impunctato, fusco; elytris subparallelis, punctato-striatis, sutura, marginibus, fasciisque duabus transversis (interdum etiam elytrorum basi) flavis; antennis piceis, ad basin flavis; pedibus flavis.

♂ Long. corp. 3 lin., lat. 1 lin.

Oblong-oval, subdepressed, parallel, black, shining. *Head* very small, not elongated; eyes *large*, distant, prominent, reaching laterally nearly as far as the apical angle of the thorax; between the eyes, above the insertion of the antennæ, is a small obsolete longitudinal impression; the surface impunctate; near the inner and posterior margin of the eyes are two subcircular obsolete fuscous spots. *Thorax* transverse, rectangular, in front very slightly emarginate; the anterior angles are subacute and depressed; the sides marginate, most distinctly anteriorly; at the base is a transverse linear fovea, nearly parallel to the margin, which does not extend to the lateral margination, but is abruptly deflected to the base; surface impunctate, flavous. *Scutellum* triangular, impunctate, shining. *Elytra* parallel, somewhat depressed, punctate-striate, black; the lateral margination (which is distinct) and the suture (except as either approaches the base) are flavous: two transverse regularly formed fasciæ of the same colour are situated, the one medially (which is slightly deflected towards the base as it approaches the margination), the other nearer to the base, at the distance from the former of its own breadth: in some examples the apex also is flavous. *Antennæ* filiform, as long as the elytra, the joints being severally of the form of those of allied species; first to fourth flavous, the rest fuscous or piceous.

The above description is from a male. Although several examples of the species were captured by Mr. Gray and myself in the immediate neighbourhood of Petropolis (Organ Mountains, Rio Janeiro), none of them were females.

I name this handsome species after my friend and fellow-traveller John Gray, Esq., to whom, for many personal kindnesses, I am happy to acknowledge my obligations.

5. Monoplatus Miersii.

M. *oblongo-ovalis, robustus, rufus, nitidus; capite parvo, depresso, oculis magnis, haud exstantibus, ad basin capitis attingentibus, impunctato, rufo-fusco; thorace transverso, marginato, angulis anterioribus acutis, ad basin transverse subdepresso et foveolato, fusco-rufo (inter foveam basinque nigro); elytris subdepressis, punctato-striatis, nitidis, fasciis duabus nigris (ad suturam interruptis), hac ad humeros lata, ad marginem attenuata, illa ad medium parva, inconstanti (aliquando maculas duas tantum efficienti); antennis fuscis, ad basin rufis; pedibus rufis, tarsis tibiisque anterioribus nigris.*

♀ Long. corp. 3 lin., lat. 1½ lin.

Oblong-oval, robust, rufous, shining. *Head* transverse, very slightly produced, impunctate, rufo-fuscous; eyes large, prominent, at some distance from each other, and almost touching posteriorly the thoracic margin. *Thorax* transverse, rectangular in front, slightly emarginate; the anterior angles slightly produced and curved *outwards* in the shape of a tooth; the sides distinctly marginate; at the base is a regular transverse groove, parallel to the margin, which is deflected abruptly towards the base of the elytra before it reaches the humeral angle; the base of the thorax (between this groove and the margin) is very dark fuscous or even black. *Scutellum* triangular, impunctate, rufous. *Elytra* broader than the thorax, robust, subcylindrical, ovate, finely punctate-striate, rufous: two irregular black transverse fasciæ are interrupted at the suture, and do not reach the margin; the anterior fascia reaches at its upper margin nearly to the base of the scutellum, and thence obliquely decreases in breadth towards the margin; it is separated from the suture by the breadth of a single stria, and from the margin by the distance of three striæ; the posterior fascia is hardly so broad as the anterior, and in one example takes the form of two oblong irregular postmedial spots. *Antennæ* filiform, fuscous, with the basal joints rufous. *Legs* rufous, with the anterior tibiæ and tarsi, and also the outer edge of the posterior tibiæ darkly-fuscous.

Brazil. In the collections of Messrs. Miers and Murray.

In general appearance this insect approaches to *M. Grayii*; it may be readily separated by its rufous colour and completely different arrangement of the transverse bands. Both the examples which have come before me of this species are females.

6. Monoplatus apicatus.

M. *oblongo-ovalis, parallelus, subdepressus, testaceo-rufus, nitidus; capite parvo, oculis exstantibus, magnis; thorace transverso, rectangulari, marginato, ad basin transverse foveolato; elytris parallelis, punctato-striatis, ad basin nigris; antennis filiformibus, fuscis, ad basin flavis; pedibus flavis, fusco adumbratis.*

♂ Long. corp. 2½ lin., lat. 1¼ lin.
♀ Long. corp. 3¼ lin., lat. 1¾ lin.

Oblong-ovate, depressed, parallel, rufo-testaceous, shining. *Head* transverse, not produced; eyes very large, prominent, but not extending laterally as far as the anterior angles of the thorax; between the eyes and above the insertion of the antennæ is a small, *obsolete*, longitudinal depression; surface impunctate, black, shining; two circular dark-fuscous ocelli-like markings are faintly apparent at the posterior and inner margin of the eyes. *Thorax* transverse, rectangular; the anterior angles depressed, but slightly prominent; the sides marginate; posterior angles distinct; parallel to the base is a transverse narrow fovea which terminates abruptly before it reaches the margination; surface impunctate, rufo-testaceous, slightly suffused (in the examples before me) with fuscous; shining. *Scutellum* distinct, triangular, impunctate, fuscous. *Elytra* subcylindrical, slightly depressed, rounded at the apex, punctate-striate, with the humeral and scutellar angles broadly gibbous; rufo-testaceous (slightly paler than the thorax), with the apex black (this colouring at the apex occupies about one-fifth of the whole surface of the elytra, and is defined by a regular transverse margin, the line of which inclines in the direction of the base, as it approaches the margination). *Antennæ* filiform, of the length of the elytra; the first joint long, and incrassated at the apex; the second short, ovate; the third and fourth nearly equal; the first to fourth (with the exception of the upper part of the first and second) testaceous, the rest fuscous. *Legs* rufo-testaceous throughout, the femora being more or less suffused with fuscous.

The above description is taken from a *male*. The *females* are more robust, less parallel; the legs, especially the posterior pair, somewhat shorter in proportion to the body; the head larger, but the eyes smaller and less prominent, and the antennæ shorter.

Specimens of both sexes were captured by Mr. Gray and myself in the immediate neighbourhood of Petropolis (Organ Mountains, Rio Janeiro), February 1857.

7. Monoplatus bimaculatus. (Tab. I. fig. 3.)

M. *oblongo-ovalis, robustus, impubescens, cervinus, nitidus; capite brevi, subpunctulato, ad basin leviter nigro-vittato, oculis prominulis, haud exstantibus; thorace transverso, rectangulari, angulis anterioribus depressis, subacutis, marginato, ad basin transverse foveolato, glabro, nigro-irrorato; elytris robustis, punctato-striatis, ad medium maculis duabus circularibus nigris; antennis filiformibus, elytris brevioribus, art. secundo et tertio flavis, ceteris fuscis; pedibus nigro-fuscis, femoribus ad basin flavis.*

♀ Long. corp. 4 lin., lat. 1¾ lin.

Oblong-oval (the *female*), robust and subcylindrical, of a fawn-colour throughout, impubescent, shining. Head short, transverse, impunctate (by means of a high power of the microscope fine punctures are visible); above the base of the antennæ, and between the eyes, is an obsolete but distinctly impressed transverse fovea; obliquely subsinuate, or medially angulated; at the base is a narrow transverse band or collar of black, extending along the margin from eye to eye: eyes tolerably large, distant; their outer margin does not reach, laterally, the line of the anterior angle of the thorax. *Thorax* transverse, rectangular, anteriorly *sub*emarginate; the anterior angles are subacute and depressed; the sides marginate and slightly arcuate, and the basal angles distinct, but closely contiguous to the elytra; at the base is a deep and well-defined transverse fovea, not extending to the sides, but abruptly deflected before it reaches the humeral angle, and terminating in the line of the base; surface somewhat globose, finely punctate, especially at the base, irrorated irregularly throughout with black. *Scutellum* small, triangular, impunctate, shining. *Elytra* robust, much broader than the thorax, subcylindrical; the surface near the scutellar angles turgescent; punctate-striate, with two circular black spots slightly in front of the middle, and extending laterally from the second to the sixth stria. *Antennæ* filiform, not so long as the elytra; the first joint long, dilated, and inflected outwards at the base, black, or dark fuscous; second short, ovate, flavous; the third longer than the first, fine, and flavous; the rest dark fuscous. *Legs* dark fuscous throughout, the base of the femora being flavous.

The above description is taken from a female.

A single specimen of this fine species was captured by Mr. Gray in February 1857 at Petropolis (Organ Mountains, Rio Janeiro).

8. Monoplatus croceus. B.M.

M. *oblongo-ovalis, croceus, nitidus; capite brevi, minuto, fovea inter oculos obsoleta longitudinali, impunctato, glabro; oculis magnis, exstantibus; thorace transverso, rectangulari, angulis anticis pro-*

minulis, marginato, ad basin distincte foveolato; elytris mediocribus, parallelis, subdepressis, ad basin apud humeros, etiam prope scutellum distincte subglobosis; antennis filiformibus, fuscis, ad basin rufis vel rufo-flavis; pedibus flavis aut croceis, tarsis tibiisque anterioribus nigris.

♂ Long. corp. $2\frac{1}{4}$ lin., lat. $1\frac{1}{4}$ lin.
♀ Long. corp. $3\frac{1}{4}$–$3\frac{1}{2}$ lin., lat. $1\frac{1}{2}$–$1\frac{3}{4}$ lin.

Oblong-ovate, slightly depressed, subparallel, impubescent, pale yellow, shining. *Head* short, small, transverse, not produced in front; eyes large, globular, and prominent (not extending laterally so far as the humeral angle of the thorax); between the eyes, and above the insertion of the antennæ, is an obscure longitudinal depression; surface impunctate, testaceous, somewhat clouded with fuscous, glabrous. *Thorax* transverse, rectangular, in front distinctly emarginate; the anterior angles depressed, but subacute; the sides marginate; at the base is a narrow transverse thread-like fovea, which is deflected abruptly into the margin of the base before it reaches the humeral angles; surface impunctate, of the same colour as the head, shining. *Scutellum* triangular, impunctate, flavous. *Elytra* parallel, subcylindrical, the sides distinctly marginate; punctate-striate; the surface near the scutellary angles slightly gibbous, croceous (in different examples the shade of yellow varies; in some it has the depth of colour of the yellow band of *Trichius fasciatus*, while in others it is almost pale flavous). *Antennæ* filiform, of the length of the elytra; the first joint large, inflected outwards and dilated at the base; the rest as in the adjoining species; the first to the fourth rufo-ferruginous, the rest fuscous. *Legs* flavous or croceous, with the tarsi and (more or less) the anterior tibiæ black.

Var. A. *Head* and *thorax* rufous; *elytra* flavous, irrorated (especially towards the apex) with black; *antennæ* rufous, with the fifth to the eleventh joints fuscous; *legs* rufous, the tarsi and anterior tibiæ being black.

The above description of the insect was taken from a male; that of the variety from a female. The different sexes of this species have the same characteristics that obtain among its congeners. The *males* are smaller, less robust, more depressed; the head is smaller, while the eyes are larger and *more prominent*; the *legs* have slightly, in reality (as well as when contrasted with the different size of the bodies), a longer development; and the *antennæ* are very apparently more produced.

This species is evidently subject to great variation in the shades of its colouring; in the examples before me, no two specimens absolutely agree in *every* point. It is at once separated from *jucundus*, to which alone it approaches in colouring, by the striation on the elytra (which is *entirely obsolete* in *jucundus*) and by the *puncturing* of the striæ, which is distinct, broad, and deep.

Taken by Mr. Gray and myself, abundantly, in the neighbourhood of Petropolis (Organ Mountains, Rio Janeiro), February 1857. A single specimen has also been found by Mr. Squire in the neighbourhood of Rio Janeiro.

9. Monoplatus jucundus.

M. *oblongo-ovatus, latus, subdepressus, impubescens, rufus; capite brevi, inter oculos longitudinaliter depresso, impunctato; thorace transverso, ad basin foveolato, impunctato; elytris latis, leviter striato-punctatis; antennis filiformibus, fuscis, ad basin ferrugineis; pedibus ferrugineis, tibiis tarsisque anterioribus, tarsisque posticis nigris.*

♀ Long. corp. 3 lin., lat. 1¾ lin.

Oblong-ovate, broad, depressed, impubescent, of a bright rufous colour throughout. *Head* short, depressed, not produced in front; eyes large, situated at the base of the head, not extending laterally as far as the anterior angle of the thorax; between the eyes and above the insertion of the antennæ is a distinct longitudinal depression; the surface impunctate. *Thorax* transverse, rectangular, in front obsoletely emarginate; the anterior angles very much depressed, subacute, produced laterally *beyond* the line of margination; the sides marginate, especially towards the apical angles, subsinuate; at the base a narrow transverse fovea extends parallel to the margin and terminates on either side in an abrupt inflection towards the base; the surface impunctate. *Scutellum* large, triangular, impunctate. *Elytra* broad (much broader than the thorax), robust, and depressed, with rows of very fine punctures arranged as striæ; the surface near the scutellary angles is somewhat raised, and the striæ-like punctures become almost obsolete; the sides distinctly marginate. *Antennæ* shorter than the elytra, filiform; the joints arranged as in the allied species, the first to the third ferruginous, the rest fuscous. *Legs* ferruginous, with the anterior tibiæ, tarsi, and the posterior tarsi black.

Captured by Mr. Miers in the neighbourhood of Rio Janeiro. In the collection of Mr. Miers and also of the Rev. H. Clark.

M. jucundus not only differs in its colour (being much more brightly and uniformly rufous) from *croceus*, but also in the punctuation of its elytra; there is, in this species, a total absence of any appearance of striæ, and the punctures themselves are very much more minute.

10. Monoplatus sexsignatus. (Tab. I. fig. 4.)

M. *oblongo-ovatus, subparallelus, impubescens, pallide flavus; capite transverso, impunctato, ad apicem fulvo, ad basin nigro; thorace transverso, rectangulari, ad latera marginato, ad basin transverse lineato, impunctato, glabro, flavo-ferrugineo; elytris parallelis, punctato-striatis, flavis, ad basin lineis duabus longitudinalibus, ad apicem tertia subrectangulari, nigris; antennis filiformibus, fuscis, ad basin flavis; pedibus flavis.*

Long. corp. 3 lin., lat. 1½ lin.

Oblong-ovate, subparallel, impubescent, pale flavous. *Head* transverse, subproduced; eyes large, prominent, situated at the base of the head; surface impunctate, shining at the apex and fulvous, above black. *Thorax* transverse, broader than the head, rectangular; the anterior angles distinctly defined and subdepressed; the sides marginate; at the base, and parallel to the basal line, is a well-defined thread-like fovea, which terminates abruptly before it reaches the lateral margins, being deflected at right angles to the basal line; the surface impunctate and glabrous; the colour flavo-ferruginous. *Scutellum* triangular, flavous, suffused in the middle with fuscous. *Elytra* broad, robust, parallel, distinctly punctate-striate; impunctate and glabrous between the striæ; the colour pale flavous: at the base, between the third and fifth striæ, is a longitudinal marking, which extends from the shoulders one-quarter of the whole length of the elytra; at the shoulders, at the eighth stria (immediately above the outer margination), is a second linear marking, extending longitudinally nearly one-half of the whole length of the elytra; at the apex is a third marking, between the fourth and the seventh striæ, subrectangular, irregular in outline, situated at about the same distance from the extreme apex as it is from the suture, approaching more nearly to (though not reaching) the margination; these markings are black, slightly suffused at their margins with rufous. *Antennæ* fine, filiform, fuscous; the basal joints flavous. *Legs* flavous throughout.

Brazil. In the collection of M. Chevrolat.

11. Monoplatus quatuor-notatus. (Front. fig. 2.)

M. *oblongo-ovatus, parallelus, subcylindricus, punctato-striatus, pallide testaceus, glaber; capite oblique foveolato inter oculos, impunctato, nigro, nitido; thorace transverso, ad basin transverse foveolato, rufo-flavo, impunctato, nitido; elytris parallelis, punctato-striatis, pallide testaceis, maculis duabus ad humeros, alterisque versus apicem nigris; antennis filiformibus, fuscis, ad basin flavis; pedibus flavis.*

♂ Long. corp. 3 lin., lat. 1 lin.

Oblong-ovate, parallel, subcylindrical, punctate-striate, of a pale testaceous colour. *Head* transverse, slightly produced; between the eyes (*immediately* adjoining the base of the antennæ) is a minute obliquely angulated fovea, in the form of the letter V; between these two depressions is an obsolete elongated puncture (medial and longitudinal); the eyes are large, prominent, and globose, situated at the base of the head, and extending laterally nearly as far as the anterior angles of the thorax; surface impunctate, black, glabrous; near the posterior and inner margins of the eyes are two obscure fuscous spots. *Thorax* transverse, rectangular, hardly emarginate in front; the anterior angles are subacute and depressed; the sides marginate; at the base is a narrow and well-defined transverse groove, extending parallel to the line of the base, which terminates abruptly (before it reaches the sides) by being inflected at right angles to the posterior margin; the surface is impunctate throughout and rufo-flavous. *Scutellum* triangular, impunctate, flavous. *Elytra* broader than the thorax, parallel, subdepressed, slightly acuminated at the apex, punctate-striate (the striæ being almost obsolete, and the punctures distinct and evenly distributed throughout); an obsolete antemedial depression (apparent when viewed laterally) gives a prominence to the surface near the base: two transverse black fasciæ (the one at the base, the other near the apex) are interrupted at the suture, and thus form four black spots; those at the base are distant from the suture by the breadth of rather more than a single stria; they extend towards the apex one-sixth of the whole length of the elytra (or two-fifths of a line), their posterior margin being subsinuate in outline; at the sides they reach, but do not colour, the line of margination : the *apical* markings are separated by a single stria from the suture, and immediately approach, but do not reach, the apex; in form these are subcircular. *Antennæ* long, filiform; the joints one to four flavous, five to eleven fuscous. *Legs* flavous throughout.

From the neighbourhood of Petropolis (Organ Mountains), Feb. 1847; the only example taken by us being a male.

12. Monoplatus semichalybeus.

M. *oblongo-ovatus, parallelus, punctato-striatus, ferrugineo-rufus, glaber; capite brevi, inter oculos transverse foveolato, impunctato; thorace transverso, ad basin subconstricto et transverse foveolato, ad latera marginato, impunctato; elytris parallelis, punctato-striatis, ad apicem dimidio nigro-cyaneis; antennis filiformibus, nigro-fuscis, art. 1–3 rufo-flavis; pedibus rufo-flavis.*

♂ Long. corp. $2\frac{1}{2}$–$2\frac{3}{4}$ lin., lat. 1 lin.

Oblong-ovate, subparallel, subdepressed, minutely punctate-striate, glabrous, ferrugineo-rufous. *Head* short, depressed, very slightly produced; above the labrum is a transverse linear depression; *immediately* above the base of the antennæ is a transverse depression which gives a prominence to two obsolete oblique elevations between the eyes, forming together (broadly, and at an obtuse angle) the character of the letter V; eyes large, globose, prominent, situated at the base of the head, extending laterally as far as the anterior angles of the thorax; the surface at the base of the head impunctate and glabrous. *Thorax* transverse, rectangular, slightly constricted at the base, hardly emarginate in the front; the anterior angles are depressed and subacute, the sides marginate; parallel to the basal line is a well-defined transverse fovea, which terminates abruptly before it reaches the sides by being deflected into the line of the base; the surface is impunctate, ferrugineo-rufous, clouded sparingly and minutely with fuscous. *Scutellum* triangular, impunctate, rufous. *Elytra* broader than the thorax, robust, subparallel, very faintly punctate-striate (the striæ being almost obsolete, and the punctures frequent and very minute): from the humeral angles extend two longitudinal carinations parallel to the margination, one between the eighth and ninth, the other at the eleventh stria; these carinations become obsolete as they approach the apex; an antemedial depression extends transversely as far as the first carination, which (when viewed laterally) gives an appearance of prominence to the surface near the scutellum: the antemedial elytra are in colour ferrugineo-rufous, clouded minutely and sparingly with fuscous; the apical portion of the surface is dark cyaneous; the line of demarcation being somewhat antemedially transverse, and falling away obliquely towards the apex as it approaches the line of margination. *Antennæ* long, filiform, of a dark fuscous colour, the three basal joints being rufous. *Legs* flavo-rufous throughout.

In one of the examples of this species, the azure-blue of the apical half of the elytra is represented by black, the anterior tibiæ and tarsi also being black.

This species, and those immediately allied to it, approach in colouring to *M. apicatus*. Of the latter, the *apex* only (that is, hardly *one* line of the $2\frac{1}{2}$ lines—the length of the elytra) is black: in *M. semichalybeus*, more than half of the elytra is deep azure or black (that is, $1\frac{1}{4}$ line of $2\frac{1}{4}$—the length of the elytra). This distinction obtains so exactly and so uniformly in the different examples of either modification of colouring (of which I have both sexes), that of itself (without any reference to well-defined though minute structural differences) it is almost sufficient to render it impossible that one should be constituted merely a variety of the other.

13. Monoplatus semiviolaceus.

M. *oblongo-ovatus, subparallelus, impubescens, glaber, rufo-testaceus; capite oblique foveolato, ad basin impunctato, antice granulato; thorace transverso, marginato, ad basin transverse foveolato, impunctato; elytris subtiliter striato-punctatis, ad apicem fusconigris, ad basin rufo-testaccis; antennis filiformibus, flavis; pedibus flavis.*

♂ Long. corp. 2½ lin., lat. 1⅓ lin.

Oblong-ovate, subparallel, subrobust, impubescent, glabrous, rufo-testaceous. *Head* short, transverse, not produced; labrum broad; eyes large, prominent, situated at the base of the head: between the eyes an indistinct but well-defined *semicircular* fovea extends on either side obliquely and upwards to their inner margins (in *semichalybeus* this fovea is more angulated, and its direction transverse): the surface in front coarsely granulated, at the base impunctate, glabrous. *Thorax* transverse, broader than the head, the anterior angles depressed, the sides marginate: at the base a transverse and well-defined fovea runs parallel to the line of the base, but is abruptly terminated before it reaches the lateral margins by being deflected at right angles towards the basal line; this transverse fovea is at a *greater distance from the basal line* than in *semichalybeus*: the surface impunctate, glabrous. *Elytra* broader than the thorax, subparallel, glabrous: under a high power faint punctures may be discerned, arranged in the form of striæ; these punctures are much more obsolete than in *semichalybeus*: the apical half of the surface is bright fuscous-black, the line of boundary in each elytron being in a subcircular form (that is, receding towards the apex as it approaches the suture). *Antennæ* filiform, flavous. *Legs* flavous throughout.

Cayenne. In the collection of M. Chevrolat.

The above description (pointing out the angulated transverse fovea in the head, and also punctures on the elytra almost obsolete) sufficiently distinguishes this species from *semichalybeus*.

14. Monoplatus nigricans.

M. *oblongo-ovatus, subparallelus, subdepressus, impubescens, flavorufus; capite brevi, inter oculos minute transverse foveolato, impunctato; thorace transverso, impunctato, ad basin foveolato;*

elytris subtilissime striato-punctatis, fusco suffusis; antennis filiformibus, rufis, ad apicem fusco-rufis; pedibus flavo-rufis.

♂ Long. corp. 3 lin., lat. 1¼ lin.

Oblong-ovate, subparallel, subdepressed, impubescent, glabrous, flavo-rufous, suffused with fuscous. *Head* short, transverse, hardly produced in front; the eyes large, globular, black, extending laterally nearly as far as the anterior angles of the thorax; between the eyes is a minute and directly transverse fovea, which when viewed under a high power is medially subsinuate (not distinctly angulated, as in *M. semichalybeus*; or semicircular, as in *M. semiviolaceus*); surface impunctate, flavo-rufous, *obsoletely* suffused with fuscous; glabrous. *Thorax* transverse, rectangular, anteriorly slightly emarginate, the anterior angles subacute, and slightly depressed; the sides marginate; at the base is a transverse thread-like fovea, which is deflected at right angles (before it reaches the humeral angle) to the base; surface impunctate. *Scutellum* triangular, impunctate, glabrous. *Elytra* parallel, subdepressed, rounded at the apex, impunctate, except under a high power, when rows of minute punctures may be discerned, arranged in the form of striæ; these striæ-like punctures are much more minute than in *M. semichalybeus*, and more distinct at the base than in *M. semiviolaceus*; the colour is dark-fuscous, suffused irregularly throughout, and especially near the base, with flavous. *Antennæ* filiform, rufous, at the apex fusco-rufous. *Legs* flavo-rufous throughout.

Brazil. In the collection of M. Chevrolat.

From *M. semichalybeus* this species is separated by its *minute* punctures on the elytra, and from *M. semiviolaceus* by its larger size, more elongated form, and its different markings on the head; it differs, in addition, from all the species which approach it by the *irregularly clouded flavo-fuscous* colouring of its elytra: it may be a question, whether this latter, if alone, would be a permanent specific character, or whether it is only the accidental variation of a single individual.

15. **Monoplatus nigrimanus.**

M. *oblongo-ovatus, subparallelus, subdepressus, rufo-flavus, glaber; capite brevi, impunctato,* lævi, *haud foveolato; thorace transverso, rectangulari, ad basin transverse foveolato; elytris* subtiliter *striato-punctatis, rufo-flavis, ad apicem fuscis; antennis fuscis, art. basalibus rufis; pedibus rufis, tarsis anterioribus fusco suffusis.*

♂ Long. corp. 2½ lin., lat. 1⅓ lin.

Oblong-ovate, subparallel, subdepressed, rufo-flavous, glabrous.

Head short, transverse, not produced in front; eyes globose, situated nearly at the base of the head; between the eyes, above the base of the antennæ, the surface is impunctate, and *unmarked by any transverse fovea*. *Thorax* transverse, rectangular, the anterior margin distinctly emarginate (more apparently so than in the allied species *M. nigricans* and *M. semiviolaceus*); the sides marginate, especially near the anterior angles; at the base is a transverse fovea, well defined, abruptly terminating before it reaches the margin by being deflected (at right angles) to the basal line; the surface is impunctate throughout and rufo-flavous. *Scutellum* triangular, impunctate. *Elytra* broader than the thorax, subparallel, subdepressed, marked throughout with very minute striæ-like punctures (which are not discernible except under a high power); the colour is rufo-flavous, at the apex broadly fuscous,—the line of demarcation between the two being medial, and slightly inclining towards the apex at the suture and at the margination; the line itself is not so distinctly defined as in *M. semiviolaceus*. *Antennæ* fuscous, the basal joints being rufous. *Legs* rufous, the anterior tarsi being suffused with fuscous.

Brazil. In the collection of M. Chevrolat.

This species most closely approaches to *M. semiviolaceus*, both in general colouring and in the details of sculpture. The absence of any transverse fovea on the head sufficiently characterizes it as a species, inasmuch as this—the character of the transverse markings between the eyes—seems to be constant throughout the group, and of considerable importance in the determination of species. From *M. semichalybeus* it is easily separated by the minuteness of the punctuation on its elytra, and by the *direction* of the transverse line of separation between the two colours on the elytra.

16. Monoplatus dimidiatipennis.

M. *oblongo-ovatus, subparallelus, subdepressus, rufo-flavus, glaber; capite brevi, antice haud producto,* inter oculos haud foveolato; *thorace transverso, impunctato, ad basin transverse foveolato; elytris parallelis, striato-punctatis, haud ad latera carinatis, glabratis, ad apicem nigro-fuscis; antennis fuscis, ad basin flavis; pedibus flavis, posticis tibiis tarsisque piceo suffusis.*

♂ Long. corp. 2¾ lin., lat. 1¼ lin.

Oblong-ovate, subparallel, subdepressed, rufo-flavous, glabrous. *Head* short, transverse, not produced in front; eyes large, globular, situated at the base of the head; the surface above the base of the antennæ is impunctate, and unmarked by foveæ. *Thorax* transverse, rectangular; the anterior margin is slightly emarginate (less distinctly so than in *M. semichalybeus*); the sides marginate, especially anteriorly; the surface impunctate and glabrous; at the base is a transverse fovea (less deep and somewhat less distinct than in *M. semichalybeus*), terminating, as in other species, by being deflected into the basal line before it reaches the margin of the thorax. *Scutellum* triangular and impunctate. *Elytra* subparallel, rounded at the apex, impressed throughout with tolerably distinct punctures arranged in the form of striæ, of equal distinctness with those of *semichalybeus*; it differs, however, from this species in having the surface entirely equate and smooth—not raised into longitudinal keel-like ridges parallel with, and closely adjoining the lateral margination; the colour is rufo-flavous, at the apex broadly fuscous,—the line of boundary between the two colours being medial, and slightly inclined towards the apex as it approaches the margination. *Antennæ* fuscous, the four basal joints being flavous. *Legs* flavous, the posterior tibiæ and tarsi as well as the termination of the femora being suffused with piceous.

Brazil. In the collection of M. Chevrolat.

This species differs from all others allied to it in colour by the depth of the punctuation of the elytra, and also generally by its unfoveolated head; from *semichalybeus*, to which it is closely allied, by its punctuation, and the absence of any keel-like ridges at the sides of the elytra.

I believe that this group of six species (which have their elytra rufo-flavous, the apex being broadly fuscous) are all specifically distinct; their differences rest on small, but well-defineable and apparently permanent characters.

17. Monoplatus angulatus.

M. *oblongo-ovatus, subparallelus, testaceo-rufus, glaber; capite brevi, inter oculos subtiliter foveolato; thorace transverso, ad basin transverse foveolato, punctulato; elytris punctato-striatis, ad apicem fusco-nigris, ad basin testaceo-rufis; antennis filiformibus, fuscis, ad basin rufo-flavis; pedibus rufo-flavis.*

Long. corp. 2 lin., lat. ¾ lin.

Oblong-ovate, subparallel, testaceo-rufous, glabrous. *Head* short, hardly produced in front; labrum subattenuated and rounded at the apex; eyes large, prominent, situated at the base of the head, and extending laterally nearly as far as the anterior angles of the thorax; from the insertion of the antennæ a faint medial longitudinal fovea extends nearly to the base, which is bisected at right angles by a transverse fovea connecting the inner margins of the eyes (these two lines together forming the character of a cross); the surface impunctate, glabrous. *Thorax* transverse, the anterior angles subacute and depressed, the sides broadly and distinctly marginate; at the base is a well-defined transverse groove parallel to the line of the base, but *subsinuate*, and terminating abruptly before it reaches the lateral margination by being deflected at right angles into the line of the base; the surface very finely punctate, glabrous. *Scutellum* triangular, impunctate. *Elytra* slightly broader than the thorax, subrobust, punctate-striate, the striæ becoming obsolete near the sides, and the punctures being distinct and well-defined; the apical half of the surface is of a bright fuscous-black colour. *Antennæ* filiform, fuscous, the three basal joints being rufo-flavous. *Legs* rufo-flavous throughout.

Brazil. In the collection of M. Chevrolat.

This species closely approaches *semichalybeus*, being however abundantly distinct, not only by its smaller size and more pronounced punctures on the elytra, but also by the *sinuation in' the basal fovea* of the thorax, by which latter character it separates itself from all other species of the group with which I am acquainted.

18. Monoplatus impunctatus.

M. *oblongo-ovatus, parallelus, striato-punctulatus, niger, nitidus; capite brevi, inter oculos transverse foveolato, impunctato, flavo; thorace transverso, rectangulari, ad basin transverse foveolato, ad latera marginato, impunctato, flavo; elytris parallelis, striato-punctatis, ante medium oblique depressis, nigris, nitidis; antennis fuscis, art. 1–3 flavis; pedibus flavis.*

♂ Long. corp. 2½ lin., lat. ¾–1 lin.

Oblong-ovate, subrobust, parallel, punctate, black, shining. *Head* short, transverse, slightly produced; above the labrum is a transverse depression, bisected medially by a longitudinal carination; on either side of the insertion of the antennæ (adjoining the inner surface of the eyes) is a minute depression; between the eyes (midway between the basal line and the insertion of the antennæ) is a transverse thread-like and very minute fovea; eyes large, globose, extending laterally as far as the anterior angles of the thorax; surface impunctate and rufous. *Thorax* transverse, in front hardly emarginate; the anterior angles are depressed and subacute, the sides marginate; at the base a transverse fovea (distinct, narrow, and thread-like) extends parallel to, and joins the line of the base by an abrupt deflection near the posterior angles; surface impunctate and flavous. *Scutellum* triangular, impunctate, fulvo-flavous. *Elytra* broader than the thorax, subparallel, depressed, with striæ-like punctures disposed evenly throughout the surface (these punctures are extremely minute, and can only be seen under a very high power); an antemedial transverse shallow depression (when viewed laterally) gives an appearance of prominence to the surface near the scutellum; at the shoulders near the seventh stria is a short and well-defined longitudinal depression. *Antennæ* filiform; the first joint long and broadly developed, especially medially and anteriorly, and slightly curved (not geniculated) outwardly; the second shorter and narrower, ovate; the third longer than the first; these three basal joints are fulvous; the rest (which are shorter) are fuscous. *Legs* flavous, the anterior tibiæ and tarsi being fuscous.

A single example of this species, from "Brazil," is in the collection of Mr. Murray.

Genus 2. ROICUS*.

LABRUM *transversum.*
PALPI MAXILLARES *elongati, subcylindrici, ad apicem attenuati.*
PALPI LABIALES *paralleli, subelongati, art. 2° elongato.*
ANTENNÆ *robustæ, filiformes, approximatæ.*
OCULI *subglobosi, ad latera capitis, distantes.*
CAPUT *subdepressum, subelongatum, haud attenuatum.*
THORAX *capite latior, quadratus, antice subemarginatus, ad latera distincte angulatus.*
ELYTRA *sat robusta, subparallela, ad apicem attenuata, haud ante medium transverse depressa.*
PEDES *robusti, tibiæ incurvatæ—posticis, apicem juxta, dente brevi armatis.*

Labrum transverse, truncated at the extremities.
Mandibles concealed.
Maxillary palpi (Tab. I. fig. 5 *m*) elongate, parallel, not geniculated; the first joint minute; the second subparallel, slightly constricted at the base; the third longer than the second, cylindrical, not rounded at the extremities; the apical *minute*, one-third of the breadth of the second, and its length being hardly greater than its breadth, in form conical.

Labial palpi (Tab. I. fig. 5 *n*) elongate, parallel, the basal joint shorter than the second; the second subparallel, slightly attenuated towards the base, the length nearly double the breadth; the apical joint minute.

* ῥοικὸς, valgus.

Antennæ situated at the front of the head, at some distance from the inner margin of the eyes, approximate, robust, filiform, of nearly the same length as the elytra; the basal joint incurved outwards, dilated and rounded, the breadth near the apex being half its length; the second joint short, subovate, its breadth being half the breadth of the basal joint, and its length not greater than its breadth, abruptly truncate, and not rounded at its apex; the third longer than the first, of the same breadth as the second, slightly dilated at the apex and obliquely truncate; the fourth joint to the eighth of the same form, but slightly shorter than the third; the ninth and tenth less robust; and the terminal joint finely attenuate at its extremity.

Eyes subglobose, situated at the sides of the head (at some distance from each other), and at some distance from the basal line.

Head depressed at right angles to the plane of the elytra; when viewed from above, transverse; elongated in front; the lateral margins being parallel, and the apex broad and transversely truncate, not attenuated.

Thorax broader than the head, quadrate (almost elongate), anteriorly very slightly emarginate; the sides finely but evenly marginate, produced antemedially into a broad and distinct lateral angular projection, thus giving to the thorax the form of an almost equilateral hexagon.

Scutellum large, triangular, impunctate.

Elytra broader than the thorax, subparallel, robust, slightly attenuated towards the apex, with no trace of a medial transverse depression; in *sexmaculatus* very finely punctate, impubescent, glabrous.

Legs robust and long, very finely pubescent (when seen under a high power). The *anterior femora* robust, subdilated medially, impunctate. The *tibiæ* robust, *incurved* distinctly but gradually through their whole length, and subincrassated towards and at the apex. The *tarsi* (Tab. I. fig. 5 *d*) short, and clothed with thick pubescence; the first joint is broad, dilated, and subcordiform; the second of half the breadth, short and ovate; the third not larger than the second, bilobed; and the apical impubescent, slightly and gradually dilated towards the apex, and incurved. The claw (Tab. I. fig. 5 *e*) is bifid, simple, at right angles to the shank, and its two members widely apart; the base of each is thickened at the inner side, but without any trace of an inner tooth, as in other neighbouring genera. The *posterior femora* (Tab. I. fig. 5 *f*) are broad and dilated; when viewed laterally, rounded at the upper margin, and at the lower tolerably rectilinear in outline; the apex is broadly and obliquely truncate. The *tibia* (Tab. I. fig. 5 *g*) is robust, of equal length with the anterior tibiæ, gradually incurved downwards and inwards through its whole length, subdilated towards the apex: when viewed obliquely, the posterior surface is flattened, having the appearance of being in form triangular rather than subcylindrical; the edges of this flattened side are distinctly marginate; in the *inner* margination, near the apex, is a well-developed angular projection; while at the apex itself, immediately behind the insertion of the tarsus, is a prominent and robust tooth-like claw. The *tarsus* (Tab. I. fig. 5 *h*) is short, the first joint being subelongate, and attenuated at the base; the second and third are narrower and much shorter, ovate (the third joint being somewhat smaller, and not bilobed); the apical joint is elongate, impubescent, *gradually* incrassated from the apex, terminating at its extremity in a bladder-like inflation which partially conceals the terminal claw. The claw is bifid; at the inner surface there is a greater tendency to a tooth-like prominence than in those of the anterior legs.

1. Roicus sexmaculatus. (Tab. I. fig. 5.)

R. *oblongo-ovalis, subcylindricus, parallelus, flavus, nitidus; capite brevi, inter oculos transverse foveolato; thorace magno, subelongato, ad latera in medio angulato, impunctato; elytris punctis minutis, veluti in striis, ordinatis, maculis sex rufotestaceis; antennis fusco-flavis; pedibus robustis, tibiis curvatis, his (cum tarsis) rufo-fuscis, femoribus testaceis.*

Long. corp. 3⅓ lin., lat. corp. 1⅓ lin.

Oblong-oval, subcylindrical, elongated, testaceous. *Head* short, depressed, very slightly produced; the eyes are situated at some distance from the back of the head; insertion of the antennæ contiguous; above the insertion and between the eyes is a transverse depression (deepest and broadest in the middle) extending obliquely to the upper surface of the eyes; mouth and maxillary palpi ferruginous; lower part of the head testaceous, the upper part impunctate, testaceous. *Thorax* quadrate; from the anterior, and also from the posterior angles, the sides gradually expand, forming at the side, antemedially, a prominent angle, slightly marginated; surface medially depressed (although it seems *doubtful* whether the depression, in the example before me, be not the result of accident), impunctate, glabrous; flavous, at the sides very slightly suffused with rufous. *Scutellum* triangular, impunctate, rufo-fuscous. *Elytra* not much broader than the thorax, parallel, subcylindrical, with very faint and obsolete punctures arranged as striæ (these are only visible under a high magnifying power), the surface appearing under an ordinary lens to be impunctate; pale testaceous, with six large and distinctly defined *rufo-testaceous* spots, arranged at equal distances one from the other and midway between the suture and margination—two (circular) at the *base*, two larger (and approaching the form of a *parallelogram*) at the *middle*, and two (subcircular) at the *apex*; margination of the elytra rufo-flavous; surface obsoletely pubescent. *Antennæ* filiform, long, tolerably robust, and slightly tapering towards the apex; the first joint is much broader than the others, curved outwards and dilated at the extremity; flavous, the rest rufo-fuscous, with the three terminal joints rufo-testaceous. *Legs large* (compared with the magnitude of the body); the tibiæ, which are singularly robust, are all distinctly curved or bent inwards; femora testaceous, tibiæ and tarsi rufo-fuscous.

A single specimen was captured by Mr. Bates in the district of the Amazon, and is in that gentleman's cabinet.

Genus 3. **EUPHENGES**[*].

LABRUM *subcirculare*.
PALPI MAXILLARES *filiformes, art. 3us elongatus, et 4us brevis, et ad basin latus haud productus.*
PALPI LABIALES *filiformes.*
ANTENNÆ *ad medium subincrassatæ, subpubescentes.*
CAPUT *inclinatum, transversum.*
THORAX *elongatus vel quadratus, rectangularis, ad basin constrictus, ad latera depressus et marginatus.*
ELYTRA *sat lata, ad apicem attenuata, aliquando fortiter ante medium oblique depressa; plerumque glabra.*
PEDES *robusti; tarsorum antic. art. 2us brevis; tibiæ posticæ ad apicem dentibus duobus armatæ.*

Labrum subcircular, narrower than the base of the head; the surface is sprinkled with a few separate and strong hairs.

Mandibles robust, partially concealed.

Maxillary palpi (Tab. I. fig. 7 *m*) filiform, elongate, not geniculated; the basal joint minute, abruptly truncate at its apex; the second slightly dilated towards the apex; the third somewhat longer than the second, subparallel; the apical joint larger in proportion than that of *Roicus*, but minute, much narrower than the second, and conical.

Labial palpi (Tab. I. fig. 7 *n*): the second joint is slightly dilated medially, and the third subelongate and conical.

[*] εὐφεγγής, præclarus.

Antennæ (Tab. I. fig. 7 *a*) more or less incrassated and subpubescent, in length equal to two-thirds of that of the elytra; the first joint is narrow at the base, dilated medially, and distinctly curved outwards; the second short and ovate; the third elongated, of greater length than the second, fine, and very *slightly* incrassated towards the apex; the fourth of the same form (but hardly so long) as the third; the fifth to the eighth short, distinctly dilated, the breadth of the seventh being almost equal to its length; the apical joints are more attenuated: all are (when viewed under a high power) subpubescent, the apex especially of each joint being clothed with a few distinct and strong hairs. The antennæ are approximate at their base, situated immediately below and between the eyes.

Eyes large, subglobose, situated nearly at the base of the head.

Head transverse; when viewed from the side, inclined at right angles to the plane of the elytra; not produced in front, deeply and thickly punctate.

Thorax elongate, slightly broader than the head, rectangular, somewhat constricted towards the base; the sides are depressed and deeply marginate: very deeply and coarsely punctate.

Scutellum triangular, impunctate, situated below the plane of the elytra.

Elytra considerably broader than the thorax, robust, slightly attenuated towards the apex: in *Lemoeides*, a few deep and scattered punctures are found antemedially, grouping themselves around a deeply incised medial oblique depression.

Legs robust; under a high power very finely pubescent. The *anterior femora* are *slightly* incurved, with a tendency to dilatation medially and near the apex. The *tibiæ* are straight, and of the same breadth throughout. The *tarsi* (Tab. I. fig. 7 *d*) are short, more distinctly pubescent; the basal joint is broad, cordiform; the second smaller than either the first or the third, and ovate; the third is shorter than the first, but somewhat broader, fringed throughout with a thick and close pubescence, not bilobed; the apical joint is elongate, gradually incrassated towards the apex. The terminal claw is simple, not toothed in its inner surface. The *posterior femora* are (when viewed transversely) oviform, considerably incrassated throughout, but most so medially. The *tibia* (Tab. I. fig. 7 *g*) is short, of equal breadth throughout, slightly incurved at its immediate base; and beyond the insertion of the tarsus (where it is somewhat dilated) more distinctly sinuated, and produced at the extremity into two curved, short, and robust teeth; the insertion of the tarsus is at between one-sixth and one-fifth of its total length. The *tarsus* (Tab. I. fig. 7 *h*) is more elongate than the anterior, and considerably narrower; the first joint elongate, attenuated, subdilated, and truncate at the apex; the second shorter, and of the same form; the third subovate, not bilobed; the whole densely fringed with close pubescence; the last joint terminates in a bladder-like inflation, which, from above, completely conceals the terminal claw, and which (more distinctly seen when viewed obliquely) itself is terminated in a pseudo-claw, similar in form and size to the claw which it protects.

1. **Euphenges sericeus.** (TAB. I. fig. 6.)

E. *oblongo-ovatus, latus, robustus, impubescens, rufo-ferrugineus; capite brevi, transverso, elongatulo, super basin antennarum oblique (in litteræ V forma) carinato, subtiliter pubescenti, ad apicem flavo-rufo, ad basin fusco-rufo; thorace quadrato, angulis subacutis, ad basin transverse depresso, impunctato, glabro, ad latera fulvo-pubescenti; elytris latis, ad apicem subattenuatis, striato-punctatis, ante medium oblique depressis, hac fovea obliqua, apice, et marginatione lurido-pubescentibus; antennis filiformibus, robustis, art.1–5 fulvis, 6–11 piceis; pedibus robustis, pallide rufis, femoribus posticis nigro adumbratis.*

Long. corp. 3 lin., lat. 1⅔ lin.

Oblong-ovate, broad, robust, impubescent, of a palish brown-red colour throughout. *Head* transverse, narrow, elongated in front: between the upper part of the labrum and the base of the antennæ is a triangular carination, which is bisected by a longitudinal medial carination from the base of the antennæ: above the base of the antennæ and between the eyes is a V-shaped ridge, extending in an oblique direction towards the inner and upper margin of the eyes; this ridge is most apparent when seen obliquely: eyes tolerably large, situated at a short distance from the base of the head, and not extending laterally as far as the angles of the thorax: the surface very obsoletely clothed (when viewed under a very high magnifying power) with flavous pubescence, especially near the inner margin of the eyes; the colour below the base of the antennæ flavo-rufous; above, of a darker brown rufous. *Thorax* quadrate, rectangular, rectilinear, slightly broader than the head, considerably narrower than the elytra; the anterior and posterior angles subacute; the anterior angles subdepressed, the sides marginate, while at the base is a broad and very shallow transverse depression; the surface is impunctate, glabrous, and thickly clothed at the sides with a close tawny pubescence. *Scutellum* triangular, fuscous, indistinctly clothed with flavous pubescence. *Elytra* much broader than the thorax, slightly attenuated towards the apex; punctures, arranged in the form of striæ, become almost entirely obsolete near the apex: a little in front of the middle is an obliquely transverse depression, extending from the first or second stria towards the shoulders; this depression is abrupt in form, and clothed with thick tawny pubescence; the base also, broadly (that is, for about a third of the whole length of the elytra), and the margination (more broadly and distinctly behind the shoulders) are similarly clothed with thick pubescence of an ashy-fulvous colour. *Antennæ* long, robust, the length of the joints from the third to the eleventh being nearly equal; the joints 1–5 fulvous, 6–11 piceous. *Legs* robust, pale rufous,—the apex of the posterior femora being tipped with black, and the tarsi being suffused with piceous.

Brazil. In the collection of M. Chevrolat.

2. Euphenges Lemoeides. (Tab. I. fig. 7.)

E. *oblongo-ovatus, punctatus, ferrugineus, nitidus; capite brevi, ad basin antennarum bituberculato, crebre punctato; thorace quadrato, rectangulari, ad basin transverse depresso, punctato; elytris apicem versus attenuatis, ad basin punctatis, ad medium oblique fossulatis, ad apicem impunctatis; antennis robustis, art. 5–8 incrassatis; flavis, art. 6–8 nigris; pedibus fulvis, tibiis posticis incurvatis.*

Long. corp. 1¾ lin., lat. ¾ lin.

Oblong-ovate, coarsely and sparingly punctate throughout, bright ferrugineous. *Head* short, slightly produced; eyes large, prominent, situated at the base of the head; below the insertion of the antennæ is a transverse triangular plane depression; immediately above the base of the antennæ are two contiguous obsolete tubercles; surface coarsely and very thickly punctate. *Thorax* quadrate (almost elongated), rectangular, subcylindrical; the anterior angles are depressed; sides marginate; at the base is a broad, transverse, shallow depression; surface coarsely punctured (the punctures being less frequent than on the head). *Scutellum* small, triangular. *Elytra* at the shoulders broader than the thorax, and gradually diminishing in breadth towards the apex; impunctate; from the base four lines of broad and coarse punctures (three near the humeral angle, and one at the suture) terminate in a very deep abrupt channel, which is deepest and broadest near to the mid suture, thence extending upwards obliquely towards the humeral angle. *Antennæ* short, robust, incrassated; the first joint broad, medially dilated; the second very short, narrower; the third fine, twice the length of the first; the fourth nearly as long as the third; the fifth to eighth gradually incrassated; all subpubescent; the first joint rufo-flavous, the second rufo-fulvous, the third and fourth flavous (clouded with testaceous), the fifth to eighth black, the ninth to eleventh flavo-testaceous. *Legs* tolerably robust; the posterior femora subelongate, robust, parallel, with an oblique fovea on the outer side near the apex; the posterior tibiæ robust, *incurved, produced* considerably *beyond the insertion of the tarsi*; colour fulvous throughout.

This species closely resembles in its general form that of the genus *Lema*, and in this respect differs from the preceding species. By the characters of its mouth (combined with the form of the elytra and of the posterior tibiæ) it proves itself clearly to be separated generically from other neighbouring species.

From the Amazon River. In the collection of Mr. Bates.

Genus 4. PHYSONYCHIS*.

Dej. Cat. (1837) p. 408.

Ovatus, subparallelus, impubescens.

LABRUM *subcirculare.*

PALPI MAXILLARES *elongati, art. 3° subcylindrico (ad apicem leviter dilatato), ultimo abbreviato.*

PALPI LABIALES *minuti, haud elongati.*

ANTENNÆ *robustæ, subincrassatæ, art. 1, 2, 8 et 11 compressis et dilatatis (in ♀ simplicibus).*

CAPUT *haud productum, depressum, breve.*

THORAX *latus, transversus, ad latera marginatus.*

ELYTRA *parallela, subdepressa, ad apicem rotundata.*

PEDES *robusti, tibiarum apicibus in ♂ dilatatis.*

Labrum subcircular, more subcircular and relatively smaller than in the preceding genus, *Euphenges.*

Mandibles robust; at their inner edge is a slight tooth-like projection; concealed.

Maxillary palpi (Tab. I. fig. 8 *m*) elongate, geniculated probably at the apex of the second joint; the basal joint obsolete; the second parallel, subdilated and truncate at its apex, which receives the insertion of the third joint; the third joint is longer, subcylindrical, slightly dilated towards the apex, broader than the second (its length being nearly double its breadth); the apical joint is abbreviated, conical, at the base equal in diameter to the apex of the third joint.

Labial palpi minute, not elongated; the apex of the terminal joint rounded.

Antennæ (Tab. I. fig. 8 *a*) robust, filiform, pubescent, subincrassated;

* φυσάω, inflo; ὄνυξ, unguis.

the basal joint very long and broadly developed, the breadth being half its length, and nearly three times the length of the second joint; flattened, not cylindrical; the sides parallel; and the apex, not attenuated, but broadly and transversely subsinuate; at the *angle* of the apex is the insertion of the second joint, which is short and ovate; the third joint to the sixth are elongate, subdilated towards the apex (the fourth, fifth and sixth being each distinctly longer and more robust than the third); the seventh is incurved and obliquely truncate at the apex, thus causing the insertion of the eighth to be not in the same line as that of the others; the eighth is broader and much shorter than the seventh, its breadth being almost equal to its length, sinuate in form, dilated at the inner side of the base, and broadly truncate at the apex; the ninth and tenth are of equal breadth with, but shorter than, the eighth; and the eleventh is greater in length than the ninth and tenth together, somewhat narrower, curved outwards at the base, and slightly attenuated towards the apex. In the *females* the antennæ are filiform, robust and simple,—the first joint being, however, considerably flattened and dilated, although not so much as in the males, and the fourth joint longer and more robust than the others.

Eyes large, subglobose, situated nearly at the base of the head, and distant.

Head short, transverse, very slightly produced in front, and inclined at right angles to the plane of the elytra.

Thorax much broader than the head, transverse, in front distinctly emarginate; the sides broadly marginate, and converging towards the front; the line of the base is somewhat rounded—that is, parallel to the line of the anterior margin.

Scutellum large, triangular,—the apex being subcircular, impunctate, and glabrous.

Elytra broader than the thorax, parallel, subdepressed, rounded at the apex, at the sides marginate, covered throughout with minute and very thickly disposed punctures; along the surface are two obscurely defined longitudinal ridges, in some specimens almost obsolete.

Legs robust, impunctate. The *anterior femora* are tolerably robust, hardly dilated, cylindrical. The *tibiæ* shorter than the femora, dilated towards the apex, rounded at their inner margin, and flattened or somewhat hollowed out at the outer margin,—armed in both sexes around the socket that receives the apex of the tarsus with a row of strong, upright, closely arranged teeth, resembling rigid hairs, or the teeth of a comb. In the males the apex of the tibiæ (Tab. I. fig. 8 *c*) is very considerably dilated, and produced at its anterior margin into an obtuse angle, broadly truncated at the apex; around this truncation (which is much more prominent than in the females) is a row of closely arranged spines, while the angle of truncation itself is armed with an acute spur, and the whole surface clothed with thick and very strong pubescence. The *tarsus* is short, and in both sexes robust; the basal joint is broad and short, somewhat rounded; the second more minute, and triangular; the third joint is somewhat broader than the basal, broadly triangular, not bilobed; the fourth joint is elongate, slightly incurved, and gradually incrassated towards the apex; the apical claw being bifid, and armed at the inner surface of each limb with a short, strong spur-like process. The *posterior femora* are broad, dilated, and when viewed obliquely from beneath, very much rounded above, and almost hollowed out at their lower margin. The *tibiæ* are straight, abruptly bent at the immediate base and gradually dilated towards the apex; the terminal socket (at the insertion of the tibiæ) is armed on either side with minute comb-like teeth. The *posterior tarsi* are short, and less dilated than the anterior; the first joint being triangular; the second of similar form, but more minute; the third shorter, but broader than the first, almost circular, not bilobed; and the apical joint attenuated (shorter than the posterior), and terminating above the apical claw in a globular inflation.

In *Physonychis* the sexual characteristics are the dilatation of the antennæ in the males (the basal, and eighth to eleventh joints), and the lateral projection at the apex of the anterior tibiæ; there is a slight difference also between the sexes in coloration.

1. **Physonychis smaragdina.** (Tab. I. fig. 8.) B.M.

P. (♂) *oblongo-ovata, parallela, subcylindrica, crebre punctata, viridi-ænea aut ænea, glabra; capite brevi, inter oculos longitudinaliter foveolato, ad basin variolato, flavo-ferrugineo, ad basin fusco; thorace lato, transverso, ad latera marginato, ad basin transverse depresso, punctato, flavo-ferrugineo; elytris parallelis, ad apicem rotundatis, crebre punctatis; antennis robustis, ad apicem dilatatis, art. 7 et 11 plus minus incurvatis, art. 1–5 flavis, 6–11 fuscis; pedibus sat robustis, flavis, femorum posticorum apicibus fusco suffusis.*

♂ Long. corp. 3¾ lin., lat. 1¾ lin.
♀ Long. corp. 3¼–4 lin., lat. 1½–2 lin.

Oblong-ovate, parallel, subcylindrical, rounded at the apex, deeply and thickly punctate, of a bright metallic-green colour. *Head* short, transverse, depressed, hardly produced in front; immediately above the labrum is a broad deep and transversely depressed plane, extending at its upper surface to the base of the antennæ; above the base of the antennæ is a longitudinal deep fovea, on either side of which (closely adjoining the margin of the eyes) is a more minute longitudinal depression, which is most distinct at the immediate base of the antennæ; the medial fovea is bounded on either side by a somewhat raised and glabrous surface, and terminates abruptly before it reaches the base of the head; the surface at the base is thickly and very coarsely variolated; colour flavo-ferrugineous, the basal line being distinctly fuscous; the eyes are large and prominent. *Thorax* broader than the head, transverse and contracted in front, anteriorly very slightly emarginate; the anterior angles depressed and minutely prominent; the sides broadly marginate; at the base is a transverse depression closely adjoining the basal line (more distinctly apparent medially than at the sides), and corresponding in breadth and depth to the lateral marginations; the surface is finely and thickly punctate throughout; flavo-ferrugineous. *Scutellum* triangular, rounded at the apex, impunctate, darkly flavo-ferrugineous. *Elytra* broader than the thorax, parallel, very slightly attenuated towards the apex, which is rounded; the surface is covered throughout with exceedingly close and tolerably distinct punctures; from the shoulders to the apex are two almost obsolete and *indistinct* longitudinal ridges, hardly perceptible except when under a high magnifying power; the colour throughout is of a bright metallic emerald-green, shaded medially (in most specimens) with a tinge of copper colour. *Antennæ* robust and tolerably long, dilated towards the apex; the first joint broad, ovate, and very distinctly *flattened*; the second short and narrow; the third to the sixth elongated, and of equal breadth throughout; the seventh is *slightly incurved*, and extends apically somewhat beyond the insertion of the eighth; the eighth is shorter, broadly dilated, especially on the side of the apex of the seventh joint, and by this lateral dilatation, as well as by its proceeding from the side (rather than from the end) of the last joint, the seventh joint forms a *geniculation*, or elbow, in the line of the antennæ; the ninth and tenth joints are broad and flattened, their outline being angulated at the apex and slightly rounded off at the base; the eleventh and terminal joint is somewhat narrower than these, but equal in length to both of them united: in form *slightly incurvated*, the whole of the joints of the antennæ appear to be flattened, rather than of a cylindrical form; in colour the joints 1–5 are flavous and 6–11 fuscous. *Legs* tolerably robust, flavous throughout,—the apex of the posterior femora being suffused with fuscous.

The above description is taken from a male specimen. The females have (as we might expect) *filiform* and *simple* antennæ, though of equal length with those of the males; the legs also (especially the anterior tibiæ) are not quite so robust. All the examples which I have seen differ also sexually in shade of colour, there being in the females an entire absence of a metallic coppery hue; and the emerald green colour, so conspicuously beautiful in the males, being represented by blue.

This handsome species is not uncommon on the western coast of Africa,—Guinea, Senegal, and Old Calabar.

Genus 5. RHINOTMETUS*.

Dej. Cat. (1837) p. 407.

CORPUS *elongato-ovale vel subovatum, convexum.*

LABRUM *transversum, integrum.*

MANDIBULÆ *robustæ, reconditæ, ad apicem ipsum sæpius fissæ, necnon intra apicem dente armatæ.*

PALPI MAXILLARES *elongati, subincrassati, art. 3^{tio} ad apicem oblique truncato.*

PALPI LABIALES *minuti, art. 2^{ndo} lato.*

ANTENNÆ *filiformes, articulis 1mo et 3^{tio} inter se æqualibus (illo distincte robusto), 2^{ndo} brevi, ultimo ad apicem acuminato.*

CAPUT *plus minus antice productum, subattenuatum.*

THORAX *elongatus, haud transversus, elytris plerumque multo angustior, antice rotundatus et subcontractus, ad latera depressus et marginatus.*

ELYTRA *sat robusta, punctato-striata, modo vestita, modo nuda.*

ABDOMEN *e segmentis quatuor compositum.*

PEDES *saltatorii (femoribus posticis valde incrassatis); tibiis anterioribus ecalcaratis, posticis calcari singulo unciformi armatis; tarsis pseudotetrameris, anterioribus subtus dense vestitis, artic. 1mo et 3^{tio} dilatatis (hoc valde bilobo), posticis haud dilatatis, brevibus, articulis 1mo, 2^{ndo} et 3^{tio} subæqualibus (2^{ndo} et 3^{tio} inter se subarctius connatis), subtus leviter productis, articulo ultimo ad apicem ipsum in globulum subito aucto, unguiculis minutis subtus munito, superne e visu reconditis.*

Labrum transverse or subsinuate, rounded at the lateral margins, narrower than the base of the head.

Mandibles small, robust, concealed from above.

Maxillary palpi (Front. fig. 3 *m*, 5 *m*) elongate, subincrassated; the basal joint small; the second ovate, truncate at the apex, and gradually attenuated towards the base, the length being not quite double the breadth; the third is of the same form as, but slightly longer and wider than, the second, broadly truncate at the apex; the terminal

* ῥίν, nasus; τέμνω, seco.

joint is short, conical, its base being much smaller than the apex of the third joint, and its length being greater than its breadth.

Labial palpi (Front. fig. 4 *n*, 5 *n*) minute ; the basal joint attenuated ; the second broader, and transversely truncate ; the apical joint minute, shorter and much narrower than the second.

Antennæ robust, filiform, tolerably approximate, situated below and within the inner margin of the eyes ; the basal joint dilated (in some species more than in others) ; the second is short and ovate, narrower than the first ; the third is not broader than the second, of equal length with the first ; the rest are subequal, slightly shorter as well as broader than the third, parallel, rounded at the base and truncate at the apex ; the terminal joint is more attenuated and produced.

Eyes large, subglobose, situated at the side of the head, at some distance from the base.

Head (Front. fig. 3 *k*) narrower than the thorax, elongated, broadly produced in front : this apical elongation varies in different individuals in length, but is in all instances very marked, as compared with the form of *Monoplatus* and other allied genera.

Thorax elongate, attenuated in front, distinctly broader than the head, but narrower than the elytra ; the anterior angles are more or less depressed ; the sides are always tolerably parallel (except at the apex, where they are constricted, and rounded at the angle) and evenly submarginate ; the anterior margin is rounded more or less, never in any degree emarginate ; and the anterior *angles* are rounded (not, as in *Tetragonotes*, distinctly acute); the surface is either glabrous or pubescent.

Scutellum triangular, occasionally subcordiform, generally impunctate, and placed below the plane of the elytra.

Elytra much broader than the thorax, subparallel, or in some species robust, punctate-striate, with an antemedial transverse depression (which is more or less distinct) extending obliquely upwards towards the shoulders, and giving an appearance of prominence to the scutellary angles ; the surface is generally punctate-striate.

Legs sufficiently robust ; when seen under a high power, subpubescent for the most part. The *anterior femora* subcylindrical, of nearly equal breadth throughout. The *tibiæ* (Front. fig. 5 *b*) are inflected immediately at the base, straight, gradually and slightly incrassated towards the apex ; at the apex itself (when seen from above) attenuated. The *tarsi* (Front. fig. 5 *d*) are shorter than the tibia ; the basal joint short and broad (not broader than the dilated part of the tibia); the second of the same form as the first, but smaller ; the third distinctly bilobed, the breadth being greater than the length ; these three basal joints are densely fringed with thick pubescence ; the terminal joint elongated, gradually thickened and incurved towards the apex : the claw is bifid (Front. fig. 5 *e*), each limb being cleft into two separate teeth ; it would seem that these two limbs are separable more or less from each other in different examples. The *posterior femora* (Front. fig. 4 *f*) are somewhat flattened, but (when seen transversely) very short, in form ovate, truncate broadly at the apex, and generally pubescent. The *tibia* (Front. fig. 4 *f*) is robust, straight, considerably shorter than the femur, somewhat incurved downwards at the immediate base ; the surface (when viewed from behind) is flattened, and longitudinally keeled or marginated: in each of these marginations, near the apex, behind the insertion of the tarsus, is a single broadly defined tooth (corresponding exactly with the *row* of tooth-like prominences in the females of *Monoplatus*); this margination is continued on either side to the apex or socket which receives the tarsus, where it is armed with a row of short, sharp, and closely arranged teeth, and at its *extreme* apex armed further with a *single* (not double, as in other genera) incurved, robust claw. The *tarsus* (Front. fig. 4 *h*) is about two-thirds the length of the tibia, and constricted ; the first joint attenuated, and subdilated at the apex ; the second of the same form as the first, but somewhat longer and narrower ; the third much shorter and considerably broader, not bilobed ; these three are all margined, and clothed on the under surface with a slight pubescence: from a hollowed socket in the middle of the third joint proceeds the apical joint, elongated, gradually incurved, and terminating in a large globular inflation, which is above (and completely conceals) the apical claw ; this claw (Front. fig. 4 *i*) is bifid, each member consisting of two distinct teeth, cleft nearly to the base.

This genus approaches *Physonychis* in the peculiar construction of the apex of the posterior tibiæ ; there is the same terminal claw and the same fringe of sharp and closely disposed teeth around the hollowed socket that receives the base of the tarsus ; and by the parallel and elongated facies of some of its species (as *R. marginatus, R. cruciatus,* and *R. spectabilis*) it forms a connecting link between this, the preceding group, and the following genus, *Tetragonotes*.

1. **Rhinotmetus leptocephalus.**

Œdionychis leptocephalus, *Perty, Conspectus Anim. Artic.* p. 110. tab. 22. fig. 5.

R. *oblongo-ovatus, subcylindricus, subelongatus, flavo-pubescens, niger ; capite elongato, ad apicem carinato, ad basin granulato, rufo ; thorace elongato, elytris angustiori, antice subattenuato, punctato, flavo-pubescenti, rufo ; elytris robustis, leviter punctato-*

*striatis, pilo flavescenti dense obtectis, maculis utrinque duabus
(apud humeros et post medium) nigro-violaceis denudatis; antennis
filiformibus, fuscis, ad basin rufo suffusis, corporis dimidio haud
longioribus; pedibus anterioribus piceis, posticis rufo-griseis.*

Long. corp. $3\frac{1}{2}$–$3\frac{3}{4}$ lin., lat. $1\frac{3}{4}$ lin.

Oblong-ovate, robust, subcylindrical, subelongate, covered for the most part with a fine flavous pile; black. *Head* short, transverse, produced broadly in front; above the labrum, extending to the base of the antennæ, is a longitudinal medial carination, divided at the insertion of the antennæ, and thence taking on either side an oblique direction; near the labrum (extending to this medial ridge) are two other oblique carinations; immediately above the insertion of the antennæ (adjoining the inner surface of the eyes) are two minute depressions; eyes tolerably large, situated nearly at the base of the head; the surface granulated, rufous, suffused (especially in front) with fuscous, the labrum being flavo-rufous. *Thorax* quadrate (almost elongate), broader than the head, but constricted towards the apex, so as to meet anteriorly (and almost in the same line) the lateral margin of the head; the surface is depressed (as compared with the surface of the elytra); the anterior angles are almost obsolete, and much depressed as well as constricted; the sides are faintly marginate; at the base (when viewed laterally) is an obsolete transverse depression; the surface is finely punctate, darkly rufous, and covered (probably) throughout with a fine thick flavous pubescence. *Scutellum* triangular, impunctate, fusco-pubescent. *Elytra* considerably broader and more robust than the thorax, subattenuated towards the apex, punctate-striate (the striæ being obsolete and the punctures deeply impressed and distinct); at the shoulders, near the seventh stria, is a short and well-defined longitudinal channel, which gives a square and well-developed form to the extreme apex of the shoulder; the surface is clothed throughout with a thick flavo-fulvous pubescence, except near the scutellary angles, where a considerable surface (denuded of this pubescence), of a circular form, is glabrous and black; also, postmedially, a transverse regularly defined fascia is formed (broadest near the suture) by a similar absence of this pubescence; at the shoulders (at the extreme apex) is an obscure suffused spot of rufous. *Abdomen* rufo-ferrugineous. *Antennæ* robust, filiform, fuscous, the basal joint being rufo-fuscous. *Legs* clothed, more sparingly than the elytra, with flavous pubescence; the anterior fuscous, sparingly suffused with rufous; the posterior rufous, the base of the tibiæ and the inflated posterior claw being rufo-fuscous.

Taken by Spix and Martius in the Minas province (Serra do Caraça), and by others sparingly in the neighbourhood of Rio Janeiro.

2. Rhinotmetus marginatus. (Front. fig. 3.)

R. *oblongo-ovatus, subparallelus, subcylindricus, pubescens, niger; capite elongato, antice carinato, super basin antennarum foveolato, flavo-pubescenti, ad basin granulato; thorace quadrato, antice constricto, subtiliter punctato, glabro; elytris sat latis et robustis, punctato-striatis, ad latera fascia dense rufo-testacea sericea marginatis; antennis filiformibus, nigro-fuscis, ad basin rufo suffusis; pedibus nigris, femoribus anterioribus ad basin, posticisque tibiis et tarsis rufo-testaceis (tibiis basalibus rufo-fuscis).*

Long. corp. 3 lin., lat. 1 lin.

Oblong-ovate, subparallel, subcylindrical, less robust than *R. leptocephalus*, faintly pubescent, black. *Head* narrow, broadly elongated in the front: above the labrum is a medial longitudinal keel-like ridge, which extends to the base of the antennæ; on either side of this, two obliquely transverse carinations are produced to the lateral margins of the labrum; above the base of the antennæ is an obsolete and short longitudinal fovea: eyes large and tolerably prominent, situated at some little distance from the base of the head; at their upper and inner margins is a very slight tubercle-like elevation, which is rufous; the surface between the eyes is sparingly flavo-pubescent, and at the base coarsely granulated. *Thorax* quadrate (almost elongated); the sides parallel, and narrowed *in front* so as to meet the base of the head (not, as in *R. leptocephalus*, *gradually* constricted), broader than the head, with the anterior angles much depressed, constricted, and obsolete; the sides submarginate; near the basal angles is a broad and obsolete depression; a faint medial longitudinal impression is apparent when viewed obliquely with a high power; the surface very finely punctate and glabrous. *Scutellum* triangular, impunctate, fuscous-black. *Elytra* broader than the thorax, parallel, subelongate, rounded at the apex; the surface near the scutellary angles is very slightly raised; punctate-striate (the punctures being almost entirely concealed by a short and closely squamose pubescence); from the fifth stria to the ninth (at the distance of two striæ from the lateral margination) is a longitudinal band of close yellow or rufo-testaceous pile, completely clothing the surface, commencing at the shoulders and extending nearly to the apex. *Antennæ* robust, filiform, faintly subpubescent, fuscous, the basal joints being suffused with rufous. *Legs* black, the anterior femora being at their base and extreme apex flavo-ferrugineous, and the posterior tibiæ and tarsi rufo-testaceous (the base of the tibia, and the globular inflation immediately above the posterior claw being rufo-fuscous).

I took a single specimen of this beautiful and distinct species by beating in the forests near to Constancia (the English boarding-house kept by Mr. R. Heath, in the heart of the Organ Mountains), December 1856.

3. Rhinotmetus cruciatus. (FRONT. fig. 4.)

R. *oblongo-ovatus, subparallelus, elongatus, fulvo-pubescens, punctato-striatus, niger; capite antice producto et ad medium carinato, ad basin antennarum bituberculato, fulvo-pubescenti, ad basin granulato, inter oculos nigro, ad basin fusco-rufo; thorace elongato, subdepresso, lateribus parallelis, antice constricto, plus minus fulvo-pubescenti, rufo, ad marginem et ad medium fusco; elytris robustis, distincte punctato-striatis, nigris, pilo flavo testaceo brevi dense vestitis, apud humeros macula subcirculari nigra, et apicem juxta altera oblongo-ovali, his maculis quatuor denudatis; antennis filiformibus, nigro-fuscis, art. 2-4 rufo suffusis; pedibus nigro-fuscis, posticorum tibiis tarsisque rufo-flavescentibus.*

Long. corp. 3 lin., lat. 1 lin.

Oblong-ovate, subparallel, subelongate, for the most part flavo-fulvous, pubescent, punctate-striate, black. *Head* narrow (as compared with the thorax), produced broadly in front (the labrum being abruptly narrower than the apex of the head): from the base of the antennæ are two oblique carinations extending to the outer margins of the labrum; between these is a medial longitudinal carination which reaches the base of the antennæ; immediately above the base are two longitudinal tubercular elevations, divided the one from the other by an abrupt and short fovea: eyes tolerably large and globose, situated at some little distance from the base of the head; the surface between the eyes is fulvo-pubescent; at the base distinctly granulated; near the insertion of the antennæ the colour is black, at the base rufous or fusco-rufous. *Thorax* broader than the head, elongate, subdepressed; the sides parallel, constricted in front, and slightly marginate; the base (when viewed laterally) is subdepressed; the anterior angles are obsolete; the surface is clothed throughout with a fine fulvous pubescence (more distinctly near the base and sides); in colour fulvo-rufous, the margins, and also a medial longitudinal line, being fuscous. *Scutellum* triangular, impunctate, flavous. *Elytra* broader than the thorax, subparallel, tolerably robust, rounded at the apex, punctate-striate (the striæ being, except at the sides, obsolete, and the punctures deep and distinct); the colour is black,—a broad antemedial band, the apex, and also the suture, being rufous; these cause the rest of the surface to constitute four large and subcircular black spots (those at the apex extending from the shoulders nearly to the medial elytra, and the postmedial pair extending nearly to the apex); these spots are well-defined and subcircular; the rufous surface which separates them is clothed throughout with thick fulvous pubescence. *Antennæ* robust, filiform, fuscous, the basal joints being suffused with rufous. *Legs* sparingly pubescent, fuscous; the base of the anterior femora being flavous, and the posterior tibiæ and tarsi being rufous suffused with piceous.

A single example of this species was taken by Mr. Gray and myself near Petropolis (Organ Mountains, Rio Janeiro), February 1857.

4. Rhinotmetus spectabilis. (Tab. II. fig. 1.)

R. *oblongo-ovatus, parallelus, subdepressus, flavo-pubescens, punctato-striatus, niger; capite producto, ad apicem longitudinaliter carinato, ad basin antennarum bituberculato, flavo-pubescenti, granulato, inter oculos nigro, ad basin rufo-fusco; thorace elongato, antice constricto, ad angulos basales depresso, sparsim flavo-pubescenti, nigro, ad basin rufo-fusco; elytris subcylindricis, punctato-striatis, flavo-pubescentibus, nigris; antennis robustis, filiformibus, piceis, ad basin rufis; pedibus fuscis, tibiis tarsisque posticis pallide ferrugineis.*

Long. corp. 3 lin., lat. 1 lin.

Oblong-ovate, parallel, robust, subdepressed, fusco-pubescent, punctate-striate, black. *Head* produced, elongated in front; from the labrum a deep longitudinal carination extends upwards to the base of the antennæ, on either side of which are two others obliquely transverse: immediately above the base of the antennæ are two short longitudinal tubercular elevations (more distinctly apparent by a deep medial fovea between them); between these and the basal line is an obsolete medial carination: the surface is finely flavo-pubescent and granulated; above the insertion of the antennæ black, at the base of the head rufo-fuscous; eyes large, prominent, globose, situated at some distance from the posterior margin. *Thorax* produced (almost quadrate); the anterior angles are very much depressed and obsolete; the sides parallel, marginate, and constricted in front; near the basal angles is a broad and shallow depression; the surface is finely and sparingly flavo-pubescent, more distinctly so at the base and sides; black, the posterior margin being rufo-fuscous. *Scutellum* small, triangular, fuscous. *Elytra* parallel, robust, subcylindrical, punctate-striate (the punctures being quite obliterated, and the striæ partially concealed by a thick golden-flavous pubescence); the surface beneath this pile is black. *Abdomen* somewhat pubescent and black. *Antennæ* robust, filiform; the four basal joints are rufous, the rest piceous. *Legs* fuscous,—the base of the anterior femora, as well as the base of the tibiæ, being rufous, the posterior tibiæ and tarsi pale ferrugineous, and the globular inflation of the posterior claw brightly rufo-fuscous.

I captured a single specimen of this species at Petropolis (Organ Mountains, Rio Janeiro), in the month of February 1857.

5. Rhinotmetus crucifer.

R.: *oblongo-ovatus, attenuatus, parallelus, pubescens; capite antice producto, ad apicem carinato, flavo-pubescenti; thorace elongato, antice constricto, angulis anterioribus obsoletis, depressis, flavopubescenti, nigro; elytris parallelis, punctato-striatis, holosericeis (nisi maculis duabus ad humeros, alterisque postmediis; hæ quatuor rotundatæ, pilo* nigro-fusco *obtectæ); antennis filiformibus, fuscis; pedibus fulvis, tarsis tibiisque ad basin anterioribus fusco suffusis, tibiis tarsisque posticis rufo-fulvis.*

Long. corp. 2¾ lin., lat. 1 lin.

Oblong-ovate, attenuated, parallel, subcylindrical. *Head* produced, elongated in front; below the base of the antennæ are two oblique carinations extending to the lateral margins of the labrum; above the base of the antennæ is a minute longitudinal fovea; eyes large, prominent, situated at some distance from the base of the head; the surface finely pubescent throughout. *Thorax* elongate, the sides parallel, and constricted in front; the anterior angles obsolete and much depressed; the sides submarginate; when viewed under a high power, a medial longitudinal fovea may be faintly traced, extending from the apex to the scutellum; the surface is finely and thickly flavo-pubescent throughout, and black (not, as in *R. cruciatus*, *sparingly* flavo-pubescent and *rufous*). *Scutellum* triangular, impunctate, and fuscous. *Elytra* parallel, subdepressed, punctatestriate (the punctures being entirely, and the striæ almost entirely concealed by a thick pubescence which clothes the surface *throughout*); the markings on this pubescence closely resemble the pattern of *R. cruciatus*, the antemedial transverse fascia and the sutural band together forming the boundaries of four large ovate spots. There are, however, these points of difference between the two species: in *R. crucifer* the medial fascia is broader, the pubescence of which it is composed is shorter, more dense, and flavous; the surface of the elytra is black, and not rufous; and the surface of the four ovate spots is (not, as in *R. cruciatus*, glabrous and impubescent, but) clothed throughout with a short and thick squamose pubescence. *Antennæ* robust, filiform, and fuscous throughout. *Legs* flavous,—the tarsi and base of the anterior tibiæ being suffused with fuscous, and the posterior tibiæ and tarsi rufo-fulvous.

After much hesitation, I have satisfied myself that this ought properly to be recognized as specifically distinct from *R. cruciatus*. At first sight it appears almost absolutely identical; but the peculiar squamose pubescence on the elytra (which is represented in the other species by complete impubescence), combined with other points of difference, are too peculiar to admit of the one being constituted merely a variety of the other.

The only example that I have seen of this species is in the cabinet of Mr. Fry, taken by him at Morro Queimado, Brazil.

6. Rhinotmetus cyaneus. (Tab. II. fig. 2.)

R. *oblongo-ovatus, latus, robustus, subcylindricus, antice attenuatus, punctato-striatus, nigro-cyaneus; capite elongato, longitudinaliter (et ad basin oblique) carinato, nigro; thorace elongato, antice constricto, subtiliter punctato, nigro, glabro; elytris latis, robustis, ante medium transverse* subd*epressis, punctato-striatis; antennis robustis, filiformibus, nigris; pedibus nigris.*

Long. corp. 2½–3 lin., lat. 1½–1¾ lin.

Oblong-ovate, broad, robust, attenuated in front, rounded at the apex, punctate-striate, glabrous, of a dark metallic-blue colour. *Head* elongated, produced anteriorly: from the angles of the labrum to the base of the antennæ are two oblique, acutely-defined carinations; between them a longitudinal keel-like ridge extends upwards to the base of the antennæ; this, between the eyes, is divided into two ridges (suboblique and then transverse), which terminate at the upper and inner margins of the eyes: eyes large, tolerably prominent, situated near the base of the head; the surface (which is entirely occupied by these ridges) is impubescent and black. *Thorax* elongated (almost quadrate); the anterior angles much depressed and *constricted*; the sides parallel and marginate; at the base (when viewed laterally) is an obsolete transverse shallow depression; the surface (as seen under a high power) is finely and sparingly punctate; black, glabrous. *Scutellum* triangular, black. *Elytra* considerably broader than the thorax, robust, convex; a slight transverse antemedial depression extends obliquely upwards towards the humeral angles, giving an appearance of prominence to the surface near the scutellum (in some examples this depression is less apparent); the surface finely punctate-striate throughout, the interstices being very finely punctured; the colour is of a deep cyaneous hue, in some examples almost black. *Abdomen* black, sparingly clothed throughout with pale fulvous pubescence. *Antennæ* robust, filiform, black. *Legs* black, with slight griseous pubescence; the claws bifid, or with an inner tooth produced nearly as far as (and occasionally of the same size as) the outer tooth.

This brilliant species is in habits very active, using its wings in the hot sunshine with as much readiness almost as a *Lebia*. The species was tolerably abundant in the Organ Mountains in February 1857; it is represented in most cabinets.

7. Rhinotmetus assimilis.

R. *oblongo-ovatus, latus, robustus, antice attenuatus, punctato-striatus, purpureo-cyaneus, nitidus; capite elongato, longitudinaliter carinato, ad basin rugoso, nigro; thorace quadrato, sub-elongato, antice constricto, ad basin punctato, nigro; elytris latis, ovatis, robustis, punctato-striatis, purpureo-cyaneis; antennis robustis, filiformibus, nigro-fuscis; pedibus fuscis.*

Long. corp. 3 lin., lat. 1½ lin.

Oblong-ovate, broad, robust, attenuated in front, punctate-striate, of a deep purple colour, glabrous. *Head* transverse, produced in front: from the angles of the labrum two obliquely transverse carinations extend in the direction of the base of the antennæ; between these is a medial longitudinal carination (hardly so abrupt as in *R. cyaneus*), produced upwards between the basal joints of the antennæ, thence separating into two *slightly diverging* lines, is at last transversely deflected towards the upper and inner margins of the eyes; this marking is considerably less prominent than in *R. cyaneus*, and the surface above it, at the base of the head (which is rugose), is considerably broader: impubescent, black. *Thorax* quadrate (almost elongate); the anterior angles are much *constricted* and depressed; the sides parallel and slightly marginate; at the base (when viewed laterally) is a transverse depression (more distinct than in *R. assimilis* and in *R. depressus*), terminating at the humeral angles in a somewhat deeper fovea; the surface is subconvex and impunctate, except at the base and sides, where it is distinctly punctate (thus differing from *R. cyaneus* and *R. depressus*, which are impunctate throughout); impubescent, black. *Scutellum* triangular, black. *Elytra* broader than the thorax, ovate, robust, antemedially very slightly depressed, deeply punctate-striate, the colour being a rich deep purple. *Abdomen* black, with griseous pubescence; the segments are broad, extending at tolerably equal distances along the abdomen —not so much accumulated together as in *R. cyaneus*. *Antennæ* robust, filiform, of a fuscous-black colour. *Legs* robust, clothed more or less sparingly with fine pale-fuscous pubescence, of a black colour throughout.

Brazil.

The only example of this species which I have seen (in the collection of Mr. Baly) has the joints of the antennæ shorter, and the whole length of the antennæ very apparently shorter (in proportion to its body) than is the case in *R. cyaneus*. We shall be right, I think, in viewing this difference as *sexual* (the example of *R. assimilis*, with the shorter antennæ, being of course a female); and if this be the case, we are able to gather further, by an inspection of the two insects, that in *no other respects do the sexes of this genus differ*, either in robustness of legs, or in the relative lengths of the posterior tibiæ, or in the comparative size of the body: it is possible, however, that the male specimens may be found to have the transverse depression on the elytra more distinct and less obsolete than the females.

R. assimilis is readily separated from all its congeners (to many of which it would seem, at first sight, to be very closely allied) by the *distinct striation* as well as by the rich purple colour of its elytra.

8. Rhinotmetus depressus. (Front. fig. 5.)

R.. *oblongo-ovatus, robustus, subconvexus, antice attenuatus, punctatus, cyaneus; capite elongato, longitudinaliter carinato, ad basin punctato, nigro; thorace ad apicem constricto, quadrato, angulis anticis obsoletis et depressis, ad medium longitudinaliter subtiliter striato, nigro; elytris latis, subparallelis, ad medium oblique depressis, striato-punctatis; antennis robustis, filiformibus, nigris; pedibus robustis, fusco-subpubescentibus, nigris, tibiis posticis fusco suffusis.*

Long. corp. 2½ lin., lat. 1¼ lin.

Oblong-ovate, robust, subconvex, attenuated in front, punctate, shining, of a bright blue colour. *Head* transverse, produced in front: from the angles of the labrum two oblique carinations extend to the base of the antennæ; between these is a medial longitudinal keel-like ridge, which diverges slightly into two subparallel raised lines, and then is further produced at right angles to the upper and inner surface of the eyes; the eyes are large, subglobular, situated at some distance from the base of the head; the base is deeply punctate: black, glabrous. *Thorax* broader than the head, quadrate, and constricted in front; the anterior angles much depressed and obsolete; the sides marginate; at the base there is no trace of a transverse depression (as in *R. assimilis* and *R. cyaneus*); at the basal angles there is an obsolete group of punctures, and (when viewed obliquely) a faint medial longitudinal channel may be traced from the apex to the base; the surface, when seen under a high magnifying power, finely punctate, glabrous, black. *Scutellum* small, triangular, black. *Elytra* robust, broader than the thorax, and subparallel; from the antemedial suture a well-defined and somewhat deep depression extends obliquely upwards towards the humeral angles, giving an appearance of prominence to the surface near the scutellum (this depression is more distinctly impressed than in *R. cyaneus* and *R. assimilis*): the surface is covered throughout with punctures arranged in the form of striæ; these punctures are tolerably deep and apparent. *Antennæ* robust, filiform, of a fuscous-black colour. *Legs* robust, clothed more or less sparingly with pale fuscous pubescence; black, the posterior tibiæ and tarsi being suffused with piceous.

Closely allied to the two former species; but abundantly separated from either by its smaller size, by the distinct obliquely transverse depression on the elytra, and by the absence of any striæ on the elytra.

This species was taken by Mr. Gray and myself at Constancia, in the Organ Mountains, in January 1857. It has been taken by Mr. Fry and other collectors also in the neighbourhood of Rio Janeiro.

9. Rhinotmetus Waterhousii.

R. *oblongo-ovatus, elongatus, parallelus, nigro-cyaneus; capite valde producto, ad apicem longitudinaliter carinato, glabrato, superne granulato, rufo-fusco; thorace elongato, antice rotundato, impunctato, fusco; elytris subparallelis, punctis veluti in striis ordinatis, ante medium transverse depressis, nigro-cyaneis, nitidis; antennis robustis, nigris; pedibus nigris, femoribus nigro-fuscis.*

Var. A. *Capite et thorace nigris.*

Long. corp. 2¼ lin., lat. 1 lin.

Oblong-ovate, subcylindrical, elongated, sides parallel, of a dark-blue colour. *Head* considerably produced; eyes large, prominent, extending laterally beyond the apex of the thorax; from the upper lip a longitudinal acute ridge extends medially upwards to the insertion of the antennæ, and there (above the insertion) terminates in a V-shaped fork; surface of the head above finely granulated, darkly rufous. *Thorax* elongate, broader than the head, rounded and depressed anteriorly; sides slightly marginate;. surface with a very slight medial longitudinal fovea, impunctate, very darkly rufo-fuscous. *Scutellum* small, obscure, darkly fuscous. *Elytra* oblong, parallel, subconvex, with punctures arranged in the form of striæ; an antemedial transverse shallow depression extends obliquely towards the shoulders, giving the appearance of prominence to the surface near the scutellum; colour dark bright blue. *Antennæ* robust, filiform, black. *Legs* black, the femora being dark fuscous.

The colour of the head and thorax of this insect is evidently subject to slight variation; occasionally it is, instead of dark fuscous, a perfect black.

Distinguished at once by its *much smaller size* from all its congeners with which I am acquainted.

Brazil; the Island of S. Paulo. In the collections of M. Deyrolle and Mr. Waterhouse.

10. Rhinotmetus ruficollis.

R. *oblongo-ovatus, robustus, antice attenuatus, punctato-striatus, niger; capite transverso, producto, antice carinato, super basin antennarum transverse foveolato, ad basin rugoso, rufo; thorace elongato, antice subattenuato, ad basin depresso, impunctato, glabro; elytris sat latis, punctato-striatis, purpureo-nigris; antennis robustis, filiformibus, piceis; pedibus robustis, piceis, femoribus posticis fusco suffusis.*

Long. corp. 3¼ lin., lat. 1½ lin.

Oblong-ovate, robust, subcylindrical, attenuated in front, impubescent, punctate-striate, black. *Head* transverse, produced in front; from the margins of the labrum two carinations extend obliquely towards the base of the antennæ, while between them an acute longitudinal ridge is produced upwards between the insertion of the two basal joints, less prominent above the base, and terminating in a transverse fovea, which connects the upper and inner margins of the eyes (sometimes the upper portion of this medial ridge is obsolete); eyes tolerably large and prominent, situated at some distance from the base of the head; the surface at the base rugose, and the colour throughout darkly rufous. *Thorax* elongate, subattenuated and rounded in front; the anterior angles obsolete and much depressed; the sides parallel at the base and marginate; at the base is a broad transverse depression (sometimes represented by two subcircular depressions, one on either side of the medial line); the surface impunctate, rufo-glabrous. *Scutellum* triangular, impunctate, and rufo-fuscous. *Elytra* considerably broader than the thorax, robust, ovate, deeply punctate-striate, impubescent, black (sometimes shaded with a purple hue). *Antennæ* robust, filiform, piceous. *Legs* robust, piceous, the posterior femora being suffused with fuscous.

Brazil (the neighbourhood of Rio Janeiro).

This species may be at once recognized among its congeners by its rufous prothorax, darkly cyaneous elytra, and piceous legs.

11. Rhinotmetus cyanipennis.

Rhinotmetus cyanipennis, *Dej. Cat.* (1837) p. 407.
—— archiepiscopalis, *Chevr.*

R. *oblongo-ovatus, subconvexus, antice elongatus, punctatus, niger, nitidus; capite producto, antice carinato, inter oculos foveolato, granulato, rufo; thorace elongato, antice rotundato et subattenuato, impunctato, rufo; elytris parallelis, punctis minutis* (ad basin obsoletis), *velut in striis dispositis, nigro-cyaneis; antennis filiformibus, fuscis; pedibus fulvis.*

Long. corp. 3 lin., lat. 1½ lin.

Oblong-ovate, robust, attenuated in front, punctate, black (generally with a bluish hue), shining. *Head* produced (so that the insertion of the antennæ is placed about midway between the base and the apex); from the labrum (which is light fulvous) to the insertion of the antennæ is a longitudinal carination, on either side of which is another, oblique, and less distinct; between the eyes, and above the insertion of the antennæ, is an obsolete T-shaped, or sometimes Y-shaped, depression; surface impunctate, at the base granulated, the colour rufous. *Thorax* subelongate; the anterior angles depressed and rounded; the sides submarginate; the surface impunctate (with a very high magnifying-glass, sparingly and finely punctured), rufous. *Scutellum* small, triangular, fuscous. *Elytra* broader than the thorax, robust, ovate, with punctures (which are fine and sometimes even obsolete) arranged in the form of striæ, obscurely pubescent, of a bright cyaneous colour. *Antennæ* filiform; the first joint being long, incrassated at the base, and deflected outwards; the second short, ovate; the third narrower than those that follow, and shorter than the first; the remainder of nearly the same breadth as the first; the first and second rufo-fuscous, the rest fuscous. *Legs* entirely fulvous throughout.

This species differs from *R. sulcicollis* (to which, in general appearance, it is closely allied) and also from *R. ruficollis* by the *fineness of the punctuation* and the absence of striæ on the elytra (the punctures being *minute* and distinctly marked upon a bright *glabrous* ground), and also by the almost complete absence of any antemedial transverse depression on the surface of the elytra.

A beautiful small variety was taken by Mr. Gray and myself at Constancia, January 1857, having the colour of the legs brightly rufous, the elytra of a purple-cyaneous colour, and the antennæ rufous with the apex fuscous.

A common species in the neighbourhood of Rio Janeiro.

12. Rhinotmetus sulcicollis.

R. *oblongo-ovatus, robustus, antice attenuatus, punctatus, niger; capite producto, ad apicem carinato, inter oculos transverse foveolato, ad basin punctato, rufo; thorace elongato, antice coarctato, apud angulos basales obsolete depresso, ad medium longitudinaliter foveolato, impunctato, rufo; elytris sat magnis, ante medium oblique depressis, striato-punctatis, nigro-cyaneis; antennis filiformibus, robustis, fuscis, ad basin nigris; pedibus rufis.*

Long. corp. 2½ lin., lat. 1¼ lin.

Oblong-ovate, robust, attenuated in front, punctate (more deeply than in the preceding species), glabrous, black. *Head* produced anteriorly: from the angles of the labrum is an oblique carination extending to the base of the antennæ; between these is a third, obsolete and medial: above the base of the antennæ is a well-marked longitudinal and also a transverse fovea, forming together the character of the letter T; this fovea is the more apparent from having its sides raised: eyes large and prominent; the surface at the base thickly and finely punctate; the colour throughout is rufous. *Thorax* subelongate (almost quadrate), coarctate in front; the anterior angles much depressed and obsolete, the sides marginate; near the basal angles is an obsolete depression, while a medial longitudinal fovea extends from the base of the head to the scutellum; the surface is impunctate and rufous, glabrous. *Scutellum* triangular, impunctate, rufo-fuscous. *Elytra* broader than the thorax, robust, subparallel; a broad antemedial depression extends obliquely upwards towards the shoulders, giving a prominence to the surface near the scutellary angles; the surface is covered throughout with punctures arranged in the form of striæ—fine, yet not so obsolete as in *R. cyanipennis*; the colour is black with a deep purple hue. *Antennæ* robust, filiform, fuscous, the three basal joints being rufous. *Legs* rufous throughout.

This species is broader and more robust than *R. elegantulus*; it is not striated (as to its elytra) like *R. ruficollis*; the punctures on the elytra are coarser than in *R. cyanipennis*; besides which distinctions, the longitudinal thoracic fovea sufficiently distinguishes it from all adjoining species.

Found in the neighbourhood of Rio Janeiro.

13. Rhinotmetus elegantulus.

R. *oblongo-ovatus, subattenuatus, punctatus, niger, nitidus; capite producto, antice carinato, inter oculos transverse foveolato, punctato, rufo; thorace subelongato, antice constricto, apud angulos basales leviter depresso, et ad medium longitudinaliter striato, rufo; elytris subattenuatis, parallelis, striato-punctatis, ante medium oblique depressis, nigro-cyaneis; antennis robustis, filiformibus, fuscis; pedibus fuscis, femoribus posticis rufo suffusis.*

Long. corp. 2¼ lin., lat. 1 lin.

Oblong-ovate, narrower than the preceding species, subparallel, finely punctate, black, shining. *Head* produced in front; from the angles of the labrum an oblique carination extends to the base of the antennæ, between which is a third, longitudinal and more obsolete: immediately above the base of the antennæ two minute tubercular elevations are apparent when viewed laterally; between these is a longitudinal fovea terminating in another, transverse, which meets the upper and inner margins of the eyes, thus forming together the character of the letter T: the surface is thickly punctate and rufous; the eyes are tolerably large, and situated at some distance from the base of the head. *Thorax* subelongate, constricted and rounded in front; the anterior angles much depressed and obsolete, the sides broadly marginate (more broadly than in the allied species): near the basal angles is an obsolete depression; while, medially, from the anterior margin to the base is a distinct longitudinal stria: the surface impunctate, rufous. *Scutellum* triangular, impunctate, fuscous. *Elytra* broader than the thorax (more attenuated than in the adjoining species), parallel, with punctures arranged throughout in the form of striæ; these punctures are minute, on a smooth and glabrous surface, resembling more closely than the others those of *R. cyanipennis*; an antemedial transverse depression extends obliquely upwards towards the humeral angles, giving an appearance of prominence to the surface near the scutellum; of a deep dark-blue colour. *Abdomen* ferrugineous. *Antennæ* robust, filiform, fuscous. *Legs* fuscous, the posterior femora being suffused with rufous.

Distinguished from all others by its *more attenuated* form; it differs also from all, except *R. cyanipennis*, in the minute punctures of the elytra, while from this latter insect it may be separated (*inter alia*) also by its thoracic longitudinal fovea.

From the Island of St. Paul's (on the coast of Brazil).

14. Rhinotmetus inornatus.

R. oblongo-ovatus, nigro-fuscus, nitidus; capite antice producto, granulato, inter oculos bituberculato; thorace elongato, ad medium longitudinaliter subfoveolato, lateribus marginatis, cylindricis, impunctato, nigro; elytris punctis velut in striis ordinatis, ad medium oblique et transverse depressis ; antennis brevibus, nigro-fuscis ; pedibus nigris, posticis tibiis tarsisque fusco adumbratis.

Long. corp. $2\frac{1}{2}$ lin., lat. 1 lin.

Oblong-ovate, impubescent, dull dark red, shining. *Head* narrow, produced in front; eyes large, somewhat prominent, situated at some little distance from the base of the head: from the labrum to the insertion of the antennæ (when viewed from above) is a central longitudinal ridge; this, at the base of the antennæ, divides itself into two diverging elevated lines (in form together resembling the letter V); at their upper extremities these oblique carinations terminate in two large and still more transverse tubercles which are situate at the upper and inner margin of the eyes: surface of the head granulated and black. *Thorax* somewhat elongate, with the lateral margins anteriorly depressed, and therefore apparently somewhat constricted; sides slightly marginate, subcylindrical; from the apex to the base is an obsolete medial longitudinal channel; surface shining, impunctate (under a higher power minute and irregularly distributed punctures are apparent, especially at the base), black. *Scutellum* very small, almost obsolete, depressed below the plane of the elytra, fuscous. *Elytra* parallel, slightly depressed, with rows of distinct punctures arranged in the form of striæ; a transverse broad antemedial depression is on either side inclined obliquely towards the shoulders (and also, less apparently, along the line of the suture to the scutellum), which gives a degree of prominence to the base. *Antennæ* filiform, short, black; the first joint dilated at the apex; second short, ovate; third, fourth, and fifth nearly equal. *Legs* black, with the posterior tibiæ and tarsi clouded with fuscous.

Brazil. In the collection of M. Deyrolle.

15. Rhinotmetus Deyrollii.

R. *oblongo-ovatus, elongatulus, punctato-striatus, flavo-fulvus ; capite producto, glabro ; thorace subelongato, antice coarctato, ad basin depresso ; elytris subdepressis, parallelis ; antennis robustis, filiformibus ; pedibus robustis, flavo-fulvis.*

Long. corp. 2 lin., lat. $\frac{3}{4}$ lin.

Oblong-ovate, subparallel, slightly elongate in front, subdepressed, punctate-striate, impubescent, of a flavo-fulvous colour throughout. *Head* transverse, produced in front; below the base of the antennæ is an obliquely transverse groove; above the base of the antennæ and between the eyes are two tolerably large, distinct, tubercular elevations, rendered more apparent by an intervening fovea and an

E

obsolete depression above; the surface is finely punctate, and at the apex glabrous; eyes tolerably large, globose, situated at some little distance from the base of the head. *Thorax* elongate (almost quadrate), the anterior angles much depressed and coarctate; the sides parallel and marginate; at the base is a broad transverse depression; the surface throughout is finely punctate. *Scutellum* triangular, impunctate. *Elytra* somewhat broader than the thorax, parallel, subdepressed, punctate-striate (the punctures being deep, and the striæ (comparatively) obsolete); an antemedial depression extends obliquely upwards towards the humeral angles, giving a somewhat turgid appearance to the surface near the scutellum. *Antennæ* robust and filiform. *Legs* tolerably robust, the globular inflation of the posterior claw being rufo-flavous.

Brazil.

16. Rhinotmetus humilis.

R. *oblongo-ovatus, subcylindricus, fulvus, lurido-pubescens; capite producto, punctulato, rufo-fulvo; thorace elongato, antice rotundato (etiamque ad latera), depresso, punctato; elytris subelongatis, punctis minutis velut in striis ordinatis, lurido-pubescentibus; antennis filiformibus, sat robustis, fulvis; pedibus fulvis.*

Long. corp. $2\frac{1}{2}$ lin., lat. $1\frac{1}{4}$ lin.

Oblong-ovate, somewhat depressed, fulvous, covered (throughout?) with a lurid squamose pubescence. *Head* elongated in front, depressed, pubescent; eyes large, prominent. *Thorax* elongated, sides slightly marginate, contracted towards the head; the anterior angles rounded; surface plane, anteriorly depressed, finely punctate; clothed throughout (as is the head) with a close, squamose, lurid pubescence. *Scutellum* almost obsolete. *Elytra* subelongate, subcylindrical, with shallow punctures arranged in the form of striæ; covered (probably throughout) with close, squamose, lurid pubescence, which partially conceals an under-clothing of bright fulvous pubescence. *Antennæ* filiform, short, fulvous. *Legs* fulvous.

The specimen from which this description is drawn is somewhat old and rubbed. Perfect specimens, I doubt not, will be found to be clothed throughout with a flavous pubescence, which is covered more or less with a fuscous and squamose pubescence.

From the neighbourhood of Rio Janeiro. A single specimen, in the collection of Mr. Miers.

17. Rhinotmetus pallipes.

R. *oblongo-ovatus, subparallelus, subcylindricus, flavo-pubescens; capite transverso, antice producto, granulato, nigro, ad basin sub-*

pubescenti et rufo-ferrugineo ; thorace elongato, ad basin transverse depresso, flavo-pubescenti, nigro; elytris parallelis, punctato-striatis, flavo-pubescentibus ; antennis filiformibus, pallide ferrugineis ; pedibus pallide flavis, tarsis anterioribus fusco suffusis.

Long. corp. 2⅔ lin., lat. 1¼ lin.

Oblong-ovate, subparallel, subcylindrical, covered throughout with a pale yellow silky pubescence. *Head* transverse, produced broadly in front: from the sides of the labrum two oblique carinations extend upwards, joining one another immediately below the base of the antennæ ; the transverse triangular plane which is thus formed is bisected by a medial longitudinal ridge: the eyes are large and prominent, situated at the base of the head: the surface is finely granulated, and pubescent at the base ; black, the base (between the eyes) being rufo-ferrugineous. *Thorax* elongated, the anterior angles attenuated and depressed; at the base is a broad transverse depression; the surface (which is black) is clothed at the sides with a pale flavous pubescence. *Scutellum* triangular, fuscous. *Elytra* parallel, subcylindrical, punctate-striate, the striæ being almost concealed by a thick silken pubescence of a pale flavous colour. *Antennæ* robust, filiform (with a slight tendency to dilatation); the first joint is ovate and broad ; the second shorter ; the third and fourth fine, of equal length, and slightly longer than the first; the rest (the fifth to the eleventh) robust, of equal breadth, and slightly shorter than the basal joint ; the colour pale ferrugineous. *Legs* pale flavous, the anterior tarsi being suffused with fuscous.

Brazil. In the collection of M. Chevrolat.

18. Rhinotmetus flavidus.

R. *oblongo-ovatus, subparallelus, subcylindricus, flavo-pubescens, fulvo-ferrugineus ; capite brevi, producto, subtiliter granulato ; thorace elongato, antice rotundato, ad angulos basaels obsolete depresso, granulato ; elytris parallelis, punctato-striatis ; antennis filiformibus, flavis ; pedibus flavis.*

Long. corp. 2⅓ lin., lat. 1¼ lin.

Oblong-ovate, subparallel, subcylindrical, clothed throughout with a pale flavous pubescence, fulvo-ferrugineous. *Head* short, transverse, broadly elongated in front; between the labrum and the base of the antennæ is a transversely triangular plane; above the base of the antennæ and between the eyes are two minute contiguous tubercles ; the eyes are prominent and black ; the surface is finely granulated, clothed at the inner margin of the eyes with pale flavous pubescence, in colour fulvo-ferrugineous. *Thorax* elongate, rounded and attenuated in front; the anterior angles depressed; the sides marginate; at the basal angles are two obsolete depressions of a triangular form; the surface (which is finely granulated) is clothed throughout, but more distinctly at the margins, with a pale flavous pubescence. *Scutellum* small, almost obsolete. *Elytra* parallel, subcylindrical; from the antemedial suture a *shallow* oblique depression extends upwards towards the humeral angles; punctate-striate, the striæ being almost entirely concealed by a fine silken flavous pubescence. *Antennæ* robust, filiform, flavous. *Legs* flavous throughout.

This species is readily distinguished from *pallipes* by the arrangement of the depressions on the thorax and the different markings on the head, as well as by the colour of its pubescence.

Brazil. In the collection of M. Chevrolat.

19. Rhinotmetus canescens.

R. *oblongo-ovalis, subdepressus, pubescens, flavus; capite producto; thorace antice rotundato, elongato; elytris punctato-substriatis, flavo-pubescentibus; antennis pedibusque flavis.*

Long. corp. $2\frac{1}{4}$ lin., lat. $\frac{3}{4}$ lin.

Oblong-oval, very slightly depressed, pubescent, flavous throughout. *Head* narrow, produced anteriorly, apparently impunctate, distinctly clothed with fine flavous pubescence; eyes large, prominent, situate at the base of the head; antennæ at their base contiguous. *Thorax* considerably narrower than the elytra, elongated, subattenuated in front, with the anterior angles slightly rounded; sides hardly marginate, flavo-pubescent. *Scutellum* small, triangular. *Elytra* with punctures arranged as striæ (at the shoulder, and towards the margin, the striation is distinctly visible under the pubescence); the humeral angles distinct, but not prominent; the surface is clothed, apparently throughout (but especially at the margins and base), with a fine, thick, velvet flavous pubescence. *Antennæ* filiform, with a tendency in the ultimate joints to become incrassated, flavous. *Legs* flavous.

Brazil. In the cabinet of Mr. Baly.

20. Rhinotmetus nigricornis.

R. *oblongo-ovatus, subparallelus, antice attenuatus, punctato-striatus, niger; capite producto, ad apicem carinato, granulato, nigro; thorace quadrato, ad basin transverse depresso, impunctato, rufo; elytris parallelis, punctato-striatis, nigris; antennis robustis, filiformibus, nigris, ad basin fusco suffusis; pedibus nigris, tibiis tarsisque posticis ferrugineo suffusis.*

Long. corp. 2 lin., lat. $\frac{3}{4}$ lin.

Oblong-ovate, subparallel, attenuated in front, punctate-striate, impubescent, black. *Head* produced in front; from the apex to the base of the antennæ is an obsolete longitudinal ridge, while immediately above their insertion are (when viewed obliquely) two longitudinal tubercular elevations; eyes large, situated at the base of the head; the surface granulated and black. *Thorax* quadrate (subelongate), anteriorly rounded (more abruptly and less broadly than in preceding species, thus forming an obscure angle, and showing a tendency to assume the form represented in the following genus, *Tetragonotes*); the anterior angles much depressed, the sides broadly marginate, and the base transversely depressed; this depression is *distinct*, and not obsolete as in other species: surface impunctate, *finely* flavo-pubescent, rufous. *Scutellum* triangular, impunctate, black. *Elytra* broader than the thorax, parallel, punctate-striate, finely subpubescent, of a deep dead-black colour. *Abdomen* black. *Antennæ* robust, filiform, black, the basal joints being suffused with fuscous. *Legs* black, the posterior tibiæ and tarsi suffused with ferrugineous.

This species is an interesting connecting link between *Rhinotmetus* and the following genus, *Tetragonotes*. In facies it is abundantly a *Rhinotmetus*, but in the form of the thorax it approaches very near to the following genus.

I captured a single example of this species at Petropolis (Organ Mountains), February 1857.

Genus 6. **TETRAGONOTES***.

CORPUS *elongatum, depressum, subparallelum.*
LABRUM *constrictum, transversum.*
PALPI MAXILLARES *elongati, art. 3° ovato.*
PALPI LABIALES *subovati.*
ANTENNÆ *filiformes, sat robustæ.*
CAPUT *breve, antice (in ♂ præsertim) productum.*
THORAX *elongatus, rectangularis, haud antice rotundatus, ad latera marginatus et angulatus.*
ELYTRA *subparallela, depressa, apicem versus subattenuata.*
PEDES: *femora postica incrassata; post. tibiæ breves, subincurvatæ, juxta apicem haud dentatæ, ut in genere* Rhinotmeto, *sed sinuatæ.*

Labrum transversely subcircular, narrower than the head.
Mandibles robust, with a slight tooth-like prominence at their inner surface, concealed.
Maxillary palpi (Tab. II. fig. 3 m) elongate, the second joint being

---

* τέτρα (= τέσσαρες), quatuor; γωνία, angulus.

broader and longer than the basal joint, dilated slightly antemedially, truncate at the apex; the third longer than the second, ovate; the apical joint elongate, narrower at its base than the apex of the third, conical.

Labial palpi (Tab. II. fig. 3 *n*) ovate, elongate; the second joint of greater length than breadth, broader than the first; the apical joint short and conical.

Antennæ filiform, sufficiently robust; contiguous, situated immediately below and between the eyes; in the males rather more elongate than the females; the first joint broad, dilated and deflected outwards towards the apex; the second short, ovate; the third subattenuated at the apex, gradually incrassated, longer than the first, in the ♂ more evidently longer than in the ♀; the fourth joint in the females is manifestly short; the fifth to the eleventh are of the same form and size, subcylindrical, slightly attenuated towards the apex; the apical joint is more attenuated and tapering.

Eyes tolerably large, very globose, prominent, situated at the base of the head, and extending laterally almost beyond the anterior thoracic angles.

Head short, transverse, broadly produced in front (but not produced so far as in *Rhinotmetus*), depressed at an obtuse angle to the plane of the elytra; generally deeply longitudinally carinated.

Thorax broader than the head, elongate, rectangular, anteriorly not emarginate; the anterior angles are much depressed and *acute* (not, as in *Rhinotmetus*, rounded and obsolete); the sides are broadly marginate, and produced antemedially into a lateral tooth-like projection (of the same form as that in *Octogonotes*); the anterior portion of the disc is generally more or less raised, and at the base transversely depressed.

Scutellum triangular, generally impubescent.

Elytra broader than the thorax, subparallel, slightly attenuated at the apex, at the sides finely marginate; generally punctate-striate.

Legs: the *anterior femora* robust, medially slightly dilated when viewed transversely. The *tibiæ* are subincurved, and slightly dilated towards the apex; the hollowed socket, admitting the base of the tarsus, is *simple* (not armed with a claw, or comb-like teeth, as in *Rhinotmetus*). The *tarsus* (Tab. II. fig. 4 *d*) is short, the basal joint broader than the tibia (in the males), and triangular; the second triangular, but more minute; the third broad, and distinctly bilobed; these three are thickly clothed on the inner surface, and fringed at their margins with close and strong pubescence; the apical joint is attenuated, elongate, and slightly incurved, admitting at its subdilated apex the terminal claw, which is bifid, and armed at the inner base with a short and robust tooth: this bifid claw is, with regard to the relative position of its two members, flexible. The *posterior femora* are laterally subcompressed, but, when viewed transversely, broadly dilated, at the apex subattenuated. The *tibiæ* (Tab. II. fig. 4 *g*) are considerably shorter than the femora, subincurved throughout, more distinctly at the immediate base; when seen from behind, the surface is flattened longitudinally (or, in some examples, almost hollowed out) and distinctly marginate; near the apex this margination is in outline slightly subsinuate, and terminates in the formation of an apical socket, the edges of which are armed with a row of very minute and short teeth, separate from each other (not *close* and elongate, as in preceding forms); the apex of the socket is prolonged into *two* abbreviated spurs. The *posterior tarsus* (Tab. II. fig. 5 *h*) is short and attenuated. I am unable to trace, after much careful examination, any sexual differences in the relative size of the different joints: the basal joint is dilated towards the apex (narrower than the tibia) and broadly truncate; the second is attenuate, elongate, *slightly* incrassated at the apex; the third is short, almost circular, clothed at its margins and under-side with a thick fringe of stout hairs; from its centre proceeds the terminal joint, which is *elongate* and attenuate, gradually dilated into a globose inflation above the apical claw; the claw is not robust, armed at its inner margin (*near the base*) with a short and robust tooth.

In general appearance this genus approaches *Rhinotmetus*—in its subcylindrical elytra and elongated head: its *more depressed* facies, however, and the abrupt anterior *angles* of the thorax, will (without other points of divergence) sufficiently characterize it. It approaches closely to *Octogonotes* in the lateral margin of the thorax; but from this it is separated widely by the form of the maxillary palpi, its less robust facies, and the elongate (not transverse) form of the thorax.

1. **Tetragonotes elegans.** (Tab. II. fig. 3.)

T. *oblongo-ovata, subelongata, punctato-striata, nigra; capite producto, antice carinato, inter oculos oblique foveolato et carinato, punctato; thorace elongato, ad latera marginato et ante medium angulato, ad apicem bituberculato, punctato, nigro; elytris subelongatis, punctato-striatis; antennis robustis, filiformibus, flavofuscis; pedibus nigris, femoribus ad basin flavis, tibiisque posticis pallide testaceis.*

Var. A. *Capite et thorace rufis.*

Long. corp. 3 lin., lat. 1 lin.

Oblong-ovate, subelongate, slightly depressed, punctate-striate, black. *Head* produced (not so prominently as in the preceding genus, *Rhinotmetus*); above the labrum is a transverse carination, intercepted by a longitudinal medial ridge, which extends upwards to the base of the antennæ; above the base of the antennæ this ridge is divided into two slightly diverging (almost parallel) carinations, which recede from one another gradually, so as to terminate transversely at the upper and inner margins of the eyes; eyes tolerably large, globose, situated at some little distance from the base of the head; the surface is deeply punctate, and black; *immediately* above the base of the antennæ, and also at the upper and inner margins of the eyes, are two minute flavo-suffused spots. *Thorax* elongate, subcylindrical, slightly broader than the head; the anterior angles depressed and subprominently acute; the sides finely marginate, with a lateral angular projection, antemedial and prominent: at the centre of the disc are two large, well-defined tubercular elevations; these are antemedial, not extending however to the anterior margin, which is not elevated at all above the plane of the thorax: the surface is sparingly but deeply punctate throughout, of a rufo-ferrugineous colour. *Scutellum* small, triangular, impunctate, fuscous. *Elytra* broader than the thorax, subelongate, subcylindrical, punctate-striate (the punctures being deep, and the striæ almost obsolete), both striæ and punctures becoming obsolete near the apex; impubescent, black. *Antennæ* robust, flavo-fuscous, the four basal joints being suffused with rufous. *Legs* black, the base of the femora being flavous, the terminal joint of the tarsi suffused with rufous, and the posterior tibiæ pale testaceous.

A beautiful variety is found, somewhat smaller in size, identical in form and sculpture, with the head and thorax of a pale rufous colour. Constancia (Organ Mountains); taken by Mr. Gray and myself in January 1857.

2. Tetragonotes atra.

T. *oblongo-ovata, subparallela, subelongata, impubescens, punctato-striata, atra; capite antice producto, carinato, supra basin antennarum oblique carinato, punctato, nigro; thorace elongato, lateribus marginatis, ante medium angulatis, haud ad medium distincte elevato, impunctato; elytris subelongatis, punctato-striatis; antennis robustis, filiformibus, rufo-piceis; pedibus piceis, femoribus ad basin flavis, tibiisque posticis testaceis.*

Long. corp. 2½ lin., lat. 1 lin.

Oblong-ovate, subparallel, subelongate, impubescent, punctate-striate, black. *Head* short (produced in front); from the labrum to the base of the antennæ is a medial longitudinal carination, which extending above the base slightly diverges, until it reaches the inner margins of the eyes; eyes tolerably large and prominent, situated near the base of the head; the surface is deeply punctate, and black. *Thorax* broader than the head, elongate, subparallel; the anterior angles are depressed and distinct; the sides are finely but evenly marginate, with a lateral angulated projection, antemedial, and broadly defined; the surface of the thorax is more *equate* than in *T. elegans*; the sides are broadly depressed, and there is an absence of any abrupt elevations on the anterior disc; the surface is deeply punctate throughout, and black. *Scutellum* triangular, rounded at the apex, impunctate, black. *Elytra* broader than the thorax, subelongate, punctate-striate, and (when seen under a high power) clothed with a very fine squamose pubescence. *Antennæ* robust, filiform, rufo-piceous. *Legs* piceous, the base of the femora being flavous, and the posterior tibiæ testaceous.

T. atra is almost identical in the details of its structure with *T. elegans*, except in the *formation of the surface of its thorax*; there is here such a complete difference, that I have not hesitated in deciding them to be two distinct species. Constancia; taken by Mr. Gray and myself, January 1857.

3. Tetragonotes calceata.

T. *oblongo-ovata, subparallela, subpubescens, flavo-ferruginea; capite elongatulo, ad medium (infra antennarum basin) longitudinaliter carinato, supra oblique carinato; thorace elongato, angulis anterioribus subacutis, ad latera marginato et (ad medium) dentato, punctato, nigro; elytris subparallelis, punctato-striatis, flavo-pubescentibus, flavo-ferrugineis, ad humeros, latera, suturam, et macula longitudinali media inter strias 5 et 7, nigris; antennis filiformibus, fuscis; pedibus nigris.*

Long. corp. 2¾ lin., lat. 1 lin.

Oblong-ovate, subparallel, slightly depressed, finely pubescent, flavo-ferrugineous. *Head* broadly subelongated; from the upper part of the labrum a longitudinal medial carination extends upwards to the base of the antennæ, from whence it diverges on either side in an oblique direction, terminating at the inner margin of the eyes; the surface finely punctate. *Thorax* elongate, not much broader than the head; the anterior angles subacute and depressed; the sides marginate, depressed, and produced antemedially into an obsolete tooth; at the base transversely depressed; the antemedial centre of the disc is elevated into two obsolete and glabrous tubercles; the surface is coarsely and irregularly punctate, black. *Scutellum* triangular, fuscous. *Elytra* subparallel, broader than the thorax, finely punctate-striate, the punctures being frequent, and the striæ almost obsolete; clothed throughout with a fine silky flavous pubescence; flavo-ferrugineous; at the humeral angles, along the margination, and along the suture (more broadly at the apex), black; between the fifth and seventh striæ also is a longitudinal suffused marking of fuscous, which does not extend either to the humeral angles or the apex. *Antennæ* filiform, robust, fuscous. *Legs* black.

Brazil. In the collection of M. Chevrolat.

4. Tetragonotes subanchoralis. (Tab. II. fig. 5.)

T. *oblongo-ovata, subdepressa, impubescens, testacea, nitida; capite brevi, subproducto, inter oculos* T *foveolato, impunctato, nigro; thorace quadrato, ad latera marginato, dentato, lævi, impunctato, rufo-ferrugineo; elytris oblongis, subdepressis, striato-punctatis, flavis, ad basin, ad suturam, et ad marginem (tenue), maculis etiam quatuor (postmediis circularibus, ad apicem oblongis), nigris; antennis robustis, nigro-fuscis; pedibus piceis, suffuso-ferrugineis.*

Long. corp. $3\frac{1}{4}$ lin., lat. $1\frac{1}{2}$ lin.

Oblong-ovate, parallel, subdepressed, impubescent, testaceous, shining. *Head* short, transverse, slightly and broadly produced; below the base' of the antennæ the surface is transversely depressed; eyes tolerably prominent, situated nearly at the base of the head; above the base of the antennæ and between the eyes is a transverse and also a longitudinal depression, which form together the character of the letter T; the surface impunctate, black. *Thorax* quadrate; the anterior angles subacute, the sides marginate and extending laterally (a little in front of the middle) into a broad and distinct tooth-like projection; the surface smooth, impunctate, rufo-ferrugineous, shining. *Scutellum* triangular, impunctate, black. *Elytra* oblong, parallel, subdepressed, finely marked with rows of punctures in the form of striæ, impubescent, flavous; at the base a broad and suffused black band extends across the shoulders, and also along the suture for about a third of its length: two circular spots are situated postmedially near the margin, between the fourth and eighth rows of punctures; and at the apex two other oblong markings (extending in an oblique direction) are separated from the margination, but join the suture; these four spots (with a narrow margin along the line of margination of the sides, and another, more distinct, at the suture) are fuscous-black. *Antennæ* robust, dark fuscous. *Legs*: the femora flavo-ferrugineous (the apex and upper part of the femora being suffused with piceous); the tibiæ and tarsi piceous; on the outer longitudinal margins of the posterior tibiæ, near the insertion of the tarsi, is a small *obsolete* tooth-like projection; the globular inflation above the posterior claw brightly rufo-piceous.

Venezuela. In the collection of M. Chevrolat.

5. Tetragonotes angulicollis. (Tab. II. fig. 4.)

T. oblongo-ovata, rufo-ferruginea; capite brevi, transverso, subproducto, inter oculos transverse foveolato, punctato, nigro; thorace elongato, angulis anticis depressis, fortiter truncatis, ad latera et basin depresso, impunctato, flavo-ferrugineo; elytris latis, subparallelis, punctato-striatis, rufo-ferrugineis, ad basin et apicem nigris; antennis filiformibus, robustis, nigris, articulis (ad basin) 1 et 2 rufo-fuscis; pedibus rufis; tibiis et tarsis piceo-suffusis.

Long. corp. 1¾ lin., lat. 1¼ lin.

Oblong-ovate, impubescent, nigro-ferrugineous. *Head* short, transverse, slightly and broadly produced in front; immediately above the base of the antennæ and between the eyes is an obliquely transverse carination; surface thickly punctate, black; at the inner margin of the eyes (near the termination of the transverse carination) are two suffused circular spots of rufous colour. *Thorax* elongate; the anterior angles depressed and very broadly truncate (the truncation giving to the antemedial margination the appearance of a distinct tooth-like projection); the sides subdepressed and marginate; at the base is a slight transverse depression, above which (near the centre of the disc) are two distinct elevations; the surface impunctate, flavo-ferrugineous. *Scutellum* small, triangular, fuscous. *Elytra* broad, subparallel, subdepressed, punctate-striate; the surface is somewhat raised near the scutellary angles; the colour is rufo-ferrugineous, with the apex and the base broadly black. *Antennæ* robust, filiform, black, the basal joint being rufo-fuscous. *Legs* rufous, the tibiæ and tarsi being suffused with piceous.

Brazil. In the collection of M. Chevrolat.

6. Tetragonotes vittata. (Tab. II. fig. 6.)

T. oblongo-ovata, parallela, subpubescens, punctato-striata, flava; capite inter oculos oblique carinato, ad basin punctato, fusco, ad apicem, et ad oculorum marginem superiorem, fulvo; thorace elongato, ad latera angulato, ad medium obsolete bituberculato, testaceo, vitta longitudinali media, marginibusque fulvis; elytris parallelis, punctato-striatis, tenue pubescentibus, testaceis, vitta longitudinali lata, etiamque sutura et marginibus fuscis; antennis filiformibus, piceis; pedibus testaceis, tibiis tarsisque anterioribus (femorumque posticorum apicibus) fusco suffusis.

Long. corp. 2¾ lin., lat. 1 lin.

Oblong-ovate, parallel, subdepressed, very finely pubescent, punctate-striate, fusco-flavous. *Head* produced in front; from the labrum to the base of the antennæ longitudinally carinated; above the base are two *oblique* carinations, extending to the upper and inner surface of the eyes; eyes tolerably large, extending laterally as far as the anterior angles of the thorax; between the eyes, immediately above the oblique carination, is a transverse depression, most apparent when viewed transversely; the surface is deeply and closely punctate; of a dark fuscous colour, the anterior portion of the head and also two subcircular spots at the upper and inner margin of the eyes being fulvous. *Thorax* elongate, rectilinear, the anterior angles subdepressed, the sides marginate, with an antemedial angulated projection; the basal angles are slightly truncate; when viewed from behind, a slight transverse basal depression gives distinctness to two faintly raised antemedial prominences; finely and sparingly pubescent; the colour testaceous, with a broad longitudinal medial fascia and also the margination on the sides fulvous. *Scutellum* fuscous. *Elytra* rather broader than the thorax, parallel, punctate-striate, the striæ being obsolete near the apex, clothed sparingly with obsolete pubescence; the colour is testaceous, with a broad longitudinal band from the shoulders nearly to the apex fuscous; the suture also and the lateral margins are narrowly fuscous. *Abdomen* fuscous, with the apex and three terminal segments testaceous. *Antennæ* somewhat elongate, filiform, piceous. *Legs* testaceous, the anterior tibiæ and tarsi and the apex of the postical femora being suffused with fuscous.

Taken by Mr. Gray and myself at Constancia (Organ Mountains), January 1857; also by Mr. Fry and other collectors in the same district.

7. Tetragonotes hexagona.

T. *oblongo-ovata, subparallela, elongata, tenue subpubescens, pallide ferruginea; capite producto, ad basin antennarum bituberculato, granulato; thorace elongato, angusto, ad latera marginato et dentato, ad basin depresso, ad medium subelevato, punctato; elytris parallelis, tenue punctato-striatis, et pube flava vestitis; antennis robustis, filiformibus, nigris; pedibus nigris, femoribus tarsisque posticis lurido-flavis.*

Long. corp. 3 lin., lat. 1$\frac{1}{5}$ lin.

Oblong-ovate, subparallel, elongate, when viewed under a high magnifying power finely pubescent, of a lurid or pale ferrugineous colour. *Head* produced and depressed in front, broad; above the labrum is a faint medial longitudinal carination extending to the insertion of the antennæ; immediately above the base of the antennæ are two oblong tubercles, situated obliquely in the direction of the inner surface of the eyes; the surface finely granulated; eyes large and prominent. *Thorax* elongate, narrow, the anterior angles depressed and subacute; the sides subdepressed, marginate, and produced antemedially into a distinct tooth; the base broadly and transversely depressed; the antemedial centre of the disc is (when viewed from the front) slightly elevated into two obsolete and glabrous tubercles, the rest of the surface coarsely and unevenly punctate. *Scutellum* small, triangular. *Elytra* broader than the thorax, elongate, parallel, finely punctate-striate, and clothed throughout with a very fine pale flavous pubescence. *Antennæ* robust, filiform, black. *Legs* robust, black, the base of the femora and also of the posterior tarsi of a lurid yellow colour.

Brazil. In the collection of M. Chevrolat.

Genus 7. PACHYONYCHIS*. (Tab. II. fig. 7.)

Dej. Cat. p. 408, ed. 3, 1837.

Labrum *transversum, breve.*

Palpi maxillares *sat robusti, art. 2^{ndo} et 3^{tio} ad apicem oblique truncatis.*

Palpi labiales *elongati, minuti.*

Antennæ *approximatæ, breves, ad apicem dilatatæ, art. 2^{ndo} haud brevi, attenuato, art. 4to quam 3^{tim} longiori, reliquis dilatatis.*

Oculi *magni, globosi, ad basin capitis positi.*

Caput *breve, transversum, haud productum.*

Thorax *transversus (subquadratus), antice constrictus, et ad latera coarctatus, lævis, glaber.*

Elytra *lata, depressa, subparallela, marginata.*

Pedes *sat robusti, tarsorum ant. art. basali lato, 2^{ndo} minuto; tibiis posticis brevibus, apicem versus robustis et oblique truncatis, ad ipsum apicem calcaratis.*

Labrum short, transverse.

Maxillary palpi (Tab. II. fig. 7 *m*) tolerably robust, apparently slightly geniculated; the second and third joints subparallel, somewhat thickened towards the apex, and obliquely truncate; the apical joint narrower and conical.

Labial palpi (Tab. II. fig. 7 *n*) elongate.

* παχὺς, robustus; ὄνυξ, unguis.

Antennæ (Tab. II. fig. 7 *a*) short, robust, gradually dilated towards the apex; the basal joint is longer than the others, and broad; the second (not thick, ovate, and shorter than the rest, but) *narrow, and of length equal to that of the apical joints*; the third and fourth subequal in length, attenuated at the base, *the fourth being almost longer than the third*; the fifth and following are gradually dilated, moniliform, short, robust (the breadth being equal to the length), rounded at the base and transversely truncate at the apex; the whole (when viewed under a high power) very finely pubescent: the antennæ are in their insertion approximate, and situated between (not below) the inner margins of the eyes.

Eyes large, globose, situated at the base of the head, and not extending laterally as far as the anterior angles of the thorax.

Head very short, transverse, inclined at right angles to the plane of the elytra; not produced in front.

Thorax transverse, almost quadrate, broader than the head, in front hardly perceptibly emarginate; the sides are gradually constricted in front, and immediately within the anterior and basal angles coarctate, so as to give an angular or subcircular form to the middle; the anterior angles are subacute and considerably depressed; the surface is smooth and glabrous.

Scutellum subtriangular, convex.

Elytra broad, depressed, broader than the thorax, the sides subparallel, and evenly marginate.

Legs: the *anterior femora* robust. The *tibiæ* inflected at their immediate base, and gradually thickened towards the apex. The *tarsi* (Tab. II. fig. 7 *d*) are short and sufficiently robust; the basal joint is dilated, broader than the apex of the tibia, rounded at the base, and in front transversely truncate, convex (rather than flattened, as in other groups); the second is minute, triangular, *very considerably smaller than the first*; the third is equal to the second, deeply bilobed, and fringed at its margin with rigid pubescence; the fourth is elongate and attenuated, gradually thickened, and incurved towards the extremity; the apical claw is bifid. The *posterior femora* are broadly incrassated, gradually tapering towards the apex. The *tibiæ* (Tab. II. fig. 7 *f*) are short, distinctly inflected at their immediate base, and sensibly thickened towards the apex, which is obliquely truncate, terminating, behind the insertion of the tarsi, in a single, robust, tooth-like spur. The *tarsi* are short; the first joint broad and triangular; the second more minute; the third subcircular and bilobed, margined with rigid pubescence; the apical joint is attenuate, and produced ultimately into a globular inflation which completely conceals (from above) the terminal claw; the claw is (like the anterior) bifid and simple, not armed at its inner surface with any second tooth.

This genus has several well-defined characters, which, combined, abundantly separate it from allied forms. In the *antennæ* the second joint is longer and narrower relatively than in other groups, and the fourth joint is rather longer than the third. The sides of the *thorax* are coarctate, in front and near the base; and in the *anterior tarsus* the first joint is broadly dilated, and the second joint minute.

1. Pachyonychis paradoxus. (Tab. II. fig. 7.)

Pachyonychis dimidiaticornis, *Dej. Cat.*

P. *oblongo-ovatus, latus, depressus, punctatus, nigro-æneus; capite brevi, haud producto, inter oculos transverse foveolato, impunctato, glabro; thorace quadrato, sed antea constricto, impunctato, nitido, nigro; elytris latis, depressis, punctatis; antennis robustis, ad apicem incrassatis, art. 1–4 flavis, 5–8 fuscis, 9–11 pallide flavis; pedibus flavis, tarsis anterioribus fusco suffusis.*

Long. corp. 1¾ lin., lat. ¾ lin.

Oblong-ovate, broad, depressed, thickly punctate, of a dark olive-green colour which approaches to black. *Head* short, transverse, not produced between the eyes: between the eyes is an obsolete, transverse, irregular groove, which is connected medially with the base of the antennæ by a fine longitudinal fovea; the two, together, forming the impression of the letter T: the surface impunctate, glabrous. *Thorax* quadrate in general form, but considerably constricted anteriorly; this constriction, commencing from the middle of the sides, gives the appearance of a very broad truncation of the anterior angles; the anterior angles subacute, very much depressed; the sides marginate, more distinctly near the posterior and anterior angles; surface impunctate, shining, black. *Scutellum* triangular, large, and distinct; the sides slightly rounded, impunctate. *Elytra* broader than the thorax, depressed; the sides broadly marginate; the surface thickly and coarsely punctate throughout. *Antennæ* robust, incrassated towards the apex; the first joint elongate, and dilated near the apex; the second ovate; the third as narrow as, but rather longer than, the second; from the fifth to the eleventh short, and dilated; in colour, the first to the fourth flavous (the first and fourth being slightly suffused with fuscous), the fifth to the eighth dark fuscous, the ninth to the eleventh very pale flavous. *Legs* flavous throughout, the anterior tarsi being suffused with fuscous.

North America (Philadelphia). In the collection of M. Chevrolat.

Genus 8. **EUTORNUS***. (Tab. II. fig. 8.)

Labrum *breve.*

Palpi maxillares *robusti, elongati, art.* 2^{ndo} *quadrato,* 3^{tio} *elongato, ad apicem subdilatato, ultimo conico.*

Palpi labiales *elongati, attenuati.*

Antennæ *breves, robustæ, subincrassatæ.*

Caput *breve, transversum, deflectum.*

Thorax *latus, transversus, antice valde emarginatus et constrictus, ad latera marginatus; rotundatus, fortiter punctatus.*

Elytra *lata, robusta, rotundata, punctata.*

Pedes *robusti; femoribus anterioribus brevibus, tibiis ad basin incurvatis; femoribus posticis incrassatissimis, tibiis brevibus, simplicibus, tarsis attenuatis.*

Labrum short, subcircular.

Maxillary palpi (Tab. II. fig. 8 *m*) robust, elongated, subdilated; the first joint narrow and abbreviated; the second almost quadrate, dilated at the apex; the third longer, distinctly subdilated at the apex; the terminal joint shorter and conical.

Labial palpi (Tab. II. fig. 8 *n*) elongate, slender.

Antennæ (Tab. II. fig. 8 *a*) short, robust, slightly incrassated; the first joint subelongated, dilated, and inflected outwards; the second narrower, ovate; the third shorter than the first, but narrower; the following short, almost transverse, truncate, and gradually dilated towards the apex.

Eyes tolerably large, situated at the base of the head, extending laterally not so far as the anterior angles of the thorax.

Head short, transverse, deflected at right angles to the plane of the elytra, not produced in front.

Thorax broad, transverse, broader than the head, in front distinctly emarginate, at the sides broadly marginate, and constricted towards the apex; the base is subcircular (almost parallel to the anterior margin); the anterior angles considerably depressed and subacute; the surface is rounded and deeply punctured.

Scutellum broadly triangular, impunctate, glabrous, in the same plane as the elytra.

Elytra broad, robust, somewhat broader than the thorax, rounded at the apex, punctate.

Legs: the *anterior femora* broad, short. The *tibiæ* are robust, short, incurved at their immediate base, and gradually thickened towards the apex, which is transversely truncate. The *tarsi* are

---

* εὖ, bene; τόρνος, convolutus.

short and dilated; the basal joint triangular, the breadth being equal to that of the base of the tarsi; the second of similar form, but more minute; the third broadly ovate, hardly bilobed; from its centre proceeds the terminal joint, attenuate, incurved, slightly thickened towards the extremity, which terminates in a bifid claw, simple, and acute; at its inner surface, near the base, abruptly thickened. The *posterior femora* are much incrassated and short, tapering gradually towards the apex. The *tibiæ* are short, straight, unarmed by any postical spur above the insertion of the tarsi, slightly thickened towards the apex, which is obliquely truncate, and armed on either side of the socket which receives the tarsus with a row of minute comb-like teeth. The *tarsus* short, of the same form as, but more attenuate than, the anterior; the ultimate joint terminating in a globular inflation above the apical claw.

1. Eutornus Africanus. (Tab. II. fig. 8.)

E. *ovatus, latus, punctatus, impubescens, niger; capite parvo, multum depresso, inter oculos carinato, fusco, ad basin rufo; thorace lato, depresso, antice emarginato, ad latera antice constricto et valde depresso, marginato, punctato, rufo-ferrugineo; elytris latis, robustis, punctatis, nigris, longitudinaliter flavo-bivittatis; antennis brevibus, robustis, incrassatis, fuscis; pedibus fuscis, femoribus posticis ad basin rufo-flavis.*

Long. corp. 2¾ lin., lat. 1½ lin.

Ovate, broad, subspherical, punctate, impubescent, black. *Head* minute, transverse, depressed at right angles to the plane of the elytra, not produced: above the insertion of the antennæ is a transverse carination, extending obliquely upwards to the inner and upper margins of the eyes; connecting this with the basal line is a longitudinal medial fovea: eyes large, subglobose, lateral, situated a little below the anterior margin of the thorax; surface finely punctate, dark fuscous, the base being broadly rufo-ferrugineous. *Thorax* broad, transverse, depressed, considerably constricted in front; the anterior angles rounded; the anterior margin broadly emarginate, the sides marginate; the surface deeply punctate, rufo-ferrugineous, suffused medially sparingly with fuscous. *Scutellum* broadly triangular, situated in the plane of the elytra, impunctate, black. *Elytra* broader than the thorax, robust, convex, rounded at the apex, deeply punctate throughout, black: a longitudinal rufo-flavous band, accurately parallel with the suture, extends at a short distance from it on either side from the base to the apex; at the apex it extends transversely to the margination, which also is (not so broadly) rufo-flavous. *Antennæ* short, robust, incrassated towards the apex,

F

darkly fuscous, the third and fourth joints being rufo-fuscous. *Legs* robust, fuscous, the base of the posterior femora being broadly rufo-flavous.

A single example of this fine species was taken by the late Mr. Foxcroft, in the neighbourhood of Sierra Leone, and is in the cabinet of Mr. Baly.

Genus 9. **PHÆDROMUS***. (Tab. III. fig. 1.)

Labrum *transversum.*

Palpi maxillares: *art. 2^{ndo} ad basin attenuato, ad apicem dilatato et oblique truncato, 3^{tio} elongato et contracto, 4to minuto.*

Palpi labiales *elongati.*

Antennæ *filiformes, sat robustæ.*

Oculi *globosi, ad latera capitis positi.*

Caput *breve, haud antice productum.*

Thorax *transversus, latus, ad latera angulatus, glaber.*

Elytra *subparallela, depressa, elongata, ad apicem rotundata.*

Pedes: *tarsis anterioribus latis, artic. 3^{tio} haud bifido; femoribus posticis incrassatis, tibiis ad apicem longitudinaliter marginatis, tarsis attenuatis.*

Labrum transversely subcircular.

Mandibles robust, short, with an inner obsolete tooth at their inner margin, concealed.

Maxillary palpi (Tab. III. fig. 1 *m*): the basal joint obsolete, obscure; the second narrower at the base than the apex of the basal joint, dilated and broadly truncate at the apex, the length being more than twice the greatest breadth; the third more elongate, and narrower, subdilated towards the apex, and broadly truncate; the apical joint is minute, subconical, considerably smaller at the base than the apex of the penultimate joint, the length equalling 1½ of its breadth.

Labial palpi (Tab. III. fig. 1 *n*) corresponding in form to the maxillary; the second joint elongated, and gradually dilated towards the apex; the apical joint minute, smaller at the base than the apex of the second joint, narrower and distinctly more elongate than the ultimate maxillary joint.

Antennæ filiform, sufficiently robust; the basal joint elongate, incurved outwards, and gradually dilated towards the apex, the apex broadly and transversely truncate; the second much narrower than the first, short, and ovate; the third shorter than the first and

* φαίδρομος, agilis.

narrower, attenuated, but subincrassated near the apex; the fourth and fifth are of the same form as, but shorter than, the third; the sixth to the eleventh are shorter, more ovate, less truncate at the apex; the apical joint being acuminated: the whole are sparingly clothed with fine pubescence, two or three longer and separate hairs being discernible at the apex of each joint.

Eyes large and globose, situated at the base of, and at the sides of the head, distant, extending laterally somewhat beyond the anterior angles of the thorax.

Head short, transverse, narrower than the thorax, not produced in front.

Thorax transverse, broader than the head, anteriorly not emarginate; the sides are finely marginate, and produced in front of the middle into a broad, well-defined obtuse angle, of the same form as, but more transverse than, the thoracic angle in the genus *Roicus*; the surface is flattened throughout and subdepressed at the base.

Scutellum almost obsolete, in the same plane as the elytra, impunctate.

Elytra subparallel, slightly broader than the thorax, depressed, rounded and not attenuated at the apex; at the sides evenly marginate, in *P. Waterhousii* finely punctate.

Legs: the *anterior femora* tolerably robust, hardly incrassated. The *tibiæ* are inflected downwards at their immediate base, and gradually incurved though their whole length, slightly dilated near the apex. The *tarsi* are broad; the first joint subtriangular, and of the same breadth as the apex of the tibia; the second of the same form, but more minute; the third broader than the first, transversely triangular, not bilobed: all three are densely clothed with a thick pubescence on their under sides and at their margins. The *posterior femora* are broadly incrassated and ovate, tapering gradually towards the apex. The *tibia* (Tab. III. fig. 1 *g*) is of the same form as the anterior, slightly incurved throughout, and gradually increasing in thickness towards the apex; the hinder surface (when viewed posteriorly) is flattened and longitudinally marginate; near the apex the outline of this margination is slightly sinuate (not dilated into a tooth, as in preceding forms), and extended to the extreme apex, so as to form the socket for the insertion of the base of the tarsus; this socket is broadly truncate, terminating ultimately in two short claw-like teeth: the surface is clothed sparingly throughout with a bristle-like rigid pubescence. The posterior *tarsus* is attenuated; the basal joint is narrow, subdilated towards the apex; the second of the same form as, but shorter than the first; the third broad, subcircular; the whole of these three joints being clothed at their apex (marginally and at their under sides) with a dense pubescence: from the centre of the third proceeds the base of the ultimate joint, which is long, attenuated, slightly inflected, and gradually dilated into a globular inflation completely concealing from above the apical claw; this claw is bifid, being armed at the base of its inner surface with a small tooth-like projection.

This genus approaches, in the form of its thorax, to *Tetragonotes* and *Octogonotes*: from the latter it is separated at once by the elongated form of its palpi; from the former it abundantly differs in its transverse and more distinctly hexagonal form of thorax.

The parallel and depressed form of *Phædromus* abundantly separates it from all other allied genera.

1. Phædromus Waterhousii. (Tab. III. fig. 1.)

P. *oblongo-ovatus, depressus, parallelus, impubescens, niger; capite transverso, depresso, inter oculos transverse foveolato, tenue punctato, nigro; thorace transverso, ad latera angulato, impunctato, flavo, glabro; elytris depressis, parallelis, punctato-striatis; antennis robustis, subincrassatis, nigris; pedibus flavo-fuscis, femoribus anticis flavis, tarsisque posterioribus rufo-fuscis.*

Long. corp. 3 lin., lat. 1 lin.

Oblong-ovate, depressed, parallel, impubescent, black, shining. *Head* transverse, very slightly produced, and depressed almost at right angles to the plane of the thorax; immediately above the base of the antennæ is a V-shaped carination, extending obliquely towards the inner margin of the eyes, and containing within it (when viewed under a high magnifying power) a minute longitudinal fovea, which connects it with a broad *transverse* and tolerably distinct depression extending between the upper margins of the eyes; eyes large and prominent, extending laterally beyond the anterior angle of the thorax; the surface finely punctate, glabrous, black. *Thorax* broader than the head, transverse, the anterior angles obsolete, but subacute; the sides (which are submarginate) are produced laterally into a distinct and prominent angle; behind this angle, which is antemedial, the lateral margins slightly approach one another towards the base; at the base is a broad but very shallow transverse depression, which extends obliquely upwards towards the anterior angles; the surface is impunctate and glabrous, of a flavous colour. *Scutellum* small, fuscous-black. *Elytra* slightly broader than the thorax, depressed, parallel, and rounded at the apex, punctate-striate, the striæ being subobsolete; at the shoulders (between the fifth and seventh striæ) is a longitudinal depression; at the apex both the striæ and the punctures are obsolete. *Antennæ* robust, subincrassated near the apex, black. *Legs* flavo-fuscous, the anterior femora being flavous and the posterior tarsi rufo-fuscous.

South Carolina, United States. In the collection of Mr. Waterhouse.

Genus 10. **PHYSIMERUS***. (Tab. III. figs. 2-7.)

Dej. Cat. ed. 3, 1837, p. 407.

Labrum *transverse subrotundatum.*
Palpi maxillares *elongati, art.* 2^{ndo} *subovato,* 3 *ampliori.*
Palpi labiales *elongati, subcylindrici.*
Antennæ *approximatæ, robustæ, filiformes aut subincrassatæ.*
Caput *breve, antice subproductum, plerumque inter oculos tuberculatum aut foveolatum.*
Thorax *quadratus aut elongatus, rarissime transversus; angulis anterioribus acutis, haud ut in* Rhinotmeto *rotundatis.*
Elytra *lata, subparallela, punctato-striata aut punctata.*
Pedes: *femoribus anter. ad apicem dilatatis, tarsorum art.* 1mo *triangulari,* 2^{ndo} *brevi, minuto; femoribus posticis incrassatis, ovatis; tibiis brevibus, apicem versus dilatatis, plerumque simplicibus (haud ad marginationem calcaratis); tarsis brevibus et attenuatis.*

Labrum transversely subrotundate.

Maxillary palpi (Tab. III. fig. 3 *m*, fig. 4 *m*) elongate, more or less subincrassated; the basal joint is minute; the second subovate, the apex being truncate; the third joint is larger than the second, and also ovate; the terminal joint is smaller than the others, and conical. The different species of this group seem, while exhibiting a manifest relationship in the general form of the maxillary palpi, to be subject to more variation *inter se* respecting them, than is found in the other genera: possibly they may be hereafter subdivisible into different sections.

Labial palpi (Tab. III. fig. 3 *n*, fig. 4 *n*) elongate, subcylindrical; the basal joint is, in outline, parallel; the antepenultimate slightly dilated towards the apex, and the terminal joint elongate and attenuated.

Antennæ tolerably approximate, situated under and between the inner margins of the eyes; robust; generally filiform, or, in a very few species, *su*bincrassated; the first joint is elongate, dilated and incurved outwards towards the apex; the second short, narrower than the first, ovate; the third as long as (and in the males somewhat longer than) the first, attenuated, subincrassated at the apex:

---

* φύσις, natura; μέρος, pars.

the fourth and fifth of equal length, somewhat shorter than, and of similar form to, the third; the sixth to the eleventh slightly more robust, and shorter.

Eyes distant, situated at the base of the head, tolerably globose, extending laterally beyond the anterior angles of the thorax.

Head short, depressed at oblique angles to the plane of the elytra, very slightly produced in front; for the most part tuberculated or foveolated between the eyes.

Thorax broader than the head; quadrate or elongate, in hardly any instances transverse; the anterior angles are considerably depressed and *distinct* (not rounded or obsolete, as in *Rhinotmetus*), and the sides are more or less broadly marginate.

Scutellum triangular.

Elytra broader than the thorax, robust, and rounded at the apex, generally punctate-striate, and clothed more or less with pubescence.

Legs: the *anterior femora* subdilated towards the apex. The *tibiæ* shorter than the femora, incurved downwards at the immediate base, slightly incrassated towards the apex, and broadly truncate. The *tarsus* is considerably shorter; the first joint is triangular, attenuated at the base; the second of the same form as the basal joint, but smaller; the third broader than the first, transverse, and subcircular (very seldom bilobed): the under surface of these three joints is clothed and the margins of them densely fringed by a thick rigid pubescence: the terminal joint is elongate, attenuated at the apex, and slightly incurved as well as incrassated towards the apex; the terminal claw is bifid, the inner margin of each tooth being armed at its inner surface near the base with a short and blunt tooth-like process. The *posterior femora* are thickly incrassated, subattenuated towards the apex, and generally (when seen transversely) of a regular ovate form. The posterior *tibia* is short, abruptly bent at the immediate base, gradually subdilated towards the apex; the surface (when viewed from behind) is flattened, and on either side longitudinally marginate: this margination near the apex is not developed into teethlike spurs, but is in most species simple; occasionally, however, its outline is subsinuate: the socket at the apex (which receives the insertion of the tarsus) is armed at its margin by a series of minute teeth arranged like the teeth of a comb, terminating ultimately in a single abrupt claw. The posterior *tarsus* is short and attenuated; the basal joint is elongate, and dilated towards the apex, where it is broadly truncate; the second is narrower than, and of equal length to the first, attenuated, and truncated at the apex; the third joint is minute and subcircular; from the centre of the third proceeds the ultimate joint, which is elongated, subcurved, and dilated at its extremity into a globular inflation, which entirely conceals from above the apical claw; this claw is of the same form as the anterior.

The only sexual distinction that I can trace in this group is the slightly elongated antennæ of the males: this is discernible especially in the third joint, which is rather longer than (instead of being equal in length to) the first.

1. Physimerus impressus.

P. *oblongo-ovalis, subdepressus, niger, nitidus; capite brevi, leviter producto, ad basin tricanaliculato, granulato, rufo-ferrugineo; thorace transverso, rectangulari, ad latera marginato, a posteriori transverse depresso, punctato, rufo-ferrugineo; elytris sat latis, leviter striato-punctatis, ante medium transverse, et ad humeros oblique fossulatis, nigris, nitidis; antennis filiformibus (subincrassatis), art. 1 et 2 fuscis, 3–5 flavis, 6–8 nigris, 9 et 10 flavis ultimoque nigro; pedibus anterioribus fuscis, fulvo-geniculatis, posticis femoribus nigris pubescentibus, tibiis tarsisque ferrugineis.*

Long. corp. $2\frac{1}{2}$ lin., lat. $1\frac{1}{4}$ lin.

Oblong-oval, slightly depressed, somewhat robust, black, shining. *Head* transverse, slightly produced; at the base (at a sensible distance above the base of the antennæ) three slightly raised ridges form together the figure of a trident—the outer ones being produced obliquely to the inner superior margin of the eyes, the medial being continued to the basal margin; these elevated ridges are lævigate, the rest of the surface being granulated; the colour is ferrugineous, at the apex fulvous. *Thorax* transverse (almost quadrate) and rectilinear; the sides marginate; at the base are two slight postmedial transverse depressions; punctate, ferrugineous. *Scutellum* triangular, fuscous. *Elytra* robust, broader than the thorax, with faint punctuation arranged irregularly as striæ (this punctuation is obsolete at the apex); a deep antemedial depression extends obliquely upwards towards the base (reaching it at the sixth line of punctuation), and gives an appearance of prominence to the humeral and also the scutellary angles; black, shining. *Antennæ* filiform, robust, slightly incrassated towards the apex; the first and second joints are fuscous, third to fifth flavous, sixth to eighth black, ninth and tenth flavous, the apical joint black. *Legs*: the anterior femora black; the tibiæ fuscous, with their superior surface clouded with black; the tarsi fuscous: of the postical, the femora are black, the tibiæ and tarsi ferrugineous.

Taken at Petropolis (Organ Mountains, Rio de Janeiro) by Mr. Fry, and in that gentleman's cabinet.

2. Physimerus vittatus.

Physimerus vittatus, *Dej. Cat.* (ed. 3) p. 407 (*auctore Chevr. Coll.*).

P. *oblongo-ovatus, subdepressus, flavus; capite brevi; thorace transverso, ad latera marginato, ad basin depresso, punctato; elytris parallelis, punctato-striatis, fulvis, quatuor vittis flavis a humeris usque ad apicem; antennis elongatulis, fuscis; pedibus flavis.*

Long. corp. 2¾ lin., lat. 1 lin.

Oblong-ovate, somewhat depressed, parallel, subpubescent, flavous. *Head* short, transverse, slightly depressed; eyes black, somewhat prominent, distant, and extending at their outer margin laterally as far as the line of the thorax; between the eyes is a transverse depression (which varies somewhat as to its breadth in different examples); the upper and posterior surface of the head thickly punctate. *Thorax* transverse; the sides marginate and slightly convex; the anterior angles distinct and subacute; the surface complanate, thickly punctured, with a broad transverse basal depression extending upwards and outwards towards the anterior angles. *Scutellum* small, triangular. *Elytra* punctate-striate, darkly fulvous, with four longitudinal bands extending from the shoulders to the apex, and clothed with (apparently formed by) a covering of bright silky flavous pubescence; these bands are generally equal in breadth to the spaces which separate them, and are parallel, not to the striæ, but to the suture: throughout the whole surface of the elytra are distributed long, distinct, upright hairs. *Antennæ* somewhat fine and elongate, fuscous; first joint thick and dilated; the second short and ovate; the fifth the length of the first; the fourth longer than the fifth, and the third than the fourth. *Legs* flavous, with the upper surface more or less marked with shadings of brown.

Closely allied to *quatuor-lineatus*, but separated from it by the different arrangement of the depressions on the head, and the absence of any marking along the suture.

Brazil (in the province of Rio Janeiro). In the collections of Mr. Fry, M. Chevrolat, and the Rev. H. Clark.

3. Physimerus quatuor-lineatus.

Octogonotes quadrilineatus, *Règne Anim.* 1820, *Guér. Méneville*, (vol. v. p. 154).

P. *oblongo-ovatus, subparallelus, subtiliter pubescens, pallide flavus; capite brevi, subelongato, inter oculos in forma crucis foveolato, impunctato; thorace transverso, lato, ad basin subdepresso; elytris punctato-striatis, vittis duabus longitudinalibus, hac inter strias 2 et 4, brevi, illa apud marginem a humero ad apicem; antennis art. 1 et 2 flavis (reliqui desunt); pedibus flavis.*

Long. corp. 2½ lin., lat. 1⅕ lin.

Oblong-ovate, subparallel, very finely pubescent, of a pale flavous colour. *Head* short, transverse, subelongated in front, and reflected downwards (at the insertion of the antennæ) at a right angle to the plane of the elytra; between the eyes is a distinct transverse groove, and crossing it at right angles is another (longitudinal and medial), extending from the insertion of the antennæ to the base; the surface impunctate: eyes tolerably prominent, black, situated at the base of the head. *Thorax* transverse, extending beyond the outer margin of the eyes; the anterior angles depressed and subacute, but almost obsolete; the sides marginate, slightly dilated medially; at the base is a transverse depression; the surface is impunctate and (when viewed under a high power) very finely flavo-pubescent. *Scutellum* small, triangular, impunctate. *Elytra* subparallel, punctate-striate; between the second and the fourth striæ is a longitudinal band of darker fulvous parallel to the suture, and which does not extend to the apex; along the margination is another, narrower band, which extends from the shoulders in a somewhat irregular line to the apex; these four longitudinal lines are glabrous, the rest of the surface being clothed with a fine pale flavous pubescence. *Antennæ*: the first two joints flavous (the rest are wanting). *Legs* flavous throughout.

Brazil. In the collection of M. Chevrolat.

This species approaches very nearly to *vittatus*; it differs, however, in the form and position of the longitudinal markings on the elytra: in *quatuor-lineatus* these occur from the second to about the fourth striæ, and again along the margination; while in *vittatus* the medial marking is along the sutural line, and the exterior marking, not along the line of margination, but between the fourth and sixth striæ: the form of the depressions on the head also sufficiently distinguishes it.

4. Physimerus virgatus.

P. *oblongo-ovatus, latus, robustus, pubescens, fuscus; capite elongatulo, supra basin antennarum granulato, nigro; thorace transverso, rectilineari, apud angulos posticos, etiamque longitudinaliter ad medium foveolato, nigro; elytris latis, punctato-striatis, flavo-pubescentibus, quatuor-lineatis; antennis ad apicem incrassatis, nigris; pedibus piceis.*

Long. corp. 2 lin., lat. 1 lin.

Oblong-ovate, broad, robust, very finely pubescent, fuscous. *Head* short, transverse, elongate in front; between the upper part of the labrum and the base of the antennæ is a triangular depressed and glabrous plane; above the base of the antennæ and between the eyes the surface is irregularly and coarsely granulated; the colour black: eyes tolerably large, situated at the base of the head. *Thorax* transverse, broader than the head, but much narrower than the elytra, rectangular, rectilinear; the anterior angles depressed; the sides submarginate; at the basal angles is a broad, distinct and tolerably deep depression, while, medially, a longitudinal fovea extends from the anterior margin to the base; the surface (when viewed under a high power) is clothed throughout sparingly with short pale fulvous pubescence; the colour black. *Scutellum* triangular, fuscous. *Elytra* much broader than the thorax, robust, punctate-striate, clothed throughout with a fine and thick brightly-flavous pubescence: this pubescence is broken by several bands of piceous colour, extending from the shoulder to the apex; the first (which is between the suture and the first stria) extends nearly to the apex; the second (between the second and third striæ) does not reach the apex; the third (between the fourth and fifth striæ) extends only two-thirds of the length of the elytra; the fourth (between the sixth and seventh striæ) is longer than the third, but shorter than the second; the fifth (between the eighth and ninth striæ) is as long as the second, becoming somewhat obsolete as it approaches the apex; and, lastly, the line of margination which extends from the shoulders to the apex; these intermediate (with the sutural and marginal) lines are all of equal breadth. *Antennæ* tolerably robust, incrassated towards the apex, black. *Legs* piceous throughout.

Columbia; Bogota. Taken by M. Parzudaki. In the collection of M. Chevrolat.

5. Physimerus labialis.

P. oblongo-ovatus, subattenuatus, pubescens, brunneus; capite brevi, transverso, ad basin antennarum T foveolato, granulato, impubescenti; thorace transverso, ad basin oblique depresso, subpunctato, sparsim pube vestito; elytris subparallelis, punctato-striatis, pubescentibus; antennis filiformibus, fuscis; pedibus flavis, fusco suffusis.

Long. corp. 2 lin., lat. 1 lin.

Oblong-ovate, subattenuated, very finely pubescent, of a tawny-brown colour throughout. *Head* short, transverse, very slightly produced in front; between the labrum and the base of the antennæ is a transverse plane (impunctate and of a pale rufous colour); immediately above the base of the antennæ are two minute tubercles, giving distinctness to a transverse and to a longitudinal fovea, which form, together, the character of the letter T; the surface throughout granulated and impubescent. *Thorax* transverse (almost quadrate);

the anterior angles depressed, the sides marginate; at the base is a transverse depression which extends obliquely upwards towards the humeral angles; the surface is finely punctate, sparingly clothed throughout with pubescence. *Scutellum* minute. *Elytra* subparallel, slightly broader than the thorax, and attenuated at the apex; punctate-striate, and clothed throughout with a very fine and sparingly distributed silken pubescence. *Antennæ* filiform, fuscous. *Legs* flavous, suffused irregularly with fuscous.

Mexico. In the collection of M. Chevrolat.

6. Physimerus ambiguus. (Tab. III. fig. 2.)

P. *oblongus, subdepressus, subparallelus, robustus, nigro-cyaneus; capite brevi, rufo; thorace transverso, ad basin depresso, punctato, rufo; elytris punctatis (striis pene obsoletis); antennis filiformibus, robustis, fuscis, ad basin rufis; pedibus nigris.*

Long. corp. 2 lin., lat. ¾ lin.

Oblong, slightly depressed, subparallel, robust, of a dark metallic-blue colour. *Head* short, depressed, very slightly elongated; between the eyes is a transverse canaliculation, the extremities of which are deflected upwards towards the upper and inner margins of the eyes; this canaliculation is shallow and almost obsolete: eyes slightly prominent, large, and distant; maxillary palpi dark fuscous; surface of the head roughly punctate and rufous. *Thorax* rectangular, transverse (almost quadrate); the sides are slightly marginate and (when viewed laterally) considerably depressed in front; the surface of the thorax subconvex, with an obscure transverse basal depression, coarsely punctate and rufous. *Scutellum* triangular, black. *Elytra* distinctly punctate, the punctures being arranged in the form of striæ (the striæ themselves being almost obsolete, not so distinct as in *P. agilis*), smooth, of a metallic bright blue, clothed very sparingly throughout (more distinctly at the apex) with pubescence; an antemedial transverse and shallow depression (which extends upwards on either side towards the humeral angles) gives an appearance of prominence to the shoulders. *Antennæ* filiform, fuscous, with the base of the terminal joints rufous; the first joint dilated towards its extremity and curved outwards; the second short, oval; the third, fourth, and fifth attenuate; the sixth to the eleventh with a *slight tendency* to dilatation. *Legs* black, with the base of the tarsal joints and the posterior apical claw rufous.

There are apparently two forms of this insect: one (the typical form), in which the thorax is transverse (almost quadrate), and the length of the insect 2–2¼ lin.; the other, in which the thorax is quadrate, and the length 1¾ lin. At first sight they appear to be decidedly different species; more careful examination, however, fails in detecting any real distinctive characters except these; and these fail as a specific distinction from the fact that there are intermediates both in size and form, and that the quadrate thorax and the smaller size are not *always* found together in the same example.

Apparently a common insect in Brazil. In the cabinets of Messrs. Fry, Baly, Gray, and the Rev. H. Clark. Examples of this species were captured by Mr. Gray and myself at Constancia (the English boarding-house of Mr. Heath, Organ Mountains), January 1857.

7. Physimerus agilis.

P. *oblongus, subparallelus, robustus, niger; capite transverso, subelongatulo, punctato, fusco; thorace quadrato, rectangulari, ad basin obsolete transverse depresso, punctato, rufo-testaceo; elytris sat latis, subparallelis, punctato-striatis; antennis filiformibus, robustis; pedibus rufis, fusco suffusis, femoribus posticis nigrofuscis.*

Long. corp. 2¼ lin., lat. 1 lin.

Oblong, somewhat depressed, subparallel, robust, of a greenish-black or black colour. *Head* transverse, short, depressed, hardly elongated in front; between the eyes (extending upwards on either side in a semicircular form towards their upper and inner margins) is a transverse shallow fovea, which is connected medially by a longitudinal channel with the space between the insertion of the antennæ; eyes distinct, slightly prominent and distant, situate at the base of the head; surface of the head punctate and fuscous. *Thorax* quadrate, rectangular; sides slightly marginate, and (when viewed laterally) gradually deflected from the humeral angles to the outer and lower margins of the eyes; at the base is an almost obsolete transverse depression; the surface is punctate throughout and rufo-testaceous. *Scutellum* triangular, fuscous. *Elytra* tolerably broad and subparallel, distinctly punctate-striate, with a broad and obsolete antemedial transverse depression, very darkly fuscous or nearly black. *Antennæ* filiform, short, robust; the first joint dilated and slightly deflected outwards; the second short and ovate (but somewhat longer than in *P. ambiguus*); the third narrower than the others and longer than the first: a tendency to dilatation is evident in the ultimate joints. *Legs* rufous, marked more or less on their upper surface with a darker shade of brown; posterior femora very darkly fuscous; on the inner margin of the claws the spur is large and distinctly visible; the bladder-like inflation of the posterior claw darkly and brightly red.

There is a great similarity as to general appearance between this insect and *P. ambiguus*; the *darker* and *less brilliant colour*, as well as the *very distinct striation* on its *elytra* (and the rufous colour of its anterior legs), abundantly separate the species.

I captured a single specimen of this insect at Constancia (Organ Mountains), January 1857.

8. Physimerus revisus.

P. *oblongo-ovatus, impubescens, nigro-cyaneus ; capite brevi, ad basin antennarum* T *impresso, punctulato ; thorace quadrato, rectangulari, ad basin constricto et transverse depresso ; elytris subparallelis, striato-punctatis, impubescentibus ; antennis filiformibus, nigris ; pedibus nigris.*

Long. corp. 2¼ lin., lat. 1⅓ lin.

Oblong-ovate, impubescent, of a bright dark cyaneous colour. *Head* transverse, slightly produced; above the labrum is a transverse triangular subdepression; immediately above the insertion of the antennæ (when viewed in front) is a longitudinal channel, bisecting at its upper extremity a transverse fovea, which form together the character of the letter T; eyes situated at the base of the head; the surface is finely and very sparingly punctate, flavous. *Thorax* quadrate, rectangular, the sides slightly constricted towards the base and marginate; the base transversely subdepressed; the surface impubescent, sparingly and very finely punctate, more thickly towards the base. *Scutellum* triangular. *Elytra* subparallel, with distinct punctures arranged in the form of striæ, impubescent, glabrous. *Antennæ* filiform, black. *Legs* black.

Brazil. In the collection of M. Chevrolat.

This species may be separated from *P. ambiguus*, *P. agilis*, and other allied species by its *total absence of pubescence, and also of striæ* on the elytra ; it differs also materially in the form of the head, and in the form, markings, and relative size of the thorax.

9. Physimerus luteicollis.

P. *ovalis, depressus, subpubescens, fuscus ; capite brevi, haud producto, luteo, punctato, oculis magnis, distantibus ; thorace quadrato (angulis acutis), ad basin transverse depresso, punctato, luteo ; elytris punctato-striatis, subpubescentibus ; antennis fuscis (ad basin articulorum flavis) ; pedibus flavis, femoribus tibiisque posticis elongatulis.*

Long. corp. 1¼ lin., lat. ⅘ lin.

Oval, slightly depressed, subparallel, clothed throughout with a fine and indistinct ashy pubescence, fuscous. *Head* short, transverse, and (when viewed laterally) very slightly produced; the eyes are large, prominent, and distant; between the eyes is a distinct transverse groove, inclining obliquely upwards in the direction of the upper and inner margins of the eyes, and connected by a medial horizontal fovea with the insertion of the antennæ; surface of the head thickly and coarsely punctured or granulated, flavo-rufous. *Thorax* quadrate (with the anterior and posterior angles distinct and subacute); sides marginate, slightly constricted towards the base, subpubescent, flavo-rufous. *Scutellum* triangular, fuscous. *Elytra* indistinctly but broadly punctate-striate, obsoletely pubescent; a slight antemedial depression gives an appearance of prominence to the shoulders; fuscous. *Antennæ* filiform, somewhat elongate; the first joint broad, and dilated near the apex; the second short, ovate; the third, fourth, and fifth of nearly equal length, and thinner than the basal or apical joints; the first, second, and third flavous, the rest fuscous. *Legs* slightly pubescent, flavous throughout.

Corcovado. Rio de Janeiro. I know only of one example of this species, in the cabinet of Mr. Fry.

10. Physimerus inornatus.

P. *oblongo-ovatus, subconvexus, parallelus, niger; capite brevi, punctato, rufo; thorace transverso, ad basin leviter constricto etiamque late depresso, punctato, ad basin flavo-pubescenti; elytris parallelis, punctato-striatis, subtiliter pubescentibus, nigris; antennis filiformibus, nigris; pedibus flavis.*

Long. corp. 2 lin., lat. ¾ lin.

Oblong-ovate, parallel, subconvex, black, pubescent. *Head* short, almost vertical; eyes large, prominent, extending laterally as far as the margin of the thorax; between the eyes and above the insertion of the antennæ is an obscure obliquely-transverse depression; surface finely punctate, rufous. *Thorax* transverse (almost quadrate), slightly constricted at the base; the anterior angles are depressed, the sides slightly marginate; at the base is a broad transverse depression; the surface is very finely punctate, at the base flavo-pubescent, rufous. *Scutellum* oblong, triangular, black. *Elytra* parallel, coarsely punctate-striate, clothed throughout with very fine ashy pubescence, black. *Antennæ* filiform, black. *Legs* flavous throughout; the globular inflation of the posterior claw bright fulvous.

This species differs from *P. minutus* not only in its larger size, but in the form and clothing of the thorax; it is less constricted at the base, and more distinctly pubescent: from other species it will be readily distinguished by the distinct colour of its elytra.

From the district of the Amazon. In the collection of Mr. Bates.

11. Physimerus minutus.

P. *oblongus, ovalis, depressus, parallelus, niger; capite brevi, impunctato, rufo; thorace brevi, transverso, ad basin constricto et depresso; elytris subcylindricis, punctato-striatis, pallide pubescentibus; antennis filiformibus, nigris; pedibus flavis, posticorum femorum apicibus fuscis.*

Long. corp. 1¾ lin., lat. ¾ lin.·

Oblong, oval, depressed, parallel, black. *Head* short, hardly produced; eyes large, prominent, extending beyond the line of the thorax; between the eyes and above the base of the antennæ is a depression in the form of the letter T; surface impunctate, rufous. *Thorax* small, transverse, considerably constricted at the base; the anterior angles much depressed, and concealed below the outer margin of the eyes; the sides are slightly marginate; at the base is a broad transverse depression; the surface is flavo-pubescent and rufous. *Scutellum* triangular, black. *Elytra* broader than the thorax, subelongated, parallel, coarsely punctate-striate, black, clothed throughout with fine ashy pubescence. *Antennæ* filiform, black. *Legs* flavous throughout; the tips of the posterior femora fuscous.

This species differs from *P. luteicollis* in its black elytra, by its more transverse thorax, and by its smaller size; from *P. inornatus* by its impunctate head, by the fineness, as well as *ashy* (instead of flavous) pubescence on the elytra, and also by its smaller size.

From the Amazon district.

12. Physimerus obscurus.

P. *oblongo-ovatus, parallelus, subpubescens; capite brevi, elongatulo, inter oculos longitudinaliter foveolato, granulato, rufo; thorace elongato, subcylindrico, angulis anterioribus subacutis, ad latera marginato, ad basin depresso et subcoarctato, granulato, rufo-ferrugineo; elytris punctis crebris in striis ordinatis, transverse complanatis, nigris; antennis filiformibus, art. 1–4 ferrugineis, cœteris fuscis; pedibus fuscis, tarsis tibiisque posticis ferrugineis.*

Long. corp. 1½ lin., lat. ½–¾ lin.

Oblong-ovate, parallel, subpubescent, black. *Head* short, slightly elongated and compressed in front; eyes large and prominent; immediately above the base of the antennæ is a short abrupt longitudinal fovea; the surface is granulated and rufous. *Thorax* elongated, rectangular, subcylindrical; the anterior angles depressed, the sides marginate; at the base is a transverse depression, giving a rounded form to the anterior disc; the surface granulated and rufous. *Scutellum* triangular, black. *Elytra* parallel, with broad and large punctures arranged in the form of striæ; a slight oblique depression is apparent antemedially near the suture; the surface is obscurely and finely pubescent, of a black or bluish-black colour. *Antennæ* filiform, tolerably robust, the joints (the second is the shortest) being nearly equal in length; first to fourth ferruginous, fifth to eleventh fuscous. *Legs* fuscous; the posterior tibiæ and tarsi ferruginous.

Morro Queimado (Brazil). In the collection of Mr. Fry.

13. Physimerus fascicularis.

P. *oblongo-ovatus, parallelus, glaber, niger; capite subproducto, ad basin antennarum transverse foveolato, punctulato, nigro (ad basin fulvo); thorace transverso, lateribus ad angulos posteriores et anteriores obsolete coarctatis, punctato, flavo, antice fuscato; elytris parallelis, punctis (ad apicem obsoletis) in striis ordinatis, nigris, ad medium transverse vitta ferruginea fasciatis; antennis filiformibus, art.* 1–5 *flavis,* 6–8 *piceis,* 9–11 *testaceis; pedibus flavis.*

Long. corp. 2 lin., lat. ¾ lin.

Oblong-ovate, subelongated, parallel, glabrous, black. *Head* short, depressed, slightly produced in front; below the base of the antennæ is a broad triangular transverse depression; immediately above the antennæ (between the eyes) is a transverse fovea, which is bisected at its upper margin by a short longitudinal fovea, giving together the appearance of the letter T inverted; eyes large, prominent, extending laterally as far as the anterior angles of the thorax; the surface finely punctate, black,—the base (from the insertion of the antennæ to the line of the thorax) being fulvous, the margins behind the eyes black. *Thorax* transverse, the anterior angles depressed and subacute; the sides marginate and (close to the anterior and posterior angles) obsoletely coarctate; surface punctate, especially at the sides and base, flavous (suffused with fuscous along the line of the apex). *Scutellum* triangular, ferruginous. *Elytra* parallel, with punctures (which are more obscure towards the suture and apex) arranged in the form of striæ, an appearance of striation being perceptible towards the margination; impubescent, black, divided medially by a broad transverse ferruginous band. *Antennæ* filiform (with a slight tendency to dilatation towards the apex); the first joint broad and dilated at the apex, and of the same length as the fifth and sixth;

the second short, ovate; the third much longer than the fourth or first; the first to the fifth flavous (the first and second being suffused with ferrugineous); the sixth to the eighth piceous (the base of the sixth being ferrugineous); the ninth to the eleventh testaceous. *Legs* flavous, the terminal joint of the anterior tarsi (which is more broadly bilobed than in the allied species) fuscous, and the apex (on the outer side) of the posterior femora suffused with fuscous.

Petropolis (Organ Mountains, Rio Janeiro). In the collection of Mr. Fry.

14. Physimerus trivialis.

P. *oblongo-ovatus, parallelus, subpubescens, ferrugineus; capite brevi, inter oculos transverse foveolato, punctato; thorace transverso, rectilineari, subtiliter punctato; elytris punctato-striatis; antennis filiformibus, nigris; pedibus nigris.*

Long. corp. 1¾ lin., lat. ½–¾ lin.

Oblong-ovate, somewhat depressed, subparallel, of a dull ferrugineous colour throughout. *Head* short, transverse, slightly depressed in front; eyes large, prominent, distant, their extreme lateral margin extending as far as (or even slightly beyond) the sides of the thorax: between the eyes is very faintly apparent a fovea in the shape of the letter T; this fovea is almost obsolete: the surface of the head distinctly punctured. *Thorax* transverse (almost quadrate), rectangular, rectilinear; the anterior and posterior angles distinct and subacute; surface somewhat depressed, very finely punctate throughout, and (under a high power) finely though sparingly pubescent. *Scutellum* triangular. *Elytra* distinctly punctate-striate, subpubescent. *Antennæ* filiform, with a distinct tendency to incrassation towards the apex; the first joint dilated, and inflected outwards; the second short, ovate; the third and fourth of nearly equal length; black. *Legs* black.

I have only seen a single specimen of this insect, from St. Paul, Brazil. In the cabinet of M. Deyrolle.

15. Physimerus juvencus. (Tab. III. fig. 3.) B.M.

Physimerus juvencus, *Dej. Cat.* (ed. 3) p. 407 (*auct. Chevr. Coll.*).

P. (♂) *oblongus, subdepressus, robustus, subpubescens, niger; capite brevi, inter oculos transverse depresso, punctato, rufo-ferrugineo; thorace transverso, subtiliter pubescenti, punctato, flavo; elytris robustis, subcylindricis, punctato-striatis, nigris, vittis duabus a humeris usque ad apicem albo-pubescentibus, hac ad suturam, hac ad marginem; antennis filiformibus, ferrugineis, art. 4–8 fuscis; pedibus flavis.*

G

Var. A (♂). *Elytris fuscis vel cyaneo-fuscis, vitta ad suturam flava.*

Var. B (*plerumque* ♀). *Elytris fere fulvis vel flavo-fulvis, haud ad suturam vel marginem vittatis.*

Long. corp. 2¼ lin., lat. ¾–1 lin.

Oblong, subdepressed, robust, somewhat pubescent, black. *Head* short, transverse, deflected anteriorly, with a shallow transverse depression extending from the insertion of the antennæ to the upper and inner margins of the eyes; eyes slightly prominent, distant, extending laterally as far as the anterior angles of the thorax; surface of the head thickly and coarsely punctured, rufo-ferrugineous. *Thorax* transverse; the sides parallel and marginate: when viewed laterally, the margination is deflected from the humeral angles to the outer and posterior margin of the eyes; at the base is a subobsolete fovea, which is expanded on either side into a more distinct and broader depression: surface of the thorax clothed with very fine pubescence (invisible except under a high power of the microscope), thickly but *finely* punctured, flavous. *Scutellum* triangular, apparently clothed with very fine cinereous pubescence. *Elytra* robust, subcylindrical, punctate-striate, black, with a metallic tinge (in certain lights) of blue: on either side of the suture, from the scutellum (where they are confluent), are two regular longitudinal bands, separated from the suture by a single stria, slightly increasing in breadth towards the centre, and terminating in a point (at a greater distance from the suture) near to the apex; these bands are formed by a fine thick velvet pubescence of pale cinereous colour, the surface of the elytra below the pubescence being more or less distinctly luteous: from the humeral angle, parallel to, but not approaching the margin, is another, more obsolete band of pubescence, which reaches to, and clothes the whole of, the extreme apex of the elytra; this pubescence is of the same colour as that of the sutural band, but on a bright black instead of a luteous ground. *Antennæ* filiform, sufficiently robust, ferrugineous, with the fourth to the eighth joints fuscous; the first joint elongated, inflected outwards, and dilated towards its apex; the second short, ovate; the third and fourth of nearly equal length, the latter being rather longer than the first. *Legs* flavous, with the bladder-like inflation on the posterior claw bright red.

The above description is taken from a male specimen (the third and fourth joints of the antennæ being distinctly more elongated as well as attenuated than in other examples). The species is evidently subject to great variation in colour: other examples of males have the elytra much less decidedly black, with the sutural band of pubescence flavous instead of ashy-grey; the females (for the most part) have the elytra entirely flavous, with very faint traces, if any, of longitudinal bands of pubescence.

Amazon River; Ega. Taken by Mr. Bates. In the collection of the British Museum and other cabinets.

16. Physimerus ephippium. (Tab. III. fig. 4.) B.M.

P. *ovalis, elongatus, ferrugineus, impubescens; capite brevi, inter oculos transverse et oblique foveolato, punctato, glabro; thorace quadrato, ad basin coarctato et transverse obsolete depresso, punctato, subtiliter pubescenti, ferrugineo; elytris latis, punctato-striatis, fuscis, ad humeros macula undique pallide ferruginea, elytrorum etiam apice pallide ferrugineo; antennis filiformibus, fulvis; pedibus flavis.*

♂ Long. corp. 2½ lin., lat. 1½ lin.
♀ Long. corp. 2 lin., lat. 1 lin.

Oval, elongate, slightly depressed, ferrugineous, shining. *Head* short, transverse; eyes subprominent, distant, extending laterally beyond the line of the anterior margin of the thorax: between the eyes is a transverse fovea, the terminations of which are obliquely inclined to the upper and inner margins of the eyes; this fovea is medially connected with the space between the insertion of the antennæ by a distinct longitudinal channel: the surface of the head is sparingly punctured throughout and glabrous. *Thorax* quadrate (almost elongate), at the base coarctate; the anterior angles depressed and subacute; the sides subsinuate, constricted at the base and finely marginate; a broad and shallow transverse postmedial depression gives prominence to the anterior surface; the surface punctate throughout, subpubescent, ferrugineous. *Elytra* distinctly broader than the thorax, somewhat depressed, punctate-striate, fuscous, shining; two large and somewhat irregularly-defined circular spots of a pale ferrugineous colour are situated antemedially, separated by the distance of two striæ from the suture, extending laterally to the margin, and reaching obliquely to the humeral angle; the apex also of the elytra is broadly ferrugineous. *Antennæ* filiform, fulvous. *Legs* flavous throughout.

From the Amazon district. Taken by Mr. Bates.

17. Physimerus suboculatus.

P. *oblongo-ovatus, subelongatus, rufo-fuscus; capite brevi, inter oculos Y foveolato; thorace quadrato, ad basin constricto et trans-*

verse depresso, punctato ; elytris punctato-striatis, fusco semicirculariter notatis ; antennis rufo-flavis ; pedibus flavis.

Long. corp. 2⅓ lin., lat. 1 lin.

Oblong-ovate, subelongate, subparallel, rufo-fuscous. *Head* short, depressed, hardly produced; between the labrum and the base of the antennæ a smooth subtriangular depression extends transversely; above the base of the antennæ, between the eyes, is a medial longitudinal fovea, which, at its upper extremity, extends obliquely towards the upper and inner margins of the eyes, thus forming the character of the letter Y; eyes large, prominent, situated at the base of the head, and extending laterally as far as the anterior angles of the thorax; the surface very finely punctate, glabrous. *Thorax* quadrate, considerably constricted towards the base; the anterior angles depressed; the sides marginate; the base broadly and transversely depressed; the surface sparingly and finely punctate, glabrous. *Scutellum* small, triangular, rufo-fuscous. *Elytra* considerably broader than the thorax, subparallel, punctate-striate, the striæ becoming almost obsolete as they approach the apex, clothed throughout (when viewed under a high power) with a fine and sparingly distributed pubescence; the colour rufo-fuscous, with a distinct subcircular marking of darker fuscous, which, commencing at the antemedial margination, extends laterally in the direction of the suture, whence it approaches in a semicircular direction, but does not reach, the humeral angle; the extremity of the humeral angle is also suffused with fuscous. *Antennæ* filiform, rufo-flavous. *Legs* flavous throughout.

This insect in general appearance closely approaches *P. ephippium*; in form, however, as well as in pattern of colour it is abundantly distinct.

Para. In the collection of M. Chevrolat.

18. **Physimerus adumbratus.** B.M.

P. *ovatus, latus, subdepressus, rufo-ferrugineus, nitidus ; capite brevi, punctato ; thorace subelongato, prope basin coarctato ; elytris latis, punctato-striatis, fusco-ferrugineis, fasciis duabus transversis latis flavo-ferrugineis indistinctis ; antennis pedibusque flavis.*

Long. corp. 1¾ lin., lat. 1 lin.

Ovate, broad, slightly depressed, rufo-ferrugineous throughout. *Head* short, transverse, shining, distinctly punctate; eyes prominent and distant; between the eyes is a transverse depression, which is inflected upwards towards its extremities along the upper and inner margins of the eyes. *Thorax* quadrate; the anterior angles distinct and slightly prominent; the sides submarginate, postmedially coarctate, the basal angles being subacute; the surface sparingly punctured; a broad basal depression (somewhat more thickly punctured than the rest of the thorax) is coextensive with the lateral constriction; impubescent, rufo-ferrugineous, with a medial longitudinal fuscous spot at the base. *Scutellum* triangular, rufo-ferrugineous. *Elytra* broad, somewhat depressed, punctate-striate, shining, with a slight antemedial transverse depression extending obliquely upwards towards the shoulders; fusco-ferrugineous; a broad and indeterminate fascia, of somewhat paler colour, extends from the shoulders obliquely to the antemedial suture, from which it is separated by the distance of a single stria; the whole of the apical half of the elytra is also more or less distinctly pale ferrugineous, adumbrated, however, by a transverse and indeterminate shading of darker colour. *Antennæ* filiform; the first joint long, and dilated towards the apex; the second short, ovate; third, fourth, and fifth of nearly equal length; fulvous. *Legs* pale testaceous throughout, with the bladder-like inflation of the posterior terminal claw bright ferrugineous.

At first sight, this species appears to be a small variety of *P. ephippium*; after much examination, however, I have resolved to register it, provisionally at least, as a distinct species. Not only is the insect considerably smaller, but its markings do not correspond to those in *P. ephippium*; and the posterior femora and tarsi are more elongate. In that species there is no trace of any other fulvous marking besides the two humeral spots, and at the apex of the elytra these are *distinct*, and well-defined upon a black ground; in *P. adumbratus*, however (not to notice the *variation* in colour), the fulvous colouring at the apex extends nearly halfway up the elytra, and is itself divided transversely by an irregularly-defined ferrugineous marking. The great difference also in the size of the insects (in a group which seems hardly ever to admit of any variation in size among the examples of a species), together with the somewhat more elongated posterior femora and tibiæ, strongly support the conclusion that the two insects are specifically distinct.

Amazon district, Villa Nova. Collected by Mr. Bates.

19. Physimerus brevicollis.

P. *ovatus, latus, depressus, subtiliter pubescens, rufo-fuscus; capite brevi, depresso; thorace transverso, ad medium constricto, punctato, rufo-flavo, ad medium rufo-fusco; elytris latis, punctato-*

striatis, fuscis, ad basin, ad medium transverse, et ad apicem rufis; antennis filiformibus, flavis; pedibus testaceis.

Long. corp. 2 lin., lat. 1 lin.

Ovate, broad, depressed, very finely pubescent, rufo-fuscous. *Head* short, depressed, hardly produced; eyes large, prominent, situated at the back of the head: antennæ approximate; above their insertion are two small tubercles, while immediately above these (extending to the base) is a medial longitudinal ridge; surface punctate, rufous, the medial ridge being rufo-piceous. *Thorax* transverse (not, as in *P. adumbratus*, quadrate), slightly constricted in the middle; the anterior angles depressed and subacute; the sides marginate; surface finely punctate, obsoletely pubescent, and rufo-flavous,—the margination, and a medial longitudinal line, being rufo-fuscous. *Scutellum* small, triangular, fuscous. *Elytra* broader than the thorax, punctate-striate (the striæ being almost obsolete, and the punctures large and deep), indistinctly clothed with ashy pubescence, fuscous, —the base of the elytra (from the humeral angle to the scutellum), a medial, broad, indeterminate fascia (which does not reach the suture), and the apex of the elytra, being rufous. *Antennæ* filiform, robust, flavous, with the fifth and sixth joints rufo-flavous. *Legs* testaceous throughout.

This species, in its general facies and in the disposition of its markings, almost entirely resembles *P. adumbratus*; it may be, however, without hesitation, separated from it by the medial longitudinal ridge on the head, and by its transverse (not quadrate and constricted) thorax.

The Amazon district. Taken by Mr. Bates.

20. **Physimerus angulo-fasciatus.**

P. *oblongo-ovatus, latus, depressus, subpubescens, rufo-ferrugineus; capite brevi, subproducto, ad basin longitudinaliter carinato, punctato, flavo-rufo; thorace transverso, punctato, flavo-rufo; elytris sat latis, punctato-striatis, transverse et oblique bivittatis; antennis filiformibus, rufo-flavis; pedibus flavis.*

Long. corp. 2 lin., lat. 1 lin.

Oblong-ovate, broad, depressed, subpubescent, rufo-ferrugineous. *Head* short, somewhat produced in front, vertical (slightly reflected backwards); eyes large, prominent, black, extending laterally as far as the line of the thorax; between the eyes, and above the insertion of the antennæ, is a minute Y-shaped depression, while above it (extending as far as the base of the head) is an obsolete medial longitudinal carination; the surface finely punctate, flavo-rufous. *Thorax* transverse, rectilinear, at the base slightly constricted and transversely depressed; the anterior angles subacute; the surface finely flavo-pubescent, punctate, flavo-rufous. *Scutellum* triangular, fuscous. *Elytra* much broader than the thorax, depressed, punctate-striate (the punctures being broad and shallow, and the striæ almost obsolete: at the apex the punctures are obsolete); the surface rufo-flavous, clothed throughout (more or less) with a fine ashy pubescence: two transverse bands of a rufo-piceous colour (the one at the humeral angle, and the other medially) extend from the margins to about the fifth stria, where they are obliquely inflected (in the direction of the apex) to the suture; these angulated fasciæ are broader and more prominent in some examples than in others; in all they are well-defined. *Antennæ* filiform, sufficiently robust, flavous, the first, and also the sixth and seventh joints being rufo-fuscous. *Legs* flavo-testaceous throughout.

From the district of the Amazon. In the collection of Mr. Bates and the Rev. H. Clark.

Besides the differences in colouring and marking (which appear to be tolerably constant) between this and other allied species, structural differences are apparent: in *P. angulo-fasciatus* the base of the thorax is more constricted than in *P. brevicollis*, and the surface of the thorax is more equate than in *P. bituberculatus*; in the sculpturing of the head, also, important differences may be traced.

21. Physimerus bituberculatus.

P. oblongo-ovatus, latus, depressus, subpubescens, flavo-rufus; capite brevi, ad basin longitudinaliter carinato, punctato; thorace transverso, rectangulari, ad basin depresso, antice elevato, rufo-fusco, antice et ad latera rufo; elytris latis, depressis, punctato-striatis, rufo-fuscis, ad humeros, et juxta apicem transverse rufo-flavis; antennis filiformibus, flavis; pedibus flavis, femoribus posticis fusco suffusis.

Long. corp. 2 lin., lat. 1 lin.

Oblong-ovate, broad, depressed, subpubescent, flavo-rufous. *Head* short, transverse, slightly depressed, hardly produced; eyes large and prominent; between the eyes, and above the insertion of the antennæ, is a small T-shaped depression, while above it, extending to the base of the head, is a longitudinal carination; surface finely punctate. *Thorax* transverse, rectangular; the anterior angles depressed; this depression extends in an oblique direction to the mid-base, giving a prominence to the anterior part of the thorax, which divides itself (very distinctly by colour, and also, less distinctly, by form) into two slightly elevated tubercles; surface punctate, rufo-fuscous,—the raised anterior surface and the sides being rufous. *Scutellum* triangular, fuscous. *Elytra* broader than the thorax, depressed, punctate-striate, subpubescent, rufo-fuscous,—the shoulders (from the humeral angle to the scutellum), and also a *broad*, suffused, transverse band (*near to the apex*), being rufo-flavous. *Antennæ* filiform, tolerably long, flavous, with the sixth and eleventh joints fuscous. *Legs* flavous, the posterior femora being pubescent, and suffused with dark fuscous; the inflation of the terminal claw bright rufo-ferrugineous.

This species may be separated from those nearly allied to it (all of which, at first sight, closely resemble one another) by the *form* of, and the *markings* on, the surface of the thorax.

From the Amazon district. Taken by Mr. Bates.

22. Physimerus bilineatus. (Tab. III. fig. 5.)

P. *oblongo-ovatus, subparallelus, pubescens, punctato-striatus, nigro-fuscus; capite brevi (ad basin antennarum leviter producto), granulato, nigro; thorace quadrato, angulis anticis subtruncatis, ad basin constricto et transverse depresso, subtiliter pubescenti, fusco, ad latera flavo; elytris subcylindricis, punctato-striatis, pubescentibus, nigris, lineis duabus fusco-pubescentibus; antennis filiformibus, tenuibus, fuscis, art. 4 et 8–10 testaceis; pedibus pallide testaceis, tarsis anterioribus rufo-testaceis, femorumque posticorum basibus fuscis.*

Long. corp. 2 lin., lat. $\frac{3}{4}$–1 lin.

Oblong-ovate, subparallel, pubescent, darkly fuscous. *Head* short, abruptly depressed and slightly produced: between the labrum and the base of the antennæ is a triangular glabrous plane, which is bisected by a medial longitudinal carination; the base of the antennæ is situated immediately on the angle of abrupt deflection, giving it the appearance, when viewed laterally, of a *Loxoprosopus*: eyes large, situated at the base of the head, extending laterally beyond the anterior angles of the thorax; the surface above the base of the antennæ finely granulated; the colour of the labrum rufo-flavous, of the head black. *Thorax* quadrate; the anterior angles subtruncate; the sides marginate, and slightly constricted towards the base: a broad transverse depression (which is well-defined and abrupt at its upper margin) extends along the line of the base; this depression is most narrow medially, becoming slightly broader as it approaches the margination: the surface subdepressed, very finely pubescent, fuscous, with a broad lateral margination of flavous. *Scutellum* small, triangular, fuscous. *Elytra* subcylindrical, punctate-striate, finely pubescent, black: a line of fuscous pubescence extends longitudinally between the first and the third striæ, gradually diverging from the suture, and extending laterally at the apex; between the fourth and seventh striæ is another longitudinal line, *more distinctly flavous*, which extends (near the shoulders) as far as the margination, and terminates before it arrives at the base: antennæ filiform, long and slender; joints one to three and five to seven piceous, four, and eight to ten pale testaceous, the eleventh fuscous. *Legs* pale testaceous; the anterior tarsi (and base of the tibiæ) rufo-testaceous; the base of the posterior femora is fuscous, and the globular inflation above the posterior claw bright rufous.

Tunantius, in the district of the River Amazon. In the collection of Mr. Bates.

23. Physimerus Batesii. (Tab. III. fig. 6.)

P. *oblongo-ovatus, latus, robustus, subparallelus, subpubescens, nigro-ferrugineus; thorace quadrato, ad basin constricto et transverse depresso, linea media longitudinali picea; scutello triangulari, fusco; elytris robustis, subcylindricis; antennis filiformibus, rufo-flavis; pedibus flavis, posticis rufo- et piceo-suffusis.*

Long. corp. 1½ lin., lat. ¾ lin.

Oblong-ovate, broad, robust, subparallel, subpubescent, dark ferrugineous. *Head* short, transverse, slightly produced; above the labrum transversely and obliquely canaliculated; antennæ at their insertion approximate; eyes large and prominent; the surface thickly punctate, rufo-ferrugineous. *Thorax* quadrate, considerably constricted at the base; the anterior angles subtruncate; the surface at the base broadly and transversely depressed, finely pubescent throughout; rufo-ferrugineous, with a medial longitudinal line of piceous. *Scutellum* triangular, fuscous. *Elytra* robust, subcylindrical, punctate-striate, transversely and obliquely depressed from the antemedial suture towards the shoulders; finely pubescent throughout. *Antennæ* filiform, fine, rufo-flavous. *Legs*: the anterior flavous; the posterior rufo-flavous, suffused with piceous.

Var. A. Surface throughout dark flavous instead of ferrugineous.

Amazon district (Santarem and Obydos). In the collection of Mr. Bates and the Rev. H. Clark.

24. Physimerus irroratus. (Tab. III. fig. 7.)

P. *oblongo-ovatus, latus, robustus, subparallelus, subpubescens, fusco-ferrugineus; thorace transverso (subquadrato); elytris latis, punctato-striatis, maculis quatuor obscurissime notatis; antennis longiusculis, tenuiter dilatatis, art.* 1–5 *ferrugineis,* 6–8 *piceis,* 9–11 *testaceis; pedibus flavis, femoribus posticis rufo-ferrugineis.*

Long. corp. 1¾ lin., lat. 1 lin.

Oblong-ovate, broad, robust, subparallel, fusco-ferrugineous, finely pubescent. *Head* short, transverse, depressed, slightly elongate; above the labrum is a transverse plane depression; above the insertion of the antennæ is an obsolete medial carination; eyes situated at the base of the head, not extending laterally so far as the anterior angles of the thorax; the surface finely and thickly punctate; near the inner margin of the eyes flavo-pubescent. *Thorax* transverse (almost quadrate); the anterior angles subtruncate; the sides marginate, and slightly constricted at the base; the surface thickly clothed with a fine ashy pubescence. *Scutellum* triangular. *Elytra* broad, robust, punctate-striate, antemedially very slightly transversely depressed, clothed throughout with a fine ashy pubescence; postmedially are two circular obscure spots between the third and the sixth striæ, and two others, nearer to the base (smaller and less distinct, between the first and third striæ), which are formed by the absence of this ashy pubescence. *Antennæ* filiform, slightly dilated towards the apex; joints one to five ferrugineous (the first being suffused with fuscous), six to eight piceous, nine to eleven testaceous. *Legs*: the anterior flavous; the posterior femora rufo-ferrugineous, and the tibiæ rufous.

Ega (district of the Amazon). In the collection of Mr. Bates.

25. Physimerus nebulosus.

P. *oblongo-ovatus, latus, parallelus, subpubescens, piceus; capite brevi, rufo-ferrugineo; thorace quadrato, ad basin constricto et transverse depresso, ad latera rufo-flavo; elytris latis, punctato-striatis, vitta antemedia transversa cinereo-pubescenti, ad latera et ad suturam ampliori; antennis subdilatatis, art.* 1–5 *flavis,* 6–11 *rufo-flavis; pedibus rufo-flavis.*

Long. corp. 1½ lin., lat. ⅔ lin.

Oblong-ovate, broad, robust, parallel, very finely pubescent, piceous. *Head* very short, depressed, not elongated at the apex; eyes tolerably large, prominent, situated at the base of the head, extending laterally as far as the anterior angles of the thorax; surface at the inner margin of the eyes flavo-pubescent, thickly punctate, rufo-ferrugineous. *Thorax* quadrate; the anterior angles subacute and depressed, the sides submarginate and considerably constricted towards the base; a broad postmedial depression extends along the line of the base; at the sides finely flavo-pubescent and rufo-flavous (more darkly piceous on the line of margination). *Scutellum* small, triangular. *Elytra* broad, punctate-striate, clothed throughout with a very fine pubescence (which in some parts can only be traced under a high magnifying power): a broad irregular antemedial band extends transversely from the suture to the margination; near the suture, and also near the line of margination, it considerably increases in breadth (extending in front at these points nearly to the shoulders and scutellum); this band is formed by an ashy-grey pubescence; the apex also is similarly clothed with pubescence. *Antennæ* filiform, tolerably long, subdilated towards their apex; joints one to five flavous, six to eleven rufo-flavous. *Legs*: the anterior flavous; the posterior rufous, the femora being suffused with piceous.

From the neighbourhood of Rio Janeiro. Collected by Mr. Squire. In the collection of Mr. Baly.

26. Physimerus pruinosus.

P. *oblongo-ovatus, subparallelus, fuscus ; capite brevi, subproducto; thorace elongato, rectangulari, ad basin constricto, ad latera depresso ; elytris punctato-striatis, ante medium oblique depressis, ad latera irregulariter cinereo lineatis; antennis longiusculis, subincrassatis, art.* 1, 2, 6–8 *dilatatis et fuscis,* 3–5 *et* 9–11 *rufoflavis ; pedibus rufo-fuscis.*

Long. corp. 2 lin., lat. ¾ lin.

Oblong-ovate, subparallel, punctate-striate, impubescent, dark fuscous. *Head* short, slightly produced; below the base of the antennæ is a transverse triangular depression: eyes large, situated at the base of the head, and extending laterally as far as the anterior angle of the thorax; between the eyes, and immediately above the base of the antennæ, is a V-shaped depression, rendered more distinct by an ashy-grey pubescence: the surface finely punctate; at the inner margin of the eyes is a line of fine grey pubescence. *Thorax* elongate, constricted at the base, rectangular; the anterior angles depressed; the sides marginate; at the base is a broad transverse antemedial depression ; the surface (under a high magnifying power) is obsoletely pubescent, more distinctly at the sides, which are marked (from the base of the head immediately behind the eyes to the posterior angle) with a longitudinal line of ashy-grey pubescence. *Scutellum* small, triangular, glabrous. *Elytra* broad, subcylindrical, distinctly punctate-striate ; an antemedial depression extends obliquely upwards towards the humeral angles ; throughout the surface are scattered several long and isolated single hairs, which are more frequent on the sides and at the base; near to the line of margination (at the sixth and seventh striæ) is an irregular line of pale pubescence from the shoulder to the apex; medially, also, between the second and third striæ is a minute longitudinal marking of the same colour. *Antennæ* filiform, slightly dilated; the joints 1, 2 and 6 to 8 subdilated and darkly fuscous, 3 to 5 elongate and rufo-ferrugineous, 9 to 11 flavous. *Legs* rufo-fuscous, the posterior femora being suffused with piceous, and the globular inflation over the apical claw bright rufous.

Colombia. In the collection of Mr. Baly.

27. Physimerus griseostriatus.

P. *oblongo-ovatus, fuscus; capite subproducto, leviter reflecto-punctato, nigro; thorace quadrato, antice subrotundato, ad basin transverse depresso, pubescenti, flavo, ad medium longitudinaliter fusco; elytris subparallelis, punctato-striatis, pube admodum brevi vestitis, ad latera flavo-vittatis; antennis filiformibus, art. 1–3 fusco suffusis, 4 testaceo, 5–8 fuscis, 9–11 testaceis; pedibus flavis, femoribus posticis ad basin fusco suffusis.*

Long. corp. 1¾ lin., lat. ¾–1 lin.

Oblong-ovate, subparallel, deeply punctate-striate, pubescent, fuscous. *Head* short, transverse, somewhat produced in front; eyes large, prominent, situated at the base of the head, and extending laterally beyond the angles of the thorax; the antennæ are inserted between the eyes, and (as in *Loxoprosopus*) immediately upon the angle (which is somewhat abrupt) that is formed by the depression of the anterior part of the head; surface thickly punctate, black. *Thorax* quadrate, with the anterior angles depressed and obsolete; the sides submarginate and slightly contracted at the base, which is transversely and postmedially depressed; the surface subpubescent throughout, flavous, with a medial longitudinal marking (broad and suffused) of flavo-fuscous. *Scutellum* minute, triangular, fuscous. *Elytra* broad, subparallel, punctate-striate, clothed throughout (as is apparent under a high magnifying power) with a fine pubescence, but more distinctly so at the margin: a broad band of flavous pubescence is continued along the line of margination from the shoulders to the apex; this band is irregular and (apparently) uncertain in form: colour fuscous. *Antennæ* tolerably long, filiform; the first three joints suffused with fuscous; the fourth testaceous; the fifth to eighth dark fuscous; the ninth to eleventh pale testaceous. *Legs* flavous throughout, the apex of the femora being suffused with fuscous.

This species, in form and markings, is not unlike *P. pruinosus*; it may, however, be readily distinguished by its more transverse and more pubescent thorax, as well as by the less deep striation of the head.

From the neighbourhood of Ega (River Amazon). Taken by Mr. Bates.

Genus 11. GLENIDION*.

LABRUM *breve, subcirculare.*

PALPI MAXILLARES *elongati, robusti, art. 2do et 3^{tio} ad apicem oblique truncatis, apicali attenuato, conico.*

PALPI LABIALES *elongati, minuti, attenuati, subcylindrici.*

ANTENNÆ *filiformes (?), art. 3^{tio} et 4to æque ac 2^{ndo} brevibus, 5to et 6to longioribus, attenuatis (reliqui desunt).*

CAPUT *breve, productum, vix depressum.*

THORAX *transversus, rectilinearis, ad basin leviter constrictus, ad latera marginatus.*

SCUTELLUM *minutissimum.*

ELYTRA *parallela, elongata, subdepressa, glabra.*

PEDES : *tarsi anteriores attenuati, vix dilatati, femora postica elongata ; tibiæ etiam elongatæ et longitudinaliter (ad apicem) excavatæ ; tarsi, art. basalis productus et sat attenuatus (art. reliqui desunt).*

Elongate, subparallel, depressed.

Labrum short, narrower than the base of the head, subcircular.

Maxillary palpi elongate ; the basal joint minute, almost quadrate; the second longer, obliquely truncate at the apex ; the penultimate somewhat broader, more cylindrical, and also obliquely truncate at the apex; the terminal joint elongate and conical.

Labial palpi elongate, minute.

Antennæ approximate, inserted between the lower margins of the eyes, probably filiform ; the basal joint elongate, dilated, and subincurved towards the apex ; the second shorter, somewhat narrower, ovate ; the third *as short as the second,* and narrow ; the fourth and fifth elongate, longer than the basal joint; the rest are wanting in the example before me.

Eyes lateral, large, subglobose, situated at some distance from the base of the head, and extending laterally as far as the anterior angles of the thorax.

Head short, transverse, not so much depressed from the plane of the thorax as the preceding genus, *Physimerus* ; somewhat porrect.

Thorax transverse (almost quadrate), rectilinear, slightly constricted towards the base ; the anterior margin is obsoletely emarginate ; the anterior angles depressed, the sides evenly marginate ; the base

* γλήνη, longurio.

transversely foveolated in *G. rubronotatum*; the surface equate, subcylindrical.

Scutellum almost obsolete, much more minute than in *Physimerus*, depressed below the plane of the elytra, triangular.

Elytra broader than the thorax, elongated, subparallel, depressed, glabrous; in *G. rubronotatum* punctate.

Legs: the *anterior femora* when viewed from the front robust, subdilated medially. The *tibiæ* elongate, at the base inflected, and gradually subdilated; the apex is obliquely truncate, and armed (beyond the insertion of the tarsus) with a robust incurved spur. The *tarsi* are elongated, almost attenuate, narrower than the base of the tibia; the basal joint is long, *slightly* dilated towards the apex; the second is of the same form, but shorter; the third is ovate, shorter than the second, not bilobed; the terminal joint is produced, and gradually thickened towards the apex, where it terminates in a bifid claw, the inner surface of which is armed *at the base* with a robust spur. *Posterior femora* incrassated and produced, regularly ovate, reaching nearly to the apex of the elytra. The *tibiæ* also are elongate, at the immediate base inflected, and gradually thickened towards the apex; when viewed obliquely from behind, the posterior surface is longitudinally flattened and postmedially hollowed out, gradually increasing in depth of concavity, until at the apex it forms a socket for the reception of the tarsus; the margination of this elongated channel is subsinuate near the apex and more broadly developed; towards the insertion of the tarsus it is armed with a series of comb-like spurs, close and porrect; the extreme apex terminates in a robust and short single spur. The *tarsus* is unfortunately, in the only example I have before me, mutilated; the basal joint is *very elongate*, and slightly thickened towards the apex.

Owing to the unfortunate mutilation of the posterior tarsus in the specimen of *G. rubronotatum*, I am not able to assure myself, by actual inspection, of the presence of the inflation above the terminal claw, and hence of the propriety of introducing it into this section of Halticidæ. I am well satisfied, however, from the previous examination of the example by Mr. Baly when in his possession, that it belongs to this group; this being the case, its affinities are evidently more with *Physimerus* than with other forms. Its general facies is almost identical, were it not for its *produced* posterior femora and tibiæ. The necessity of separating it, however, from this genus is abundantly manifest; the striking peculiarity of the third *abbreviated* joint of the antennæ, combined with the *elongated* postical femora and elongated and grooved postical tarsi, is sufficient to constitute it the basis of a separate genus.

1. Glenidion rubronotatum.

G. *oblongo-ovale, parallelum, depressum, nitidum, nigrum; capite brevi, subproducto, fovea incisa inter oculos, impunctato, rufo-ferrugineo, lævi; thorace quadrato, ad latera et postice marginato, ad basin constricto et transverse foveolato, impunctato, rufo-ferrugineo; elytris depressis, punctis velut in striis ordinatis, nigris, apud medium et ad apicem (juxta suturam) litura ferruginea umbratis; antennis filiformibus, art.* 2–4 *abbreviatis,* 5 *et* 6 *elongatis,* 1–3 *ferrugineis,* 4–6 *fuscis* (*reliqui desunt*); *pedibus flavis, femoribus posticis fuscatis, tibiisque elongatis.*

Long. corp. 2¼ lin., lat. 1 lin.

Oblong-oval, parallel, depressed, black, shining. *Head* short, transverse, depressed, hardly elongate in front, impunctate; eyes large, subprominent, distant; between the eyes and above the insertion of the antennæ, which are contiguous, are two small abrupt transverse foveæ, while above them a third (broader and more distinct) extends upwards in a longitudinal direction. *Thorax* quadrate; sides marginate, slightly constricted towards the base; the anterior angles are subacute; close to the basal line is a narrow transverse groove (which does not terminate, as in the genus *Monoplatus*, before it reaches the humeral angle, but which extends along the whole of the basal line, and connects itself with the lateral margination); surface impunctate, rufo-ferrugineous. *Scutellum* triangular, minute, fulvo-rufous. *Elytra* depressed, parallel, with rows of punctures arranged in the form of striæ (the striæ being obscurely apparent near the shoulders and at the margination); the colour is black, on either side of the suture, postmedially, and especially towards the base, irregularly shaded off into rufo-ferrugineous, this decoloration around the postmedial suture being indeterminate and irregularly defined. *Antennæ* filiform; the first joint dilated and subelongated; the second short, ovate; both of these fulvous; the third attenuate, abbreviated, *hardly longer than the second*; the fourth and fifth elongate (the rest are wanting); colour fusco-fulvous. *Legs*: the posterior elongated, flavous, with the apex of the posterior femora and tibiæ clothed with fuscous.

Brazil. In the collection of Mr. Baly.

Genus 12. HYPANTHERUS*.

PALPI MAXILLARES *elongati, art.* 3ᵗⁱᵒ *producto et cylindrico.*
PALPI LABIALES *elongati, attenuati.*
ANTENNÆ *plus minus dilatatæ, robustæ, approximatæ.*

* ὑπό, sub; ἀνθηρός, coloratus.

Oculi *distantes, ad basin capitis, subglobosi.*

Caput *breve, robustum, vix ad apicem productum, depressum.*

Thorax *transversus, aliquando subquadratus, depressus.*

Elytra *lata, robusta, plerumque punctato-striata et leviter pube vestita.*

Pedes : *ant. tibiis ad basin incurvatis, ad apicem dilatatis et oblique truncatis ; ant. tarsis brevibus, art. 2^{ndo} minuto ; femoribus posticis valde incrassatis ; tibiis longitudinaliter marginatis, et ante apicem ecalcaratis.*

Labrum transverse, subrotundate at the margins.

Maxillary palpi (Tab. IV. fig. 1 *m*) subelongate ; the basal joint minute ; the second ovate, and broadly truncate at the apex ; the third longer and broader than the second, and subcylindrical ; the apical joint is broadly conical.

Labial palpi (Tab. IV. fig. 1 *n*) subelongate, narrower than, but of the same form as, the maxillary.

Antennæ robust, approximate, inserted below and somewhat between the lower margins of the eyes, more or less dilated medially ; the first joint is incrassated, and slightly incurved outwards towards the apex ; the second short and *broad* ; the third and fourth are subequal, longer and narrower than the first ; the fifth is shorter than the fourth ; the sixth to the eighth are shorter and generally more robust ; the ninth to the eleventh are gradually attenuated towards the extremity.

Eyes tolerably large, situated at some little distance from the base of the head and not extending laterally so far as the anterior angles of the thorax.

Head short, robust, narrower than the thorax, hardly elongated in front, depressed at almost right angles to the plane of the elytra.

Thorax transverse (in some species almost quadrate), broader than the head, rectangular ; the sides marginate, narrower relatively than in *Thrasygœus, Eupeges,* and even *Phylacticus* ; the anterior angles are more or less depressed,—its whole surface being inclined at a very apparent angle to the plane of the elytra.

Scutellum triangular, impunctate, generally impubescent.

Elytra robust, more manifestly broader than the thorax than in the subsequent genera, punctate-striate, generally clothed with pubescence, and depressed antemedially and obliquely, so as to give an appearance of prominence to the scutellary surface.

Legs: the *anterior femora* tolerably robust and subcylindrical, slightly incurved near the apex. The *tibia* (Tab. IV. fig. 1 *c*) is abruptly incurved immediately at the base and gradually dilated towards the apex, where it is broadly obliquely truncate. The *tarsi*

(Tab. IV. fig. 1 *d*) are short and broad, the basal joint being broadly ovate; the second of the same form as the basal joint, but more minute; the third broader than the first, broadly ovate, not bilobed; these three basal joints are densely margined with thick rigid pubescence; from the centre of the third proceeds the base of the terminal joint, which is attenuated and gradually incrassated, terminated by the apical claw, the two members of which are simple, and unarmed at their inner margin by any basal tooth. The *posterior femora* are very robust, and incrassated, slightly attenuated towards the apex, broadly truncate. The *tibia* (Tab. IV. fig. 1 *g*) is short and robust, abruptly bent at the immediate base, and, when viewed from behind, longitudinally flattened; this flat longitudinal surface is on either side marginate; the marginations are produced immediately above the insertion of the tarsus into an obtuse spur, and continued to the extreme apex, where they terminate in two robust claws; the insertion of the tarsus is at some little distance from the apex, and the socket which contains it is armed with minute teeth, like the teeth of a comb. The *tibiæ* (Tab. IV. fig. 1 *h*) are short and attenuate, the first and second joints being ovate, and the third broadly subcircular; the fourth is elongate, subincurved, and produced above into a broad globular inflation, which completely conceals from above the apical claw. This claw is bifid and, like the anterior claw, simple.

The general appearance of the insects composing this genus will (without reference to structural details) at once separate them from others. They are more robust, more cylindrical, and less depressed than in *Physimerus*; the thorax is narrower and more rectangular than in *Phylacticus*, which at first sight it closely resembles; and from *Thrasygœus* the genus is at once separated by its *much smaller size*, as well as by its more contracted thorax.

1. Hypantherus concolor. (Tab. IV. fig. 1.)

H. *oblongus, latus, sat robustus, flavo-pubescens, rufo-ferrugineus; capite brevi, super antennarum basin* T *foveolato, punctato, ad medium rufo-fusco suffuso; thorace transverso, rectangulari, ad basin transverse depresso, punctato; elytris latis, robustis, ad medium oblique depressis, punctato-striatis; antennis brevibus, incrassatis, rufo-testaceis, art. 6–8 nigris; pedibus robustis, subpubescentibus, rufo-ferrugineis.*

Long. corp. 2⅔ lin., lat. 1⅓ lin.

Oblong, broad, tolerably robust, flavo-pubescent, rufo-ferrugineous. *Head* short, transverse, slightly produced; between the mouth and the base of the antennæ is a transverse subtriangular depression; immediately above the insertion of the antennæ is an obsolete longitudinal fovea, which joins at its upper extremity a broader transverse shallow depression: the surface below the antennæ almost impunctate; above, strongly punctate, rufo-ferrugineous, medially suffused with rufo-fuscous. *Thorax* a little broader than the head, transverse, rectangular; the anterior angles depressed; the sides marginate; at the base is an obsolete shallow transverse depression; the surface flavo-pubescent, finely punctate. *Scutellum* triangular, flavo-pubescent. *Elytra* tolerably broad, robust, medially subdepressed, punctate-striate, flavo-pubescent. *Antennæ* short, robust, incrassated; the first joint broad and long; the second short, ovate; the third nearly as long as, but more slender than, the first; the fourth and fifth shorter and slightly broader than the third; the sixth, seventh and eighth broadly dilated; rufo-testaceous, sixth to eighth black. *Legs* robust, subpubescent, rufo-ferrugineous.

From the district of the River Amazon. In the collections of Mr. Bates and the Rev. H. Clark.

2. Hypantherus ambiguus.

H. oblongo-ovatus, sat robustus, fusco-ferrugineus; capite brevi, super antennarum basin bituberculato, ad basin crebre punctato, rufo-ferrugineo, in medio rufo-fusco; thorace transverso, lævigato, flavo-pubescenti; elytris robustis, punctato-striatis, flavo-pubescentibus; antennis brevibus, incrassatis, art. 1–5 flavis, 6–8 nigris, 9–11 flavis; pedibus anterioribus flavis; femoribus posticis rufo-fuscis, tibiis ad apicem obsolete dentatis, et (cum tarsis) rufo-fulvis.

Long. corp. 2¾–3 lin., lat. 1¼ lin.

Oblong-ovate, sufficiently robust, of a dark-brown ferrugineous colour throughout. *Head* short, slightly produced; above the mouth is a transverse subtriangular depression: immediately above the insertion of the antennæ is a deep longitudinal fovea, giving prominence to two oblong shining tubercles, one on either side of it; above this fovea there is no trace of a transverse depression, as in *H. concolor*: the surface in front levigate, above thickly and deeply punctured; rufo-ferrugineous, suffused medially with rufo-fuscous. *Thorax* transverse, rectangular; the anterior angles depressed; the sides marginate; the surface levigate, flavo-pubescent. *Scutellum* triangular, flavo-pubescent. *Elytra* robust, longer and proportionally narrower than in *H. concolor*, antemedially transversely subdepressed, punctate-striate, flavo-pubescent (the punctures being somewhat finer and the pubescence closer than in *H. concolor*). *Antennæ* short, robust, incrassated, the third and fourth joints being slender, and of the length of the first; the sixth to the eighth dilated; the colour of the first and second rufo-flavous, the third to fifth flavous, the sixth to eighth black, the ninth to eleventh flavous. *Legs*: the anterior flavous throughout; on the outer edge of the *posterior* tibiæ, near the apex, is a *minute* spur-like projection; the femora pubescent, rufo-fuscous; the tibiæ and tarsi rufo-fulvous.

In form and general appearance this insect is closely allied to *H. concolor*; it may be separated, however, by its greater length, its proportional narrowness, as well as by the difference of its colouring,—by the difference of the sculpturing at the apex of the head, and by the character of its punctuation and pubescence on the elytra.

From the district of the Amazon. In the collection of Mr. Bates.

3. Hypantherus assimilis.

H. *oblongo-ovatus, robustus, flavo-pubescens, rufo-ferrugineus; capite brevi, inter oculos V carinato, impunctato; thorace transverso, æquato, rectangulari; elytris latis, subcylindricis, punctato-striatis, ante medium transverse depressis; antennis filiformibus, ferrugineis, art. 6–11 fuscis; pedibus rufo-ferrugineis.*

Long. corp. 2 lin., lat. 1 lin.

Oblong-ovate, robust, finely flavo-pubescent, rufo-ferrugineous. *Head* short, transverse, slightly produced in front; between the labrum and the base of the antennæ are a longitudinal medial and also two oblique carinations; above the base and between the eyes are also two oblique carinations, forming together the character of the letter V; eyes lateral, globose, situated nearly at the base of the head; the surface is subpubescent, more distinctly at the inner margin of the eyes, at the base impunctate, and rufous. *Thorax* transverse (almost quadrate); the anterior angles depressed and subacute, the sides marginate and subparallel; the surface is inclined, equate, and subpubescent. *Scutellum* small, triangular, fuscous. *Elytra* broad, robust, subcylindrical, slightly tapering towards the apex, finely punctate-striate, evenly and obsoletely pubescent; when viewed obliquely, a shallow transverse antemedial depression is apparent. *Antennæ* robust, filiform, slightly thickened near the apex, ferrugineous, the sixth to the eleventh joints being fuscous. *Legs* robust, rufo-ferrugineous, and subpubescent.

A single example of this species was taken by Mr. Squire in the neighbourhood of Rio Janeiro, and is in the cabinet of Mr. Baly. It differs from *H. ambiguus* by its filiform (not broadly incrassated) antennæ, by its shorter and comparatively more robust form, and by the obsolete striæ on the elytra.

4. Hypantherus Batesii.

H. *oblongo-ovatus, robustus, obsolete pubescens, rufo-ferrugineus; capite brevi, antice subproducto, inter oculos bituberculato, ad basin punctato; thorace transverso, rectangulari; elytris robustis, ante medium obsolete depressis, punctato-striatis; antennis robustis, flavis, art. 6–8 incrassatis et nigris; pedibus rufo-flavis.*

Long. corp. 2⅔ lin., lat. 1¼ lin.

Oblong-ovate, robust, obsoletely pubescent, rufo-ferrugineous. *Head* short, transverse, slightly produced in front; below the base of the antennæ is a transverse triangular plane depression; above the base are two short tubercular elevations (not produced longitudinally, as in *H. ambiguus*); at the base of the head deeply punctate (not granulated, as in *H. ambiguus*); the eyes are lateral and globose, situated nearly at the base of the head: in colour the apex is flavous, and the transverse depression below the antennæ fuscous (in *H. ambiguus*, the anterior part of the head is uniformly rufo-ferrugineous); the base is ferrugineous, medially fuscous. *Thorax* transverse, rectangular; the anterior angles depressed and subacute; the sides parallel and evenly marginate; the surface equate, thickly punctate, and obsoletely pubescent (less distinctly so than in *H. ambiguus*), rufo-ferrugineous, medially broadly piceous. *Scutellum* triangular, fuscous. *Elytra* broad, robust, antemedially transversely depressed, rufo-ferrugineous (not fuscous, as in *H. ambiguus*); finely pubescent, punctate-striate, the striæ being deep, and the punctures obsolete. *Antennæ* robust, medially dilated, flavous, the sixth to the eighth joints being incrassated and black. *Legs* robust, subpubescent, rufo-flavous.

The above description indicates the several points of difference between this species and *H. ambiguus*, to which it is very closely allied. *H. Batesii* may be separated not only by the colour and striation of the elytra, and the colour of the thorax, but by the form of the tubercular markings about the base of the antennæ.

Taken by Mr. Bates in the district of the River Amazon, and in that gentleman's collection.

5. Hypantherus Deyrollii. (Tab. IV. fig. 2.)

H. *oblongo-ovatus, subpubescens, flavus; capite ad basin antennarum foveolato; thorace transverso, ad basin depresso; elytris punctato-striatis, ad apicem flavo-pubescentibus; antennis filiformibus, robustis; pedibus posticis brevibus.*

Long. corp. 2 lin., lat. ¾–1 lin.

Oblong-ovate, subrobust, parallel, subpubescent, flavous. *Head* short, slightly produced; between the eyes and above the base of the antennæ is an obsolete fovea in the form of the letter T; the surface is finely pubescent and thickly punctate. *Thorax* transverse (almost quadrate); the anterior angles depressed and somewhat rounded; the sides marginate; near the base are two broad postmedial depressions, while from the head to the scutellum extends an obsolete (almost imperceptible) longitudinal impression. *Scutellum* small, triangular. *Elytra* broad, parallel, punctate-striate (the punctures being broad and the striæ shallow); clothed throughout with a fine flavous pubescence, which can only be traced by a high magnifying power, except at the apex, where it is *more distinctly* apparent. *Antennæ* filiform, tolerably robust. *Legs*: the posterior short; the apex of the tibiæ (which does not extend beyond the elytra) being produced beyond the insertion of the tarsi; the globular inflation above the posterior claw bright red.

This species differs considerably in detail from *H. rufo-testaceus*, which in general facies it resembles; it is narrower in form, the anterior angles of the thorax are less acute, the striation on the elytra is more distinct, the pubescence on the surface is closer, and on the elytra there is hardly any trace of a transverse antemedial depression.

Island of St. Paul, Brazil. In the cabinet of M. Deyrolle.

6. Hypantherus rufo-testaceus.

H. *oblongo-ovatus, robustus, subpubescens, rufo-testaceus; capite inter oculos tricarinato; thorace quadrato, ad apicem coarctato, ad basin transverse depresso, punctato; elytris robustis, striato-punctatis, ad basin flavo-pubescentibus; pedibus subpubescentibus, rufo-flavis, femoribus (et tibiis ad basin) posticis fusco suffusis.*

Long. corp. 2⅓ lin., lat. 1¼ lin.

Oblong-ovate, robust, sparingly pubescent, rufo-testaceous. *Head* short, somewhat produced; between the insertion of the antennæ is a longitudinal carination, which extends on either side obliquely in the direction of the upper margin of the eyes; within this V-shaped ridge is another medial longitudinal carination, which extends to the line of the base; the surface thickly punctate. *Thorax* quadrate; the anterior angles slightly truncate; sides anteriorly slightly coarctate, marginate, the margination shortly and abruptly contracted immediately behind the anterior angle; surface at the base transversely subdepressed, punctate. *Scutellum* small, triangular, rufo-fuscous. *Elytra* broad, robust, with punctures arranged in the form of striæ; a transverse antemedial depression extends obliquely upwards towards the humeral angles; the surface glabrous except at the sides, and more evidently at the apex, where it is distinctly flavo-pubescent. *Antennæ* wanting, with the exception of the first two joints; the first broad, dilated towards the apex, and reflected backwards; the second short and truncate, both rufo-testaceous. *Legs* tolerably robust, subpubescent, rufo-flavous, the extreme apex of the posterior femora and the base of the posterior tibiæ being suffused with fuscous.

Brazil. In the cabinet of M. Deyrolle.

Genus 13. THRASYGŒUS*.

LABRUM *breve, transversum.*

PALPI MAXILLARES *elongati, subcylindrici; art. 3^{tio} subparallelo, et ad apicem truncato, 4to minuto, elongato.*

PALPI LABIALES *art. 2^{ndo} subdilatato, ultimo elongato, attenuato.*

ANTENNÆ *filiformes.*

CAPUT *breve, haud antice productum, verticale.*

THORAX *latus, transversus, antice subconstrictus, ad latera marginatus et rectilinearis.*

ELYTRA *subdepressa, lata, punctato-striata.*

PEDES *femoribus anterioribus sat robustis, tarsis brevibus, art. 1mo triangulari, 2^{ndo} brevi, lato, 3^{tio} lato et bilobo; femoribus posticis incrassatissimis, tibiis longitudinaliter depressis (haud cylindricis) et marginatis, simplicibus, haud dente ad marginem armatis.*

Labrum short, transverse, abruptly rounded at the margins.

Maxillary palpi (Tab. IV. fig. 3 *m*) elongate, subcylindrical; the basal joint quadrate, minute; the second broader, dilated, and obliquely truncate near the apex; the third somewhat broader than the second, subparallel, and transversely truncate at the apex; the apical joint minute and elongate.

Labial palpi (Tab. IV. fig. 3 *n*): the basal joint dilated at the apex; the second less parallel than in the maxillary, transversely truncate; and the terminal joint elongate and attenuated.

Antennæ filiform; the basal joint slightly dilated and inflected outwards from the base; the second not ovate, but of the same form as, and shorter than, the first; the third to the fifth of equal length, nearly equal in length to the first, more attenuated, slightly incrassated towards the apex, and obliquely truncate; the terminal joints are somewhat more attenuated; the whole very finely pubescent: the

* θρασύς, fortis; γυῖον, membrum.

antennæ are at their insertion approximate, and immediately below and between the inner margin of the eyes.

Head small, transverse, not produced in front, inclined at right angles to the plane of the elytra.

Thorax broader than the head, and relatively broader than in the adjoining groups, transverse, slightly constricted in front; the anterior angles considerably depressed; the surface subequate; the sides rectilinear and marginate; the basal line sinuate.

Scutellum triangular, impunctate.

Elytra broad, robust, subdepressed, punctate-striate; in some species finely pubescent, and variegated in colour.

Legs: *anterior femora* sufficiently robust, slightly dilated antemedially. The *tibiæ* are straight (inflected at the immediate base), longitudinally ribbed or marginate, slightly dilated towards the apex. The *tarsus* (Tab. IV. fig. 3 *d*) is short; the first joint subelongate, triangular, of breadth equal to that of the tibia; the second shorter, broader; the third broader still, transversely bilobed, margined with rigid pubescence; the apical joint is elongate, slightly incurved, and incrassated towards the apex. The terminal claw is bifid, each member consisting of a *double* claw of equal length. The *posterior femora* are very broadly incrassated, ovate, gradually attenuated towards the apex; at the base broadly truncate—the junction of the femur to the metathorax being at an *angle* of this truncation. The *tibiæ* (Tab. IV. fig. 3 *g*) are short and straight; the surface is not cylindrical, but trilateral—the posterior surface being, near the apex, subsinuate in outline; the apical socket, in which the tarsus is inserted, is elongate and truncate. Of the *tarsi* (Tab. IV. fig. 3 *h*) the basal joint is elongate, and widened towards the apex, obliquely truncate; the second of the same form, but shorter; the third subcylindrical.

This genus is allied to *Eupeges* in the form of its thorax, as well as of the posterior femora and the maxillary palpi. Its totally different facies however (less ovate and less parallel), the thorax relatively smaller, and the elytra more robust, besides some difference in the form of the posterior tibia, compel us to feel that it ought to constitute a separate, although a closely allied genus.

1. Thrasygœus eximius. (Tab. IV. fig. 3.)

T. oblongo-ovalis, latus, sat robustus; capite haud producto, brevi, antice glabro, ad basin granulato, nigro; thorace transverso, antice constricto etiamque depresso, angulis anterioribus subacutis, ad basin transverse depresso, subpubescenti, punctulato; elytris robustis, punctatis (haud striatis), pubescentibus, nigris, maculis quatuor magnis (duabusque minutis ad scutellum) pallide flavis;

antennis filiformibus, tenuibus, articulis 1–4 rufo-flavis, 5–7 fuscis, 8–11 pallide cinereis; pedibus flavis.

Long. corp. 3¾ lin., lat. 2 lin.

Oblong-oval, broad, robust, subdepressed. *Head* short, depressed (almost vertical), not produced; below the base of the antennæ is a transverse triangular glabrous depression; the surface between the eyes granulated, with two more distinct wart-like prominences; at the base *thickly* punctate, black. *Thorax* transverse, constricted in front; the anterior angles depressed, hardly extending laterally beyond the eyes; the sides marginate; at the base is a broad shallow medial depression; the surface subpubescent and finely punctate, flavous, slightly suffused with black towards the apex. *Scutellum* triangular, black. *Elytra* robust, somewhat broader than the thorax, with punctures arranged in the form of striæ, finely and closely pubescent; black, with four large and two smaller white markings; the two smaller oval, close to the scutellum between the first and third striæ; of the *larger*, two (broad and transverse) are situated antemedially between the second and the ninth striæ, while two are similarly situated nearer to the apex. *Antennæ* filiform, attenuated; first to fourth joints rufo-flavous (on the upper surface of the apex fuscous), fifth to seventh fuscous, eighth to eleventh very pale cinereous, almost white. *Legs* flavous throughout; the apex of the posterior femora dark fuscous; the bladder-like inflation of the posterior claw bright ferrugineous.

This insect, at first sight, resembles *Octogonotes sumptuosus*; it differs, however, in its more robust form, in the deeper and more distinct punctuation at the back of the head, and by the absence of any tooth-like projection in the margination of the thorax, in the fuscous colour of the scutellum, and in the disposition and colouring of the markings on the *elytra*, as well as in the great contrast of form of the maxillary palpi.

A single specimen, captured by Mr. Bates in the Amazon district, is in that gentleman's cabinet.

2. Thrasygœus exaratus.

T. *oblongo-ovatus, latus, punctato-striatus, nigro-cyaneus; capite brevi, transverso, super basin antennarum bituberculato, punctato, fulvo-rufo; thorace transverso, antice attenuato, ad basin transverse depresso, sparsim punctato, rufo; elytris latis, punctato-striatis, nigro-cyaneis; antennis filiformibus, nigris; pedibus robustis, piceis, femoribus fusco suffusis.*

Long. corp. 4 lin., lat. 2 lin.

Oblong-ovate, broad, punctate-striate, dark blue, glabrous. *Head* short, transverse, depressed, not produced in front; above the labrum is a transverse triangular depressed plane; immediately above the insertion of the antennæ are two small obsolete tubercles, while between them is an indistinct linear depression extending towards, but not reaching, the base of the head; surface punctate, fulvo-rufous. *Thorax* transverse, considerably constricted in front; the anterior angles much depressed; the sides marginate, and near the anterior angles subsinuate; at the base is a broad transverse medial depression (not extending to the margins) on either side of the centre of the disc; near to the anterior angles is a small circular depression; the surface is glabrous, finely and sparingly punctate, rufous. *Scutellum* triangular, fusco-rufous. *Elytra* broad, robust, punctate-striate, of a deep dark-blue colour, glabrous. *Antennæ* filiform, black, the first joint being suffused with rufo-fuscous. *Legs* robust, piceous, the femora being suffused with fuscous.

Brazil. In the collection of M. Chevrolat.

3. Thrasygœus obscurus.

T. *oblongo-ovatus, robustus, subparallelus, subpubescens, pallide flavus; capite brevi, supra antennarum basin tenue bituberculato, granulato; thorace transverso, lato, rectangulari, punctato; elytris punctato-striatis, subpubescentibus; antennis robustis, filiformibus; pedibus subrobustis.*

Long. corp. 2½ lin., lat. 1¼ lin.

Oblong-ovate, robust, subparallel, very finely pubescent, of a pale flavous colour throughout. *Head* broad, transverse, depressed, slightly produced; above the labrum is a transverse and triangular plane; immediately above the base of the antennæ are two obscure but somewhat broad tubercles, forming between them and above them a fovea of the shape of the letter T; the surface below the tubercles pale flavous, above coarsely granulated and fuscous. *Thorax* broad, transverse, rectangular, rectilinear; the anterior angles depressed and distinct; the sides submarginate; the surface finely punctate. *Scutellum* triangular, impunctate, fulvo-flavous. *Elytra* somewhat broader than the thorax, subparallel, punctate-striate, clothed throughout with a *fine* thick pubescence. *Antennæ* tolerably long, robust, filiform; the first joint long, and broadly dilated at the apex; the second short, ovate, inserted at the outer margin of the first; the third longer than the first, pale flavous. *Legs* tolerably robust, pale flavous throughout.

Brazil. In the collection of Mr. Baly.

4. Thrasygœus undatus.

T. *oblongo-ovatus, latus, subdepressus, subtiliter pubescens, rufo-ferrugineus; capite subelongato, granulato; thorace transverso, ad apicem subconstricto, ad basin et ad angulos anticos depresso; elytris latis, punctato-striatis, vittis duabus transverse notatis inconstantibus undatis flavis, hac ante medium, illa ad basin; antennis robustis, ad apicem dilatatis, art. 1–6 fusco suffusis, 7–9 piceis, 10 et 11 testaceis; pedibus flavis.*

Long. corp. $2\tfrac{2}{3}$ lin., lat. $1\tfrac{1}{2}$ lin.

Oblong-ovate, broad, subdepressed, very finely pubescent, of a dark fawn or ferrugineous colour. *Head* transverse, subelongated; above the labrum is a transverse triangular plane, extending upwards nearly to the base of the antennæ: above the antennæ are two broad and obsolete tubercles, extending to the inner margin of the eyes; above them is a slight transverse depression: the surface granulated, of a dark brown colour,—the upper and inner margins of the eyes, and a small circular spot medially at the base, being of a paler hue: eyes large, prominent, situated at the base of the head, extending laterally nearly as far as the angles of the thorax. *Thorax* transverse, rectangular (slightly contracted towards the apex), rectilinear; the anterior angles depressed; the sides marginate; at the base is a broad transverse shallow depression, which is most distinctly apparent near the basal angles; in front, also, are three depressions,—one medial longitudinal, distinct and deep, the others lateral and more obsolete; the surface very finely punctate throughout; the colour a dark brown. *Scutellum* large, triangular, impunctate. *Elytra* much broader than the thorax, depressed, punctate-striate, the punctures in the striæ being almost obsolete, and clothed throughout (when viewed under a high power) with a very fine pubescence; the surface of a deep-brown colour, which is broken antemedially and near the base by two irregularly-formed transverse markings of a pale flavous colour: the one which is antemedial is obliquely transverse, extending in the direction of the scutellum; it consists of several (four to six) short longitudinal lines, connected one with the other anteriorly; the postmedial transverse marking is also very irregular in form, and does not extend to the suture: at the margin of the shoulders, also, is an indication of this same pale flavous colour. *Antennæ* robust, dilated towards the apex; the joints one to six flavous, suffused with fuscous; seven, eight and nine piceous, ten and eleven testaceous. *Legs* flavous throughout, the apex of the femora and the tibiæ and tarsi being suffused with piceous.

Venezuela. In the collection of M. Chevrolat.

Genus 14. EUPEGES*.

LABRUM *breve, subcirculare.*

PALPI MAXILLARES *minuti, art. 3^{tio} elongato, et ad apicem dilatato, art. ultimo conico.*

PALPI LABIALES *attenuati.*

ANTENNÆ *approximatæ, sat robustæ, filiformes.*

CAPUT *transversum, antice haud productum.*

THORAX *transversus, latus, ad latera subrotundatus.*

ELYTRA *sat robusta, subparallela et cylindrica.*

PEDES: *ant. tarsi breves, art. 3^{tio} lato et bilobo; tibiæ posticæ simplices, nec sinuatæ nec dente armatæ; tarsi breves et attenuati, art. 1mo et 2^{ndo} subæqualibus, 3^{tio} minuto et subcirculari.*

Labrum short, subcircular.

Mandibles robust, sinuated or dentated at the inner margin near the base, at the apex acuminate.

Maxillary palpi (Pl. IV. fig. 4 *m*) elongate, minute; the basal joint obsolete; the second slightly dilated at the apex; the third longer than the second, the length being equal to three times the breadth, and dilated at the apex; the apical joint conical.

Labial palpi (Pl. IV. fig. 4 *n*) attenuated, filiform.

Antennæ approximate, situated *below* the inner margin of the eyes, sufficiently robust, filiform; the first joint elongate, slightly inflected outwards, and subdilated towards the apex; the second short, ovate; the third not quite so long as the first, narrow, subdilated at the apex; the fourth and fifth equal in length.

Eyes globose, situated at the base of the head.

Head depressed (not porrect), transverse, narrower than the thorax, not produced anteriorly.

Thorax transverse, much broader than the head, relatively broader (as compared with the head and the elytra) than in *Hypantherus* and *Thrasygœus*, constricted in front; the sides subsinuate and marginate.

Elytra robust, perceptibly, but not considerably, broader than the thorax, slightly rounded at the sides, finely punctate or impunctate, glabrous.

Scutellum triangular, situated on the same plane as the elytra.

Legs: the *anterior femora* and *tibiæ* robust. The *tarsi* short; the first and second joints not so broad as the apex of the tibiæ, subequal in length; the third broader and distinctly bilobed; the apical claw

---

* εὖ, bene; πήγνυμι, firmo.

is bifid, and armed at its inner surface with an obsolete tooth. The *posterior femora* are incrassated. The *tibia* (Tab. IV. fig. 4 *g*) is short, inflected at its immediate base, and gradually thickened towards the apex; when viewed from behind, the posterior surface is *slightly* grooved longitudinally, simple (not sinuate or armed with a spur); the apex is obliquely truncate and simple at the extremity, without any terminal claws. The *tarsi* (Tab. IV. fig. 4 *h*) are attenuate and short; the first and second joints subequal; the third shorter and circular; the apical joint is broadly inflated at its extremity.

This genus is distinguishable from all others (except *Hydmosyne*) by its robust, subparallel and ovate form, depressed (not cylindrical), by the breadth of its thorax, and by its *unarmed* posterior tibiæ; from *Oinops* it may be separated by its less porrect head, by the structure of its maxillary palpi, and also by its unarmed tibiæ. The species composing it will probably, hereafter, be subdivided into two separate genera. There is a manifest contrast in facies between *E. præclara* and the two other species: the former insect is distinctly *oval*, the humeral angles of the elytra are less prominent, and the lateral line of the thorax is almost continued in the line of margination of the elytra; in *E. scabrosa* the shoulders are prominent, the sides of the elytra are more parallel, and the thorax is less broadly transverse; the ultimate joint of the anterior tarsus is also, in the former species, more deeply bilobed.

1. Eupeges præclara. (Tab. IV. fig. 4.)

E. ovalis, robusta, subcylindrica, nitida ; capite lato, transverso, depresso, punctato, rufo ; thorace transverso, sat magno, ad basin lato, sensim versus caput constricto, impunctato, rufo ; elytris robustis, punctis obsoletis veluti in striis ordinatis, purpureo-cyaneis, nitidis ; antennis haud elongatis, robustis, rufo-testaceis ; pedibus etiam rufo-testaceis.

Long. corp. $3\frac{1}{2}$ lin., lat. $1\frac{3}{4}$ lin.

Oblong, oval, robust, shining. *Head* transverse, short, depressed, much narrower than the thorax; eyes small, prominent, not extending to the anterior margin of the thorax; above the base of the antennæ is a transverse ridge (rendered more distinct by a medial depression behind it); surface of the head punctate, rufous. *Thorax* transverse, equate; the anterior angles (which project beyond the head) are subacute and depressed; the sides marginate; the basal angles are in close proximity to the shoulder of the elytra; the form of the thorax (*broad* at the base) is gradually constricted towards the anterior angles, although even at the apex it is considerably broader than the head; surface impunctate, rufous. *Scutellum* triangular, very darkly rufous. *Elytra* broad, robust, with punctures (very minute and obsolete) arranged in the form of striæ; glabrous, of a dark metallic blue colour. *Antennæ* short, robust, with a tendency to dilatation towards the apex (from the fifth to the eleventh joints); the first joint dilated, inflected outwards, and nearly as long as the third and fourth together; rufo-testaceous. *Legs* rufo-testaceous throughout.

A single specimen, taken in the Amazon district by Mr. Bates, is in that gentleman's collection.

2. Eupeges scabrosa.

E. *ovalis, robusta, nigra; capite brevi, ad basin antennarum bituberculato, punctato, fusco-rufo; thorace transverso, punctato, fuscorufo; elytris subcylindricis, punctato-striatis, granulatis, nigris; antennis filiformibus, fusco-nigris; pedibus rufis, tibiis tarsisque fuscis.*

Long. corp. 3¼ lin., lat. 1½ lin.

Oblong, oval, subparallel, robust, black. *Head* short, transverse, slightly produced; below the base of the antennæ is a transverse triangular plane; above the base of the antennæ are two prominent tubercular elevations, which are more prominent by reason of a medial longitudinal fovea, and above them a transverse depression; eyes globose, situated nearly at the base of the head; the surface of the head strongly punctate, impubescent, fusco-rufous. *Thorax* transverse, in front slightly emarginate; the anterior angles are subacute and much depressed; the sides are marginate, and in outline subsinuate; near the basal angle (when viewed obliquely) is an obsolete depression; the surface is deeply punctate, impubescent, and fusco-rufous. *Scutellum* triangular, pubescent, rufo-fuscous. *Elytra* subcylindrical, parallel, punctate-striate; the punctures are entirely, and the striæ almost, concealed by a clothing of short and coarse pubescence, which gives a generally scabrous appearance to the whole surface; the colour black. *Antennæ* robust, filiform, the second and third joints being slightly attenuated; fuscous-black, the two basal joints being suffused with rufous. *Legs* rufous, the anterior tibiæ and tarsi fuscous.

Brazil.

3. Eupeges nigrifrons.

E. *oblongo-ovata, subparallela, depressa, subtiliter pubescens, pallide flava; capite brevi, transverso, oblique foveolato, granulato, flavo, ad basin nigro-fusco; thorace transverso, æquato, subgranulato; elytris robustis, punctato-striatis; antennis filiformibus, fuscis, ad basin flavis; pedibus flavis; tibiis tarsisque fusco suffusis.*

Long. corp. 2½ lin., lat. 1¼ lin.

Oblong-ovate, subparallel, slightly depressed; when viewed under a high power clothed with a *very fine* pubescence throughout; of a pale flavous colour. *Head* short, transverse, hardly produced; above the labrum (which is fuscous) is a triangular plane depression; at the insertion of the antennæ is a minute, but distinct V-shaped carination, immediately above which is a transverse fovea; a subcircular or obliquely angulated fovea extends between the *upper* and inner margins of the eyes: the surface finely granulated throughout; at the base fuscous-black, and below the insertion of the antennæ flavous. *Thorax* transverse, rectangular, rectilinear; the anterior angles subdepressed; the sides submarginate; the surface equate, somewhat flat, and finely granulated. *Scutellum* triangular, impunctate, fuscous. *Elytra* rather broader than the thorax, subparallel, punctate-striate, clothed throughout with a pale flavous pubescence, so fine that it does not conceal the striæ or the punctures. *Antennæ* robust, filiform, fuscous, the three basal joints being flavous. *Legs*: the anterior rufo-flavous, the posterior pale flavous, the tibiæ and tarsi being suffused with fuscous.

Brazil. In the collection of M. Chevrolat.

Genus 15. PHYLACTICUS*.

LABRUM *transversum, subsinuatum.*

PALPI MAXILLARES *elongati, filiformes, art.* 2^{ndo} *et* 3^{tio} *ad apicem dilatatis.*

PALPI LABIALES *subcylindrici.*

ANTENNÆ *filiformes, sat robustæ, aliquando ad apicem obsolete incrassatæ.*

CAPUT *verticale, vix productum, plerumque inter oculos foveolatum aut carinatum.*

THORAX *transversus (interdum subquadratus), ad apicem plus minus constrictus, depressus.*

ELYTRA *robusta, brevia, ad apicem aliquando subattenuata.*

PEDES: *tibiæ anteriores ad basin ipsum curvatæ, haud ad apicem dilatatæ; tarsi breves, art.* 2^{ndo} *minuto,* 3^{tio} *lato: femora postica incrassatissima, subovata; tibiæ ad apicem subdilatatæ, simplices, haud dente munitæ; tarsi breves, attenuati, art.* 2^{ndo} *et* 3^{tio} *minutis.*

* φυλακτικὸς, vigilans.

Labrum transversely subsinuate.

Maxillary palpi (Tab. IV. fig. 5 *m*, fig. 6 *m*) elongate, filiform; the basal joint obscure; the second subdilated towards the apex and obliquely truncate; the third longer and slightly broader (at the apex) than the second; the apical joint attenuate, much narrower than the apex of the third.

Labial palpi (Tab. IV. fig. 5 *n*, fig. 6 *n*) attenuate, subcylindrical, the penultimate joint in *P. modestus* being somewhat more dilated than in *P. pollenosus* or *P. olivaceus*.

Antennæ sufficiently robust, filiform (slightly dilated towards the apex); the basal joint subelongate, inflected outwards, and slightly incrassated; the second short and ovate; the third attenuated, and somewhat longer than the first.

Eyes prominent, situated at some distance from the base of the head, lateral.

Head depressed at right angles to the plane of the elytra, hardly produced in front; impubescent, and generally deeply marked transversely or obliquely between the eyes.

Thorax broader than the head, transverse (sometimes almost quadrate), not emarginate in front; the sides are depressed and marginate, and towards the apex more or less constricted; the surface is generally equate, and impubescent.

Scutellum triangular.

Elytra robust, broader than the thorax; the humeral angles prominent, slightly tapering towards the apex; for the most part distinctly punctate-striate, covered with a *fine* pubescence.

Legs: anterior *femora* robust, subcylindrical, slightly incrassated near the apex. *Tibiæ* inflected at their immediate base, straight (not incurved), finely pubescent, cylindrical, not dilated towards the apex; the insertion of the tarsus is at the *extreme* apex. The *tarsus* (Tab. IV. fig. 5 *d*) is short; the basal joint is triangular, not broader than the tibia; the second joint of the same form, but *much more minute*; the third is more transverse, subcircular, the breadth being double that of the basal joint, and almost bilobed; these three joints are densely clothed with rigid pubescence: the terminal joint is attenuate and incurved, *slightly* dilated towards the apex, shorter in length than in the adjoining genera: the claw is broadly bifid, and simple, unarmed by any inner tooth. The *posterior femora* are (when viewed transversely) incrassated, in form subovate. The *tibiæ* (Tab. IV. fig. 6 *g*) are short and robust, somewhat thickened at the apex and base; at the apex *obliquely* truncate, and terminating below the insertion of the tarsus in a strong, double, hook-shaped process; the lateral margination is entirely unarmed by any spurs. The *tarsus*

(Tab. IV. fig. 6 *h*) is short and attenuated; the basal joint elongated, and towards the apex slightly incrassated; the second is minute, almost triangular; the third is not larger than the second, circular, —from the centre of which proceeds the terminal joint, which is elongate, and terminating at the apex in a globular inflation, which completely conceals the claw when viewed from above.

The *robust* and abbreviated form, the (generally) anteriorly compressed thorax, and the simple filiform antennæ at once point out this genus. The details of structure are yet more evidently distinct. Its unarmed post-tibia, and *minute* second and third joints of the post-tarsus are sufficient of themselves to separate it.

1. Phylacticus modestus. (Tab. IV. fig. 5.) B.M.

P. ovatus, subcylindricus, brevis, robustus, pubescens, stramineus; capite depresso, haud producto, punctato, inter oculos foveolato, labro nigro, oculis parvis, haud prominentibus, ad basin punctato; thorace quadrato, antice subconstricto, angulis prominulis, haud truncatis, ad latera obsolete marginato, ad basin complanato, et transverse depresso, punctato; elytris robustis, punctato-striatis, pubescentibus; antennis filiformibus, robustis, art. 1mo lato, 2^{ndo} brevi, minuto; pedibus stramineis.

Long. corp. 3 lin., lat. 1 lin.

Ovate, short, robust, punctate-striate, finely pubescent, of a pale straw colour throughout. *Head* minute, vertical, hardly produced; below the base of the antennæ is a transverse triangular depressed plane; immediately above, or almost between the basal joints, are two oblique well-defined carinations, rendered more distinct by a deep medial fovea, and by two lateral depressions adjoining the inner margins of the eyes; eyes small, lateral, situated at the base of the head; the surface at the base punctate. *Thorax* transverse, robust, constricted in front; the anterior angles are much depressed and almost obsolete; the sides marginate; the base (when viewed obliquely) is broadly depressed; the surface throughout is punctate and very finely pubescent. *Scutellum* somewhat cordiform, impunctate. *Elytra* robust, broader than the thorax, punctate-striate, at the base obsoletely gibbous, clothed throughout with a *fine* flavous pubescence, sparingly distributed. *Antennæ* filiform. *Legs* sufficiently robust; the globular inflation of the posterior claw of a bright rufous colour.

Very closely allied in form to its congeners, but distinguishable at once by its *pale flavous* elytra and larger size, as well as by the *markings on the head* and the form of its thorax.

Santarem (Amazon River). A single specimen, taken by Mr. Bates, is in the cabinet of the British Museum.

2. Phylacticus ustulatus.

P. *oblongo-ovatus, robustus, impubescens, olivaceo-viridis; capite brevi, ad basin antennarum tenue bituberculato, punctato; thorace transverso, antea depresso et attenuato, crebre punctato; elytris robustis, punctato-striatis, inter strias punctis minutissimis et crebris instructis, ad basin rufo-fuscis; antennis tenuibus, filiformibus, brevibus, flavo-ferrugineis; pedibus flavo-ferrugineis, femoribus posticis olivaceo-viridibus, ad apicem rufo-fusco suffusis.*

Long. corp. 3¾ lin., lat. 1¾ lin.

Oblong-ovate, robust, impubescent, of a dull brown green colour. *Head* short, transverse, obliquely depressed, broadly but slightly elongate; immediately above the labrum is a transverse impunctate plane, of a pale but more clear green colour than the rest of the insect; above the base of the antennæ are two apparently slightly raised tubercles, which are formed by a somewhat deep and well-defined medial and longitudinal fovea, and also by two other shallower depressions near the inner surface of the eyes: eyes tolerably prominent; the surface above the base of the antennæ coarsely punctate. *Thorax* transverse, broader than the head, narrowed and considerably depressed in front; the sides distinctly marginate; the surface finely and closely punctate. *Scutellum* triangular. *Elytra* robust, subclongated towards the apex, punctate-striate, the surface between the striæ being very finely punctate; the colour of a dark dull olive-green; at the apex broadly rufo-fuscous, bounded by a suffused line of *darker* fuscous, the boundary-line between the two colours being situate at the distance from the apex of one-third of the whole length of the elytra. *Antennæ* fine, filiform, short, the second and third joints being equal in length, and shorter than the first; flavo-ferrugineous. *Legs* flavo-ferrugineous; the posterior femora being of an olive-green colour, at the apex suffused with rufo-fuscous. *Abdomen* flavo-ferrugineous, at the apex suffused with rufo-fuscous.

Cayenne. In the collection of M. Chevrolat.

3. Phylacticus olivaceus. (TAB. IV. fig. 6.)

P. *ovalis, latus, robustus, olivaceus; capite brevi, elongatulo, inter oculos oblique foveolato, punctato; thorace transverso, ad basin lato, apicem versus sensim attenuato, angulis anticis depressis, punctato; elytris latis, ad humeros thorace paulum latioribus, punctato-striatis; antennis filiformibus, fuscis; pedibus ferrugineis, fusco suffusis.*

Long. corp. 2¾ lin., lat. 1½ lin.

Oval, broad, subdepressed, of a brownish-green colour throughout.

Head short, depressed, very slightly elongated in front; labrum and anterior surface of a paler colour (almost cinereous): eyes black, slightly prominent, distant; between them, and extending longitudinally as far as the insertion of the antennæ, is a medial Y-shaped fovea: surface finely and closely punctate. *Thorax* transverse (almost quadrate); sides marginate, broad at the base, but considerably constricted anteriorly; the margination (when viewed laterally) is abruptly depressed from the humeral angle in the direction of the outer margin of the eyes; a very faint medial longitudinal line is indistinctly apparent (when viewed in some lights), and the basal transverse depression (so distinct in many of the allied species) is almost obsolete; surface finely punctate. *Scutellum* triangular, fuscous. *Elytra* robust, distinctly punctate-striate, with the humeral angles less prominent, and more closely rounded off from the thorax than in other species of this group. *Antennæ* filiform, with the first joint dilated towards the apex and inflected outwards; the second short, ovate; the third longer than the first, flavo-ferrugineous; the fifth and sixth joints more distinctly fuscous. *Legs* pale ferrugineous; suffused on the upper surface of the anterior tarsi and tibiæ, as well as at the apex of the posterior femora, with fuscous.

Of a dark-green colour in recently captured specimens; this colour would seem, however, to be evanescent; one example before me has almost entirely lost it, and is of a faint pale-green colour.

This species is almost identical with the figure and description of *Œdionychis viridis* of Perty (Delectus Anim. Arctic. p. 110. tab. xxii. fig. 6); it wants, however, the flavous marking on the head and thorax. I subjoin Perty's description, which has reference, doubtless, to an allied species of this genus*. Taken by Mr. Bates, in the district of the Amazon. In the cabinets of Mr. Bates and the Rev. H. Clark.

---

* "Œdionychis viridis. Œ. *subtus et femoribus posticis flavus, supra pallide viridis; elytris punctato-striatis.* Long. 2¼′′′, lat. hum. 1¼′′′.

"*Habitat* in Brazilia æquatoriali.

"Habitu *Lemis* affinis. Caput viride linea utrinque flava, oculis fuscis. Thorax viridis, elytris pæne duplo angustior, vitta utrinque flavicante, scutellum flavicans. Elytra pallide viridia, subparallela, insigniter punctato-striata, ad dorsum deplanata; subtus cum ore flavus. Mesostethium linea impressa. Antennæ flavicantes, corporis dimidio parum longiores. Femora et tibiæ anteriores virides; tarsi flavicantes. Pedes postici femoribus flavis, articulo tarsi ultimo valde inflato unguiculisque minutissimis brunneis."

4. Phylacticus prasinus.

P. *oblongo-ovatus, robustus, punctato-striatus, impubescens, olivaceus; capite inter oculos* Y *foveolato, ad basin fortiter punctato ; thorace transverso, angulis anticis* acutis, *punctatis ; elytris robustis, punctato-striatis ; antennis filiformibus, fuscis ; pedibus olivaceis.*

Long. corp. 2⅔ lin., lat. 1½ lin.

Oblong-ovate, robust, punctate-striate, impubescent, of a dull green colour throughout. *Head* slightly produced in front; immediately above the labrum is a transverse depression: eyes tolerably large, situated at the base of the head; between the eyes, and immediately above the base of the antennæ, is a longitudinal well-defined fovea, which is terminated at its upper extremity by two oblique canaliculations extending to the inner margins of the eyes, thus together forming (more distinctly and deeply than in the allied species, *P. olivaceus*) the character of the letter Y; the surface between it and the base of the head is broader and more deeply granulated: in colour of a uniform dull green, with the exception of the labrum and the insertion of the antennæ, which are flavous. *Thorax* transverse (not constricted anteriorly as in *P. olivaceus*), the anterior angles depressed and distinctly acute; the sides are very finely marginate; the surface finely and thickly punctate. *Scutellum* triangular, impunctate, of a fuscous olive-green colour. *Elytra* somewhat broader than the thorax, robust, deeply punctate-striate, impubescent. *Antennæ* robust, filiform, dark fuscous. *Abdomen* flavous. *Legs* robust, of a dull-green colour throughout.

P. prasinus differs but slightly from *P. olivaceus*; the modified form of the thorax and of the basal part of the head seem sufficiently to separate it as specifically distinct.

Para. In the collection of M. Chevrolat.

5. Phylacticus pollinosus.

P. *oblongo-ovalis, parallelus, subconvexus, flavo-fulvus ; capite haud producto, ad basin punctato et nigro ; thorace transverso, punctato, pubescenti ; elytris punctato-substriatis, pubescentibus ; antennis nigris ; pedibus testaceis, tibiis tarsisque anterioribus femoribusque posticis (ad basin) fuscis.*

Long. corp. 2½ lin., lat. 1 lin.

Oblong-ovate, robust, subpubescent, flavo-fulvous. *Head* short, depressed, not produced; eyes large, distant, extending laterally nearly to the anterior angle of the thorax; surface of the head finely granulated; at and below the insertion of the antennæ pale fulvous, at the base black. *Thorax* transverse, rectangular; the anterior angles depressed, the sides submarginate; the surface equate (with an obsolete thread-like fovea at the base), finely and thickly punctured, and clothed throughout with a short downy pubescence. *Scutellum* triangular, dark fuscous. *Elytra* oblong, subelongated at the apex, very finely punctate-striate, of a somewhat deeper colour than the thorax; clothed throughout with a close, short, flavous pubescence. *Antennæ* filiform, black. *Legs* pale testaceous, with the anterior tibiæ and tarsi (and the base of the posterior femora) fuscous, and the posterior tibiæ and tarsi rufo-fuscous.

This species abundantly differs from *P. olivaceus* in its colour (flavous, instead of olive-green), in the form of its thorax, which is not contracted in front, and in the character of the punctuation of the elytra.

Morro Quèimado (Rio Janeiro). A single example, in the collection of Mr. Fry.

6. Phylacticus amabilis.

P. *oblongus, subdepressus, robustus, pubescens, fulvo-ferrugineus (interdum etiam fulvus); capite brevi, penitus verticali, inter oculos in forma literæ* Y *foveolato; thorace transverso, apud angulos anteriores depresso, pubescenti; elytris punctato-striatis, pubescentibus; antennis filiformibus, fulvis, ad apicem flavis; pedibus flavis.*

Long. corp. $2\frac{1}{2}$ lin., lat. 1–$1\frac{1}{4}$ lin.

Oblong, subdepressed, pubescent, fulvo-ferrugineous. *Head* short, depressed (almost vertical); eyes large, situated at the back of the head; above the insertion of the antennæ, and between the eyes, is a broad Y-shaped fovea; the surface at the base is finely granulated. *Thorax* transverse, rectangular; the anterior angles depressed and distinct; sides rectilinear and slightly marginate; the surface equate, and covered with a bright flavous pubescence. *Scutellum* minute. *Elytra* punctate-striate, the punctures being entirely concealed by concolorous thick fulvous (or in other examples ferrugineous) pubescence. *Antennæ* filiform; fulvous, with the apex flavous. *Legs* flavous.

The colour of this species is subject to some variation in hue, ranging from ferrugineous to flavous.

From the district of the Amazon River. In the collection of Mr. Bates and the Rev. H. Clark.

Genus 16. HOMAMMATUS*.

LABRUM *breve, transversum.*

PALPI MAXILLARES *elongati, art.* 2^{ndo} *ad apicem dilatato,* 3^{tio} *longiori et cylindrico.*

* ὦμος, humerus; ἅμματος (ἅμμα), nodus.

PALPI LABIALES *filiformes.*
ANTENNÆ *approximatæ, ad apicem dilatatæ aut subdilatatæ.*
CAPUT *plus minus attenuatum, antice productum, verticale.*
THORAX *transversus (subquadratus), antice rotundatus.*
ELYTRA *robusta, lata, abbreviata, ante medium transverse depressa.*
PEDES: *tibiæ anteriores ad apicem subincrassatæ ; tarsi, art.* 2^{ndo} *minuto ; tibiæ posticæ longitudinaliter marginatæ, et ad marginem subsinuatæ ; tarsi breves et attenuati, art.* 1mo *et* 2^{ndo} *subæqualibus.*

Labrum narrow, transverse.

Maxillary palpi (Tab. IV. fig. 7 *m*, fig. 8 *m*) elongate; the first joint minute; the second dilated at the apex; the third longer and broader than the second, more cylindrical; the apical joint nearly the length of the second, and attenuate.

Labial palpi (Tab. IV. fig. 7 *n*, fig. 8 *n*) fine, elongate, the medial joint being filiform.

Antennæ (Tab. IV. fig. 8 *a*) approximate, situated below the inner margin of the eyes, robust, medially dilated; the basal joint is broadly dilated and incurved towards the apex; the second robust and short; the third as long as the first, attenuate, especially at the base; the fourth of the same form as the third, but shorter; the fifth to the seventh distinctly dilated and short; the terminal joints less robust and abbreviated.

Eyes large, globose, situated at the base of the head, extending laterally not so far as the anterior angles of the thorax.

Head more or less attenuated, produced in front, more distinctly vertical than in any other genus of the group, or (in *H. turgidus*) subvertical.

Thorax transverse (almost quadrate); the anterior margin rounded; the sides finely marginate.

Scutellum triangular, situated somewhat below the plane of the elytra.

Elytra robust, considerably broader than the thorax, abbreviated, antemedially transversely depressed, punctate or finely punctate-striate.

Legs: the *anterior femora* sufficiently robust, subincrassated towards the middle. The *tibiæ* (Tab. IV. fig. 7 *c*) are inflected at their immediate base, and gradually thickened towards the apex, where (below the insertion of the tarsus) they are terminated by two incurved claws. The *tarsi* (Tab. IV. fig. 7 *d*) are short, slightly broader than the base of the tibia; the first joint is triangular; the second of the same form as, but rather smaller than, the first; the third is deeply bilobed, broader, circular: the apical claw is bifid, and armed at its inner surface with a basal tooth. The *posterior femora* are incrassated, but not so broadly as in allied genera. The *tibiæ* (Tab. IV. fig. 8 *g*) are inflected at their immediate base; when viewed from behind, the posterior surface is longitudinally grooved; the margination of this groove is *subsinuate* above the insertion of the tarsus; the apex is armed with a series of comb-like teeth, and terminates in a robust incurved claw. The *tarsus* (Tab. IV. fig. 8 *h*) is short and attenuate; the first and second joints subequal, dilated at their apex; the third minute, almost circular; the ultimate joint is produced into a globular inflation: the claw is armed at its inner surface with a short basal tooth.

The two species which constitute this genus widely differ from all other forms. Their *very robust* elytra (medially obliquely depressed), and their *small* angulated thorax, designate them, *prima facie*, as quite distinct from all other adjoining groups; they differ, however, *inter se*, and will probably at some future time, when we know more of South-American insect-life, form the basis of two separate genera. In *H. turgidus* the head is depressed, but not so abruptly vertical; the antennæ are obsoletely, not distinctly, incrassated (perhaps rather filiform); and the thorax is more constricted in front, and, as compared with the head, narrower. There is an absence, also, of that peculiar glabrous and entirely impunctate surface of the thorax. There may be traced moreover (under the microscope) a slight variation in the relative forms and lengths of the joints of the palpi.

1. Homammatus turgidus. (Tab. IV. fig. 7.)

H. *ovalis, latus, subrotundatus, piceus; capite parum producto, ad apicem oblique canaliculato; thorace quadrato, antice subconstricto, pube flava sparsim obtecto, punctato; elytris striato-punctatis, ante medium complanatis, rotundatis, ad latera tenuiter pubescentibus; antennis robustis, filiformibus, art. 1mo–5to, 9no et 10mo flavis, 6to, 7mo, 8vo et ultimo nigris; pedibus flavis, femoribus posticis tarsisque anterioribus fuscis.*

Long. corp. $2\frac{1}{2}$ lin., lat. $1\frac{1}{4}$ lin.

Oval, somewhat broad and robust, piceous. *Head* small, and slightly produced; from the base of the antennæ two raised carinations extend obliquely to the upper and inner margin of the eyes, while between them is a third longitudinal carination which approaches medially the margin of the thorax: eyes prominent, situated at the base of the head, not extending laterally as far as the anterior angles of the thorax: surface rugose. *Thorax* small, quadrate; the anterior angles subacute and distinctly depressed; the sides marginate; the surface is punctate, and clothed (as is apparent under a high power) with fine ferrugineous pile. *Scutellum* triangular, impunctate, fuscous. *Elytra* broad, robust (considerably broader than the thorax), with punctures arranged in the form of striæ; a broad antemedial depression extends transversely and obliquely upwards towards the humeral angles, giving an appearance of prominence to the scutellary angles; the surface glabrous, except at the sides and apex, which are subpubescent. *Antennæ* sufficiently long and robust, filiform; the third and fourth joints slightly attenuated; first to fifth flavous, sixth to eighth black, ninth and tenth flavous, eleventh black. *Legs* flavous, the anterior tarsi and posterior femora being fuscous.

I captured a single example of this insect at Tejuca (near Rio Janeiro) in January 1857.

2. Homammatus nitidus. (Tab. IV. fig. 8.)

H. *ovatus, robustus, glaber, rufus; capite parvo, depresso, impunctato, nigro; thorace transverso, pœne quadrato, ad basin depresso, impunctato, nigro; elytris latis, levissime punctatis, antemediis transverse (et oblique humeros versus) depressis, impubescentibus, rufis; antennis robustis, subincrassatis, nigro-fuscis; pedibus anterioribus piceis, posticis rufis.*

Long. corp. $2\frac{1}{4}$ lin., lat. $1-1\frac{1}{4}$ lin.

Ovate, broad, glabrous, of a bright red colour. *Head* short, transverse, produced and attenuated anteriorly; eyes very large (in comparison with the breadth of the head), situated close to the basal line, and extending laterally not so far as the anterior angles of the thorax: below the insertion of the antennæ is a longitudinal medial carination, and two others (one on either side of it) obliquely transverse; above the base of the antennæ is a distinct V-shaped carination, extending obliquely upwards nearly to the base of the head; on either side of this, the margin of the eyes is bounded by a minute and regular fovea, which extends parallel to their inner and upper circumference: the surface is black and impubescent, at the base punctate. *Thorax* transverse (almost quadrate); the anterior angles depressed and subtruncate; the sides marginate; at the base is a slight transverse depression, which gives to the anterior part of the thorax a subcylindrical form; surface impunctate, bright glabrous, black. *Scutellum* small, triangular, rufous. *Elytra* much broader than the thorax, robust, subdepressed; under a high magnifying power very finely punctate, the punctures being arranged in the form of striæ: an antemedial transverse depression is continued upwards and obliquely towards the inner part of the shoulder, causing the base (near to the scutellary angles) to appear raised and prominent; within this depression the punctures are much more distinctly apparent: surface impubescent, glabrous, brightly rufous. *Antennæ* robust, medially somewhat incrassated; the first joint broad and dilated; second short, ovate; third longer than the first and narrow; fourth to eighth gradually incrassated: the colour fuscous black, the third joint and the ninth to eleventh being suffused with piceous. *Legs*: the posterior tibiæ are somewhat long, and produced beyond the insertion of the tarsi; the anterior piceous, the posterior rufous.

From Choco, Colombia. In the collection of Mr. Baly.

I believe that these two species, *H. turgidus* and *H. nitidus*, although generally allied to each other, will hereafter form two distinct genera. In *H. nitidus*, *inter alia*, the head is more produced, the thorax is anteriorly rounded, and the antennæ have a more decided tendency to dilatation; in the absence of other species, however, I do not venture to separate them.

Genus 17. HOMOTYPHUS*.

PALPI MAXILLARES *cylindrici, art. 2^{ndo} et 3^{tio} subæqualibus, apicali attenuato.*

PALPI LABIALES *elongati, art. penultimo subdilatato.*

ANTENNÆ *approximatæ, ad apicem subincrassatæ, art. 3^{tio}, 4to et 5to æqualibus et attenuatis, 6to–10mo brevibus, robustis, art. ultimo plerumque attenuato.*

CAPUT *verticale, haud productum.*

THORAX *transversus, rarissime æquatus, subpubescens, et aut punctatus aut granulatus.*

ELYTRA *lata, plerumque leviter tuberculata, plus minus ante medium transverse depressa, punctato-striata, pube vestita.*

PEDES *robusti, tibiis posticis inarmatis.*

Labrum transversely subrotundate.

Maxillary palpi (Front. fig. 6 *m*) robust, cylindrical; the basal joint minute; the second and third of equal length, not incrassated at the apex (the second being somewhat narrower than the third): the apical joint is much more attenuated than the rest, being at its base *considerably* narrower than the apex of the third joint; its length is *nearly* double its breadth.

Labial palpi (Front. fig. 6 *n*) elongate; the penultimate joint slightly broader than the apical.

Antennæ approximate, situated between the lower margins of the

* ὦμος, humerus; τύφομαι, turgesco.

eyes, filiform, subincrassated towards the apex ; the first joint elongate, dilated gradually towards the apex, and (when seen under a high power) abruptly incurved and attenuated at the immediate base ; the second joint is short, much narrower as well as shorter than the first, constricted at the base and broadly truncate at the apex ; the third, fourth and fifth are *equal in length,* longer than the second, but shorter than the first, attenuate, but subdilated towards the apex; the sixth is of the same form as, but more incrassated and shorter than, the fifth; the seventh to the tenth are shorter (the length being hardly double the breadth), for the most part subdilated and cylindrical; the apical joint is somewhat narrower, and tapering at the extremity.

Eyes lateral, situated at the base of the head.

Head (Front. fig. 6 *s v*) depressed at right angles to the plane of the elytra, not produced in front, much narrower than the thorax.

Thorax broad, transverse, rectangular, anteriorly not emarginate ; the sides are depressed and marginate ; not constricted in front ; the surface is generally irregularly tuberculated and granulated.

Scutellum triangular.

Elytra broader than the thorax, robust; the shoulders being well developed and prominent, more apparently so by reason of a more or less distinct transverse antemedial depression ; punctate-striate, and for the most part clothed with obsolete pubescence, the surface being generally irregular both in sculpture and in colour of pubescence.

Legs: the *anterior femora* robust, slightly attenuated near the apex. The *tibiæ* are distinctly incurved at their immediate base, straight, gradually and slightly thickened towards the apex. The *tarsi* are short, the basal and second joints being subequal in size (the basal being almost cordiform, the second triangular and equal in breadth to the base of the tibia); the third is much broader, distinctly bilobed, and fringed with a thick and rigid pubescence ; from the base of the third proceeds the apical joint, attenuated and incurved, *slightly* dilated towards the extremity : the terminal claw is bifid, armed at its inner surface near the base with an obsolete tooth. The *posterior femora* are short, and when viewed from beneath, very robust, incrassated, the upper margin being almost circular, the lower margin almost straight, gradually attenuated towards the apex. The *tibia* is short, abruptly inflected at the base, straight, unarmed near the apex by any tooth-like spurs ; at the apex somewhat thickened and obliquely truncate ; the terminal socket which receives the tarsus being fringed with a serrated margination of closely-arranged comb-like teeth, and terminating ultimately below the tarsus in a double curved claw. The *tarsus* is short and attenuated; the basal and second joints are conical, attenuated at their base, dilated gradually towards their apex: the third is shorter, subcircular, and deeply bilobed; from its base proceeds the terminal joint, which is broadly inflated into a globular projection covering entirely the apical claw.

This genus is remarkable on account of its close alliance (with the single important exception of the form of the maxillary palpi) with *Omototus*: the few points of structural difference that present themselves *prima facie* are too few (although, so far as I can ascertain, constant) to allow, of themselves, this genus to be established separately. The rather more parallel and oblong outline, and a slight variation that can be traced in the form of the tarsi and apex of the posterior tibiæ, are not sufficient, alone, to warrant the formation of a new genus; when, however, to these constant but comparatively slight variations is added the *very pronounced contrast* of form in the *maxillary palpi*, there can be no longer any doubt that the two groups are really abundantly separate from each other. In the genus before us, the maxillary palpi are cylindrical, not dilated at the apex, and in general outline filiform: in *Omototus*, on the other hand, the maxillary palpi are broadly incrassated; the breadth of the penultimate joint exceeds its length, and considerably exceeds the breadth of the apical joints. Without, however, a careful examination of the labial, and, especially, the maxillary palpi, it will be impossible with certainty to distinguish between the two genera: in *general* features they are absolutely identical.

1. Homotyphus lacunosus. (Front. fig. 6.)

H. *subovatus, rotundatus, robustus, flavo-pubescens, ferrugineus; capite brevi, inter oculos transverse foveolato, granulato; thorace transverso, brevi, ad basin oblique depresso, ad apicem medium longitudinaliter impresso, granulato; elytris latis, robustis, fortiter punctato-striatis, ad medium transverse depressis, etiamque ad basin; antennis brevibus, ad apicem dilatatis, ferrugineis, art. 6–8 nigro-fuscis; pedibus subpubescentibus, flavis.*

Long. corp. $2\frac{3}{4}$ lin., lat. $1\frac{2}{3}$ lin.

Subovate, rotundate, robust, flavo-pubescent, dark ferrugineous. *Head* very short, depressed, not produced in front: eyes distant, slightly prominent, situate at an appreciable distance from the base: antennæ at their insertion approximate; above the insertion of the antennæ and between the eyes is an obsolete shallow depression in the form of the letter T: surface below the insertion of the antennæ flavous, at the base coarsely granulated, ferrugineous, while at the inner margin of the eyes it is clothed with a faint flavous pubescence. *Thorax* slightly transverse, rectangular; the sides submarginate; the anterior angles extending beyond the base of the head, subacute; the surface complanate; from the middle of the base a broad depression extends on either side obliquely upwards towards the apical angles; the anterior and medial surface (being thus slightly raised) is impressed longitudinally by an obsolete broad fovea; the surface is coarsely granulated, and clothed throughout with irregular flavous subpubescence. *Scutellum* small, triangular, impunctate, subpubescent, depressed below the surface of the elytra. *Elytra* broad, robust, strongly punctate-striate, sulcated: an antemedial broad and shallow transverse depression gives a prominence to the humeral angles, while another (halfway between this depression and the apex) produces two other elevations, one postmedially, and the other nearer the apex; along the *basal* transverse ridge, the space between the first and fifth striæ is distinctly raised; in the *postmedial* ridge, the surface between the second and third, the fourth and fifth, seventh and eighth is abruptly raised: the surface is clothed throughout (more or less distinctly) with bright flavous pubescence. *Antennæ* short (hardly exceeding half the length of the body), incrassated; the first joint broad and dilated; the second short, ovate, nearly as broad as the first; the third, fourth and fifth not quite so long as the first, attenuated; the sixth to eleventh dilated; the sixth to eighth dark fuscous, the rest ferrugineous. *Legs* flavous throughout, pubescent.

Captured by Mr. Gray and by myself in the forests near Petropolis (Organ Mountains, Rio Janeiro), February 1857.

2. Homotyphus Vellereus.

H. *ovatus, latus, subpubescens, flavo-ferrugineus; capite brevi, deflexo, ad basin antennarum longitudinaliter foveolato; thorace transverso, rectilineari, ad basin transverse depresso, punctato, subtiliter flavo-pubescenti; elytris latis, punctato-striatis, flavo-pubescentibus; antennis (artic. quatuor testaceis) (reliqui desunt); pedibus flavis.*

Long. corp. 2⅕ lin., lat. 1½ lin.

Ovate, broad, subpubescent, flavo-ferrugineous. *Head* small, transverse, deflected at right angles to the plane of the thorax, slightly produced; above the labrum is a transverse triangular depression; above the base of the antennæ is an obsolete short longitudinal fovea, on either side of which (near the inner margins of the eyes) the surface is subdepressed; eyes large and prominent, extending laterally as far as the anterior angles of the thorax, and situated at some little distance from the base of the head; the surface finely punctate. *Thorax* transverse, rectilinear; the anterior angles subacute and depressed; the sides marginate; at the base is a broad and shallow transverse depression; the surface thickly punctate and (when seen under a high power) finely flavo-pubescent. *Scutellum* small, transversely triangular. *Elytra* much broader than the thorax, robust, distinctly punctate-striate; a shallow transverse depression extends antemedially in an oblique direction towards the shoulders; the surface is clothed throughout with fine flavous pubescence. *Antennæ* (probably filiform); the four basal joints pale testaceous; the first and second joints are robust, and the third and fourth attenuated (the rest are wanting). *Legs* flavous throughout; the globular inflation above the posterior claw being bright fulvous.

Brazil; Minas Geraës. In the collection of M. Chevrolat.

3. Homotyphus fuliginosus.

H. *ovatus, latus, robustus, fusco-pubescens, niger ; capite brevi, inter oculos, ad basin antennarum (rufo suffusam), bituberculato, punctato ; thorace subquadrato, ad apicem leviter bituberculato, granulato ; elytris latis, striato-punctatis ; antennis ad apicem dilatatis, fulvis, art. 7mo et 8vo nigro-fuscis ; pedibus robustis, nigro-fulvis ; femoribus posticis fuscis.*

Long. corp. $2\frac{2}{3}$ lin., lat. $1\frac{1}{2}$ lin.

Ovate, broad, robust, fusco-pubescent, black. *Head* short, transverse, depressed, slightly elongated; eyes tolerably large: immediately above the insertion of the antennæ are two distinct longitudinal tubercles; above them are three obsolete lines of carination,—one medial, extending nearly to the base, the others obliquely transverse: the surface in front finely punctured, more distinctly and coarsely at the base; near the insertion of the antennæ suffused with rufous. *Thorax* quadrate (slightly transverse), the anterior angles depressed; at the apex are two slightly raised tubercles (in form resembling, but very much more obsolete than those of *H. tuberculatus*); surface granulated, covered with short pubescence. *Scutellum* small, almost obsolete, triangular. *Elytra* broader than the thorax, with punctures arranged in the form of striæ (the punctures not so coarse as in *H. tuberculatus*); the surface is covered throughout with short, squamose, dark fuscous pubescence. *Antennæ* broad, robust; from the seventh to the eleventh joints dilated, fulvous, the seventh and eighth joints being dark fuscous. *Legs* robust, dark fulvous, the posterior femora being fuscous.

Mexico. In the collections of Mr. Fry and the Rev. H. Clark.

4. Homotyphus asper. B.M.

H. *oblongo-ovatus, latus, sat robustus, fusco etiamque ferrugineo pilo vestitus, niger; capite brevi, inter oculos bituberculato, ad apicem nigro-ferrugineo, ad basin granulato et piceo; thorace quadrato, antice subcompresso, punctato; elytris punctato-striatis, robustis, pilo variegato vestitis* (ad medium *ferrugineo,* ad basin *fusco,* ad marginem *cinereo,* inter se commixtis); *antennis ad apicem incrassatis, brevibus,* art. 1 et 2 *fulvis,* 3–5 *flavo-fulvis,* 6–9 *piceis,* 10 et 11 *testaceis; pedibus nigro-fuscis, tibiis tarsisque posticis flavis.*

Long. corp. 2½ lin., lat. 1¼ lin.

Oblong-ovate, broad, complanate, irregularly clothed throughout with fuscous and also dark ferrugineous pubescence; black. *Head* short, depressed, slightly elongated in front; eyes tolerably large, situated not quite at the base of the head; between the eyes (immediately above the base of the antennæ) are two tubercles: the surface of the head in front is dark ferrugineous or piceous; at the base granulated and dark piceous. *Thorax* quadrate (slightly transverse), somewhat compressed in front; the anterior angles subacute and depressed; the surface complanate, punctate, dark piceous, clothed throughout with ferrugineous pubescence. *Scutellum* small, triangular, cinereous. *Elytra* subparallel, coarsely punctato-striate, the surface between the second and fourth striæ (close to the shoulders) being raised; clothed throughout with a dense, very short pubescence, as well as with longer, more erect and isolated hairs; this pubescence is mottled throughout—piceous, ferrugineous, and ashy grey: a transversely-oblique postmedial fascia may be traced more distinctly, as of a decided tendency to ferrugineous (bounded on either side by indications of grey), while behind this the predominant shade is fuscous. *Antennæ* incrassated towards the apex, short, tolerably robust; the first joint fulvous, suffused with piceous; the second fulvous; third, fourth and fifth flavo-fulvous; sixth to ninth piceous; tenth and eleventh testaceous. *Legs* dark fuscous, the posterior tibiæ and tarsi flavous; the globular inflation over the posterior claw being bright red.

This species appears to have a very extended range. I have examples before me from Mexico, from the Amazon district, and also from different parts of Brazil; while among all these examples there is little or no perceptible variation either in size or in colour of pubescence.

In the collections of the British Museum, Mr. Baly, Mr. Fry, and the Rev. H. Clark.

5. Homotyphus squalidus. B.M.

H. *oblongo-ovatus, robustus, subpubescens, ferrugineus; capite sub-producto, inter oculos bituberculato, punctato; thorace quadrato, ad medium bituberculato, squamoso; elytris latis, robustis, punctato-striatis, ferrugineo- et sparsim cinereo-pubescentibus, ad basin rufo-fuscis; antennis brevibus, art. 6–10 incrassatis, 1–6 flavis, 7–9 fuscis, 10 et 11 flavo-testaceis; pedibus robustis, fusco-ferrugineis.*

Long. corp. $2\frac{1}{3}$–$2\frac{1}{2}$ lin., lat. 1–$1\frac{1}{4}$ lin.

Oblong-ovate, robust, subpubescent, ferrugineous. *Head* short, transverse, slightly produced: between the eyes (immediately above the base of the antennæ) is a broad transverse ridge, divided by a medial depression so as to form two tubercles; above this ridge are three obsolete longitudinal carinations, reaching nearly to the base of the head: the surface punctate and subpubescent. *Thorax* quadrate (slightly transverse); the anterior angles depressed; the sides slightly marginate; when viewed laterally, the base appears to be transversely subdepressed; the surface in front is raised, and forms medially two tubercles; the whole being clothed with thick squamose pubescence, fusco-ferrugineous, sparingly interspersed with flavous; the surface beneath this appears to be coarsely punctate. *Scutellum* minute, triangular, flavous. *Elytra* broader than the thorax, robust, broadly punctate-striate, clothed throughout with thick, close, mottled pubescence; pale ferrugineous, being interspersed with ashy-grey; at the *base* the colour is more decidedly *rufo-fuscous*. *Antennæ* short, robust; the first joint broadly dilated; the sixth to the tenth incrassated; first to sixth flavous; the base of the sixth and seventh to ninth fuscous; tenth and eleventh flavo-testaceous. *Legs* robust, fusco-ferrugineous throughout.

This species differs from *H. tuberculatus* by its considerably smaller size, and from *H. fuliginosus* by the more ashy colour of its pubescence, as well as by the coloration of the antennæ; from *H. asper* it may be recognized by the three obsolete longitudinal carinations at the base of the head, and from *H. nodosus* by the raised transverse carination immediately above the base of the antennæ.

Mexico. In the collection of the British Museum.

6. Homotyphus holosericeus. (Tab. V. fig. 1.)

H. *suborbicularis, subpubescens, flavus; capite depresso, inter oculos foveolato, punctato; thorace transverso (pœne quadrato), ad basin transverse depresso, flavo-pubescenti; elytris subglobosis, punctato-striatis, pubescentibus, ad latera duabus maculis (et ad apicem fascia*) *suffusis, flavo-testaceis ; antennis flavis,* art. 7, 8 *et* 11 *fusco-flavis ; pedibus flavis.*

Long. corp. 2 lin., lat. 1¼ lin.

Ovate, suborbicular, subpubescent, flavous. *Head* short, and hardly produced; below the base of the antennæ is a transverse triangular impression; between the eyes is an obsolete T-shaped fovea; eyes tolerably large, globose, situated at the base of the head; surface punctate. *Thorax* transverse (almost quadrate), rectangular; the anterior angles depressed and subacute; at the base is a broad transverse postmedial depression: the surface is finely but thickly pubescent, flavous; at the margins more distinctly flavo-pubescent. *Scutellum* obsolete, flavous. *Elytra* subglobose, considerably broader than the thorax, punctate-striate, thickly clothed throughout with pubescence; flavous, with two suffused transverse bands (which become obsolete near the suture) and another near the apex (which is continued throughout) flavo-testaceous. *Antennæ* filiform, tolerably robust, flavous, with the seventh and eighth and also the eleventh joints fusco-flavous. *Legs* flavous throughout.

From the nighbourhood of Rio Janeiro. In the collection of Mr. Fry.

7. Homotyphus maculicornis.

H. *oblongo-ovatus, latus, robustus, subtiliter pubescens, punctatus, nigro-ferrugineus ; capite transverso, supra basin antennarum bituberculato, ad basin granulato ; rufo-ferrugineo, ad basin piceo ; thorace quadrato, subæquato, granulato ; elytris latis, punctato-striatis, punctis sat magnis, fulvo- et nigro-pubescentibus ; antennis ad apicem subincrassatis, articulis* 1–5 *flavis,* 7–9 *fuscis,* 10 *et* 11 *flavis ; pedibus robustis, fuscis.*

Long. corp. 2½ lin., lat. 1⅓ lin.

Oblong-ovate, broad, robust, finely pubescent, deeply punctate, of a dark ferrugineous colour throughout. *Head* transverse, deflected and slightly but broadly produced in front; between the labrum and the base of the antennæ the surface is transversely depressed; immediately above the base of the antennæ are two minute but very distinct tubercles, above which the surface is coarsely granulated: eyes tolerably large, situated at the base of the head, extending laterally not quite so far as the anterior angles of the thorax: the surface (except at the base) is glabrous and rufo-ferrugineous; at the base darkly piceous. *Thorax* broader than the head, transverse, rectangular, at the sides very finely marginate; the surface (when compared with other species in this group) is almost equate; two almost obsolete tubercles are observable medially, near the anterior margin, while on either side of these, adjoining the anterior angles, is an indistinct depression; near the basal angles, also, are two other obsolete depressions: the surface (when viewed under a high power) is very sparingly clothed with pubescence, and coarsely granulated. *Scutellum* small, triangular, rounded at the apex, impunctate, and fuscous. *Elytra* much broader than the thorax, robust, punctate-striate, the striæ being very indistinct, and near the suture obsolete, while the punctures are very large and deep: the surface is clothed with a close and very fine pubescence of a fulvo-ferrugineous colour, mottled throughout irregularly with ashy grey, and at the sides and base more distinctly fulvous. *Antennæ* incrassated at the apex; the first joint being long and dilated; the second much shorter and narrower; the third, fourth, and fifth of equal length, longer and slightly narrower than the second; the sixth to the eleventh short and dilated, broader than the first and shorter than the second: in colour the first to the fifth are flavous, the first being suffused with fuscous, and the fourth and fifth and also the base of the sixth testaceous; the seventh, eighth, and the apex of the ninth darkly fuscous; the tenth and eleventh testaceous. *Legs* robust, fuscous throughout.

This species may be distinguished from *H. squalidus* not only by its more close and differently coloured pubescence, but by the obsolete striæ on its elytra, which in the latter species are well-defined.

Mexico. From the collection of M. Chevrolat.

8. Homotyphus Wollastonii.

H. *ovatus, latus, subdepressus, fulvo-ferrugineus; capite granulato, subpubescenti, flavo-rufo; thorace transverso, rectangulari, ad basin subdepresso, granulato, flavo-rufo; elytris latis, punctato-striatis, fulvo-ferrugineis; antennis ad apicem subincrassatis, testaceis, art.* 7–11 (*subincrassatis*) *rufo-testaceis; pedibus flavis.*

Long. corp. 1⅔ lin., lat. ¾–1 lin.

Ovate, broad, subdepressed, subpubescent, fulvo-ferrugineous. *Head* short, abruptly transverse, hardly produced; above the labrum is a transverse, triangular, slightly elevated plane (black); above the base of the antennæ (which are contiguous) is an obsolete fovea, in the form of the letter Y: eyes situated at the base of the head, and extending laterally as far as the anterior angles of the thorax: the surface is finely granulated, pubescent, and flavo-rufous. *Thorax small* when compared with the breadth of the elytra, transverse, rectangular; the sides slightly marginate and parallel; at the base are two broad subdepressions; the surface is granulated, finely pubescent and flavo-rufous. *Scutellum* small, triangular, rufous. *Elytra broad*, subdepressed, punctate-striate, the punctures being concealed by a very fine ferrugineous pubescence. *Antennæ* short, attenuated, subincrassated towards the apex; the first joint long, dilated at the apex and reflected backwards; the second broad, short, ovate; the third to the sixth long and fine (the fourth to the sixth being of equal length and shorter than the third); seventh to eleventh short and subincrassated; the colour of the first to the sixth testaceous, seventh to eleventh rufo-testaceous. *Legs* flavous; the globular inflation over the posterior claw being brightly rufous.

Bahia. In the collection of the Rev. H. Clark.

Genus 18. ÆDMON*.

LABRUM *breve.*

PALPI MAXILLARES *elongati, cylindrici, art. penultimo robusto.*

ANTENNÆ *subincrassatæ, pubescentes, art.* 3–5 *brevibus, attenuatis,* 6–11 *gradatim dilatatis.*

OCULI *ad basin capitis positi.*

CAPUT *breve, fere verticale.*

THORAX *transversus, angulis anterioribus distinctis, lateribus ad basin subcompressis.*

ELYTRA *lata, robusta, ad latera subrotundata.*

PEDES: *tarsis anterioribus brevibus (art.* 1 *et* 2 *subæqualibus); tibiis posticis apicem juxta unidentatis.*

Labrum shorter than the base of the head, subcircular.

Maxillary palpi (Tab. V. fig. 2 *m*) elongate, cylindrical; the second joint short, obliquely truncate at the apex; the penultimate joint cylindrical, robust, the length being nearly three times the breadth; the apical joint minute and conical.

Labial palpi (destroyed in the single example of this genus before me).

Antennæ robust, subincrassated, clothed throughout sparingly with pubescence; at the apex of each joint are two or three rigid hairs (larger than the others) which project at almost right angles; the first joint is subrotundate, broad, and elongate; the second of the same form, but smaller; the third to the fifth are subequal in length, shorter and considerably more attenuated than the first; the sixth to the eleventh are gradually incrassated towards the apex, and shorter: the antennæ, as to their insertion, are approximate, and

* αἰδώς, verecundia.

situated between the lower margins of (not below) the eyes; eyes large, lateral, situated at the base of the head, and extending laterally nearly as far as the anterior angles of the thorax.

Head short, transverse, inclined, but not abruptly, at right angles to the plane of the elytra, impubescent.

Thorax transverse, slightly broader than the head; the anterior angles are distinct and depressed; the sides are marginate and subconstricted towards the base.

Scutellum small, triangular.

Elytra broad, robust, slightly rounded at the sides, the greatest breadth being near the middle, punctate-striate, clothed throughout with fine pubescence.

Legs: the *anterior femora* robust (constricted at the base), broadly truncate at the apex. The *tibiæ* are abruptly inflected at the immediate base, gradually thickened towards the apex. The *tarsi* are short and sufficiently broad; the first and second joints are triangular, of equal breadth with the base of the tibia, the second joint being rather smaller than the first; the third joint is broader, subcircular, slightly bilobed, and fringed with a margin of thick rigid pubescence; the apical joint is longer than the third, narrow, and inflected and gradually incrassated towards the apex: the claw is bifid, and armed at its inner surface with a broad tooth. The *posterior femora* are broadly dilated, gradually tapering towards the apex. The *tibia* (Tab. V. fig. 2 *g*) is short and robust, thickened towards the apex; immediately in front of the insertion of the tarsus, the margination of the posterior flattened side is produced into a distinct spur-like projection; the apex is obliquely truncate, and armed at its extremity with a single incurved and strong tooth. The *tarsus* is elongated and narrow, the *basal* joint being *longer and somewhat broader* than the rest, triangular in form; the second is of the same form as the first; the third is *minute* and almost circular; from its centre proceeds the insertion of the ultimate joint, which is narrow, and produced into a globular inflation above the terminal claw.

The single example from which I have formed this genus presents abundantly distinguishing characteristics. The form of its maxillary palpi (elongate and cylindrical, not dilated) separates it at once from other subsequent genera, to which, in facies, it seems to be related; while the peculiar form and hirsute antennæ, and the spur near the apex of the posterior tibia, as well as the relative lengths of the joints of the tarsus (without any reference to its general facies), forbid its being placed in any of the groups to which, by the form of its palpi, it is most nearly allied.

1. Ædmon sericellum. (Tab. V. fig. 2.)
Klug (auct. Chevr. Coll.).

Æ. oblongo-ovatum, subparallelum, sat robustum, pubescens, flavo-testaceum; capite brevi, ad basin antennarum T foveolato, punctato; thorace transverso, ad basin depresso, punctato; elytris punctato-striatis, ante medium transverse depressis, flavo-pubescentibus; antennis robustis, ad apicem incrassatis, flavis, articulis 10 et 11 fuscis; pedibus flavis.

Long. corp. ¾ lin., lat. ⅔ lin.

Oblong-ovate, subparallel, tolerably robust, finely pubescent, flavotestaceous. *Head* short, transverse, hardly produced; immediately above the base of the antennæ is a medial longitudinal fovea, which is terminated at its upper extremity by a transverse channel extending at right angles to it between the eyes, these channels forming together the character of the letter T; eyes large, black, situated at the base of the head, extending laterally not quite so far as the anterior angles of the thorax: the surface finely punctate throughout. *Thorax* transverse, the anterior angles depressed, the sides marginate; at the base is a shallow transverse depression; the surface finely punctate throughout. *Scutellum* triangular. *Elytra* somewhat broader than the thorax, subparallel, distinctly punctate-striate; an antemedial transverse depression gives an appearance of prominence to the base; the surface is clothed throughout with fine and sparingly distributed flavous pubescence. *Antennæ* robust, somewhat incrassated towards the apex, clothed distinctly with several hairs of unequal length at right angles to the joints of the antennæ; the first joint longer than any of the others, and dilated at its apex; the second broad, short, ovate; the third to the sixth of equal length, *not longer than the second*, and attenuated; the seventh to the eleventh short and dilated; in colour, the first to the ninth flavous, the tenth and eleventh fuscous. *Legs* flavous throughout.

Porto Rico. In the collection of M. Chevrolat.

Genus 19. PLEUROCHROMA*.

Mandibulæ *robustæ, simplices.*
Palpi maxillares *elongati, filiformes, haud dilatati, art. penultimo subincurvo, ultimo minuto.*
Palpi labiales *quam maxillares latiores.*
Antennæ *breves, ad apicem subincrassatæ.*
Caput *breve, verticale, plerumque inter oculos depressum.*

---

* πλευρά, latus; χρῶμα, color.

THORAX *transversus, latus, rectangularis, glaber.*

ELYTRA *parallela, lata, robusta, plerumque punctato-striata, et læte colorata, glabra.*

PEDES: *tibiis posticis brevibus, simplicibus, ad apicem, a posteriori, marginatis et subsinuatis.*

Labrum short, subcircular in outline.

Mandibles robust, simple.

Maxillary palpi (Tab. V. fig. 3 *m*) elongate, filiform, not dilated; the second joint is short, transversely truncate at the apex; the third elongate, slightly incurved, the length being three times the breadth; the ultimate joint is minute and conical.

Labial palpi (Tab. V. fig. 3 *n*) perceptibly broader than the maxillary, acuminated.

Antennæ approximate, situated below and between the inner margins of the eyes, robust, short, incrassated at the apex; the basal joint broad and elongate; the second narrower, short, ovate; the third to the fifth narrow at their base, dilated towards the apex, narrower and longer than the second; the sixth to the eleventh slightly broader, shorter, transverse at the apex and rounded at the base.

Eyes lateral, situated at the base of the head, subglobose.

Head short, transverse, depressed at right angles to the plane of the elytra, narrower than the thorax, not produced in front, generally obliquely or transversely depressed between the eyes; impubescent, glabrous.

Thorax transverse, rectangular, rectilinear, the anterior angles depressed, the sides depressed and marginate; equate; impunctate, glabrous.

Scutellum large, triangular, impunctate.

Elytra broader than the thorax, short, robust, subdepressed, the sides *somewhat* dilated medially; generally punctate-striate, glabrous.

Legs: *anterior femora* robust, slightly dilated towards the middle. The *tibiæ* are short, incurved abruptly at the immediate base, gradually and slightly thickened towards the apex. The *tarsi* are short and broad; the basal and second joints being of subequal length; the third broader and slightly bilobed, the margin being fringed with a rigid and thick pubescence; the terminal joint is narrow and slightly incurved, and dilated towards the extremity: the claw is bifid and simple. The *posterior femora* are short, incrassated, and rounded at their upper margin. The *tibiæ* (Tab. V. fig. 3 *g*) are short, not incurved, gradually but slightly thickened towards the apex; the posterior outline above the insertion of the tarsus is subsinuate (not armed with a distinct spur), and obliquely truncate at the apex. The *tarsi* are short and attenuated; the two basal joints minute and triangular; the third subcircular, and the fourth elongated, and dilated at its extremity into a globular inflation, which completely conceals from above the terminal claw.

This pretty little group of insects readily separates itself from all others: its *broad depressed* surface (not subglobose, as in *Leptotrichus* or *Homotyphus*) and its *more* filiform antennæ at once abundantly distinguish it; it differs also materially in the form of the maxillary palpi, which are somewhat more elongate than in *Homotyphus* and decidedly shorter than in *Leptotrichus*; its general facies is depressed, subparallel, broad, impubescent, and brightly coloured. From *Panchrestus* it differs in its less globose body, in the form of its antennæ, and in its simple, unarmed posterior tibiæ.

1. **Pleurochroma balteatum.** (TAB. V. fig. 3.)

P. *oblongo-ovale, robustum, subcylindricum, nigrum, nitidum; capite brevi, depresso, inter oculos rugoso, ad basin punctulato, nigrorufo; thorace transverso, antice subcoarctato, subpunctato, et obsolete vermiculato, nigro-rufo; elytris latis, punctato-striatis, ad apicem obsolete punctatis, nigris, vitta media transversa rufa; antennis brevibus, ad basin rufis, ad apicem fuscis; pedibus rufotestaceis.*

Long. corp. 2 lin., lat. 1 lin.

Oblong-oval, robust, subcylindrical, black, shining. *Head* short, depressed, not produced; eyes tolerably large, situated at the back of the head, not extending laterally as far as the line of the margin of the thorax; the surface between the eyes rugose, above sparingly punctate, dark rufous. *Thorax* not quite so broad as the elytra, transverse, rectangular, slightly coarctate in front; the anterior angles depressed; sides marginate; the surface equate, subpunctate, with short minute impressed lines thickly interspersed among the punctures; dark rufous. *Scutellum* triangular, rufous. *Elytra* somewhat broader than the thorax, subcylindrical, with rows of punctures arranged in the form of striæ (these punctures become obsolete towards the apex); black, with a broad transverse medial band of rufous extending from the margination and slightly widening as it approaches the suture. *Antennæ* short, subclavate, at the base rufous, towards the apex fuscous. *Legs* rufo-testaceous.

From the district of the Amazon. In the collections of Mr. Baly, Mr. Bates, and the Rev. H. Clark.

2. **Pleurochroma nitidulum.**

P. *oblongo-ovale, breve, robustum, nigrum; capite brevi, inter oculos T foveolato, punctato, rufo; thorace transverso, rectangulari, subpunctato, rufo; elytris robustis, striato-punctatis, nigris, nitidis; antennis subincrassatis, robustis, flavis, ad apicem fuscis; pedibus flavis.*

Long. corp. $2\frac{1}{4}$ lin., lat. $1\frac{1}{4}$ lin.

Oblong-oval, short, robust, black. *Head* short, narrower than the thorax, transverse, depressed, slightly elongated; eyes large; between the eyes, and above the base of the antennæ, is a shallow T-shaped depression; the surface punctate, rufous. *Thorax* broader than the head, but distinctly narrower than the *elytra*, equate, transverse, rectangular; the anterior angles depressed, sides marginate; surface finely punctate, rufous. *Scutellum* triangular, fuscous and rufous. *Elytra* broad, robust, slightly rounded at the sides, with rows of punctures arranged as striæ (these punctures become obsolete towards the apex); black, shining. *Antennæ* short, subclavate, robust; at the base flavous, at the apex fuscous. *Legs* flavous.

This species differs from the preceding by the form and sculpture of the thorax, and also by the absence of the rufous band on the elytra.

Amazon district. A single specimen, in the collection of Mr. Baly.

3. **Pleurochroma pallidum.**

P. *oblongo-ovale, robustum, subcylindricum, rufum; capite brevi, depresso, super antennarum basin longitudinaliter depresso, punctato; thorace transverso, ad apicem constricto, vermiculato; elytris latis, striato-punctatis; antennis brevibus, subclavatis, ad basin fulvis, ad apicem fuscis; pedibus rufo-testaceis.*

Long. corp. $2\frac{1}{4}$ lin., lat. $1\frac{1}{4}$ lin.

Oblong-oval, short, robust, subcylindrical, rufous throughout. *Head* short, depressed, not produced; eyes large, extending laterally not so far as the sides of the thorax; above the insertion of the antennæ is a longitudinal depression, dividing into two parts a transverse slightly raised plane, which is smoother than the rest of the head; surface punctate. *Thorax* transverse, rectangular, somewhat compressed towards the apex; the anterior angles depressed, sides marginate; the surface smooth, vermiculate (with short irregular impressed lines). *Scutellum* triangular. *Elytra* broad, rounded at the sides, with punctures arranged in the form of striæ; these punctures become obsolete towards the apex. *Antennæ* short, subclavate;

at the base fulvous, at the apex fuscous. *Legs* rufo-testaceous throughout.

From the Amazon district. A single specimen, in the collection of Mr. Baly.

Genus 20. LEPTOTRICHUS*.

PALPI MAXILLARES *elongati et attenuati, art. penultimo cylindrico.*
PALPI LABIALES *robustiores, art. 2^{ndo} lato et ad apicem oblique truncato.*
ANTENNÆ *dilatatæ, articulo tertio brevi, subpubescentes.*
CAPUT *breve, transversum, haud productum, verticale.*
THORAX *inclinatus, subconvexus, transversus, latus.*
ELYTRA *robusta, brevia, subcylindrica.*
PEDES: *tibiis posticis ad marginationem posteriorem inarmatis, in calcar ad apicem productis.*

Labrum narrow, subcircular.

Maxillary palpi (Tab. V. fig. 4 *m*) elongate, much more so than in *Pleurochroma*, and attenuated; the basal joint minute; the second slightly dilated towards the apex (which is obliquely truncate), the length being nearly double the breadth; the penultimate joint is nearly double the length of the second, and almost cylindrical; the apical joint is minute and conically elongate.

Labial palpi (Tab. V. fig. 4 *n*) more robust than the maxillary, the second joint being broad and (apparently) obliquely truncate both at the base and apex; the apical joint minute.

Antennæ approximate, situated at the inner and lower margin of the eyes; *broadly incrassated*, more distinctly so than in *Pleurochroma* or *Homotyphus*; the basal joint elongate, dilated gradually towards the apex, and inflected outwards; the second almost as broad as the first, short, ovate; the third is attenuate, *not so long as the first*, slightly thickened at the apex; the fourth is of the same form as, but shorter, and a trifle more robust than the third; from the fifth to the tenth the joints are shorter, very robust, transverse, and abruptly truncate; the apical joint is narrower and more elongate; the whole are clothed with a short thick pubescence.

Eyes not quite so prominent as in the preceding genera, lateral, situated at the base of the head, and extending laterally not so far as the anterior angles of the thorax.

Head short, transverse, not produced (but subattenuated) in front, depressed at right angles to the plane of the elytra.

Thorax broader than the head, robust, inclined, depressed at the

* λεπτὸς, tenuis; θρίξ, coma.

anterior angles and the sides; more convex than in the preceding genus; in form transverse, slightly compressed in front, comparatively much broader than in the next genus.

Scutellum broadly triangular, pubescent.

Elytra robust, short, subcylindrical, much more robust and broader than the thorax; more convex than in the preceding genus.

Legs: anterior femora short, robust, slightly dilated medially. The *tibiæ* are short, inflected abruptly at their immediate base, somewhat thickened towards the apex. The *tarsi* are sufficiently broad; the two basal joints subelongate and triangular (the second being smaller than the first); the third is transversely subcircular, deeply bilobed, and margined with a deep, dense fringe of rigid pubescence; the apical joint is attenuate and gradually thickened, as well as inflected towards the apex : the terminal claw is bifid, and armed at the inner surface with an obsolete basal tooth. The *posterior femora* are, when viewed transversely, broadly incrassated, short, rounded at the upper surface, extending nearly to the apex of the elytra. The *tibiæ* are short, robust, inflected at the immediate base, slightly attenuated medially; at the apex broadly obliquely truncate, and at the angle of truncation slightly dilated; the socket which receives the base of the tarsus is simple (not armed with comb-like teeth), and produced apically into a *single* well-developed spur. The *tarsus* is inserted at *some little distance* from the apex of the tibia, short, and much narrower than those of the anterior feet; the first and second joints are triangular in form and elongate; the third not broader, subcircular, and almost bilobed; the last joint is attenuated, and produced apically into a broadly inflated globular projection, which completely conceals from above the terminal claw.

This genus may be distinguished from all allied to it, by its *distinctly elongated* maxillary palpi, and also by its robust body and dilated antennæ from the preceding genus.

1. **Leptotrichus castaneus.** (Tab. V. fig. 4.)

L. *ovatus, robustus, latus, castaneus, flavo-pubescens; capite antice foveolato; thorace transverso, punctato, ad latera flavo-pubescenti; scutello pubescenti; elytris robustis, punctatis, ad apicem lateraque pubescentibus; antennis validis, fortiter incrassatis, art.* 1–5 *flavis,* 6–11 *nigris; pedibus flavis.*

Long. corp. 2¼ lin., lat. 1½ lin.

Ovate, short, robust, castaneous, flavo-pubescent. *Head* short, not produced; below the base of the antennæ is a transverse triangular depression; above the base, between the eyes, is an obsolete T-shaped fovea (forming within it two slight elevations); surface punctate, impubescent. *Thorax* broadly transverse, the upper surface subcylindrical; the anterior angles much depressed; the surface distinctly punctate, at the sides flavo-pubescent. *Scutellum* triangular, thickly pubescent. *Elytra* robust, broad; on either side is an antemedial transverse depression, which does not reach the suture; surface punctate, the punctures being less distinct at the apex and arranged in the form of striæ; at the apex and sides flavo-pubescent. *Antennæ* short, robust, broadly incrassated towards the apex; the first joint is long, deflected outwards, and dilated at the extremity; the second broad, short, ovate; the third and fourth slender, not equal in length to the first; the sixth to tenth broadly dilated; the first and second flavous, third to fifth flavo-testaceous, sixth to eleventh black. *Legs* flavous.

From the neighbourhood of Ega, River Amazon. In the collections of Mr. Bates and the Rev. H. Clark.

Genus 21. **PANCHRESTUS***.

PALPI MAXILLARES *cylindrici, robusti, haud attenuati.*
PALPI LABIALES *breves, ovati.*
ANTENNÆ *sat robustæ, dilatatæ, art. 3^{tio} et 1mo æqualibus.*
CAPUT *breve, subproductum, plerumque verticale.*
THORAX *transversus, interdum ad latera angulatus, plerumque punctatus, aut granulatus.*
ELYTRA *robusta, plerumque ante medium transverse depressa, punctato-striata, interdum obsolete pube vestita.*
PEDES: *tibiæ posticæ simplices, haud dente armatæ, breves.*

Labrum narrow, *more contracted than the base of the head*, transverse, and rounded at the margins.

Maxillary palpi (Tab. V. fig. 5 *m*) elongate, but medially somewhat more dilated, and altogether shorter and more robust than in the preceding genus; the penultimate joint is almost as broad as it is long, and the terminal joint broader at the base and less attenuated than in the genus *Leptotrichus*.

Labial palpi (Tab. V. fig. 5 *n*) short, ovate.

Antennæ approximate, situated between and below the inner margin of the eyes, sufficiently robust, medially dilated, *not so broadly as in the preceding genus*; the basal joint is long, dilated medially and towards the apex; the second shorter and narrower, ovate, transversely truncate at the apex; the third attenuated, *longer* (slightly) *than the first* (in the preceding genus this joint is distinctly

* πᾶν, omnino; χρηστὸς, bonus.

shorter than the basal joint); the fourth equal in form to, but shorter than, the third; the fifth to the eleventh of equal length with, but much broader than, the fourth; the ultimate joint being attenuated.

Eyes large, globose, lateral, distant, situated at the base of the head, and extending laterally almost as far as the anterior angles of the thorax.

Head short, transverse, somewhat produced in front, inclined at right angles to the plane of the elytra.

Thorax broader than the head, transverse, narrower in proportion and less robust than in the preceding genus; the sides depressed, marginate, and more or less obsoletely subsinuate in outline (occasionally dentate); for the most part deeply punctate or granulated, and very finely pubescent or glabrous.

Scutellum small, triangular, depressed below the plane of the elytra, sometimes apparently obsolete.

Elytra robust, broader than the thorax, not so convex as in the preceding genus; an antemedial transverse depression gives a prominence to the anterior angles; the surface is punctate-striate, and in most cases covered sparingly with obsolete pubescence.

Legs: anterior femora subcylindrical, straight, hardly dilated medially. The *tibiæ* are abruptly incurved at the immediate base, straight, gradually but slightly thickened towards the apex. The *tarsi* are short; the first joint elongate, triangular; the second shorter but *somewhat broader* than the first; the third much broader, subcircular in form, and slightly bilobed; the apical joint is not so elongate as in other genera, attenuate, slightly incurved, and incrassated towards the terminal claw, which is bifid and simple (a rudimentary tooth (almost obsolete) may be traced at the base of the inner surface). *Posterior femora* incrassated (when viewed from the side), ovate, gradually tapering towards the apex; the surface near the apex being subsinuate in outline, or hollowed out, near the insertion of the tibia. The *tibia* is short, straight, slightly incrassated at the extreme apex, where it is obliquely truncate, terminating below the insertion of the tarsus in a single, strong incurved spur. The *tarsus* is short and attenuated; the two first joints are triangular, broadly truncate at the apex; the third subcircular, broader than the basal joints, bilobed, and fringed at its margin with dense rigid pubescence; the apical joint is dilated into a globular inflation covering the ultimate claw.

This genus, more closely allied to the latter (*Leptotrichus*) than to any others, may be readily separated from it by its less convex form, less elongated and attenuated palpi, by its narrower thorax, and less incrassated form of antennæ.

1. Panchrestus pulcher.

P. *ovatus, robustus, subpubescens, rufus, nitidus; capite brevi, antice subproducto, subtiliter granulato; thorace transverso, ad latera obsolete dentato, crebre punctato; elytris brevibus, robustis, striato-punctatis, sparsim fulvo-pubescentibus; antennis brevibus, ad apicem incrassatis, art. 1–5 flavis, 6–11 nigris; pedibus pallide rufis aut flavis.*

Long. corp. $2\frac{1}{3}$ lin., lat. $1\frac{1}{3}$ lin.

Ovate, robust, subpubescent, bright red, shining. *Head* short, depressed (almost vertical), produced in front; labrum black; eyes tolerably large, distant, situate at the back of the head, and extending laterally nearly to the anterior angle of the thorax; surface closely granulated and rufous. *Thorax* transverse; the anterior angles depressed; the sides marginate and irregular in outline, projected ante-medially in the form of a tooth; surface coarsely and thickly punctured. *Scutellum* very small. *Elytra* short, broad, robust, with punctures arranged in the form of striæ, bright rufous, clothed very sparingly with fulvous pubescence. *Antennæ* short, robust, incrassated towards the apex; joints first to fifth flavous or fusco-flavous; sixth to eleventh considerably incrassated and black. *Legs* pale red or flavous throughout.

I cannot but feel it to be probable that this insect may (with others hereafter to be discovered) constitute a separate genus: in its abbreviated form (its transverse thorax and robust elytra), coupled with its short and incrassated antennæ, and the peculiar vertical form of the head (which approaches to *Loxoprosopus*), not to mention the lateral angular projection in the margination of the thorax, it presents several points of difference from its allies.

From the district of the Amazon. Collected by Mr. Bates.

2. Panchrestus rubicundus.   B.M.

P. *ovatus, robustus, rufus, subpubescens; capite brevi, inter oculos oblique foveolato; thorace crebre punctato; elytris valde punctato-striatis, subpubescentibus; antennis ad apicem dilatatis, art. 1–5 testaceis, 6–11 nigro-fuscis; pedibus testaceis.*

Long. corp. 2 lin., lat. 1 lin.

Ovate, broad, robust, rufous, subpubescent. *Head* short, slightly depressed; eyes large, somewhat prominent; below the base of the antennæ is a transverse triangular depression; immediately above the antennæ is an obsolete, obliquely transverse fovea, in the form of the letter V; surface thickly punctured. *Thorax* transverse; the anterior angles depressed; the sides marginate; surface thickly punctate, subpubescent. *Scutellum* triangular. *Elytra* broad, robust, coarsely punctate-striate, more obsoletely towards the apex (the striæ being broader and the punctures deeper than in *P. pulcher*), subpubescent (but *more distinctly* pubescent than in *pulcher*); a slight antemedial depression extends transversely behind the shoulders. *Antennæ* tolerably robust, short, dilated towards the extremity; the joints first to fifth pale testaceous, sixth to eleventh dark fuscous. *Legs* testaceous throughout.

This species closely resembles *P. pulcher*, appearing at first sight to be merely a pale and small variety of that species; it is, however, distinctly separated (as well as by its smaller form and paler colour) by the *form of its head*, which is less produced and more attenuated towards the labrum; by the *punctuation* on the elytra, which is more distinct and deep; by the general *subpubescent* (instead of glabrous) character of its surface; and by the disposition of colouring on the antennæ, the transition being *abrupt* from testaceous to fuscous, and not suffused as in the case of *P. pulcher*.

Ega (River Amazon). In the collection of Mr. Bates, and also in that of the British Museum.

3. Panchrestus inconspicuus. (Tab. V. fig. 5.)

P. *oblongo-ovalis, fusco-rufus, subpubescens; capite (inter oculos) foveolato; thorace crebre punctulato; elytris robustis, leviter punctato-striatis; antennis ad medium dilatatis, art. 1–4 ferrugineis, 5–8 dilatatis, nigris, 9 testaceo, 10 et 11 nigris; pedibus fusco-rufis.*

Long. corp. 2 lin., lat. 1 lin.

Oblong-ovate, tolerably robust, fusco-rufous, subpubescent. *Head* small, short, produced, attenuated near the mouth; eyes large, prominent, but not extending laterally as far as the angles of the thorax; immediately above the base of the antennæ is a short medial fovea, produced (when viewed from the front) in the form of an obsolete carination to the base of the head; at the inner margin of the eyes is also an oblique depression, which (in conjunction with the medial line) gives an appearance of elevation to the intermediate surface. *Thorax* transverse, rectangular; the anterior angles slightly depressed; the sides marginate; at the base is a slight depression, extending obliquely upwards towards the anterior angles; the surface finely and thickly punctate, subpubescent, especially towards the sides. *Scutellum* small, triangular. *Elytra* robust, finely punctate-striate (more obsoletely towards the apex), subpubescent, especially at the apex and sides. *Antennæ* robust, incrassated towards the middle; joints first to fourth ferrugineous, fifth to eighth (which are dilated) black, ninth testaceous, tenth and eleventh black. *Legs*: the posterior femora short and broadly dilated; the colour throughout fusco-rufous.

From the neighbourhood of Santarem (River Amazon). Taken by Mr. Bates.

4. Panchrestus rufescens. (Tab. V. fig. 6.) B.M.

P. *latus, robustus, subpubescens, punctatus, rufo-ferrugineus; capite punctulato; thorace transverso, angulis anticis subacutis, ad latera marginato et (ad medium) angulato, angulis posticis oblique truncatis, punctato; elytris striato-punctatis; antennis robustis, ad apicem subdilatatis, flavis, art. 6–11 piceis; pedibus testaceis, femoribus posticis rufo-flavis.*

Long. corp. 2 lin., lat. 1 lin.

Ovate, broad, parallel, subpubescent, punctate, of a pale rufo-ferrugineous colour throughout. *Head* short, hardly produced in front; above the labrum is a transverse triangular depression; above the base of the antennæ, between the eyes, is an obsolete Y-shaped fovea; eyes globose, oval, lateral, situated at the base of the head; the surface of the head is finely punctate. *Thorax* transverse, slightly broader than the head; the anterior angles are depressed and subacute; the sides marginate, the margination being produced antemedially and laterally into a distinct angle (somewhat resembling in form the genus *Octogonotes*); the posterior angles are distinctly obliquely truncate; at the base is an obsolete subcircular depression; the surface is coarsely impressed with shallow punctures. *Scutellum* triangular, impunctate, situated below the plane of the elytra, testaceous. *Elytra* broad, parallel, antemedially transversely depressed, punctate, sparingly flavo-pubescent. *Antennæ* robust, subincrassated towards the apex; the joints three to five are subequal in length and attenuated, the rest short and slightly dilated; flavous, the joints six to eleven being piceous. *Legs* testaceous, the posterior femora and inflation of the apical claw being rufo-flavous.

This species differs from *P. rubicundus* in its paler colour, its glabrous elytra, and the character of the punctuation on its elytra, which is not so coarse and less frequent; from *P. pulcher* it differs by its distinct (not obsolete) punctuation, while from *P. inconspicuus* it may readily be separated by the angular margination of its thorax.

A single specimen, taken by Mr. Bates at Santarem, in the district of the River Amazon, is in the collection of the British Museum.

Genus 22. **HYLODROMUS***.

PALPI MAXILLARES *breves, sat robusti, art. apicali haud elongato.*
ANTENNÆ *dilatatæ et subcomplanatæ, art. 3–6 incrassatis et brevibus, art. 7–11 elongatis et filiformibus.*
CAPUT *breve, verticale, antice subproductum.*
THORAX *transversus, ad basin constrictus et transverse depressus.*
ELYTRA *sat lata, robusta, depressa (haud convexa).*
PEDES: *tibiis posticis sensim dilatatis, et ad apicem ipsum bicalcaratis; tarsis brevibus.*

Labrum transverse, sinuate, narrow.

Maxillary palpi (Tab. V. fig. 7 *m*) short, tolerably robust; the penultimate joint cylindrical and short; the terminal joint rounded, not attenuated.

Labial palpi (Tab. V. fig. 7 *n*) obscure in the single example of this genus before me.

Antennæ very remarkably incrassated and *flattened*; the basal joint long, dilated towards the apex and inflected outwards; the second very short, ovate; the third to the sixth broadly dilated and short, the sixth being somewhat longer but narrower than the fifth, and the fifth and sixth broader than the others; the ultimate joints are *abruptly* attenuated and filiform.

Eyes large, lateral, situated at the base of the head, extending laterally as far as the lateral angles of the thorax.

Head short, transverse, *abruptly* deflected at right angles, at the insertion of the antennæ, and, when viewed transversely, approaching the form of *Loxoprosopus*; in front slightly produced.

Thorax transverse, slightly broader than the head; the anterior angles acute and prominent; at the base *constricted* and depressed.

Scutellum triangular, situated in the plane of the elytra.

Elytra broader than the thorax, robust; the anterior angles well defined; the surface is depressed (much less convex than in the preceding genera) and punctate-striate, faintly pubescent.

Legs: *anterior femora* straight, perceptibly thickened towards the middle. *Tibiæ* short, straight, cylindrical. The *tarsi* are more robust; the basal joint is elongated and triangular in form; the second shorter; the penultimate rounded, broader than the basal joint, obsoletely bilobed, and fringed around its margin with a dense rigid pubescence; from the centre of the third joint proceeds the terminal joint, elongated, sensibly thickened towards the apex, and incurved: the claw is bifid, simple, unarmed by any inner tooth. The *posterior femora* are incrassated (not so broadly as in the preceding genus, *Panchrestus*), ovate, gradually tapering towards the apex. The *tibia*

---

* ὕλη, nemus; δρόμος, cursus.

is abruptly incurved at its immediate base, straight, and at the apex sensibly dilated and obliquely truncate, terminating ultimately in *two* strong curved spurs below the insertion of the tarsus. The *tarsus* is short and attenuated; the first and second joints being elongated, and dilated at the apex (the second being somewhat smaller than the basal joint); the third is broader, subcircular, and clothed at its margins with a dense pubescence; the apical joint is elongated, and produced into a globular inflation, which quite conceals, from above, the terminal claw.

This genus is a connecting link between several of the preceding genera and *Loxoprosopus*: with the former it is connected by its nonincrassated palpi; with the latter by its parallel and depressed cylindrical body.

I have no means of ascertaining how far the extraordinary dilatation of the antennæ may be sexual, as is the case in other genera in which the form of the antennæ is abnormal,—as in *Physimerus*, where the incurved apical and broadly flattened basal joints are found only in the males, and in *Loxoprosopus*, where the males alone possess the very *elongated* antennæ.

1. Hylodromus dilaticornis. (Tab. V. fig. 7.)

H. *oblongo-ovalis, subdepressus, subpubescens, fuscus; capite brevi, ad basin antennarum prominulo; thorace quadrato, ad basin constricto, crebre punctato, subpubescenti, flavo; elytris sat robustis, subcylindricis, punctato-striatis, subpubescentibus, nigrofuscis (ad apicem rufo-suffusis); antennis, art. 1mo elongato, a 3^{tio} gradatim ad 6^{tum} maxime incrassatis, 7mo–11mo abrupte et tenue filiformibus, flavis aut fusco-rufis; pedibus, anterioribus flavis, posticis flavo-ferrugineis.*

Long. corp. 1¾ lin., lat. ¾ lin.

Oblong-ovate, subdepressed, broad, subpubescent, fuscous. *Head* not so transverse as in allied genera, vertically depressed, hardly elongated; eyes large, prominent, situated nearly at the base of the head, and extending laterally as far as the angles of the thorax: between the eyes (nearer to their lower surface) is a distinct elevation, upon which is situated the base of the antennæ; this elevation is not so angulated or abrupt as in *Loxoprosopus*: between the antennæ, at their base, a minute fovea extends upwards, and is continued in an obsolete longitudinal ridge towards the base of the head; on either side of this fovea are two depressions, nearer to the inner surface of the eyes: the surface is flavous and finely punctate. *Thorax* quadrate (slightly transverse), constricted towards the base; the anterior angles are depressed; the surface subequate, finely and thickly punctate, subpubescent, flavous. *Scutellum* small, triangular, fusco-flavous. *Elytra* broader than the thorax, subparallel, equate, punctate-striate (the punctures being broad, and the striæ almost obsolete), finely pubescent; dark fuscous, suffused with ferrugineous at the apex. *Antennæ* tolerably long, robust; the first joint broad and long (extending, when placed horizontally, beyond the outer margin of the eye); the second short, narrow; from the third to the sixth the joints are gradually but strongly incrassated, so that the sixth joint is nearly three times the breadth of the second; the rest of the joints are abruptly and finely filiform, the seventh being slightly larger, and the eighth to eleventh narrower and longer than the second; in colour, the joints first to third are flavous, the fourth to eleventh rufous, the fifth, sixth, and apex of the eleventh being rufo-fuscous. *Legs*: the anterior flavous; the postical flavo-ferrugineous.

From the district of the River Amazon.

Genus 23. CŒLOCEPHALUS*.

PALPI MAXILLARES *elongati, art. penultimo cylindrico, ad basin subconstricto, art. ultimo brevi, haud attenuato.*

PALPI LABIALES *cylindrici, minuti.*

ANTENNÆ *filiformes, elongatæ, elytris duplo longiores.*

CAPUT *breve, antice productum, verticale.*

THORAX *quadratus, rectilinearis, ad basin subconstrictus.*

ELYTRA *subcylindrica, parallela, punctato-striata, subpubescentia.*

PEDES: *tibiarum articulo secundo minuto; tarsis posticis haud dentatis, ad apicem dilatatis.*

Mandibles concealed.

Maxillary palpi (Tab. V. fig. 8 *m*) elongate; the second joint truncate at its apex; the penultimate somewhat broader, cylindrical, its length being double its breadth; the apical joint is broadly conical.

Labial palpi elongate, minute.

Antennæ approximate, situated at the anterior angle of the head, filiform, attenuate, elongated; in form, length, and position closely corresponding to the antennæ of *Loxoprosopus*; the first joint is broad, dilated, and incurved outwards towards the apex; the second short and ovate, the following elongate and attenuate, the whole being twice the length of the elytra.

Eyes globose, situated at the base of the head, and extending laterally as far as the anterior angles of the thorax.

Head resembling that of *Loxoprosopus*, short, transverse, broadly

* κοῖλος, cavus; κεφαλή, caput.

produced in front, *abruptly* inflected (near the insertion of the antennæ) at right angles to the base and thorax.

Thorax quadrate, rectilinear, broader than the head, constricted and transversely depressed at the base.

Scutellum in the same plane as the elytra, indistinct, triangular.

Elytra broader than the thorax, parallel, subcylindrical, deeply punctate-striate, and clothed sparingly with pubescence.

Legs: the *anterior femora* (when viewed from the front) tolerably robust, and attenuated towards the apex. The *tibiæ* abruptly inflected at the extreme base, straight, and gradually thickened towards the apex. The *tarsus* (Tab. V. fig. 8 *h*) is short and broad; the two basal joints are triangular, the *second being shorter and more minute than the first* (in *Loxoprosopus* the basal joint is *minute*, and the second more elongated); the third broader, short, and almost bilobed; the margins and under surface are clothed with a rigid thick pubescence; the apical joint is elongated, subincurved, and terminates in a bifid claw. The *posterior femora* are incrassated, gradually tapering towards the apex. The *tibiæ* are short, distinctly incurved at the immediate base, subattenuated medially, and broadly dilated towards the apex, which is obliquely truncate; the socket which is thus formed, is, when viewed under a high magnifying power ($\frac{1}{2}$-inch Ross), fringed at its margination with minute comb-like teeth, and terminates ultimately in a strong (not incurved) projecting spur. The *tarsi* are elongate and narrow; the first joint longer than the second (both being dilated at the apex); the third subrotundate; the fourth elongated, and terminating in a large globular inflation immediately above the apical claw.

This genus is very closely allied to *Loxoprosopus*, and is, in fact, only to be separated from it by the form (distinctly cylindrical and elongate, not abruptly dilated) of the maxillary palpi, and by the relative lengths of the joints of the anterior tarsus.

1. Cœlocephalus pulchellus. (Tab. VI. fig. 4.) B.M.

C. *oblongo-ovatus, parallelus, subtiliter pubescens, fusco-niger; capite depresso, rufo-flavo; thorace subquadrato, ad basin tenue constricto, impunctato, rufo-flavo; elytris parallelis, punctato-striatis; pedibus flavis, femoribus posticis fusco adumbratis.*

Long. corp. 2 lin., lat. $\frac{2}{3}$ lin.

Oblong-ovate, parallel, depressed, subpubescent, punctate, of a greyish-black colour. *Head* depressed, vertical; between the eyes is a longitudinal medial fovea (in different examples more or less obsolete); eyes large, globose, lateral, situated at the base of the head; the surface is finely punctate, impubescent, rufo-flavous. *Thorax* transverse (almost quadrate); the anterior angles depressed; the sides marginate; the base constricted, but not so apparently as in *C. amœnus*, and transversely depressed; the surface is impunctate, flavo-pubescent and rufo-flavous. *Scutellum* triangular, pubescent, fuscous. *Elytra* broader than the thorax, parallel, punctate-striate, the punctures being coarse and shallow; black, obsoletely flavo-pubescent. *Antennæ* approximate, filiform, fusco-ferrugineous. *Legs* flavous, the posterior femora being suffused with fuscous.

Taken by Mr. Bates in the district of the River Amazon. In the collection of the British Museum, and also in that of Mr. Baly.

2. Cœlocephalus amœnus.

C. *oblongo-ovatus, parallelus, subtiliter pubescens, nigro-fuscus; capite brevi, impunctato, flavo; thorace quadrato, ad basin constricto et transverse depresso, flavo; elytris parallelis, striato-punctatis, subpubescentibus, nigro-fuscis, sutura et apice flavo marginatis; antennis filiformibus, ferrugineis, art. 9–11 flavis; pedibus flavis.*

Long. corp. 2 lin., lat. ⅔ lin.

Oblong-ovate, parallel, depressed, obsoletely pubescent, punctate, of a dark fuscous colour. *Head* short, not produced in front, vertical, or somewhat reflected backwards below the base of the antennæ; above the labrum is a transverse triangular depression; eyes small, globose, lateral, situated at the base of the head; the surface is impunctate, of a pale flavous colour. *Thorax* quadrate, more elongate than in *C. pulchellus*, and the base more distinctly constricted; the anterior angles are depressed; the sides rectilinear; the surface transversely depressed at the anterior and basal margins, subglobose, impunctate, flavous, obsoletely flavo-pubescent. *Scutellum* triangular, flavo-pubescent, flavous. *Elytra* broader than the thorax, parallel, depressed, with rows of punctures arranged in the form of striæ; these punctures are broad and shallow; the surface is subpubescent, of a dull fuscous colour,—the line of the suture, and also the apex, being bordered with a narrow, well-defined suffused line of flavous. *Antennæ* approximate at their insertion, filiform, ferrugineous, the three apical joints being flavous. *Legs* flavous throughout, the apical inflation of the postical claw being rufo-flavous.

Closely allied to *C. pulchellus*, from which species it may be readily separated by the absence of any marking between the eyes, by the quadrate and posteriorly constricted form of the thorax, and by the sutural flavous band on the elytra.

Ega, district of the River Amazon.

3. Cœlocephalus pygmæus. (Tab. V. fig. 8.)

C. oblongo-ovalis, subparallelus, robustus, pallide testaceus; capite brevi, reflexo, juxta antennarum insertionem bituberculato, punctato, pallide testaceo, ad basin nigro suffuso; thorace quadrato, ad basin constricto et transverse depresso, punctato; elytris robustis, parallelis, punctato-striatis, leviter flavo-pubescentibus, ad basin macula nigra semicirculari notatis, etiamque post medium duabus maculis triangularibus suffusis; antennis elongatis, filiformibus, testaceis; pedibus pallide testaceis.

Long. corp. 1¾ lin., lat. ¾ lin.

Oblong-oval, subparallel, robust, pale testaceous. *Head* short, slightly produced, reflected backwards at an acute angle; eyes large, very prominent, projecting laterally beyond the margin of the thorax; the antennæ are inserted in a slight projection from the surface (which extends a little in front of the margin of the eyes); behind the insertion of the antennæ are two indistinct tubercles, which are formed by an obsolete Y-shaped fovea; the surface is punctate, especially at the base, and in colour pale testaceous; at the upper margin (between the eyes) suffused with black. *Thorax* quadrate, distinctly constricted at the base (more so than in *C. fusco-costatus*); the anterior angles are depressed; the sides submarginate; at the base is a broad transverse depression, extending to the lateral submargination; the surface is finely punctate. *Scutellum* triangular, impunctate, fuscous. *Elytra* broad, robust, parallel, punctate-striate, very finely flavo-pubescent; at the base is a large black marking, common to both elytra, semicircular in form, of the breadth of the base of the thorax: two other markings, triangular, and more suffused, are situated postmedially; these do not reach the margination, or the suture, and are at some little distance from the extreme apex. *Antennæ* fine, filiform, more than twice the length of the elytra, pale fulvo-testaceous. *Legs* somewhat long and attenuated, pale testaceous throughout.

This species differs from *C. fusco-costatus* in the form of its thorax, which is more constricted at the base, in its pale concolorous antennæ, and in the absence of any suffused marking at the margination of the elytra. Although in other respects these insects are almost identical, it is difficult to believe that these differences (differences both of form and colour) can be the result of variation, and equally difficult to believe that they are sexual, inasmuch as the length of the antennæ, which would be the principal sexual characteristic, is the same in each.

From the district of the River Amazon.

4. Cœlocephalus fusco-costatus.

C. *oblongo-ovatus, robustus, pallide testaceus; capite brevi, reflexo, inter oculos transverse depresso, punctato, inter oculos fusco suffuso; thorace quadrato (subelongato), ad basin constricto et transverse depresso, punctulato; elytris sat robustis, parallelis, punctato-striatis, ad basin medium circulariter maculatis, etiamque transverse ad mediam suturam; lateribus fusco suffusis; antennis longis, filiformibus, art. 1–3 fuscis, 4 et 5 testaceis, 6 fusco, 7 et 8 nigro-fuscis, 9–11 testaceis; pedibus pallide testaceis.*

Long. corp. 2 lin., lat. ⅔ lin.

Oblong-ovate, rather *more* parallel than *C. pygmæus*, robust, punctate-striate, subpubescent, pale testaceous. *Head* short, depressed, reflected backwards at a sharp and acute angle; eyes large, very prominent, projecting laterally beyond the margin of the thorax, situated immediately at the back of the head; the base of the antennæ is prominent, and situated directly on the angle of reflection; immediately above it, and between the eyes, is an obsolete T-shaped depression; the surface is finely punctate, more distinctly at the base, between the eyes suffused with dark fuscous. *Thorax* quadrate (slightly elongated), distinctly constricted at the base; the anterior angles depressed; the sides marginate; at the base is a broad transverse depression, which extends as far as the margination; the surface is finely punctate, subpubescent. *Scutellum* triangular, fuscous. *Elytra* broad, robust, parallel, broadly punctate-striate (the punctures being broad and shallow), subpubescent: at the base is a large semicircular spot common to each elytron and surrounding the scutellum (this marking is equal in breadth to the base of the thorax); at the line of margination is a longitudinal suffused fuscous marking, extending from the shoulders nearly to the apex, while on the suture (between the middle and the base) is a small suffused fulvous marking, obliquely transverse. *Antennæ* twice the length of the elytra, filiform; the first and second joints dilated; the first, second, and base of the third fuscous; the fourth and fifth testaceous; the sixth fuscous; the seventh and base of the eighth dark fuscous, inclined to black; the rest pale testaceous. *Legs* pale testaceous throughout; the globular inflation over the posterior claw bright ferrugineous.

This species may be distinguished from *C. pygmæus* (to which it is very closely allied) by the different form of the thorax, the colouring of its antennæ, and the fuscous margination on its elytra.

From the district of the River Amazon.

TRIBUS II.

Palpi maxillares ad apicem incrassati (articulo ultimo interdum minuto), articulo tertio subgloboso aut transverso, nunquam elongato, rarius quadrato.

Genus 24. LOXOPROSOPUS*.

Guérin-Mén. (Icon. Règne Anim. 1829–38, p. 306).
Dohrn, Linn. Ent. 1855, p. 329. tab. 2. fig. 3, 4.
Thompson, Archives, vol. i. p. 289.

LABRUM *subsinuatum, breve.*

PALPI MAXILLARES *validi, incrassati, art.* 3^{tio} *globoso, ultimo brevi.*

PALPI LABIALES *elongati.*

ANTENNÆ *filiformes, in ♂ longissimæ.*

CAPUT *transversum, antice verticale.*

THORAX *rectangularis, transversus, antea submarginatus; lateribus marginatis, et in angulum productis.*

ELYTRA *parallela, depressa, punctato-striata.*

PEDES *robusti; tibiis posticis simplicibus, haud dente armatis.*

Labrum short, transverse, subsinuate.

Maxillary palpi (Tab. VI. fig. 1 *m*) robust, short, incrassated; the second joint conical, broader than the basal, obliquely truncate at the apex; the third globose, nearly twice the breadth of the second, and the breadth not less than the length; the terminal joint is *short* and circular, broadly flattened.

Labial palpi (Tab. VI. fig. 1 *n*) elongate; the penultimate joint is slightly thickened at the apex; the terminal joint attenuate.

Antennæ filiform, in the males very long, twice the length of the body; the first joint is broadly flattened towards the apex; the second ovate; the third to the fifth subequal, attenuated, slightly thickened at the apex, nearly double the length of the basal joint; the terminal joints are somewhat shorter and narrower; the antennæ are in position approximate, situated at the frontal angle, on a transverse prolongation of the head.

Eyes tolerably large, lateral, situated at the base of the head, and extending laterally not quite so far as the anterior angles of the thorax; in the males more globose and prominent than in the females.

Head (Tab. VI. fig. 1 *k*) short, transverse, abruptly deflected backwards at less than a right angle immediately below the insertion of

* λοξὸς, obliquus; πρόσωπον, frons.

the antennæ; between this angle and the labrum (when viewed transversely) is a concave plane depression, extending across the breadth of the anterior surface; at the base also (when viewed laterally) is a transverse depression, which gives a gibbous appearance to the surface between it and the insertion of the antennæ.

Thorax broader than the head, transverse, rectangular, in front *slightly* emarginate; the sides are broadly marginate, the margination being generally produced into an angle; the base is transversely subdepressed: in the males the thorax is more quadrate and smaller than in the females.

Scutellum broadly triangular.

Elytra parallel, depressed, broader than the thorax, and rounded at the apex; the surface is equate and punctate-striate, pubescent or glabrous.

Legs: the *anterior femora* robust, subparallel, slightly attenuated towards the apex. The *tibiæ* are distinctly incurved at their immediate base, gradually incrassated towards the apex, and at the extremity transversely truncate. The *tarsi* are short and broad; the basal joint being *abbreviated*, in form broadly triangular; the second is slightly narrower, and more attenuated at the apex; the third is broader than the first and bilobed; these three joints are at their margins and undersides coarsely pubescent; the terminal joint is elongated and incurved, situated at the base of the third, and subdilated towards the apex: the claw is robust, bifid, and armed at its inner surface with a strong blunt spur. The *posterior femora* are short and (when viewed transversely) broadly dilated, tapering towards the apex, which is truncate. The *tibiæ* are robust, slightly incurved at their immediate base, and at the apex broadly flattened out into a socket, which receives the insertion of the tarsus. The *tarsus* is short and attenuate; the first joint being narrow, less produced than the second, and subdilated at the apex; the second is more elongate; the third subovate; and the terminal joint produced into a globular inflation, which completely conceals from above the apical claw.

The *Saperda*-like head and general facies, as well as the enormous length of the antennæ of the insects of this group, suggest at once the propriety of removing this genus entirely away from the Phytophaga, and placing it among the Longicornia; and, indeed, if the only data from which we could form an opinion as to its true position were, on the one side, the head and antennæ of a Longicorn, and on the other, the incrassated posterior femora of the group of Halticidæ, it would perhaps be difficult to decide as to which it had the most affinity: for while many of the Galerucidæ (i. e. *Luperus*, and, to some extent, *Calomicrus*) show a manifest tendency to an elongation of the antennæ; other groups, confessedly *not* Galerucidæ (e. g. *Hypocephalus armatus, Necrodes,* and *Sagra*), have the thickened posterior thigh; and some, like the genus *Orchestes,* have even the power of leaping. The structure of the maxillary palpi, however (combined with the globular inflation of the posterior claw), seems to be decisive, and leads us, without hesitation, to admit the genus into the present group, as very nearly allied to *Octogonotes*.

In this genus, the males are at once to be recognized from the females by their enormously elongated antennæ; the thorax, moreover, in the ♂ is less broadly transverse, more nearly quadrate, the elytra are slightly less robust, the head is narrower and longer, the eyes are larger and more globose, and in the antennæ the two basal joints are very much more robust, as well as elongated.

1. Loxoprosopus ceramboides. (Tab. VI. fig. 1.)

L. (♂) *oblongus, ovalis, subdepressus, parallelus, niger; capite leviter producto, reflexo, nigro; thorace transverso, rectangulari, ad medium depresso, rufo-marginato, nigro; elytris subpubescentibus, punctato-striatis, nigris, rufo marginatis; antennis longissimis, fusco-nigris; pedibus fusco-nigris.*

♂ Long. corp. $4\frac{1}{2}$ lin., lat. $1\frac{3}{4}$ lin.
♂ Long. antenn. 10–11 lin.

Oblong, oval, parallel, subcylindrical, slightly depressed. *Head* very short and transverse (when viewed from above); at the insertion of the antennæ (which are contiguous), the head is sharply reflected at an acute angle (the anterior part being inclined backwards in the direction of the thorax), and slightly produced; eyes tolerably prominent, not large, situated at the base of the head, extending laterally nearly to the line of the apical angle of the thorax: the antennæ (when viewed from above) appear to be situated on a gibbous projection, which stands out from beyond the line of the eyes; this projection is divided by a longitudinal channel, is well-defined, and also bounded at the base by a distinct transverse shallow groove; at the extreme apex of this projection are two globular fuscous sockets, from which spring the base of the antennæ; surface *below* the antennæ subpubescent, lævigate, black, with a narrow margin on either side pale testaceous; *above* the antennæ finely granulated, black. *Thorax* slightly broader than the head, transverse, rectangular, equate, without any important definite elevations (a slight shallow fovea is apparent at the middle of the disc); anterior angles subacute, sides marginate; surface almost impunctate, obsoletely pubescent, black; margination of the sides fulvous. *Scutellum* obscure, triangular, black.

Elytra rather broader than the thorax, parallel, subcylindrical, faintly but regularly punctate-striate, clothed throughout with short dense fuscous pubescence; black; sides evenly bounded with fuscous, more broadly behind the shoulders, and not reaching the apex. *Antennæ* filiform, very long (in the males between two and three times the length of the body), subpubescent, fuscous, with the base of each joint flavous. *Legs* tolerably robust, flavous throughout.

Guérin-Méneville (Icon. Règne Animal, Cuv.), in his description of this species, speaks, with reference to the thorax, of "près des angles antérieurs une fossette ronde au milieu en avant, et une large fossette transversale, un peu arquée près du bord postérieur." In the two examples which I have had the opportunity of examining, there is very little trace of such depressions: it is evident that in this respect the species is subject to some variation, for we cannot assume the thoracic sculpturing to be sexual, inasmuch as his specimen (as the examples before me) was clearly a male.

Rio Janeiro and the neighbourhood. A single example of this fine species in the collections of M. Chevrolat, Mr. Fry, Mr. Miers, and Herr Dohrn.

2. **Loxoprosopus marginatus.** (Tab. VI. fig. 2.)

L. oblongo-ovatus, subcylindricus, niger, subtiliter pubescens; capite brevi, transverso, antice lævigato, testaceo, triangulari macula fusca notato, superne granulato, transverse foveolato, fulvo-ferrugineo, inter oculos fusco; thorace transverso, rectangulari, punctato, fulvo, ad medium suffuso fusco; elytris robustis, punctato-striatis, pubescentibus, nigro-fuscis, ad marginem (et ad suturam obsolete) fulvis; antennis filiformibus, elongatis, nigro-fuscis, ad basin articulorum rufo-fulvis; pedibus ferrugineis, tibiis anterioribus femoribusque (ad basin) posticis nigro-fuscis.

Long. corp. 2⅛ lin., lat. 1 lin.

♂ Long. antenn. circa 4 lin.

Oblong-ovate, subcylindrical, somewhat depressed, finely pubescent, of a fuscous-black colour. *Head* short, transverse, abruptly deflected at an acute angle in front; labrum dark fuscous; the anterior part of the head (between the base of the antennæ and the mouth) is a smooth plane, lævigate, testaceous, with a triangular fuscous marking; eyes slightly prominent, distant, extending laterally as far as the line of the sides of the thorax; antennæ approximate at their insertion, which is situated on the angle caused by the abrupt inflection of the head: from the insertion of the antennæ to the base is a more or less distinct medial fovea, while crossing it at right angles (at some distance from the insertion of the antennæ) is another horizontal fovea; on either side of and below the point of intersection are two distinct and prominent tubercles: the upper surface of the head is granulated and fulvo-ferrugineous, with a dark-fuscous band above the base of the antennæ and between the eyes. *Thorax* transverse, rectangular, having the anterior and basal angles distinctly defined; the sides are parallel and straight; a broad but slight postmedial depression extends obliquely on either side in the direction of the humeral angles; the surface is distinctly punctate, fulvous, with two medial clouded markings of fuscous. *Scutellum* small, triangular, fuscous. *Elytra* robust, strongly punctate-striate, clothed at the base, and also at the sides and along the suture, with a slight ashy pubescence; in colour dark fuscous, the suture being (by reason of the pubescence) narrowly fulvous, and the sides also being marked by a fulvous line, which at the shoulder is distinct and broadly defined, but becomes obsolete as it approaches the extremity. *Antennæ* much longer than the body, filiform; the first joint narrow at the base and dilated towards the apex; the second short, ovate, not broader than the base of the first; the third, fourth, fifth and sixth very long, attenuate, somewhat dilated at the apex; in colour dark fuscous, with the base of the second, third, fourth and fifth fulvous. *Legs* ferrugineous, with the anterior tibiæ and part of the tarsi, and also the apex of the posterior femora, dark fuscous.

From the district of the River Amazon.

3. Loxoprosopus humeralis. B.M.

L. *oblongo-ovatus, parallelus, sat robustus, fulvus; capite brevi, subproducto, super basin antennarum bituberculato; thorace transverso, angulis anticis distinctis, ad basin et ad latera late depresso, punctato, fulvo, ad medium piceo; elytris parallelis, punctato-striatis, ad basin sparsim pubescentibus, fuscis, ad latera flavo-lineatis; antennis filiformibus, art. 1–5 flavo-fuscis, 6–11 fuscis; pedibus fuscis, femoribus ad basin flavis, tibiis tarsisque posticis rufo-flavis.*

Long. corp. 2 lin., lat. 1 lin.

Oblong-ovate, parallel, finely pubescent, fuscous black, occasionally fulvous. *Head* short, transverse, and, when viewed laterally, reflected in front backwards at an acute angle to the base; the anterior and lower portion of the head (which is somewhat produced) is almost impunctate, black, shining; from the labrum a triangular marking extends to the insertion of the antennæ; the antennæ are approximate, and on the angle caused by the abrupt reflection; eyes distant, situate at the base of the head, and not extending laterally as far as the line of the margin of the thorax; between the eyes (and immediately above the insertion of the antennæ) are two small transverse tubercles, while behind them (between them and the base of the head) is a medial depression; the upper surface of the head is fulvous. *Thorax* transverse, slightly constricted at the base; the anterior angles (which extend beyond the base of the head) are depressed, subacute, and distinct; sides submarginate: at the base is a broad and well-defined transverse depression, which extends obliquely upwards in a broad lateral depression towards the anterior angles; this lateral and basal depression gives a circular and subglobular form to the anterior and medial surface, which is finely and thickly punctate: fulvous, except the surface immediately in front of the basal depression, which is piceous, this darker colour adumbrating more or less the whole of the raised portion of the disc,—the line of margination and the anterior margin being also narrowly and obscurely fuscous. *Scutellum* broad, triangular, obscure, below the plane of the elytra, darkly fuscous. *Elytra* parallel, tolerably robust, coarsely punctate-striate, imperfectly clothed at the apex with fine ashy or fuscous pubescence; from the humeral angles (which extend beyond the base of the thorax) a line of flavous colouring is produced along the margination, most distinctly at the shoulders; occasionally the suture also is margined with flavous. *Antennæ* equal in length to the body; the first joint distinctly incrassated at the apex; the second short, ovate, and much less robust; the third longer than the first; the fourth and fifth nearly equal, and shorter than the first; the rest short, with a distinct tendency to dilatation, and subpubescent: the first joint is in colour rufo-fuscous; the second fuscous; the third, fourth and fifth flavous, with the apex fuscous; and the rest dark fuscous. *Legs* pale flavous, with the anterior tarsi, tibiæ, and upper portion of the femora, and also the apex of the posterior femora, fuscous.

Collected by Mr. Bates at Santarem (Amazon). A single specimen in the collection of the British Museum; in the collections also of Mr. Bates and the Rev. H. Clark.

This species is subject to considerable variation in the closeness of the pubescence, and also in the flavous margination of the elytra; in one example before me the thorax is entirely flavous, and the sutural and marginal band of flavous well-defined and broad.

4. Loxoprosopus cæruleus.

L. *oblongo-ovatus, robustus, nigro-cyaneus, nitidus; capite brevi, ad apicem reflexo, impunctato, fulvo-ferrugineo; thorace transverso, rectangulari, ad basin distincte transverse depresso, apud angulos anticos etiam obsolete depresso, nitido, fulvo-ferrugineo; elytris robustis, subcylindricis, striato-punctatis, nigro-cyaneis, ad suturam tenuiter flavo-pubescentibus ; antennis elongatis, filiformibus, art. 1–4 flavis, 5–8 fuscis, 9–11 testaceis ; pedibus flavis.*

Long. corp. 1¾–2¼ lin., lat. ¾–1¼ lin.

Oblong-ovate, robust, of a deep-blue colour, shining. *Head* very short, transverse, when viewed laterally abruptly deflected; eyes large, prominent, distant, reaching laterally as far as the line of the margin of the thorax; between the eyes and immediately above the insertion of the antennæ (which are approximate) are two distinct tubercles; the surface of the head is smooth, impunctate and fulvo-ferrugineous, with four distinct but obscure linear thread-like markings, extending each from the middle of the base, the *two outer* ones to the margin of the eyes, the *two inner* ones to the two tubercles between the eyes. *Thorax* transverse, rectangular; the sides are parallel and very slightly marginate: at the base is a broad transverse depression (with a slight depression also at the anterior angles), which gives an appearance of prominence to the anterior disc; these depressions are finely clothed with pubescence: the surface of the thorax is smooth (under a high power very finely punctate) and fulvo-ferrugineous. *Scutellum* triangular, flavous, distinct. *Elytra* robust, subcylindrical, with punctures arranged in the form of striæ, of a bright dark-blue colour; the line of the suture, by reason of a fine margin of pubescence, is pale flavous; the shoulders are slightly prominent; the whole surface is clothed with minute and sparingly distributed pubescence. *Antennæ* more than twice the length of the elytra, filiform; the first joint dilated; the second minute, short, and ovate; the four basal joints flavous, fifth to eighth fuscous, ninth to eleventh testaceous. *Legs* flavous.

Brazil, district of the River Amazon. In the collections of Messrs. Baly and Bates, and the Rev. H. Clark.

Genus 25. PERIBLEPTUS*.

LABRUM *subsinuatum aut circulare.*

PALPI MAXILLARES *elongatuli et ad apicem dilatati, art. penultimo maximo, ultimo brevi.*

PALPI LABIALES *subcylindrici.*

ANTENNÆ *filiformes, attenuatæ, in ♂ corpore fere duplo longiores, art. 3, 4 et 5 subæqualibus.*

CAPUT *breve, transversum, depressum, verticale, haud antice productum.*

---

* περίβλεπτος, omnibus admiratus, eximius : περί, circum ; βλέπω, video.

Thorax *transversus, ad basin leviter constrictus, lateribus marginatis, subsinuatis, sparsim punctatus.*

Elytra *lata, robusta, parallela, ante medium transverse depressa, punctato-striata.*

Pedes *robusti; tibiis posticis brevibus, inarmatis, ungulis apicalibus dente robusto ab infra armatis.*

Labrum short, circular or subsinuate in outline.

Maxillary palpi (Tab. VI. fig. 3 *m*) subelongate, dilated at the apex; the second joint is longer than the first, and gradually incrassated; the penultimate is considerably broader (as well as longer) than the second; the last joint is short, narrower, and more or less flattened.

Labial palpi attenuate, more or less cylindrical.

Antennæ situated between (and somewhat below) the eyes, filiform, attenuate, in the males at least twice the length of the body; the first joint is elongate, slightly thickened towards the apex, and inflected outwards; the second is shorter and more attenuate; the third distinctly longer than the first; the fourth and fifth subequal; in the males these three last-named joints are relatively as long as in the genus *Loxoprosopus*; the remaining joints are filiform and subcylindrical.

Eyes circular, globose, lateral, situate at (or close to) the base of the head.

Head short, transverse, depressed, and at the insertion of the antennæ (when viewed laterally) vertical or almost reflected backwards, not produced in front; at the insertion of the antennæ, the angle which is formed by the reflection of the head is sharp and well-defined, not rounded, thus closely resembling the preceding genus, *Loxoprosopus*; the surface is more or less punctate.

Thorax transverse, rectangular; the anterior angles subacute and depressed; the sides marginate and subsinuate, with a tendency to an angle near the middle; at the base slightly constricted; the surface, in the example before me, is coarsely and sparingly punctate and glabrous.

Scutellum large, triangular, impunctate, situated in the plane of the elytra.

Elytra broad, parallel, robust, broader and more robust than in *Loxoprosopus*, and distinguished moreover from that genus by a broad antemedial transverse depression, which extends obliquely upwards to the shoulders, and gives a prominence to the scutellary angles; the surface in the example before me is deeply punctate-striate, the striæ being obsolete near the suture and at the apex.

Legs robust. The *anterior femora* cylindrical, and slightly dilated medially. The *tibiæ* are distinctly deflected at their immediate base, cylindrical, and hardly dilated at the apex. Of the *tarsi* the first joint is broad and elongate, triangular; the second more minute; the third broader than the first, bilobed; the terminal joint is elongated, the claw being armed at its inner surface on either side near the base with a sharp tooth. The *posterior femora* are broadly incrassated. The *tibiæ* are short, robust, not incurved medially, and attenuated; the posterior surface is flattened, and hollowed out or marginate: this margination at the apex forms a socket for the insertion of the tarsus; the margins of the socket are simple; the extreme apex is armed (behind the insertion of the tarsus) with a single robust spur. The *tarsus* is short and attenuated, the two basal joints being slightly dilated at their apex; the third joint subcircular; the fourth terminating in a globular inflation.

This genus, though closely allied to *Loxoprosopus*, is certainly very distinct. The angulated or subsinuate lateral margin of the thorax, the broad and very apparent transverse depression on the elytra, and its generally robust form will at once characterize it. It is an interesting link between *Loxoprosopus* and the following genus, *Octogonotes*: to the former it is allied by its elongate antennæ and its abruptly vertical head; to the latter genus by the angular form of the lateral margins of the thorax.

1. Peribleptus lævigatus. (Tab. VI. fig. 3.)

P. *ovatus, robustus, parallelus; capite brevi, reflexo, supra basin antennarum bituberculato, punctato, antea nigro, superne flavo; thorace transverso, ad basin subattenuato, transverse depresso, punctato, flavo, antice et ad medium longitudinaliter suffuso fusco; elytris punctato-striatis (ad suturam striis obsoletis), transverse apud medium depressis, nigro-fuscis, ad humeros longitudinaliter flavo-notatis; antennis longis, tenuibus, filiformibus, flavis, art. 7 et 8 fuscis, 9–11 pallide testaceis; pedibus pallide testaceis.*

Long. corp. 2 lin., lat. 1 lin.

Ovate, robust; sides parallel. *Head* short, transverse, depressed, and (below the insertion of the antennæ) reflected; eyes tolerably large, distant, situated nearly at the base of the head, and extending laterally as far as the line of the margin of the thorax; above the insertion of the antennæ are two slightly transverse and approximate tubercles; the surface is punctate; the colour in front black, at the base flavous. *Thorax* transverse (almost quadrate), slightly narrowed towards the base; the anterior angles are prominent; the sides are marginate and, medially, slightly dilated; the posterior angles are distinct and subacute; at the base a broad shallow transverse depression extends obliquely towards the anterior angles, giving a prominence and a rotundate appearance to the disc; the surface is punctate, in colour flavous, with the anterior margins and two medial longitudinal indistinct markings rufo-fuscous. *Scutellum* triangular, distinct, flavous. *Elytra* punctate-striate (the striæ being less distinct towards the suture); an antemedial depression extends *upwards* along the suture, and obliquely to the humeral angles, giving a rotundate and subglobose form to the base of either elytron; the surface is lævigate, and of a dark-fuscous colour, gradually shading off towards the apex into testaceous; at the humeral angles (and extending partially along the margination) is a light-flavous marking. *Antennæ* of the length of the body, filiform; the first joint incrassated towards the apex and inflected outwards; the second short, ovate; the third longer than the first, fine, and slightly incrassated at the apex; fourth and fifth nearly equal; seventh to eleventh with a distinct tendency to dilatation; in colour, first to sixth flavous, seventh and eighth dark fuscous, ninth to eleventh pale testaceous. *Legs* pale testaceous, infuscated at the base of the posterior femora (suggesting, from their general appearance, the immaturity of the example); the globular inflation of the posterior claw bright red.

A single specimen was captured by Mr. Gray at Petropolis (Organ Mountains), February 1857.

Genus 26. OCTOGONOTES*.

Drap. Ann. des Sc. Phys. vol. iii. p. 181.
Dej. Cat. ed. 3 (1837), p. 407.
Laporte, Hist. Nat. des Anim. Artic. Coleopt. (1840) vol. ii. p. 519.
Hope, Coleopt. Manual, vol. iii. (1840) p. 169.
Orbigny, Dictionnaire d'Histoire Naturelle (1841, &c.).

LABRUM *latum, ad latera rotundatum.*

MANDIBULÆ *robustæ, ad apicem acuminatæ, ad basin denticulatæ.*

PALPI MAXILLARES *inflati, art. 2^{ndo} sensim incrassato, 3^{tio} abbreviato, valde dilatato, ultimo subulato, depresso.*

PALPI LABIALES *elongati, subcylindrici, ad apicem attenuati.*

ANTENNÆ *filiformes, robustæ, in ♂ subattenuatæ et productæ.*

OCULI *distantes, in ♂ globosi.*

CAPUT *haud productum, breve, depressum.*

THORAX *transversus, ad latera angulatus, plerumque complanatus.*

* ὀκτώ, octo; γωνία, angulus.

Elytra *sat robusta, parallela, ad apicem rotundata, punctato-striata.*
Pedes *robusti, tibiis posticis simplicibus, haud calcare armatis, marginatione retro subsinuata.*

Labrum broad, subcircular.

Mandibles (Tab. VI. fig. 5 *o*) robust, subconvex, broad, at the apex attenuated and produced into a sharp tooth; on the inner surface are two angulated depressions, which form a second, much smaller and more obtuse tooth.

Maxillary palpi (Tab. VI. fig. 5 *m*) globose; the basal joint minute, almost obsolete; the second short, gradually thickened towards the apex, where it is broadly obliquely truncate; the penultimate is inflated, much thicker and shorter than the second, increasing in diameter towards the apex; the apical joint is subulate, circular, and *flattened*, not acute, or conical.

Labial palpi (Tab. VI. fig. 5 *n*) minute, elongated; the second joint subcylindrical, broader than the first; the apical attenuate.

Antennæ filiform, robust (in the males very much elongated); the basal joint produced, and dilated towards the apex; the second short, ovate (these two joints in the ♀ less dilated and smaller than in the ♂); the third, fourth and fifth subequal (in the ♂ slightly attenuate).

Eyes large, situated at the base of the head, not extending laterally so far as the anterior angles of the thorax; in the males globose, in the females less prominent.

Head short, hardly produced in front, almost vertical.

Thorax broader than the head, transverse (in the males less transverse than in the females), constricted towards the apex; the sides marginate, the margination being produced antemedially (more or less distinctly) into an obtuse angle.

Scutellum large, triangular, rounded at the apex.

Elytra broad, robust, in the males slightly more attenuate than in the females, rounded at the apex, punctate-striate or punctate, clothed more or less with fine pubescence.

Legs: the *anterior femora* robust. The *tibia* incurved at its immediate base, gradually thickened towards the apex; at the extreme apex (*below* the insertion of the tarsus), on the under side, it is armed with a series of closely arranged comb-like teeth. The *tarsus* (Tab. VI. fig. 5 *d*) is broad and short; the basal joint contracted at the base, and triangular; the second is of the same form, but *larger* in dimensions; the third is broadly transverse, depressed medially, not bilobed; from its centre proceeds the terminal joint, which is elongate, gradually incurved and incrassated towards the apex: the claw is bifid, thickened at the base, not armed on the inner surface with an inferior tooth. *Posterior femora* incrassated, ovate, at the apex grooved for the reception of the tibia. The *tibia* (Tab. VI. fig. 6 *g*) short, straight: when seen from behind, the posterior surface is flattened, marginate, and near the apex depressed into a longitudinal groove; this margination is not produced (as in the genus *Monoplatus*) into a spur, but is in outline subsinuate; at the apex the tibia is dilated, and margined near the insertion of the tarsus with a series of sharp and regularly disposed comb-like teeth; the extreme apex is produced into two robust incurved claws. *Tarsi* attenuate; the first joint elongate, dilated at the apex; the second of the same form, but shorter; the third minute, ovate; the fourth produced into a globular inflation, which conceals from above the apical claw.

The sexes of this genus may be separated at once by the relative lengths of the antennæ: in the males the antennæ are longer and slightly more attenuated, the head also is narrower, the eyes are more globose, and the body somewhat less robust. There is a slight variation also in the form of the thorax: in some species the anterior angles are more or less (obsoletely) truncate, and it is the aspect of one of these examples which probably suggested the name of the genus, by giving to the thorax the semblance of being eight-sided. As a rule, and in the old typical species, *O. Banoni*, Drap., the thorax is hardly more than six-sided.

1. Octogonotes brunneus. (TAB. VI. fig. 5.)

O. *ovalis, depressus, latus, lanuginosus, brunneus; capite brevi, subdepresso, inter oculos transverse foveolato, granulato; thorace transverso, quadrato, ad latera marginato et (ad medium) leviter angulato; elytris robustis, punctato-striatis; antennis flavis (articulis 5–8 nigris); pedibus brunneis.*

Long. corp. 4¼ lin., lat. 2 lin.

Oval, broad, somewhat depressed, clothed throughout with a golden-brown pubescence, which varies in shade in different examples. *Head* short, transverse, slightly elongated in front; eyes small, distant; between the eyes and the insertion of the antennæ is a triangular irregular depression; the surface of the head is roughly granulated, very finely pubescent; of a rich golden-brown colour. *Thorax* transverse, with the anterior angles very broadly obliquely-truncate, thus considerably contracting the breadth of the anterior surface; the sides marginate, and when viewed from above (by reason of the truncation of the anterior angles), apparently projecting laterally and medially into a distinct obtuse angle; the surface of the thorax is complanate, and depressed on either side in front; at the base a broad and distinct (but not sharply defined) shallow depression extends obliquely upwards nearly to the humeral angles; thickly pubescent. *Scutellum* triangular, hardly separated from, and on the same plane as, the elytra; fuscous, pubescent. *Elytra* broad, somewhat depressed, finely punctate-striate, fulvous, and clothed throughout, like the thorax, with short golden pubescence. *Antennæ* filiform; the first joint dilated, and deflected outwards; the second short, ovate, and attenuated at the base; the third as long as the first; in colour flavous, with the fifth to the eighth joints darkly fuscous, and the ninth to the eleventh pale flavous. *Legs* entirely fuscous, the posterior femora being clothed with pubescence.

District of the River Amazon. In the collections of Messrs. Baly, Bates, and the Rev. H. Clark.

2. **Octogonotes thoracicus.**

Guérin-Mén. (*Iconogr.* 1829–38, p. 305. pl. 49 bis, fig. 9).
Dej. Cat. ed. 3. p. 407.

O. *oblongo-ovalis, parallelus, subdepressus, fusco-tomentosus ; capite abbreviato, rufo-ferrugineo ; thorace transverso, marginato, antice subcoarctato, pubescenti, rufo-ferrugineo ; elytris punctato-striatis, tomentosis, fuscis vel (a tergo) nigro-fuscis ; antennis nigris ; pedibus fulvis, nigro adumbratis.*

Long. corp. 4¼ lin., lat. 1¾ lin.

Oblong-oval, subparallel, somewhat depressed, tomentose. *Head* short, not produced in front; eyes large, fusco-ferrugineous, distant, situated at the base of the head, but not extending laterally as far as the line of the lateral margin of the thorax; between the eyes (and immediately above the insertion of the antennæ) are two small tubercles; labrum dark fuscous; above the insertion of the maxillary palpi, on either side, is a dark fulvous spot; the surface of the head is somewhat rough, slightly pubescent, rufo-ferrugineous. *Thorax* transverse; the sides marginate; the anterior angles acute; behind the anterior angles is a small marginal projection (which is more or less tooth-like in appearance in different examples); the anterior angles are obliquely truncate; a broad postmedial depression (most distinct at the base) inclines on either side obliquely towards the anterior angles; the surface of the thorax is rufo-ferrugineous, clothed throughout (and especially near the base) with a fine golden pubescence. *Scutellum* distinct, large, slightly raised

M

above the plane of the clytra, subcordiform, impunctate, dull black. *Elytra* punctate-striate, clothed throughout with a dense and short pubescence, which almost conceals not only the punctures of the striæ, but the striæ themselves; dark fuscous (when viewed from behind, almost black; when transversely, or in front, flavo-ferrugineous): the colour and denseness of this pubescence vary considerably in different examples. *Antennæ* short, subincrassated; first joint narrow at the base, but gradually dilated towards the apex, and deflected outwards; the second without the dilatation of the first, short, ovate; the third as long as the first, and gradually but slightly dilated; the fourth, fifth and sixth are slightly but sensibly still further dilated; black. *Legs* fulvo-pubescent, shaded on their upper surface (and on the upper and outer surface of the posterior femora) with dark fuscous.

Cayenne. In the cabinets of M. Deyrolle, Mr. Baly, and the Rev. H. Clark.

3. Octogonotes Banoni. (TAB. VI. fig. 6.)

Drapiez, Ann. Sci. Phys. Brux. iii. p. 191. pl. 39. f. 6.
Dej. Cat. (1837) p. 407.

O. oblongus, ovatus, subparallelus, leviter pubescens, punctato-striatus, niger; capite brevi, ad basin antennarum bituberculato, granulato; thorace transverso, ad latera marginato et angulato, ad medium basin depresso, flavo; elytris elongatis, punctato-striatis, vitta undique apud marginem lata, obliterata, a humeris usque ad apicem, flava, ad medium elytrorum in maculas duas dilatata; antennis filiformibus, nigris, art. 8–11 fulvis; pedibus flavis, nigro superne nebulosis.

Long. corp. 4 lin., lat. 1¾ lin.

Oblong, ovate, subparallel, slightly depressed, subpubescent, punctate-striate, black. *Head* short, transverse, not produced; above the labrum is a transverse carination (of a fulvous colour), while immediately above the base of the antennæ are two distinct tubercular elevations, more prominent by reason of a fovea between them, and also of a fovea, less prominent and transverse, above them; eyes globose, situated at a short distance from the base of the head; the surface is finely granulated, and black. *Thorax* slightly broader than the head, transverse; the anterior angles depressed and subacute; the sides marginate, and produced laterally (a little in front of the middle) into a tooth-like projection; the basal angles are obliquely truncate; the surface is postmedially excavated and very finely punctate; in colour flavo-testaceous, finely suffused with fuscous. *Scutellum* triangular, impunctate, black, shining. *Elytra* somewhat broader than the thorax, subelongate, slightly attenuated towards the apex, punctato-striate, very finely pubescent (the pubescence almost concealing the punctures, not the striæ); in colour black, with a marginal irregular fulvo-testaceous stripe extending from the shoulder to the apex, and expanding towards the middle into a broader and more regularly defined transverse patch. *Antennæ* robust, filiform, subincrassated towards the middle; piceous, the joints eight to eleven being fulvous. *Legs* subpubescent, flavo-testaceous; the anterior tibiæ and tarsi, and the upper surface of the femora, being piceous; the apex also of the posterior femora is black, and the globular inflation of the posterior claw of a bright rufous colour.

Cayenne.

4. Octogonotes binotatus. (TAB. VI. fig. 7.)

O. oblongo-ovalis, subparallelus, niger; capite brevi, haud producto, granulato, nigro, inter oculos verrucoso; labro nigro; oculis magnis, exstantibus; thorace transverso, complanato, angulis anterioribus fortiter, posticis leniter oblique truncatis, ad latera marginato, pubescenti, stramineo, ad medium (præsertim versus caput et scutellum) nigro adumbrato; scutello nigro; elytris parallelis, punctato-striatis, nigris, maculis duabus ad medium (stramineis, circularibus, pubescentibus); antennis robustis, filiformibus, art. 1mo valido, ad apicem subannulato, 2do brevi, 3^{tio} et 4to elongatis, 1mo ad 7mo nigris; 8vo, 9no et 10mo (forsitanque 11mo) stramineis; pedibus stramineis, tibiis tarsisque anterioribus, femoribusque a superiori parte fusco-nigris.

Long. corp. 3 lin., lat. 1¼ lin.

Oblong-oval, depressed, of a dull black colour. *Head* transverse, short, not produced; immediately above the insertion of the antennæ, which are contiguous, are two indistinct transverse and somewhat oblong tubercles, forming together in shape the letter V; eyes large, prominent, reaching nearly to the margin of the thorax; the upper and posterior surface of the head is thickly punctate and black, the front of the head pale flavous. *Thorax* broader than the head, transverse, with the anterior angles distinctly and obliquely truncate, thus forming, in appearance, a slight antemedial lateral angle; the posterior angles are *very slightly* truncate; the sides marginate; the surface is clothed throughout (but especially at the sides) with a fine silky pubescence of a cream colour; medially, and more distinctly at the apex and base, is a cloudy longitudinal fuscous marking. *Scutellum* subcordiform, black, impunctate. *Elytra* somewhat depressed, distinctly punctate-striate (the surface between the striæ is finely and thickly punctate), and clothed throughout, but especially towards the sides and apex, with a very fine yellowish pubescence (hardly discernible except under the microscope); at the middle of each elytron (separated from the suture by two striæ, and from the lateral margination by a single stria) is a regularly formed circular spot, clothed throughout with a close and distinct straw-coloured pubescence; this spot is connected with the shoulder by an obsolete longitudinal cinereous marking, which occupies the interval between the fifth and seventh striæ. *Antennæ* black; the first joint broad, dilated towards the extremity; the second short, and narrower; the third and fourth much longer than the first (all of these being indistinctly annulated with a fuscous band at their base); the eighth to the tenth, and probably the eleventh, pale cinereous. *Legs* flavous; the upper part of the anterior femora, and also the tibiæ and tarsi, fuscous; posterior claw entirely covered by a distinct globular enlargement, which is of a bright orange colour.

Cayenne.

It may be a question, whether an examination of several specimens would not resolve this into a simple variety of *O. Banoni*, Drap. The single specimen before me presents, however, apparently distinct specific characters, not only in the markings of its elytra (which consist of a single well-defined circular spot, instead of a broad longitudinal line extending from the shoulder to the apex), but also in the form of its thorax. In *O. Banoni* the basal angles of the thorax are broadly truncate, which, with the truncation of the anterior angles, gives an appearance to the lateral margin of two short, obtuse, lateral projections (the margin, between these two projections being scooped out or emarginate), while in this species (*O. binotatus*) the sides of the thorax are almost parallel. The black markings also on the thorax of *O. binotatus* are quite unrepresented in that of *O. Banoni*.

5. Octogonotes sumptuosus. (Tab. VI. fig. 8.)

O. *oblongo-ovalis, robustus, niger, nitidus; capite fovea triangulari inter oculos, sparsim punctato; thorace transverso, angulato, ad latera marginato, angulis anterioribus oblique truncatis, fulvo, aureo-pubescenti; elytris, punctis veluti in striis ordinatis, nitidis, nigris, fasciis duabus et maculis quatuor pubescentibus, auratis; fasciarum, hac ad medium, hac pone medium, haud suturam attingentibus; macularum, duabus ad humeros, tertia longitudinali ad suturam, juxta scutellum, quartaque ad apicem, communi; antennis pedibusque flavis.*

Long. corp. 3¾ lin., lat. 1¾ lin.

Oblong-oval, robust, subparallel, black, shining. *Head* short, not produced, with a T-like impression between the eyes; glabrous, sparingly punctured. *Thorax* transverse, subdepressed; the sides are marginate, produced laterally on either side (a little before the middle) into a very obtuse angle (apparently formed by the truncation of the anterior angles); the surface smooth and sparingly punctate; the colour is fulvous, clothed (especially at the base and sides) with a fine golden pubescence. *Scutellum* large, flavous. *Elytra* black, shining, with ten striæ-like rows of almost obsolete punctures; two fasciæ (the one a little before the middle, and the other at an equal distance between this and the apex), both of which are interrupted by the suture, are formed by bright golden pubescence on a fulvous ground; four spots likewise are similarly formed by this golden pubescence on the surface of the elytra: two, at (but not touching) the humeral angles; a third, oblong in form, at the basal part of the suture; and a fourth, as large as the other three united, subtriangular at the apex; these two latter are common to both elytra. *Antennæ* robust, filiform, fulvous. *Legs* fulvous; the upper surface of the anterior tibiæ and femora being obscurely clouded with black.

Ega, in the district of the River Amazon.

6. Octogonotes bicinctus.

O. oblongo-ovatus, subcylindricus, niger, nitidus; capite brevi, depresso, supra antennarum basin oblique foveolato, impunctato; thorace transverso, angulis anticis depressis, oblique truncatis, ad basin oblique depresso, impunctato, subpubescenti, flavo; elytris latis, striato-punctatis, vittis duabus (pilo albo formatis transversis), ad angulos humerales macula circulari, et juxta scutellum prope suturam linea brevi notatis; antennis filiformibus, ferrugineis, apice testaceis; pedibus fulvis, superne fuscis.

Long. corp. 3⅓ lin., lat. 1½ lin.

Oblong-ovate, robust, subdepressed, black, shining. *Head* short, depressed, almost vertical; maxillary palpi rufous; eyes prominent, situated at the back of the head, extending laterally nearly as far as the anterior angles of the thorax; below the base of the antennæ is a transverse, triangular, black glabrous depression; above the base of the antennæ (and between the eyes) is a narrow, obliquely transverse fovea; the surface is almost impunctate, black. *Thorax* rather broader than the head, transverse; the anterior angles depressed and subacute, broadly and obliquely truncate, forming medially in the margination a short angular projection; at the base a broad transverse medial depression extends obliquely towards the anterior angles; the surface is almost impunctate, subpubescent, flavous. *Scutellum* triangular, impunctate, black. *Elytra* slightly broader than the thorax, with rows of punctures arranged as striæ; black, shining; two transverse bands (which are formed by dense white pubescence) extend from the first stria to the margination, one medially, the other nearer the apex; at the humeral angles is a small circular spot, and along the suture for a short distance from the scutellum is a narrow linear marking of the same colour and formation. *Antennæ* tolerably long, filiform, ferrugineous; the joints eight to eleven being testaceous. *Legs* fulvous, on the upper surface fuscous; the inflation of the posterior claw bright ferrugineous.

This species differs from *O. sumptuosus* (to which it is nearly allied) in the colouring as well as in the disposition and size of the markings on the elytra.

From the district of the River Amazon.

Genus 27. **APALOTRIUS**[*].

PALPI MAXILLARES *robusti, breves, plerumque geniculati, art.* 3^{tio} *dilatato, globoso.*

PALPI LABIALES *cylindrici, attenuati.*

ANTENNÆ *filiformes, robustæ.*

CAPUT *breve, depressum, fere verticale.*

THORAX *latus, transversus,* rectilinearis, *antice tenue constrictus.*

ELYTRA *lata, robusta, subcylindrica, punctato-striata.*

PEDES *robusti ;* tibiis posticis *a retro super tarsi insertionem* calcare armatis.

Labrum subcircular, broad.

Mandibles robust, at the inner margin armed with a single short but acute tooth.

Maxillary palpi (Tab. VII. fig. 1 *m*) broad, robust, generally geniculated; the basal joint minute; the second gradually broader towards the apex and obliquely truncate; the third broader and not longer than the second, also obliquely truncate at the apex; the terminal joint much narrower than the third, and conical.

Labial palpi (Tab. VII. fig. 1 *n*) minute, somewhat more elongate than in the genus *Octogonotes*; the first and second joints attenuated at the base; the ultimate joint attenuate.

Antennæ approximate, situate between and below the inner mar-

[*] ἀπαλὸς, gracilis ; θρίξ, coma.

gin of the eyes, robust, filiform; the first joint is elongate and broadly dilated; the second ovate, short; the third, fourth and fifth attenuated and subequal.

Eyes globose, distant, situated almost immediately at the base of the head, extending laterally not so far as the anterior angles of the thorax.

Head short, hardly produced in front, deflected at right angles to the plane of the elytra.

Thorax broader than the head, transverse, very slightly constricted in front; the anterior angles subacute and depressed; the sides marginate; the surface equate, and in *A. pubescens* finely pubescent.

Scutellum large, triangular, impunctate, situated on the plane of the elytra.

Elytra broad, robust, subcylindrical, rounded at the apex; in *A. pubescens* deeply punctate-striate and pubescent.

Legs: the *anterior femora* sufficiently robust, attenuated at the base. The *tibiæ* are straight, incurved at their immediate base, and cylindrical. The *tarsi* are short; the basal joint triangular, of the breadth of the base of the tibia; the second of the same form, but *more minute*; the third transverse, subcircular at the apex, distinctly bilobed; these three are clothed on their under side with thick rigid pubescence; from the base of the third proceeds the last joint, which is elongated, and gradually dilated and incurved towards the apex; the joint terminates in a bifid tooth, unarmed by any spur on its inner surface. The *posterior femora* are broadly incrassated, ovate, tapering gradually to the apex, which is obliquely truncate. The *tibia* (Tab. VII. fig. 1 *g*) is short, abruptly incurved at its immediate base; the posterior surface is longitudinally grooved, and terminates in a hollowed socket for the insertion of the tarsus; the margination of this socket is armed above the insertion of the tarsus, and also below, with an obtuse spur. The *tarsus* is abbreviated; the first and second joints attenuated at the base, the second being more minute than the first; the third minute and circular; the fourth dilated into a globular inflation, which conceals from above the terminal claw.

I am unable, from the examples before me, to trace with certainty any sexual distinctions in this genus.

Apalotrius is in form closely related to *Octogonotes*, from which it may be separated by the *quadrangular* (not hexagonal) form of its thorax, by the manifestly different form of the maxillary palpi, and by the distinct spur on the margination of the postical tibia.

1. Apalotrius pubescens. (TAB. VII. fig. 1.)

A. ovalis, latus, subdepressus, pubescens, luridus; capite brevi, depresso, parum producto, inter oculos transverse foveolato, sparsim punctato, nigro, ad frontem flavo; thorace transverso, angulis anterioribus coarctatis, marginato, subcomplanato, pubescenti, flavo; elytris latis, punctato-striatis, nigro-fuscis vel nigris, nitidis, sed ad apicem et latera pube flava (inter strias 4 et 5 præsertim) vestitis; antennis pedibusque flavis, femorum posticorum apicibus exceptis nigris.

Long. corp. 3 lin., lat. 1¾ lin.

Oval, broad, robust, slightly depressed. *Head* and *thorax* much narrower than the elytra, pubescent. *Head* short, transverse, depressed in front; eyes large, globose, distant, their exterior margin extending laterally as far as the line of the margin of the thorax; between the eyes is a transverse fovea, extending in an oblique direction towards the upper margin of the eyes; the surface of the head is sparingly but deeply punctured; black, the anterior portion (in front of the insertion of the antennæ) being flavous. *Thorax* transverse, slightly narrowed in front; sides marginate, and (when viewed laterally) deflected from the humeral angle to the lower margin of the eyes; the anterior and posterior angles are subacute and distinct; the surface of the thorax is equate and very finely punctured throughout, pubescent, flavous. *Scutellum* triangular, slightly granulated, fuscous. *Elytra* broad, depressed, punctate-striate; black, shining, clothed throughout irregularly, but especially at the apex, the margins, and between the fifth and sixth striæ, with a fine silky golden pubescence (this band of pubescence between the fifth and sixth striæ is in perfect specimens very marked and distinct). *Antennæ* robust, filiform, with the first joint incrassated, and deflected outwards at the apex; the second somewhat more attenuate, short and ovate; of the rest, which are filiform, the third is longer than the fourth, and the fourth narrower than the fifth; the two basal joints are ferrugineous, the rest flavous. *Legs* entirely flavous, with the exception of the apex of the postical femora, which is black.

Several examples of this fine species have been sent home by Mr. Bates from Ega (River Amazon).

It is probable that in quite recent specimens the elytra will be found to be clothed throughout with a fine griseous pubescence, instead of being, as in the examples before me, black and shining; and that this pubescence will obscure the longitudinal band, which in these examples is so conspicuous.

Genus 28. **EXARTEMATOPUS***.

MS. Chevr. Coll.

MANDIBULÆ *infra dente brevi basali armatæ.*
PALPI MAXILLARES *robusti, incrassati, art. 3^{tio} dilatato, ultimo brevi.*
PALPI LABIALES *elongati, attenuati.*
ANTENNÆ *robustæ, sat magnæ, apicem versus dilatatæ.*
CAPUT *breve, verticale, thorace constrictius.*
THORAX *transversus*, latus, *rectangularis*, angulis anticis exstantibus, *depressus.*
ELYTRA *lata, convexa, punctato-striata, colorata, glabra.*
PEDES *robusti ; tibiis posticis simplicibus.*

Labrum subcircular.

Mandibles robust at the base, and armed on the inner margin with a short basal tooth, at the apex acuminated.

Maxillary palpi (Tab. VII. fig. 2 *m*) robust, incrassated ; the basal joint minute; the second dilated towards the apex and obliquely truncate ; the third more robust and shorter, attenuated at the base ; the ultimate joint *abbreviated*, conical.

Labial palpi (Tab. VII. fig. 2 *n*) elongate, minute ; the basal joint quadrate ; the second somewhat thickened towards the apex, and constricted at the base ; the third narrower at the base than the apex of the second.

Antennæ approximate, situated between and below the inner margin of the eyes, robust, *long*, dilated at the apex ; the basal joint elongate (extending, when placed laterally, beyond the sides of the head) and gradually dilated, and inflected towards the apex ; the second ovate, short ; the third to the sixth nearly as long as the first, more attenuate ; the seventh to the eleventh abbreviated, and more robust, gradually incrassated as they approach the apex.

Eyes large, subglobose, situated at the base of the head.

Head short, not produced, much narrower than the thorax ; when viewed laterally, depressed at right angles to the plane of the thorax.

Thorax transverse, *broad*, rectangular ; the anterior angles depressed, but *prominent* ; the sides parallel and broadly marginate ; the surface is flat, inclined at an angle of 45 degrees from the plane of the elytra.

Scutellum large, triangular, situated in the same plane as the elytra.

Elytra broad and convex, considerably broader than the thorax, rounded at the apex, punctate-striate, brightly coloured, glabrous.

Legs: the *anterior femora* robust, and slightly incurved on their inner margin near the apex. The *tibiæ* are short, robust, inflected

---
* Derivatione incerta.

at their immediate base, and gradually dilated; when viewed from above, the anterior surface is longitudinally grooved, especially near the insertion of the tarsus, where it is obliquely truncate. The *tarsus* is short and robust; the first joint transverse, triangular; the second of the same form, but more minute; the third subtriangular, hardly bilobed: in different examples the first and second joints are more or less subequal, but in all examples the terminal joint is distinctly broader than the others: the terminal claw is bifid, simple, robust, and slightly dentated at the inner margin near the base. The *posterior femora* are robust, incrassated, ovate. The *tibia* is short, inflected at the immediate base, gradually thickened towards the apex; when seen from behind, the posterior surface is longitudinally grooved, forming at the apex a socket for the reception of the tarsus, and armed at its lower extremity, below the insertion of the tarsus, with two incurved spurs. The *tarsus* is attenuated; the first joint dilated, and transversely truncate at the apex; the second of the same breadth, but shorter and more triangular; the third minute and subcircular; these three joints are clothed on their under surface with thick pubescence; from the base of the third proceeds the ultimate joint, which terminates in a broad globular inflation completely concealing from above the apical claw.

This genus has very distinct characters: the antennæ are robust, *not short*, and incrassated at the apex; the thorax is *broad*, the anterior angles are *very prominent*, and its surface is not rounded, but flat, in one plane, which is depressed at an angle of 45 degrees to the plane of the elytra: these, together with the robust form of the elytra (without reference to manifest peculiarities of structure in the palpi and tarsi), are amply sufficient to separate it generically from other forms.

1. Exartematopus nobilis. (TAB. VII. fig. 2.)

E. *oblongo-ovatus, latus, impubescens, punctato-striatus, castaneus; capite brevi, inter oculos transverse foveolato, punctato, rufoflavo; thorace transverso, angulis subproductis, antice emarginato, lateribus marginatis, rufo-flavo, maculis quatuor circularibus, lateribusque, fusco-nigris: elytris latis, subdepressis, punctatostriatis, plagis sex flavis; i. e. duabus ad humeros (a sutura ad marginem, maculas nigras duas continentibus), duabus ad marginem (apud medium, parvis, immaculatis), duabusque apicem juxta, maculam unam nigram continentibus; antennis robustis, artic.* 1–5 *ferrugineis,* 6 *nigro et subdilatato (reliqui mihi desunt); pedibus ferrugineis, femoribus posticis (antice et superne visis) castaneis.*

Long. corp. 3 lin., lat. 2 lin.

Oblong-ovate, broad, subdepressed, punctate-striate, impubescent, of a brown-castaneous colour. *Head* very short and much depressed, almost vertical; above the labrum is a triangular transverse depression; immediately above the insertion of the antennæ are two subcircular depressions, and between them is a longitudinal medial fovea, which joins a distinct transverse depression above them; eyes large and subprominent, situated at the base of the head; the surface is finely and sparingly punctate and rufo-flavous, the medial depression being suffused with fuscous. *Thorax* transverse, considerably broader than the head (when viewed transversely, depressed at a considerable angle to the plane of the elytra); the anterior margin is emarginate, the anterior angles being depressed and prominent; the sides are broadly marginate, and in outline subsinuate; near the base are two obsolete depressions: the surface is distinctly and sparingly punctate, of a rufo-flavous colour; at the anterior margin (immediately above and somewhat between the eyes) are two subcircular minute black spots; behind them (at mid distance between them and the posterior margin) are two others, occupying the obsolete depressions; the lateral margination also is broadly black. *Scutellum* triangular, impunctate, fuscous-black, glabrous. *Elytra* broader than the thorax, robust, subdepressed, punctate-striate (the punctures being deep and large, the striæ more obsolete, and both being almost obsolete near the apex): at the humeral angles, and also at the apex, large irregularly defined patches of testaceous colour extend transversely from the lateral margins to the suture; the outline of that at the base is irregularly transverse, containing two insulated black maculæ (the one near the suture, the other at the extreme angle of the shoulder); the apical marking contains a single macula at its centre; between these two (apical and humeral) patches is a third, at the mid-margin of the elytra, unconnected with, and much smaller than either, immaculate, and like them testaceous; the castaneous coloration of the elytra between this and the other patches is darkly suffused with fuscous. *Abdomen* ferrugineous. *Antennæ* robust, and apparently subincrassated; in the imperfect example before me, the five basal joints are fulvous and the sixth (which is *slightly broader* than the fifth) black. *Legs* rufo-ferrugineous; the apex of the postical femora being at its outer side suffused with rufo-fuscous.

Espirito Santo. In the collection of Mr. Fry.

2. Exartematopus scutellaris. (Tab. VII. fig. 3.)

E. oblongo-ovatus, robustus, impubescens, pallide stramineus ; capite depresso, transverso, abbreviato, supra basin antennarum T *foveolato, impunctato, glabro, nigro ; thorace transverso, antice emar-*

ginato, angulis anterioribus rotundatis, punctatis, flavo-stramineis; elytris robustis, latis, tenue punctato-striatis, glabris; antennis robustis, ad apicem dilatatis, fulvis; pedibus robustis, flavo-ferrugineis.

Long. corp. 4½ lin., lat. 2½ lin.

Oblong-ovate, robust, impubescent, of a pale stramineous colour. *Head* depressed, not produced in front; above the labrum is a transverse triangular plane depression; immediately above the base of the antennæ is a short longitudinal fovea, which joins another (extending transversely and somewhat obliquely upwards towards the upper and inner margin of the eyes), these two canaliculations forming together the character of the letter T; eyes tolerably large, situated at the base of the head; the surface impunctate, glabrous, black, with a triangular suffused marking of fusco-rufous above the transverse fovea. *Thorax* transverse, much depressed, in front distinctly emarginate; the anterior angles are rounded; the sides broadly marginate; the surface is finely and sparingly punctate, glabrous, flavo-stramineous. *Scutellum* large, triangular, impunctate, glabrous, dark piceous. *Elytra* robust, much broader than the thorax, finely punctate-striate, glabrous, of a stramineous colour throughout. *Antennæ* robust, subdilated towards the apex; the first joint long; the second short, ovate; the third to the sixth attenuate, of almost equal length, and shorter than the first; the seventh to the eleventh short, dilated; the colour fulvous, the extremity of the third and fourth joints being suffused with piceous, and the apex (from the seventh to the eleventh joints) slightly tinged with fuscous. *Legs* robust, flavo-ferrugineous throughout; body beneath black, the under part of the thorax and the abdomen being flavous.

Brazil. In the collection of M. Chevrolat.

Genus 29. **HYDMOSYNE***.

MANDIBULÆ *intra ad basin subtiliter dentatæ.*
PALPI MAXILLARES *elongati, ad apicem dilatati, art. ultimo conico, brevi.*
PALPI LABIALES *robusti, subcylindrici, minuti.*
ANTENNÆ *filiformes, robustæ.*
CAPUT *transversum, antice subproductum,* subporrectum.
THORAX *capite latior, transversus, ad apicem constrictus.*
ELYTRA *subparallela, thorace leviter ampliora.*
PEDES : *tibiis posticis a retro longitudinaliter excavatis,* rectis, *et ad ipsum apicem (pone tarsorum insertionem) ungulis duabus armatis.*

* ἰδμοσύνη, scientia, agilitas.

Labrum subcircular.

Mandibles (Tab. VII. fig. 4 *o*) robust, acuminated at the apex; the inner surface near the base is subsinuate, and forms two obsolete inner teeth.

Maxillary palpi (Tab. VII. fig. 4 *m*) elongate, dilated at the apex; the basal joint is minute; the second attenuate, thickened towards the apex; the third joint in breadth double that of the second, gradually inflated towards the apex; the terminal joint is abbreviated and conical.

Labial palpi (Tab. VII. fig. 4 *l*) minute, robust, subcylindrical; the penultimate joint being slightly thickened at the apex, and the terminal joint more slender.

Antennæ approximate, situated between and below the inner surface of the eyes, filiform, robust; the basal joint elongate and broadly dilated (more broadly than in the preceding genus, *Exartematopus*); the second narrower, and *minute*; the third joint longer than the first, and attenuate; the fourth and fifth thicker and subequal.

Eyes large and subglobose, situated at the base of the head, extending laterally not so far as the anterior angles of the thorax.

Head transverse (slightly produced in front), *hardly more depressed in front than the thorax, porrect.*

Thorax broader than the head, transverse, obsoletely excavated in front; the sides subconstricted towards the apex and marginate; the surface *generally* finely punctate and glabrous or sparingly pubescent.

Scutellum distinct, triangular.

Elytra subparallel, slightly broader than the thorax, punctate or punctate-striate, subpubescent or glabrous.

Legs: the *anterior femora* robust. The *tibiæ* incurved at their immediate base and gradually thickened towards the apex. The *tarsi* are elongated; the basal joint is triangular, not quite so broad as the apex of the tibiæ; the second of the same form, but more minute; the third broad, and almost bilobed; the apical joint is elongate, inflected, and gradually thickened; the terminal claw is bifid, and armed on its inner surface on either side with a second, more minute tooth. The *posterior femora* are broadly incrassated, gradually tapering towards the apex. The *tibiæ* are short, inflected at the immediate apex; the posterior surface is longitudinally grooved, and terminates in a deeply marginate socket for the insertion of the antennæ; this socket commences in an obtuse angle in the margination, is armed along its sides with a closely arranged series of comb-like teeth, and terminates ultimately in a double incurved claw (the outer one being larger and more prominent than the inner) below the insertion of the tarsus. The *tarsus* is short and attenuate; the two basal joints being triangular and subequal; the penultimate rounded and minute; the terminal joint dilated into a bladder-like inflation above the apical claw, which is bifid, and has each limb armed with an inner and smaller tooth.

After much examination and comparison, I have felt that this form ought to be separated generically from that which follows, to which it has a manifest affinity. The head is distinctly *porrect*, not depressed at right angles; the terminal joint of the posterior tarsus is not so broad, or so manifestly bilobed; and the longitudinal margination of the postical tibia is unarmed (except immediately at the socket) by any distinct spur. The facies also of the whole insect is different: it is broader, flatter, not so cylindrical, and, instead of being pubescent, is brightly glabrous.

1. Hydmosyne inclyta. B.M.

H. *oblongo-ovata, subparallela, punctata, viridi-œnea; capite brevi, ad basin antennarum bituberculato, granulato, rufo-flavo; thorace transverso, ad basin late depresso, punctato, rufo-flavo; elytris sat robustis, subtiliter striato-punctatis; antennis filiformibus, fuscis; pedibus flavo-ferrugineis, fusco suffusis.*

Long. corp. $4\frac{1}{4}$ lin., lat. 2 lin.

Oblong-ovate, subparallel, punctate, impubescent, of a dark metallic-green colour. *Head* short, transverse, not produced in front; above the labrum is a transverse triangular carination, and immediately above the base of the antennæ are two tubercles, more prominently distinct by reason of a fovea which separates them: eyes tolerably globose, situate at the base of the head; the surface between the eyes is finely granulated; the colour rufous. *Thorax* somewhat broader than the head, transverse; the anterior angles subdepressed and distinct; the sides marginate: at the base (when viewed obliquely) is a transverse broad depression; the surface is finely punctate and glabrous; in colour rufo-flavous. *Scutellum* triangular, impunctate, rufo-flavous. *Elytra* tolerably broad and robust, somewhat broader than the thorax, with punctures (minute and closely arranged) distributed in the form of striæ; these punctures are obsolete as they approach the apex; near the shoulders (between the sixth and seventh striæ) is a short but deep longitudinal depression. *Antennæ* filiform, fuscous. *Legs* flavo-ferrugineous, suffused with fuscous.

South America. In the collection of the British Museum.

Genus 30. **ATYPHUS**[*].

PALPI MAXILLARES *breves, dilatati, art.* 3^{tio} *subquadrato.*
PALPI LABIALES *minuti, art. ultimo elongato.*
ANTENNÆ *filiformes, sat robustæ (haud tam ut in* Hydmosyne).
CAPUT *transversum, latum, verticale.*
THORAX *transversus, rectangularis.*
ELYTRA *parallela, subcylindrica, ad apicem rotundata.*
PEDES: *tibiis posticis calcaratis, tarsis brevibus.*

Labrum short, contracted, transverse.

Maxillary palpi (Tab. VII. fig. 5 *m*): the basal joint minute, rectangular, quadrate; the second longer than the first, dilated and obliquely truncate at the apex; the third much shorter and broader than the second, almost quadrate; the terminal joint broadly conical.

Labial palpi (Tab. VII. fig. 5 *n*) minute; the second joint dilated and transversely truncate at the apex; the terminal joint elongate, and of half the breadth of the apex of the second.

Antennæ approximate, situated between the inner margins of the eyes, filiform, tolerably robust (more slender, however, than in *Hydmosyne*); the basal joint dilated (not so distinctly as in the preceding genus); the second short and ovate; the third longer than the first, and attenuated; the fourth and fifth subequal.

Eyes large, subglobose, lateral, at the base of the head, extending laterally to *nearly* the anterior angles of the thorax.

Head somewhat broad, transverse, and (when viewed laterally) deflected at right angles to the elytra (not porrect and narrowed, as in *Hydmosyne*).

Thorax transverse, rectangular, slightly broader than the head; the sides marginate and obsoletely subsinuate.

Scutellum smaller than in the preceding genus, triangular.

Elytra parallel, subcylindrical, perceptibly broader than the head, rounded at the apex.

Legs: the *anterior femora* and *tibiæ* (when viewed from in front) robust. The *tarsi* are short; the two basal joints triangular (the second being slightly shorter than the first); the penultimate joint more transverse and bilobed; these three are clothed on their inner surface with a thick and short pubescence: the terminal claw is bifid and simple, robust at the base. The *posterior femora* incrassated, at the apex *obliquely* truncate. The *tibiæ* (Tab. VII. fig. 5 *g*) are in-

[*] ἀ, non; τύφω, turgesco.

flected at their immediate base: when viewed from behind, the posterior surface is longitudinally grooved; the margination of this groove is produced near the socket (not at the socket, as in *Hydmosyne*) into an obtuse spur; the socket itself is margined on either side with a close series of comb-like (erect and fine) teeth; the ultimate apex is armed with two incurved, robust claws of *equal* size. The *tarsi* are attenuate and short; the first and second joints being nearly equal (narrow, and somewhat dilated at the apex); the third slightly broader and subcircular.

There is a manifest similarity between this genus and *Eupeges*; both are in general form subcylindrical, parallel, and sufficiently robust. The striking difference, however, between them in the form of the maxillary palpi alone would, without other distinguishing characters, amply separate them.

1. Atyphus carbonarius.

A. *oblongo-ovatus, subparallelus, punctato-striatus, impubescens, niger; capite brevi, inter oculos Y foveolato, granulato, nigro; thorace transverso, ad basin oblique depresso, punctato, flavo; elytris sat robustis, subparallelis, punctato-striatis, interstitiis subtiliter granulatis; antennis filiformibus, piceis; pedibus nigris.*

Long. corp. $3\frac{1}{4}$ lin., lat. $1\frac{2}{3}$ lin.

Oblong-ovate, subparallel, punctate-striate, impubescent, shining, black. *Head* short, transverse, not produced in front: below the base of the antennæ is a transverse triangular depression; above the base and between the eyes is a deep and distinct fovea, in the form of the letter Y: the eyes are large, tolerably globose, and situated near the base of the head; the surface is deeply granulated and black. *Thorax* broader than the head, transverse; the anterior angles acute and depressed; the sides marginate, and in outline subsinuate; at the base is a transverse depression, extending obliquely upwards towards the anterior angles: the surface (when seen under a high power) is finely punctate and glabrous; the colour flavous. *Scutellum* impunctate, triangular, black. *Elytra* somewhat broader than the thorax, subparallel, impubescent, deeply punctate-striate, the interstices being very finely granulated. *Antennæ* filiform, the third joint being more attenuated than the rest; piceous. *Legs* black.

Morro Queimado (Rio Janeiro). In the collection of Mr. Fry, M. Lacordaire, Mr. Waterhouse, and the Rev. H. Clark.

This species is subject to some variation.

Var. A. Scutellum flavous, and the elytra sparingly clothed with very fine pale pubescence.

Var. B. Scutellum flavous, and the elytra clothed with thick and short squamose pubescence.

Var. C. Scutellum black, and the elytra covered with short and thick squamose pubescence.

2. Atyphus flaviventris.

A. *oblongus, parallelus, subcylindricus, niger; capite transverso, subproducto, ad basin punctato; thorace transverso, ad basin oblique depresso, impunctato, obsolete pubescenti-flavo; elytris parallelis, subrobustis, punctato-striatis, obsolete pubescentibus, nigris; antennis filiformibus, nigris; pedibus nigris.*

Long. corp. 3 lin., lat. 1⅓ lin.

Oblong, parallel, subcylindrical, black. *Head* short, transverse, very slightly produced in front; eyes large, tolerably prominent; between the base of the antennæ and the labrum is a transverse triangular plane, bounded at its upper margin by two oblique ridges; immediately above the base of the antennæ are two obsolete elevations; the surface is coarsely punctate and black. *Thorax* transverse; the anterior angles depressed and subacute; the sides marginate; at the base is a broad and shallow transverse depression, which extends obliquely upwards towards the anterior angles; the surface impunctate and obsoletely pubescent, flavous. *Scutellum* triangular, black. *Elytra* parallel, subrobust, punctate-striate, clothed throughout (as seen under a high power) with obsolete pubescence; black. *Antennæ* filiform, black. *Legs* black.

Brazil. In the collection of M. Chevrolat.

3. Atyphus comes.

A. *oblongus, subparallelus, subpubescens, flavo-ferrugineus; capite transverso, ad basin antennarum subtiliter bituberculato, subpubescenti, granulato, fulvo-flavo; thorace transverso, ad basin et latera depresso, testaceo-pubescenti, fulvo; elytris robustis, punctato-striatis, pallide pubescentibus, fulvo-ferrugineis, lineis duabus suturaque fusco-nigris; antennis filiformibus, fuscis; pedibus fulvis, femoribus posticis tarsisque anterioribus fuscis.*

Long. corp. 2½ lin., lat. 1 lin.

Oblong, subparallel, robust, subpubescent, flavo-ferrugineous. *Head* transverse, slightly produced in front; above the labrum is a transversely triangular plane depression; between the eyes, and immediately above the base of the antennæ, are two minute subprominent tubercles, which are more apparent by being each of them surrounded by a circular fovea; eyes large and prominent, extending laterally nearly as far as the angles of the thorax; the surface (when viewed under a high magnifying power) subpubescent and finely granulated, fulvo-flavous. *Thorax* transverse, slightly broader than the head, rectangular; the anterior angles subacute and depressed; the sides marginate; at the base is a broad transverse depression, extending upwards in a subcircular form towards the anterior angles; the surface finely testaceo-pubescent, fulvous. *Scutellum* triangular. *Elytra* parallel, robust, deeply and broadly punctate-striate; the colour fulvo-ferrugineous: parallel to the suture are two well-defined bands of fuscous-black, which extend from the shoulders to the apex; these bands have the breadth of two striæ, and are at the distance from the suture of four striæ; the sutural line itself also is obsoletely fuscous. *Antennæ* filiform, fuscous. *Legs* fulvous, with the base of the posterior femora and the anterior tarsi (with part of the anterior tibiæ) fuscous.

Taken in the neighbourhood of Rio Janeiro, by the late Mr. Squire, December 1859.

4. Atyphus furcipes.

A. *ovatus, robustus, cyaneus, nitidus; capite brevi, transverso, ad basin antennarum* T *foveolato, impunctato; thorace lato, transverso, ad basin depresso; elytris robustis, punctato-striatis; antennis filiformibus, nigris; pedibus nigro-cyaneis.*

Long. corp. 3½ lin., lat. 2 lin.

Ovate, robust, of a bright dark-blue colour throughout. *Head* short, transverse, slightly produced in front; immediately above the base of the antennæ is a distinct fovea in the form of the letter T; the surface is impunctate. *Thorax* broader than the head, transverse; the anterior angles subprominent and considerably depressed; sides marginate; at the base is a broad and shallow depression of a semicircular form (extending upwards near the margins in the direction of the anterior angles); the surface is impunctate and glabrous. *Scutellum* triangular and impunctate. *Elytra* robust, broader than the thorax, deeply punctate-striate; an antemedial transverse depression (which is broad and shallow) gives an appearance of prominence to the humeral angles. *Antennæ* filiform, tolerably robust, black. *Legs* of a dark-blue colour, the tarsi being suffused with fuscous.

New Grenada. In the collection of M. Chevrolat.

This species at first sight closely resembles *Rhinotmetus* by its general character and bright blue colour. It may be distinguished, however, not only by its more robust form, but by its *transverse* (instead of elongated) thorax. It approaches more closely still to *Monoplatus*, and might readily be taken for a large and robust female of that group; independently, however, of the structural peculiarities of the mouth and tarsi, its thorax is not marked at the base by the transverse thread-like line which obtains in every example of the genus that I have been able to examine. Moreover I doubt whether any true species of *Monoplatus* are found beyond the borders of the provinces of Rio Janeiro, São Paulo, Minas Geraës, and Espiritu Santo.

Genus 31. **GETHOSYNUS***.

PALPI MAXILLARES *dilatati, art. 3° incrassatissimo, ultimo brevi.*
PALPI LABIALES *subcylindrici, elongati.*
ANTENNÆ *filiformes, sat robustæ.*
CAPUT *breve, depressum.*
THORAX *capite latior, transversus, lateribus subsinuatis.*
ELYTRA elongata, *parallela, subcylindrica, haud ante medium transverse depressa.*
PEDES *robusti; tibiis posticis super tarsorum insertionem obsolete calcaratis.*

Labrum subcircular, contracted.

Maxillary palpi (Tab. VII. fig. 6 *m*) dilated; the basal joint small and quadrate; the second longer, dilated at the apex; the third, in length, not greater than, but, at the apex, double the breadth of, the second; the terminal joint minute.

Labial palpi (Tab. VII. fig. 6 *n*) attenuated, subcylindrical, the penultimate joint being slightly dilated near the apex.

Antennæ approximate, situated immediately below the inner margin of the eyes, filiform, sufficiently robust; the basal joint is considerably dilated, more so than in the adjoining genera (approaching in character the genus *Physonychis*); the third and fourth joints are subequal, the fourth joint being slightly longer as well as more attenuate than the third.

Eyes globose, circular, lateral, situated near to the base of the head.

Head short, depressed, but not produced in front.

Thorax distinctly broader than the head, transverse; the anterior

* γηθόσυνος, lætus; à γηθέω.

angles are considerably depressed; the sides marginate and subsinuate in outline.

Scutellum triangular, situated somewhat below the plane of the elytra.

Elytra broader than the thorax, elongate, parallel, not antemedially transversely depressed, punctate, glabrous.

Legs robust. The *anterior femora* cylindrical. The *tibiæ* are inflected at the immediate base and gradually thickened towards the apex; unarmed at the extreme apex by any terminal spur. The *tarsi* are short and robust; the first and second joints subequal and triangular; the third joint broader and more circular, almost bilobed; the terminal joint is subincrassated, and slightly inflected downwards towards the apex. The *posterior femora* are ovate and short. The *tibiæ* (Tab. VII. fig. 6 *g*) are inflected at their immediate base; the posterior surface is longitudinally grooved; this groove is more distinctly marginate as it approaches the apex; the margination (immediately before the insertion of the tarsus) is distinctly sinuate, or produced into an *obsolete* tooth; the socket which contains the insertion is unarmed at its lateral margins by any pectinations, but is terminated ultimately by a single robust spur. The *tarsus* is attenuate; the basal joint minute, triangular; the second joint is of the same form as, but narrower than, the first; the third joint is shorter; from its centre proceeds the apical joint, which is broadly inflated, and entirely conceals from above the terminal claw; the claw appears to be simple, quite unarmed by any inner basal tooth.

Although this genus is formed upon a single example, I have had no hesitation whatever in separating it from the rest of the group. It is more parallel and elongate than any of the adjoining forms, and may at once be separated from them by its general facies.

1. Gethosynus sanguinicollis. (Tab. VII. fig. 6.) B.M.

G. oblongus, nitidus; capite brevi, haud producto, punctato, inter oculos biverrucato, rufo; thorace transverso, ad latera submarginato, complanato, fortiter punctato, rufo; elytris parallelis, elongatulis, punctato-striatis, nigro-viridescentibus, nitidis; antennis filiformibus, nigro-fuscis, articulis ad basin rufo annulatis; pedibus rufis, tarsis tibiisque anterioribus fuscis.

Long. corp. 3 lin., lat. 1¼ lin.

Oblong-ovate, narrow, slightly depressed; *head* and *thorax* of a dark crimson-red colour, strongly and coarsely punctate. *Head* short, transverse, not produced; between the eyes, and above the insertion of the antennæ, are two small indistinct tubercles, which give an appearance of a depression in the form of the letter T. *Thorax* transverse, rectangular; sides marginate, and parallel to each other, or very slightly convergent towards the anterior angles; surface slightly complanate, with an obscure postmedial longitudinal ridge. *Scutellum* triangular, fuscous. *Elytra* parallel, elongate, strongly punctate-striate, of a bright metallic dark-green colour, the extreme apex being somewhat tinged with fuscous, and sparingly clothed with thin pubescence. *Antennæ* filiform, robust, dark rufo-fuscous; the basal joint black, broad, especially towards the apex, and deflected outwards; the second joint short, ovate; the third longer than the fourth, and the fifth about the length of the first. *Legs* bright crimson-red, with the anterior tarsi, tibiæ, and upper part of the femora dark fuscous.

Espiritu Santo, Brazil. A single specimen is in the collection of the British Museum.

Genus 32. **ALLOCHROMA***.

PALPI MAXILLARES *elongati, apicem versus subdilatati.*

PALPI LABIALES *attenuati.*

ANTENNÆ *filiformes, plerumque subtiliter incrassatæ.*

CAPUT *breve, haud antice productum, sæpenumero pœne verticale.*

THORAX *transversus.*

ELYTRA *lata, robusta, abbreviata, aliquando ante medium transverse depressa, glabra, rarius pube vestita.*

PEDES: *tibiæ posticæ a retro visæ longitudinaliter marginatæ, sinuatæ aut rectæ, breves.*

Labrum transverse, short, subcircular; mandibles concealed, armed more or less distinctly at their inner surface with a double depression forming together a short tooth.

Maxillary palpi (Tab. VII. fig. 7 *m*) elongate, robust; the first joint short, quadrate, constricted at the base; the second longer and broader, transversely truncate; the penultimate short, transverse, robust, the breadth being greater than (or at least equal to) the length, incrassated towards the apex; the last joint conical and abbreviated.

Labial palpi (Tab. VII. fig. 7 *n*) attenuate and more or less elongate; the basal joint short; the second and third of subequal length, almost cylindrical, and attenuated towards the apex.

Antennæ situated below (or in a line with) the lower margin of the eyes, robust, filiform, with a distinct tendency in many species

* ἄλλος, diversus; χρῶμα, color.

to dilatation; the basal joint is long, and incrassated towards the apex; the second short and ovate; the third attenuate, and always longer than the first; the fourth varies in length in different species, sometimes it is shorter than (but more frequently equal in length to) the third and fifth; the rest of the joints are robust and generally subincrassated.

Eyes globose, lateral, situated at the base of the head.

Head much narrower than the thorax, hardly produced in front, depressed, frequently at right angles to the plane of the thorax.

Thorax transverse (very rarely if ever quadrate), broader than the head; the anterior angles are depressed and distinct (not obsolete or rounded, as in the genus *Rhinotmetus*); the sides are marginate and for the most part parallel; the surface is generally broad and flat rather than subcylindrical, glabrous, or in some cases sparingly clothed with obsolete pubescence.

Scutellum well-developed, triangular, situated in the same plane as that of the elytra.

Elytra broad, cylindrical, and abbreviated; always broader and more robust than the thorax; in some species antemedially transversely depressed; the surface is punctate-striate, glabrous or finely pubescent, and generally brightly coloured.

Legs robust and sufficiently elongate. The *anterior femora* subcylindrical. The *tibiæ* are inflected at the immediate base, straight, unarmed, longitudinally grooved in front. The *tarsi* are broad and short; the first and second joints are subequal, and in form triangular, in most species broader than the apex of the tibiæ; the third joint is of still greater breadth, and deeply bilobed; the terminal joint is slightly incrassated towards the apex: the claw is armed at its inner surface with a very distinct tooth. The *posterior femora* are incrassated and ovate. The *tibiæ* are distinctly incurved at the base, straight, and longitudinally grooved along their posterior surface: the margins of this groove are in no instance serrated or armed with a tooth; for the most part they are straight, rarely in outline even sinuate: the apex of the tibia is dilated and obliquely truncate: the socket for the insertion of the tarsus is unarmed laterally (as is the case in other genera) by comb-like teeth; it is terminated by two strong and very distinct spurs. The *tarsus* is short and attenuated; the two basal joints are subdilated towards their apex; the third is circular and somewhat broader; the fourth broadly inflated: the terminal claw, like the anterior, is armed at its inner surface with a basal spur.

This genus may without difficulty be separated from those adjoining it. In general facies the species composing it are shorter and more robust; the elytra are distinctly broader than the thorax, and for the most part brightly coloured. Its transverse and rectilinear thorax, together with the unarmed posterior tibiæ, will also separate it from those groups to which, from the form of the palpi, it is nearly allied.

1. Allochroma humerale.

A. *ovale, robustum, subdepressum, nigrum; capite brevi, ad apicem elongatulo, longitudinaliter carinato, punctato, ad basin penitus granulato, rufo (inter oculos nigro maculato); thorace transverso, ad apicem leniter constricto, antice (ad latera) depresso, æquato, punctato, rufo, macula longitudinali ad medium, alterisque apud angulos anticos, nigris; elytris robustis, punctato-striatis, flavo-pubescentibus, fusco-nigris, ad humeros rufo notatis; antennis rufis, art. 5–8 rufo-fuscis; pedibus rufis, tibiis anterioribus (tarsorumque apicibus) fuscis.*

Long. corp. $3\frac{1}{2}$ lin., lat. 2 lin.

Oblong, oval, slightly convex, robust, black. *Head* very short, depressed, almost vertical, slightly elongate; eyes large, but not prominent, situated at the back of the head; at the base of the antennæ (immediately above their insertion) a short longitudinal fovea is apparent; below the insertion of the antennæ is a longitudinal ridge, extending nearly to the mouth; the surface is punctate, especially at the base, where it is almost granulated; the colour is rufous, with a dark fuscous suffused spot between the eyes and close to the base. *Thorax* transverse, slightly constricted towards the head; the anterior angles considerably depressed; the sides submarginate; surface smooth and equate throughout, very thickly punctate, rufous, with a *dark* fuscous medial longitudinal line (which is broad, and widening towards the middle) extending from the head to the basal margin; the depression also of the anterior angles is of a dark fuscous colour. *Scutellum* triangular, impunctate, rufo-fuscous. *Elytra* somewhat broader than the thorax, robust, short, punctate-striate, of a dark fuscous colour, clothed throughout with a short flavous pubescence; from the base of the elytra (between the scutellum and the humeral angle) is a broad longitudinal rufous band, diminishing gradually in breadth and terminating medially at the fifth stria. *Antennæ* filiform, short, rufous, with the fifth to the eighth joints rufo-fuscous. *Legs* rufous, with the anterior tibiæ (as well as the apex of the tarsi) fuscous.

A. humerale may be distinguished from its congeners by its greater size, and more particularly by the short and thick flavous pubescence on its elytra.

From the district of the River Amazon.

2. Allochroma coccineum.

A. *oblongo-ovatum, latum, robustum, impubescens, punctato-striatum, pallide rufum, glabrum; capite brevi, haud producto, inter oculos oblique foveolato, impunctato; thorace transverso, ante submarginato, apud angulos posticos obsolete depresso; elytris latis, striato-punctatis, ante medium transverse depressis; antennis robustis, filiformibus, ad apicem subtiliter incrassatis, rufo-fuscis, art. 6–11 fuscis; pedibus anterioribus nigro-fuscis, posticis rufis.*

Long. corp. $2\frac{1}{2}$ lin., lat. $1\frac{1}{8}$ lin.

Oblong-ovate, broad, robust, impubescent; punctate-striate, of a pale rufous colour throughout, glabrous. *Head* short, transverse, not produced in front; above the labrum is a transverse plane; above the base of the antennæ and between the eyes is a distinct and subcircular groove, which extends obliquely upwards towards the upper margin of the eyes; the surface impunctate: eyes large and prominent, situated at the base of the head, but not extending laterally as far as the anterior angles of the thorax. *Thorax* transverse, broader than the head; the anterior margin slightly emarginate; the anterior angles depressed and subacute; the sides marginate; the posterior angles subacute; the surface is equate, without any transverse basal depression; two very obsolete impressions are situated submedially in the direction of the posterior angles. *Scutellum* triangular, large, rounded at the apex, impunctate. *Elytra* broader than the thorax, robust, *slightly* attenuated towards the apex, with punctures arranged in the form of striæ; a broad and shallow depression extends transversely a little above the middle, which gives an appearance of prominence to the base; at the sixth stria from the suture a short longitudinal depression (close to the shoulder) gives distinctness to the humeral angle. *Antennæ* robust, filiform, with a slight tendency to dilatation at the apex; rufo-fuscous, the sixth to the tenth joints being fuscous. *Legs*: the anterior darkly fuscous; the posterior rufous throughout.

Brazil. Taken by Mr. Fry, and also by my friend Mr. Gray and myself, in the neighbourhood of Rio Janeiro.

This species is subject to slight variation in colour, some examples being of a brighter crimson hue than others: in one example in Mr. Fry's collection the posterior legs are black, and the antennæ more distinctly incrassated and of a deep black colour throughout.

In figure and general appearance, as well as in size, this species approaches closely to *Altica chlorotica*, Oliv. (vol. vi. p. 690, species 57, plate 2. fig. 37); it wants, however, the transverse postical line on the thorax, and appears to be deeper in colour than Olivier's species.

3. Allochroma sexmaculatum. (Tab. VII. fig. 7.) B.M.

A. *oblongo-ovatum, sat robustum ; capite foveolato ; thorace transverso, ad latera marginato, ad basin depresso, punctato, fuscorufo ; elytris latis, punctato-striatis, apicem versus obsoletis, testaceis, nigro sex-maculatis ; maculis duabus ante medium obliquis, alteris duabus post medium subcircularibus, et juxta humeros duabus minutis, fusco suffusis ; antennis robustis, filiformibus, rufo-fuscis ; pedibus robustis, rufis, fusco suffusis.*

Long. corp. 3 lin., lat. $1\frac{1}{2}$ lin.

Oblong-ovate, tolerably robust, impubescent, punctate-striate, shining, testaceous. *Head* short, very slightly produced in front; above the labrum is a distinctly transverse plane depression; immediately above the antennæ is a longitudinal fovea (extending nearly to the basal line) which is bisected at right angles by a short transverse carination, these two together forming, medially, between the eyes the character of a cross; on either side of these is a lateral angulated depression almost parallel to, but not approaching, the margins of the eyes; closely adjoining the base of the antennæ is another small but deep depression; the surface is impunctate and rufous. *Thorax* somewhat broader than the head, transverse, rectangular; the anterior angles acute and depressed; the sides broadly marginate; near the basal angles is an indistinct depression, more apparent when viewed transversely; the surface is deeply punctate throughout, of a dark rufous colour suffused with fuscous. *Scutellum* triangular; the apex being somewhat rounded, impunctate, black. *Elytra* broader than the thorax, robust, punctate-striate, the punctures being large and deep, and the striæ very apparent at the humeral angles; the striæ near the middle are no longer discernible, while at the apex the punctures are almost entirely obsolete; the colour is testaceous: on either side of the suture are two irregularly formed black markings; the one, antemedial, extends obliquely from the second to the fifth stria, in form obliquely and irregularly lozenge-shaped (on either side of this, between the seventh and eighth striæ, is a minute subcircular spot of suffused black); the other, postmedial, immediately adjoining the suture, is subcircular, between the second and the seventh rows of punctures. *Antennæ* robust, filiform, rufous; the fifth and sixth joints being longer than the third. *Legs* rufous, suffused with piceous.

A. sexmaculatum has evidently a very extended range. I have before me examples from Guatemala (from the British Museum collection), St. Catharine, and other districts of Brazil.

In the collection of the British Museum, and in most private cabinets.

4. Allochroma fasciatum. (Tab. VII. fig. 8.) B.M.

A. *oblongo-ovatum, robustum, depressum, punctatum, rufum; capite ad basin T foveolato; thorace transverso, ad latera marginato; elytris sat latis, punctatis, rufis, ad humeros et pone medium nigris (i. e. fascia transversa tenui ad medium, sutura, basique rufis); antennis robustis, filiformibus, fuscis; pedibus rufis, fusco suffusis.*

Long. corp. 2¾ lin., lat. 1½ lin.

Oblong-ovate, robust, depressed, punctate, impubescent, of a dark rufous colour. *Head* short, hardly produced; above the labrum is a transverse triangular depression; above the base of the antennæ and between the eyes is a longitudinal fovea, which is terminated at its upper extremity by another, transverse (extending between the inner margins of the eyes), these two together forming the character of the letter T; eyes tolerably prominent, situated near the base of the head; the surface (when viewed under a high power) darkly rufous. *Thorax* considerably broader than the head, transverse; the anterior angles depressed and prominent; the sides broadly marginate; at the base (when viewed laterally) is an obsolete transverse depression; the surface, under a high power, is minutely punctured, of a dark rufous colour, suffused with fuscous. *Scutellum* triangular, rufous. *Elytra* broader than the thorax, subdepressed, with punctures arranged in the form of striæ; these punctures become obsolete as they approach the apex: black; a transverse medial band, and also the apex being rufous; the suture also is narrowly rufous. *Antennæ* robust, filiform, rufo-fuscous. *Legs* rufous; the anterior tibiæ and femora being suffused on their upper surface with fuscous.

This species is subject to slight variation as to colour, and also the breadth of the transverse marking on the elytra.

Mexico, and the northern portion of the continent of South America. In the cabinet of the British Museum, and in most collections.

5. Allochroma piceum.

A. *ovale, sat robustum, subdepressum, nigro-piceum, nitidum; capite brevi, haud antice elongato, inter oculos foveolato, punctulato, fusco-castaneo; thorace transverso, rectangulari, angulis subacutis, post medium transverse depresso, punctato; elytris punctis magnis velut in striis coordinatis (ad marginem striatis), ante medium transverse et oblique depressis, apud humeros, marginem, et apicem parum castaneis; antennis robustis, piceis, art. 10mo et 11mo fuscis; pedibus piceis.*

Long. corp. 2¾ lin., lat. 1¼ lin.

Oval, black, shining. *Head* short, depressed, scarcely elongated in front, dark rufous; labrum fulvous; eyes distant and slightly prominent: between the eyes, and above the insertion of the antennæ, is a longitudinal fovea which extends nearly to the base of the head (narrowed between the eyes, but broader as it approaches the basal margin); a transverse and less distinctly defined fovea (increasing in breadth near the eyes) crosses this at right angles: the surface of the head is sparingly punctate, and of a rich castaneous colour. *Thorax* transverse, with the anterior and posterior angles acute; sides marginate, subsinuate; near the base is a broad and shallow transverse depression; the surface is distinctly but sparingly punctate, piceous, shining. *Elytra* with deep and distinct punctures arranged in the form of striæ; a broad and indistinct antemedial depression (which is inflected upwards on either side towards the shoulders) gives an appearance of fullness or prominence to the anterior angles; the colour is dark piceous, fading away at the shoulders, along the margins, and especially towards the apex, into a castaneous brown. *Antennæ* filiform, robust, piceous; the apex of the first and second joints, and the tenth and eleventh fuscous. *Legs* robust, piceous throughout.

Brazil.

6. Allochroma Balii.

A. *ovale, subdepressum, nigrum, nitidum; capite et thorace rufis; capite brevi, transverso, antice elongatulo, inter oculos transverse foveolato; thorace transverso, ad latera marginato; scutello rufo; elytris latis, fascia albo-flava antemedia, ad suturam bipartita, maculisque duabus ad apicem, circularibus, marginem (haud suturam) attingentibus, punctis obsoletis veluti in striis ordinatis; antennis fuscis; pedibus fuscis, femoribus posticis flavis.*

Long. corp. 2¾ lin., lat. 1¼ lin.

Oval, broad, subdepressed, black, glabrous. *Head* slightly depressed, produced somewhat in front; eyes prominent, lateral; between the eyes is a transverse and also a longitudinal fovea, forming together the character of the letter T; the surface is impunctate, except near the basal line, where scattered punctures are apparent; the colour is rufo-castaneous. *Thorax* transverse; the anterior margin slightly emarginate; the sides broadly marginate, and (when viewed laterally) depressed; the surface is impunctate and rufo-castaneous. *Scutellum* triangular, rufous. *Elytra* broad, black, shining, with faint and sparingly distributed punctures arranged as striæ; a broad antemedial transverse fascia, of a straw colour, is interrupted at the suture; near the apex are two large circular spots of the same colour. *Antennæ* short, robust, slightly incrassated towards the apex, fuscous. *Legs* black; the posterior femora being black, and the tibiæ and tarsi fuscous.

South America. A single example in the collection of Mr. Baly.

7. Allochroma lunatum. (Tab. VIII. fig. 1.)

A. *oblongo-ovatum, latum, robustum, impubescens, punctato-striatum, flavum; capite brevi, inter oculos foveolato, punctato; thorace transverso, rectangulari; elytris robustis, punctato-striatis, macula subcirculari ad scutellum, alteraque obliqua ad apicem, nigris; antennis filiformibus, flavis, art. 5 et 6 fusco suffusis; pedibus flavis, femoribus posticis fuscis.*

Long. corp. $2\frac{3}{4}$ lin., lat. $1\frac{1}{2}$ lin.

Oblong-ovate, broad, robust, impubescent, punctate-striate, of a flavous colour. *Head* transverse, abbreviated, not produced in front; below the base of the antennæ is a transverse triangular depression (impunctate and glabrous); between the eyes is a short longitudinal fovea, bisecting at its upper extremity another transverse depression, thus forming together the character of the letter T; eyes globose, extending laterally not quite so far as the base of the head; the surface is very finely punctate. *Thorax* transverse, rectangular; the anterior angles depressed and well-defined; the sides finely marginate and rectilinear; the surface is equate, clothed sparingly with a very fine pubescence. *Scutellum* triangular, impunctate, and black. *Elytra* broader than the thorax, robust, distinctly punctate-striate; flavous, with an almost circular black marking near the scutellum, extending laterally on either side to the seventh stria, and (in the direction of the apex) the distance of one-third of the whole length of the elytra: another marking at the apex is also common to both elytra; its upper margin commencing medially, at the sides, extends obliquely towards the suture; this apical marking is interrupted at the suture by the distance on either side of one stria. *Antennæ* filiform, robust (subincrassated), flavous, the fifth and sixth joints being suffused with fuscous. *Legs* flavous; the posterior femora being fuscous (suffused at the base with rufo-flavous), and the globular inflation on the posterior claw brightly rufo-fuscous.

This beautiful species is from the district of the River Amazon. In the collections of Messrs. Baly, Bates, Herr Dohrn, M. Chevrolat, and the Rev. H. Clark.

8. Allochroma flavovittatum.

A. *ovale, latum, subdepressum, obsolete pubescens, rufum; capite brevi, inter oculos transverse foveolatum; thorace transverso, punctato, rufo; elytris latis, punctato-striatis, nigris, fascia transversa media flava, sutura quoque a fascia ad scutellum late flava; antennis filiformibus, fuscis; pedibus flavis.*

Long. corp. $2\frac{1}{4}$ lin., lat. 1–$1\frac{1}{4}$ lin.

Oval, broad, depressed, obsoletely pubescent, rufous. *Head* very short, vertical, slightly produced; eyes large, prominent, extending laterally as far as the line of the margin of the thorax: from the labrum a longitudinal carination extends upwards to the insertion of the antennæ; on either side of this are two other obliquely transverse carinations extending to the sides of the mouth; above the insertion of the antennæ, and between the eyes, is a transverse fovea: the surface in front is glabrous, near the basal margin punctate, rufous. *Thorax* transverse, rectangular, slightly constricted towards the base; the anterior angles are depressed; the surface is thickly punctate, rufous. *Scutellum* triangular, flavo-rufous. *Elytra* much broader than the thorax, depressed, coarsely punctate-striate, dark cinereous black: a broad postmedial flavous fascia extends from the margination to the suture; its lower boundary (as it approaches the suture) inclines slightly towards the apex; upon its anterior margin it is rounded off from the margination upwards, extending obliquely towards the scutellum, and bounded at the scutellary angles by the second stria; this flavous fascia is clothed throughout with yellow pubescence, the extreme apex of the elytra being clothed with *white* pubescence. *Antennæ* filiform, attenuate, fuscous, the basal joint being flavous. *Legs* entirely flavous.

From the district of the River Amazon.

9. Allochroma venustum.

A. ovatum, robustum, impubescens, punctato-striatum, flavo-ferrugineum; capite brevi, inter oculos foveolato, granulato; thorace transverso, ad basin depresso, punctato; elytris robustis, punctato-striatis (ad apicem obsolete), ante medium transverse subdepressis, subtiliter pubescentibus; antennis filiformibus, robustis, subincrassatis, flavis, art. 7–10 fuscis; pedibus flavis.

Long. corp. 2 lin., lat. $1\frac{1}{4}$ lin.

Ovate, robust, impubescent, punctate-striate, flavo-ferrugineous. *Head* short, slightly produced in front; above the labrum is a transverse triangular depression; eyes tolerably globose, black, situated nearly at the base of the head, extending laterally nearly as far as the anterior angles of the thorax; between the eyes is a medial longitudinal fovea; the surface is finely granulated. *Thorax* transverse (almost quadrate), slightly constricted towards the apex; the anterior angles are much depressed; the sides marginate; at the base (when viewed obliquely) is a broad transverse depression; the surface is finely and thickly punctate throughout. *Scutellum* triangular, impunctate. *Elytra* considerably broader than the thorax, robust, punctate-striate (the striæ becoming almost obsolete as they approach the apex); an antemedial transverse depression gives a prominence to the surface near the scutellum, extending obliquely upwards, and terminating in a short and deep longitudinal fovea at the apex of the shoulders, between the eighth and ninth striæ: the surface (when viewed under a high power) is clothed throughout sparingly with an obsolete flavous pubescence; this pubescence is more apparent near the apex. *Antennæ* filiform, robust, tolerably short, subincrassated, flavous, the joints seven to ten being fuscous. *Legs* flavous throughout.

Brazil.

A. venustum may be recognized from most of its congeners by its concolorous elytra; it is distinctly *broader* than the two following species, which also are concolorous.

10. Allochroma nigro-marginatum.

A. *oblongo-ovale, robustum, subpubescens, flavo-ferrugineum; capite brevi, ad basin carinato; thorace transverso, angulis anticis subtruncatis, punctulato, ad basin pubescenti, ad marginationem piceo; elytris latis, punctato-striatis; antennis dilatatis, art.* 1–5 *flavis,* 6–9 *rufo-piceis,* 10 *et* 11 *rufo-ferrugineis; pedibus flavo-ferrugineis.*

Long. corp. 1 lin., lat. ½ lin.

Oblong-oval, broad, robust, very finely pubescent, of a flavo-ferrugineous colour throughout. *Head* short, depressed, slightly elongated; in front of the head is an obsolete transverse triangular depression; above the insertion of the antennæ are two oblique carinations extending transversely to the base of the head; eyes situated at the base of the head; the surface is finely punctate. *Thorax* transverse; the anterior angles depressed and truncate; the sides marginate and rectilinear (very slightly subsinuate towards the base); the surface is very finely punctate, clothed with pubescence towards the sides and apex; at the margination piceous. *Scutellum* small, triangular, pubescent. *Elytra* broad, robust, finely punctate-striate, transversely and antemedially subdepressed; finely flavo-pubescent. *Antennæ* robust, slightly dilated towards the middle; the joints one to five are flavous, six to nine rufo-piceous, ten and eleven rufo-ferrugineous. *Legs* flavo-ferrugineous throughout.

Rio Janeiro. In the collection of the Rev. H. Clark.

11. Allochroma assimile.

A. *oblongo-ovatum, latum, robustum, tenuiter subpubescens, flavo-ferrugineum ; thorace quadrato, ad basin transverse depresso ; elytris punctato-striatis, ante medium subdepressis, ad latera et ad basin subpubescentibus; antennis ad apicem dilatatis, art. 1–5 flavo-rufis, 6–8 rufo-piceis (cæteri desunt) ; pedibus anterioribus flavis, posticis rufo-flavis.*

Long. corp. 1 lin., lat. ½ lin.

Oblong-ovate, broad, robust, finely subpubescent (not so distinctly and generally as in *A. nigro-marginatum*); the colour is flavo-ferrugineous throughout. *Head* short, transverse, slightly produced; above the base of the antennæ, and between the eyes, are two obsolete obliquely-transverse carinations, while between them is a third, medial, reaching to the base of the head ; the surface is finely punctate. *Thorax* quadrate; the anterior angles subacute and much depressed ; the sides marginate; the surface more distinctly pubescent than in *A. nigro-marginatum*; the base is broadly and transversely subdepressed. *Scutellum* small, triangular, flavous. *Elytra* broad, robust, subparallel, finely punctate-striate, the striæ being almost obsolete; finely pubescent at the sides and apex, and very sparingly throughout the whole surface (more sparingly than in the former species) ; a broad and faint transversely oblique depression extends antemedially in the direction of the shoulders. *Antennæ* tolerably robust, slightly dilated towards the middle and apex ; joints one to five flavo-rufous, six to eight rufo-piceous (the rest are wanting in the example before me). *Legs*: the anterior flavous; the postical rufo-flavous.

This species is at first sight closely allied to *A. nigro-marginatum*; it may without difficulty be separated by the quadrate form of its thorax, and also by its somewhat less distinct pubescence.

Rio Janeiro. In the collection of Mr. Baly.

12. Allochroma quatuor-pustulatum. B.M.

A. *ovale, subparallelum, rufo-flavum, nitidum ; capite brevi, depresso, haud producto, inter oculos in forma literæ T foveolato ; thorace transverso, angulis subacutis, ad latera marginato, sparsim punctulato crebrius ad basin ; maculæ duæ circulares nigræ ad basin appropinquant ; elytris punctato-striatis, maculis quatuor nigris circularibus ornatis, ad marginem rufo-ferrugineis ; antennis brevibus, robustis, incrassatis, art. 1–5 rufo-flavis, 6–9 nigris, 10 et 11 testaceis ; pedibus flavis.*

Long. corp. 2⅓ lin., lat. 1–1¼ lin.

Oval, rufo-flavous. *Head* short, depressed, not anteriorly produced: eyes tolerably large, distant, not extending laterally as far as the posterior angles of the thorax; parallel to the inner margin of each is a semicircular depression, while *between* these depressions a T-shaped fovea is apparent: the surface is impunctate. *Thorax* transverse, rectangular; the anterior angles are prominent and subacute; the sides marginate and depressed; the basal angles also subacute; the surface is equate, finely punctured, glabrous; at the base are two circular black spots; the margination is rufo-fuscous, and the sides suffused with rufous. *Scutellum* triangular. *Elytra* broad, deeply punctate-striate; on either side of the suture (occupying the space between the second and the sixth striæ) are two large circular spots of a dark fuscous or black colour; the margination of the elytra is rufo-fuscous. *Antennæ* short, robust, subincrassated; the first joint being long, and dilated at the apex; the second short, ovate; the third shorter than the first, and contracted; the fourth and fifth shorter than the third; the remaining joints gradually but slightly incrassated; the first to the fifth flavous, the sixth to the ninth dark fuscous, the tenth and the eleventh testaceous. *Legs* flavous throughout.

Guatemala. A single specimen, in the cabinet of the British Museum.

This species, closely resembling *A. festivum*, is separated from it not only by its larger size and the different arrangement of its maculations, but in the character of the surface of its thorax, which is much more finely and less closely punctured.

13. Allochroma festivum.

A. *ovale, sat robustum, ferrugineum, nitidum; capite brevi, haud producto, inter oculos transverse foveolato; thorace transverso, angulis anterioribus depressis, marginato, punctato, maculis duabus postmediis nigris ornato; elytris fortiter punctato-striatis, maculis quatuor nigris inter strias 2^{am} et 6^{tam}; antennis robustis, ad apicem subincrassatis, fuscis, art. 6to–9no nigris; pedibus fuscis.*

Long. corp. $2\frac{1}{4}$ lin., lat. $1\frac{1}{4}$ lin.

Oval, ferrugineous, shining; of the form of the preceding species. *Head* very short and depressed: from the base of the antennæ a short longitudinal furrow extends medially upwards, and meets a transverse fovea between and somewhat above the eyes, the two together forming the letter T; this T-shaped canaliculation is bounded on either side by a depression, which is close to, and follows the course of, the inner margin of the eyes: the surface is finely punctate. *Thorax* transverse; the anterior angles depressed; the sides marginate; the surface is punctate, more distinctly at the base: a postmedial transverse depression (which does not reach the basal line) extends to the margination; in this depression are two contiguous circular spots. *Scutellum* sufficiently large, triangular, fuscous. *Elytra* tolerably robust, coarsely punctate-striate; in the centre of the antemedial, and also of the postmedial part of the elytra (between the second and the sixth striæ) is a large insulated black macula (that nearer to the shoulders subcircular, that at the apex oval or elongate). *Antennæ* robust, short, incrassated towards the base, fuscous, with the sixth to the ninth joints back. *Legs* robust, ferrugineous.

Brazil.

A. festivum differs from all other species, except the preceding, in its four distinct markings on the elytra.

14. Allochroma sex-signatum. (Tab. VIII. fig. 2.)

A. ovatum, robustum, flavum; capite depresso, antice haud attenuato, inter oculos in forma literæ T foveolato, impunctato (ad basin punctis minutis notato), rufo; thorace transverso, rectangulari, angulis distinctis marginatis, flavis; elytris punctis veluti in striis dispositis, flavis, ad basin rufo suffusis; maculis sex nigris, ad humeros duæ, ad scutellum duæ circulares, duæque post medium transversæ; antennis robustis, subincrassatis; pedibus flavis, tarsis anterioribus (tibiisque superne visis) fuscis.

Long. corp. 2¾ lin., lat. 1¼ lin.

Ovate, robust, flavous. *Head* large, very slightly produced, depressed; eyes tolerably large, but not extending laterally to the line of the anterior angles of the thorax; between the eyes is a very distinct T-shaped fovea, the longitudinal line of which is extended *obsoletely* upwards towards the base; the surface of the head is impunctate (with a few scattered minute punctures at the base) and rufous. *Thorax* transverse, rectangular, slightly compressed towards the base; the anterior angles are prominent and subacute; the sides distinctly marginate; the posterior angles distinct; the surface is equate (without *any* depressions), impunctate, and in colour flavous. *Scutellum* distinct, triangular, large, impunctate, flavous. *Elytra* broad, robust, with rows of large and shallow striæ-like punctures; a slight and broad depression extends transversely, a little in front of the middle; the surface is flavous; the apex is broadly suffused with rufous; six large black spots are distributed on the surface: one, on either side, at the humeral angle, a second (larger and circular) near the scutellum, and the third (larger still and transverse) postmedially. *Antennæ* robust, filiform, with a tendency to incrassation towards the apex, fuscous. *Legs* flavous, with the anterior tarsi and upper part of the anterior tibiæ fuscous.

Brazil.

15. Allochroma generosum. (TAB. VIII. fig. 3.) B.M.

A. oblongo-ovale, subcylindricum, cyaneum, nitidum ; capite et thorace rufis, valde punctatis ; capite brevi, subdepresso, antice paulum producto ; thorace transverso, angulis prominulis, lateribus marginatis, ad medium sensim anguloso-undulatis, bituberculato ; elytris parallelis, punctis velut in striis ordinatis ; antennis brevibus, fuscis ; pedibus nigris.

Long. corp. 3 lin., lat. 1⅜ lin.

Oblong-ovate, somewhat cylindrical, of a dark blue colour, shining; *head* and *thorax* strongly punctate, fulvo-rufous. *Head* short, transverse, depressed, hardly elongated in front; eyes distant, slightly prominent, extending laterally as far as the line of the thorax at the anterior angles; between the eyes (most apparent when viewed in front) is a transverse depression, which is connected with the insertion of the antennæ by a short medial horizontal fovea. *Thorax* slightly transverse (almost quadrate); the sides marginate, slightly dilated at the middle; the anterior angles distinct and subacute. *Scutellum* triangular, impunctate, fulvous. *Elytra* somewhat robust; the sides are parallel, with broad and shallow punctures arranged as striæ; an appearance of prominence is given to the anterior angles by a shallow transverse depression which extends obliquely in the direction of the shoulders; the colour is cyaneous, shining. *Antennæ* short, filiform, with a slight tendency to dilatation in the fifth to the eleventh joints, all of which are short, and of similar form and equal size; the first joint is narrow at the base, but dilated at the apex, of the length of the fourth; the second short, ovate; the third attenuated, longer than the first or the fourth; black. *Legs* rufo-fuscous.

Columbia. A single example is in the collection of the British Museum.

Genus 33. CERICHRESTUS*.

PALPI MAXILLARES *globosi, art. 3^{tio} plus duplo 2^{ndo} latiori, quadrato.*
PALPI LABIALES *elongati.*
ANTENNÆ *robustæ, ad apicem attenuatæ, ad medium subincrassatæ.*
CAPUT *breve, verticale.*

---

* κέρας, (cornu), frons, facies; χρηστὸς, eximius.

THORAX *transversus, ad basin plerumque transverse depressus.*
ELYTRA *parallela, punctato-striata, plerumque tomentosa aut holo-sericea.*
PEDES : *tibiis posticis, a retro visis, longitudinaliter canaliculatis, haud calcaratis.*

Labrum transverse, sinuate.

Mandibles concealed; at their inner surface, near the base, sub-dentate.

Maxillary palpi (Tab. VIII. fig. 4 m) globose; the basal joint quadrate; the second broader, and subdilated at the apex; the third subdilated, and sometimes obliquely truncate at the apex; the third twice the breadth of the second, and quadrate; the fourth short and flattened.

Labial palpi (Tab. VIII. fig. 4 n) elongate; the first and second joints being subincrassated towards their apex; the third elongate and cylindrical.

Antennæ approximate, filiform, in some species subdilated, robust, the length in the females being not more than two-thirds that in the males; the basal joint is produced, slightly dilated, and subinflected outwards; the third, fourth and fifth are shorter than the first, and subequal.

Eyes large and prominent, situated at the base of the head; in the males more globose than in the females.

Head short, not produced in front, vertical.

Thorax transverse; the anterior angles considerably depressed; the sides parallel, not sinuate in outline; the base is generally more or less transversely depressed, and the surface for the most part clothed with pubescence.

Scutellum triangular, situated in the plane of the elytra.

Elytra broader than the thorax, parallel, sometimes subcylindrical, strongly punctate-striate, generally clothed with dark pubescence more or less concealing the punctures of the striæ; the antemedial surface is never depressed transversely.

Legs: the *anterior femora* robust, cylindrical, subdilated towards the middle. The *tibiæ* are short, inflected at their immediate base, and gradually thickened towards the apex. The *tarsi* are short; the first joint triangular, not broader than the apex of the tibiæ; the second is of the same form, but somewhat smaller; the third is broader, more transverse, and distinctly bilobed; the fourth, proceeding from the base of the third, is produced and gradually thickened towards the apex: the ultimate claw is bifid, and armed at its inner surface near the base with a projecting spur or tooth, which is much more prominent than in adjoining groups. The *posterior femora* (when viewed transversely) are very much incrassated and ovate; in the males they are distinctly more elongate than in the females. The *tibiæ* are short, inflected at the immediate base, and longitudinally grooved along the posterior surface; this groove is gradually deepened into a terminal socket for the reception of the base of the tarsus; the margination of the groove is never, I believe, dentate, but generally subsinuate; the apex is subdilated and obliquely truncate, and armed below the insertion of the tarsus with a robust double spur. The *tarsus* is short; the first joint is considerably dilated at the apex; the second more filiform; the third much shorter and subcircular; from its centre proceeds the ultimate joint, which is apically dilated into a large globular inflation completely concealing from above the terminal claw.

This genus has a facies peculiarly its own, and unmistakeable. The antennæ, which are generally filiform, are more attenuate towards the apex than in other genera; the elytra are parallel and subcylindrical, much more elongate than in the genera *Allochroma* or *Omototus*; the surface is generally clothed throughout with a thick and short pubescence.

The sexual distinctions in this genus are evident: the males are less robust in form; they have the antennæ considerably longer, the eyes slightly more globose, the posterior femora more elongate (extending nearly to the apex of the elytra), and also the basal joints of the anterior tarsi flatly and broadly dilated.

1. Cerichrestus Balii.

C. *oblongus, ovalis, parallelus, pubescens, niger; capite brevi, nigro, ad apicem fulvo, ad basin fulvo maculato; thorace transverso, subquadrato, antice coarctato, ad basin transverse depresso, nigro-pubescenti, ad latera læte aureo marginato; elytris elongatis, punctato-striatis, ad humeros fulvo notatis; antennis robustis, incrassatis, nigris, art.* 9–11 *testaceis; pedibus fuscis, femoribus (ad basin), tibiis tarsisque posticis testaceis.*

Long. corp. 3½ lin., lat. 1¼ lin.

Oblong, oval, the sides parallel and somewhat attenuated; pubescent, black. *Head* very short, depressed, slightly produced in front; eyes distant, situated at the base of the head, and extending laterally not quite so far as the anterior angles of the thorax. *Antennæ* approximate; labrum and maxillary palpi of a dark bright-fuscous colour; the lower part of the head (below the insertion of the antennæ) pale ferrugineous; above the antennæ granulated and black;

immediately behind the eyes (between them and the base of the head) is a small fulvous marking which is confluent with the marking on the thorax. *Thorax* broader than the head, but gradually compressed in front, so that the anterior angles (which are distinct and slightly prominent) are at the same distance one from the other as the eyes; the sides are slightly marginate; at the base, and extending transversely towards the anterior angles, is a broad depression: the surface is clothed throughout with a thick short black pubescence; on either side is a broad band of bright yellow or golden pubescence, which extends along the whole length of the margination, being slightly narrowed as it approaches the basal angles. *Scutellum* triangular, impunctate, black. *Elytra* elongate, deeply punctate-striate, very finely tomentose throughout; of a dull black colour; at the shoulders is a short oblique marking of the same colour as (and connected with) the lateral band of the thorax, which extends, not along the margination, but between the seventh and eighth striæ. *Antennæ* not so long as the body, incrassated, black; the first joint is strongly dilated at the apex, and deflected outwards; the second short, narrower than the first, and dilated towards the apex; the third of greater length than the first, dilated towards the apex, and clothed more distinctly with long black pubescence; the fourth, fifth and sixth of the same form and colour as the third, and similarly pubescent, the fourth being still more broadly dilated; the terminal joints are gradually attenuate, the ninth to the eleventh being of a pale testaceous colour. *Legs* dark fuscous; the base of the femora, and the posterior tibiæ and tarsi, being pale testaceous.

Brazil. A single specimen of this insect is in the collection of Mr. Baly.

2. Cerichrestus apicalis.

C. *oblongus, subparallelus, subcylindricus, subtiliter pubescens, niger; capite transverso, ad basin antennarum tenue foveolato, granulato, nigro, ad apicem flavo, et ad basin fulvo bimaculato; thorace transverso, antice subcontracto, ad baseos angulos late depresso, ferrugineo-nigro, ad latera flavo vittato; elytris elongatulis, punctato-striatis, pubescentibus, nigris, ad humeros flavo notatis; antennis sat robustis, ad medium dilatatis, nigris, art. 9no fulvo, 10mo et 11mo flavis; pedibus nigris, femoribus ad basin flavo suffusis, tibiis tarsisque posticis fulvis.*

Long. corp. 3 lin., lat. 1⅓ lin.

Oblong, subparallel, subcylindrical, under a high power very finely pubescent, black. *Head* transverse, much depressed, slightly produced in front; eyes large, prominent, situated at some little distance from the base of the head, extending nearly as far as the anterior angles of the thorax: between the labrum and the base of the antennæ, the surface is smooth, glabrous, and transversely depressed; immediately above the base of the antennæ is an obsolete longitudinal depression; the whole surface being coarsely granulated; in colour black, the space between the labrum and the antennæ being flavous: at the base of the head, immediately behind the eyes, are two transversely lateral markings of a fulvous-red colour. *Thorax* transverse, slightly contracted in front, and (when viewed laterally) subdepressed; the anterior angles are subacute and depressed; the sides marginate; at the basal angles are two broad and obsolete depressions: the surface is clothed throughout (when viewed under a high power) with a short and thick pubescence; the colour fulvous-black, with a broad margin on either side of a bright golden-flavous colour. *Scutellum* triangular, dark fuscous. *Elytra* somewhat broader than the thorax, parallel, subelongate, deeply punctate-striate, the interstice between the second and third striæ being slightly but distinctly elevated; clothed throughout with a thick close pubescence; the colour black, of a ferrugineous hue; at the shoulders is a suffused flavous marking, which (becoming more obsolete) tinges the anterior half of the line of margination; the body beneath black. *Antennæ* broad, robust, dilated, and flattened medially; the first joint broad, and gradually dilated towards the apex; the second short, subtriangular; the third longer than, but hardly so broad as the first; the fourth to the seventh gradually but broadly dilated, and the seventh to the eleventh gradually attenuated towards the apex: the colour black, finely pubescent; the ninth joint being fulvous, and the tenth and eleventh flavous. *Legs* black; the base of the femora being fulvous, or suffused with flavous; the posterior tibiæ and tarsi fulvous; the globular inflation of the posterior claw piceous.

This species very nearly approaches *C. Balii* both in disposition of markings and in general form; it is, however, shorter and broader, and the thorax is unmarked by any lateral depressions.

New Grenada. In the collection of M. Chevrolat.

3. Cerichrestus Deyrollii.

C. *oblongus, ovatus, parallelus, pubescens, niger; capite brevi, granulato, fusco-rufo, ad basin fusco; thorace quadrato, ad basin subconstricto et transverse depresso, fusco, ad latera nigro-rufo; elytris parallelis, punctato-striatis, nigris; antennis subincrassatis, nigris; pedibus rufo-fuscis, tarsis tibiisque anticis nigro-fuscis.*

Long. corp. $2\frac{1}{2}$ lin., lat. $\frac{3}{4}$–1 lin.

Oblong, ovate, parallel, subcylindrical, pubescent, black. *Head* short, transverse, deflected, slightly produced in front; eyes distant, somewhat prominent; the maxillary palpi of a rufous colour: the lower surface of the head (below the insertion of the antennæ) is flavo-rufous, between the eyes fusco-rufous, and at the base fuscous; granulated, clothed towards the base with exceedingly minute pubescence. *Thorax* quadrate, constricted at the base; the anterior angles are distinct, but not prominent; the sides marginate; at the base is a broad transverse depression; the surface is tomentose, fuscous, except marginally, where it is broadly shaded off into dark rufous. *Scutellum* triangular, black. *Elytra* parallel, distinctly punctate-striate, dull black. *Antennæ* short, robust, in the fourth, fifth and sixth joints somewhat incrassated. *Legs* rufo-fuscous, with the anterior tibiæ and tarsi nigro-fuscous.

C. Deyrollii may be separated from all others in the genus by the form and the colouring of the thorax. It appears also (although the example before me is imperfect) to be narrower, and more elongated in general form.

Cayenne. In the collection of M. Deyrolle.

4. Cerichrestus Batesii. (TAB. VIII. fig. 4.) B.M.

C. oblongus, ovatus, subcylindricus, subtiliter pubescens, niger; capite brevi, granulato, ad labrum transverse depresso, fusco, antice rufofusco, inter oculos flavo binotato; thorace transverso, ad basin subconstricto, lateribus pœne angulatis, antice globoso, ad basin transverse depresso; elytris subcylindricis, punctato-striatis; antennis filiformibus, sat robustis, nigris; pedibus fuscis, tibiis tarsisque anterioribus et femoribus posticis (suffuse) nigro-fuscis.

Long. corp. 2¾–3 lin., lat. 1½–1¾ lin.

Oblong, ovate, subcylindrical, somewhat robust, finely pubescent, black. *Head* very short, depressed, not vertical, slightly produced in front; eyes distant, somewhat prominent, extending laterally to the line of the margin of the thorax; antennæ approximate; the surface of the head is granulated; below the insertion of the antennæ is a broad transverse triangular subdepression; the colour of the head below the antennæ is rufo-fuscous, and above dark fuscous; between the eyes (situate at their inner margin, and immediately above the insertion of the antennæ) are two small flavous markings, apparently caused by pubescence. *Thorax* transverse, subconstricted at the base; the anterior angles are broadly obliquely truncate; the sides are marginate and, medially, almost angulated; at the base is a broad, transverse depression (giving a decided prominence to the medial disk); near the posterior angles are two deep and well-defined circular foveæ; the surface (with the exception of a transverse triangular black margin at the base) is clothed with a rich golden pubescence. *Scutellum* triangular, somewhat transverse, punctate, black. *Elytra* subcylindrical, parallel, distinctly punctate-striate; between the striæ (and also between the punctures) very finely granulated; dull black. *Antennæ* filiform, considerably shorter than the elytra, sufficiently robust; the first joint broad, dilated towards the apex; the second short, ovate; the third twice the length of the second, and equal in length to the first; the fourth to the seventh with a slight tendency to dilatation; black. *Legs* fuscous, with the anterior tibiæ and tarsi and the outer and lower side of the postical femora dark fuscous.

C. Batesii may be at once recognized from other species by the sculpturing of its thorax, the globose anterior disk, and the two circular depressions near the basal angles.

Ega, district of the River Amazon. In the collection of the British Museum, and also in those of Mr. Baly, Mr. Bates, and the Rev. H. Clark.

5. Cerichrestus tenuicornis.

C. *oblongus, ovalis, subdepressus, niger; capite haud producto, super basin antennarum* T *foveolato, granulato, nigro, inter oculos fulvo binotato, antice flavo; thorace subquadrato, ad basin transverse depresso, fusco, utrinque flavo late marginato; elytris oblongis, parallelis, punctato-striatis, nigris, pubescentibus, ad humeros tenue longitudinaliter flavo notatis; antennis robustis, subfiliformibus, nigris; pedibus flavo-fuscis, tibiis tarsisque anterioribus nigro-fuscis.*

Long. corp. 2¾–3 lin., lat. 1¼ lin.

Oblong, oval, slightly depressed, very dark fuscous or black. *Head* short, transverse, depressed, not elongated in front; eyes tolerably large, prominent, extending laterally to the marginal line of the anterior thoracic angles; antennæ approximate, above their insertion and between the eyes is a T-shaped fovea; the surface at the base of the head is coarsely granulated; labrum and maxillary palpi fuscous; the anterior surface of the head is ferrugineous, the upper surface black; between the eyes and adjoining their inner margin are two fulvous markings. *Thorax* transverse, almost quadrate; the anterior angles obliquely truncate; the sides marginate; at the base and also near the apical angles is a broad transverse depression: the colour is dark fuscous, marked on either side by a broad flavous band, which becomes confluent at the anterior margin; this band seems to be formed for the most part by thick flavous pubescence. *Scutellum* triangular, obscure, dark fuscous. *Elytra* parallel, punctate-striate, dull black or very darkly fuscous, tomentose: from the humeral angle is a *narrow* indistinct flavous line extending halfway towards the apex; this is very much narrower than in *C. exiguus*, and is continued (not, as in that species, *across* the striæ and along the margination, but) along the line of the striæ. *Antennæ* of the same length as the body, robust, subfiliform, although in the third to the sixth joints there is an evident *tendency* to incrassation; black, not pubescent. *Legs* flavo-fuscous, with the anterior tibiæ and tarsi darkly fuscous.

Several examples of this species have been sent home from the Amazon by Mr. Bates. In the collections of Messrs. Baly, Bates, and the Rev. H. Clark.

The above description is taken from a male example; in the female the antennæ are not more than two-thirds the length (being hardly longer than the elytra). Other sexual characters also, which we should look for, are apparent: in the *male* the body is slightly *less robust*, and the basal joints of the anterior tarsi broadly and flatly dilated; there is a manifest dilatation also (when viewed laterally) in the *posterior tibiæ* of the male.

6. Cerichrestus exiguus.

C. oblongus, ovatus, subdepressus, niger; capite brevi, transverso, granulato, inter oculos tuberculis obsoletis ferrugineis binotato; thorace transverso, ad latera subsinuato, ad basin oblique depresso, punctato, tomentoso, nigro, ad medium longitudinaliter flavo notato; elytris latis, parallelis, punctato-striatis, ad humeros longitudinaliter fulvo notatis; antennis brevibus, robustis, incrassatis, nigris, art. 9–11 fulvo-flavis; pedibus nigris, femoribus (ad basin) et tibiis posticis fulvis, tarsis posticis flavis.

Long. corp. $2\frac{1}{2}$ lin., lat. $1\frac{1}{4}$ lin.

Oblong, ovate, broad, somewhat depressed, of a dull black colour. *Head* very short, transverse, depressed, almost vertical, not elongated; between the labrum and the line of the lower margin of the eyes is a transversely concave depression; eyes prominent, large, distant, situated *near to* the base of the head; antennæ approximate: the labrum and the maxillary palpi of a dark fuscous colour; the lower portion of the head ferrugineous; immediately above the insertion of the antennæ (and caused by an intermediate depression) are two obsolete ferrugineous tubercles, bounded (towards the base) by a transverse fovea; the surface of the head above this fovea is granulated and black; at the base is a distinct circular fulvous marking. *Thorax* transverse; the anterior angles obliquely truncate, but distinct; the sides marginate, and in outline subsinuate; a very slight medial longitudinal depression extends nearly to the base, while on either side of it an equally indistinct but broader depression is produced obliquely from the base towards the anterior angles: the surface is very thickly and finely punctured throughout, tomentose, black, with a broad medial longitudinal flavous marking, gradually extending in breadth from the base to the anterior margin; the margination of the thorax is ferrugineous. *Scutellum* very small, indistinct, darkly fuscous. *Elytra* broad, parallel, distinctly punctate-striate, tomentose, of a dull black colour; at the humeral angle is a distinct and broad fulvous marking, extending halfway down the margin of the elytra, broader at the base (extending laterally to the point of contact of the posterior angle of the thorax) and thence gradually diminishing. *Antennæ* short (not equal in length to the elytra), robust, incrassated; the first joint not so long as in allied species, dilated at the apex; the second short, ovate; the third, fourth, fifth and sixth gradually but broadly dilated, and distinctly pubescent, black; ninth to eleventh fulvo-flavous. *Legs* black, with the base of the femora and also the posterior tibiæ fulvous; the posterior tarsi flavous; the inflation above the posterior claw bright fulvo-rufous.

Amazon district.

7. Cerichrestus Chevrolatii.

C. *oblongo-ovatus, parallelus, subcylindricus, subtiliter pubescens, punctato-striatus, fusco-niger; capite brevi, granulato, super oculos fulvo notato; thorace quadrato, ad basin transverse foveolato, nigro-fusco, ad latera fulvo; elytris subelongatis, punctato-striatis; antennis subfiliformibus, fuscis; pedibus fuscis, femoribus flavo suffusis.*

Long. corp. 2½ lin., lat. ⅘ lin.

Oblong-ovate, parallel, subcylindrical, under a high power obsoletely pubescent, deeply punctate-striate, fuscous-black. *Head* short, transverse, not produced; below the base of the antennæ is a transverse glabrous depression; eyes tolerably large, situated at the base of the head, extending laterally as far as the anterior angles of the thorax; the surface at the base is coarsely granulated; in colour the labrum is fuscous, the part between the labrum and the insertion of the antennæ fulvous; at the base of the head dark fuscous, with two fulvous spots at the inner and upper margin of the eyes. *Thorax* quadrate, depressed in front, *slightly* constricted at the apex; sides finely marginate, and in form subsinuate; at the base (when viewed laterally) is a deep and distinctly defined transverse fovea; the surface is dark fuscous, the lateral margins being broadly fulvous. *Scutellum* triangular, impunctate, fuscous-black. *Elytra* somewhat broader than the thorax, subelongate and parallel, deeply punctate-striate, and (when viewed under a high power) very finely covered with short obsolete fuscous pubescence. *Antennæ* robust, subfiliform, fuscous. *Legs* fuscous, the femora being suffused with flavous.

C. Chevrolatii differs from *C. exiguus* (to which it is most nearly related) by its very parallel and subcylindrical elytra, as well as by the absence of any flavous marking near the humeral angles.

South America. In the collection of M. Chevrolat.

8. Cerichrestus humilis.

C. *oblongo-ovalis, parallelus, subdepressus, punctato-striatus, subtiliter pubescens, fusco-niger; capite brevi, depresso, granulato, antice flavo, ad basin nigro; thorace transverso, ad basin subcoarctato et transverse depresso, subtiliter pubescenti, flavo, ad medium fusco adumbrato; elytris depressis, punctato-striatis, obsolete fusco-pubescentibus; antennis filiformibus, sat robustis, nigris; pedibus flavis, tibiis tarsisque fusco adumbratis.*

Long. corp. 2¼ lin., lat. 1 lin.

Oblong-oval, somewhat depressed, parallel, punctate-striate, finely clothed with obsolete fuscous pubescence, fuscous. *Head* short, vertical, slightly produced in front; below the insertion of the antennæ is a transverse triangular depression, at the base of the antennæ the surface is obsoletely raised; the base of the head is coarsely granulated, and in colour black; the eyes are large, globular, lateral, and situated at the base of the head. *Thorax* transverse, rectangular; the sides are at the base slightly constricted and marginate; at the base is a broad transverse depression; the surface is equate and thickly pubescent; the colour is flavous, being, medially, broadly adumbrated with fuscous. *Scutellum* minute, fuscous. *Elytra* broader than the thorax, depressed, parallel, punctate-striate (the punctures being obsolete, and the striæ deep), and clothed with a minute, but thick, fuscous pubescence; the colour dark fuscous. *Antennæ* filiform, tolerably robust, black. *Legs* flavous, more or less clouded with fuscous.

C. humilis differs from most of the species in the group by the absence of markings on the elytra; and from those which, like it, are concolorous as to their elytra, by its smaller size and form of thorax.

From the district of the River Amazon. Taken by Mr. Bates.

9. Cerichrestus flavicans. (TAB. VIII. fig. 5.)

C. *oblongo-ovatus, subparallelus, niger; capite brevi, depresso, inter oculos T foveolato, punctato, nigro, ad basin late flavo notato; thorace transverso, subpubescenti, punctato, ad medium late longitudinaliter flavo vittato; elytris sat latis, punctato-striatis, flavo fasciatis, et apud marginationem (a fascia transversa ad humeros) flavo vittatis; antennis robustis, subdilatatis, nigris, art.* 9–11 *testaceis; pedibus fuscis, femoribus (ad basin) et tibiis posticis flavis.*

Long. corp. $2\frac{1}{4}$ lin., lat. $1-1\frac{1}{4}$ lin.

Oblong-ovate, subparallel, subrobust, black. *Head* short, much depressed, slightly produced; eyes large, prominent, black; above the insertion of the antennæ is a T-shaped depression, forming the boundary of two obsolete tubercles; the surface at the base is finely punctate; the labrum is of a bright black colour; the surface between the mouth and the base of the antennæ is pale testaceous, above the base of the antennæ fulvous (the T-shaped depression being fuscous, and a margin to the eyes broadly black). *Thorax* transverse, rectangular; the anterior angles depressed; the sides marginate; the surface is equate, finely pubescent, and punctate; a broad medial longitudinal marking of flavous extends from the apex (where it is nearly the breadth of the whole thorax) to the base (where it is the breadth of the scutellum); the colour of the margination is fulvous. *Scutellum* triangular, flavous. *Elytra* broad, punctate-striate, finely and closely pubescent: a transverse, irregularly defined flavous fascia extends, medially, from the margination to the suture; this fascia is connected on either side with the shoulder by a broad marginal flavous band. *Antennæ* tolerably long, robust, slightly incrassated towards the middle; black, the ninth to eleventh joints being pale testaceous. *Legs* dark fuscous, with the base of the femora and the posterior tibiæ flavous.

This species, though allied to *C. marginicollis*, is clearly distinct; the colour of the thorax and the form of the marking of the elytra, besides the diversity in the *sculpturing* of the *head*, amply separate it.

From the district of the Amazon. Taken by Mr. Bates.

10. Cerichrestus marginicollis. (TAB. VIII. fig. 6.)

C. *oblongo-ovalis, sat robustus, subpubescens, niger; capite brevi, inter oculos longitudinaliter leviter carinato, ad basin granulato, inter oculos suffuse fusco bimaculato ; thorace transverso, flavo-pubescenti, flavo, ad latera (antice) rufo-fusco ; elytris robustis, subparallelis, punctato-striatis, subtiliter pubescentibus, a humeris usque ad postmediam suturam oblique flavo-vittatis ; antennis robustis, nigris, art. 9–11 pallide testaceis ; pedibus fuscis, femoribus posticis fulvis, tarsisque posticis rufo-fulvis.*

Long. corp. 2 lin., lat. 1 lin.

Oblong-oval, tolerably robust, subpubescent, black. *Head* short, depressed, subelongate ; eyes large, prominent, extending laterally as far as the anterior angle of the thorax ; between the mouth and the base of the antennæ is a transverse triangular plane depression ; above the insertion of the antennæ is an obsolete medial longitudinal ridge ; the surface below the eyes is in colour testaceous (the mouth being broadly fuscous), above the eyes it is granulated and black, with two suffused fuscous markings at the posterior margins of the eyes. *Thorax* transverse, rectangular ; the anterior angles are depressed ; the sides marginate ; the surface is depressed, equate, flavo-pubescent, and in colour flavous, with a margination (more broadly anteriorly) of fuscous, and an obsolete longitudinal medial marking of rufo-fuscous. *Scutellum* triangular, flavous. *Elytra* robust, subparallel, punctate-striate, closely and finely pubescent, black: between the fifth and the eighth striæ, a longitudinal band (which does not touch the margination) extends from the shoulders nearly to the apex (being rounded off as it approaches the apex from the margination to the suture); its inner boundary is deflected abruptly and transversely towards the suture near the middle of the elytra, the whole forming an irregular semi-ovate band, the breadth of which is considerably greatest near the apex. *Antennæ* robust, with a tendency to dilatation; in colour black; the ninth to eleventh joints pale testaceous. *Legs* fuscous; the anterior femora being testaceous, the base of the posterior femora fulvous, and the posterior tarsi rufo-fulvous; the globular inflation above the posterior claw bright piceous.

C. marginicollis and the preceding species, *C. flavicans*, are exceptions to the general character of the genus, in that they have their elytra broadly and distinctly marked with flavous colour : this species is readily separated from *C. flavicans* by the triangular marking below the base of the antennæ, as well as by the obsolete longitudinal carination at the apex of the head ; it is more obviously separated by the disposition of its markings on the thorax and the elytra.

From the district of the Amazon. In the collections of Mr. Bates and the Rev. H. Clark.

Genus 34. **CALIPEGES** *.

LABRUM *breve, subcirculare.*
PALPI MAXILLARES *incrassati, art.* 3^{tio} *pœne rotundato, lato, ultimo conico.*
ANTENNÆ *robustæ, incrassatæ, art.* $4^{to}-8^{vo}$ *dilatatis, brevibus.*
CAPUT *breve, antice attenuatum, ad basin punctatum.*
THORAX *quadratus, elytris constrictior, subglobosus.*
ELYTRA *sat lata, cylindrica, fossa transversa ante medium antice punctata, ad apicem impunctata, glabra, obsolete pube sparsim (ad latera, apicem, et depressionem transversam) vestita.*
PEDES *robusti;* tibiis posticis *brevibus, rectis, haud calcaratis; tarsis brevibus, attenuatis.*

Labrum small, narrow, subcircular.

Maxillary palpi (Tab. VIII. fig. 7 *m*) robust; the first joint minute; the second incrassated, and apparently obliquely truncate at the apex; the penultimate joint is globose, rounded at the sides, the length being equal to the breadth, transversely truncate at the apex; the last joint is smaller, although broad at the base, acuminate, the length being distinctly greater than the basal breadth.

Labial palpi elongate, minute; in the example before me hardly appreciable in consequence of injury or decay.

Antennæ (Tab. VIII. fig. 7 *a*) robust, strongly dilated; the first joint attenuate at the base, elongate, and incrassated towards the apex; the second ovate, somewhat shorter but not narrower than the first, ovate, attenuate at the base; the third of equal length with the first, *fine and attenuated* at the base, and dilated towards the apex; the fourth to the eighth considerably incrassated, clothed with fine pubescence; the ninth to the eleventh more elongated and attenuated.

Eyes lateral, situated at the base of the head, circular, subglobose.

Head short, transverse, slightly produced, and attenuate in front; below the base of the antennæ is a transverse depressed plane; above this plane is a minute longitudinal medial channel, passing between the basal joints of the antennæ; the surface of the head at the base is sparingly but deeply and coarsely punctate.

Thorax somewhat broader than the head, but considerably narrower than the elytra, quadrate in form, almost elongate; the anterior angles are somewhat rounded; the base is constricted and slightly transversely subdepressed; the surface is subglobose in *C. crispus*, sparingly punctate, and obsoletely pubescent.

Scutellum triangular, impunctate.

Elytra decidedly broader than the thorax, short, *with a deep ante-*

---

* καλὸς, bonus; πήγνυμι, firmo.

medial depression which extends transversely nearly to the margination; this depression gives a prominence to the surface near the scutellary angles, and also (viewed laterally) to the medial disk: the surface is, antemedially, deeply and sparingly punctate; postmedially, and especially near the apex, impunctate; the surface at the apex, sparingly near the sides, and in the transverse depression is flavo-pubescent.

Legs robust. The *anterior femora* are subcylindrical, attenuated at the apex and base. The *tibiæ* are short, straight, and cylindrical, hardly thickened towards the apex. The *tarsi* are short; the basal and second joint subequal in form (the second joint being shorter and *comparatively* broader); the third joint is broader, ovate, and bilobed; the apical claw is bifid, and unarmed at its under surface with any claw. The *posterior femora* are broadly incrassated, short, not extending so far as the apex of the elytra. The *tibia* is *short* and robust, straight, gradually thickened towards the apex; the posterior margination is straight; the apex is broadly obliquely truncate, and is terminated by a double robust claw below the insertion of the tarsus. The *tarsus* is also short, attenuated.

An interesting form, allied to some species of *Cerichrestus* by its distinctly dilated antennæ; but abundantly distinct by reason of its more cylindrical body, and marked transverse depression of the elytra.

1. Calipeges crispus. (Tab. VIII. fig. 7.)

C. oblongo-ovatus, subparallelus, robustus, subtiliter pubescens, castaneus; capite subproducto, punctato; thorace quadrato, ad basin constricto et transverse subdepresso; elytris parallelis, robustis, subcylindricis, ante medium fortiter *transverse depressis, striato-punctatis; antennis art.* 4–8 *incrassatis,* 1–8 *fusco-ferrugineis,* 9–11 *flavis; pedibus fulvis.*

Long. corp. 1½ lin., lat. ⅔–¾ lin.

Oblong-ovate, subparallel, robust, very finely pubescent, of a dark castaneous colour. *Head* short, transverse, slightly produced in front; above the labrum is a transverse triangular carination; and above the insertion of the antennæ, and between the eyes, is an obsolete, obliquely transverse ridge of the form of the letter V; the surface is deeply but sparingly punctate; eyes large, situated at the base of the head, extending laterally almost as far as the anterior angles of the thorax. *Thorax* quadrate (the length being perhaps slightly greater than the breadth), constricted towards the base; the anterior angles are depressed and subacute; the sides are marginate; at the base is a broad transverse depression, which is most distinct (viewed laterally) near the basal angles; the surface is sparingly punctate, clothed throughout with fine and almost obsolete fulvous pubescence. *Scutellum* minute. *Elytra* parallel, robust, subcylindrical, short: a very distinct transverse depression extends antemedially from the suture to the sixth or seventh stria; this depression gives an appearance of prominence to the surface near the base; punctures arranged in the form of striæ, which are large and distinct near the base, are almost obsolete as they approach the apex: the surface is clothed throughout very sparingly with fine long single hairs, and underneath these with a very fine flavous pubescence. *Antennæ* robust, strongly dilated; in colour, the first to the third joints are ferrugineous, the fourth to the eighth dark fuscous, the ninth to the eleventh flavous. *Legs* fulvous throughout.

Para. In the collection of M. Chevrolat.

Genus 35. OMOTOTUS*.

Dej. Cat. (1837), p. 407.

PALPI MAXILLARES *breves, subdilatati.*
PALPI LABIALES *elongati.*
ANTENNÆ *filiformes, robustæ, interdum ad apicem subtiliter incrassatæ.*
CAPUT *breve, transversum, pœne verticale, rugosum.*
THORAX *transversus, aliquando subquadratus, interdum etiam ad latera obscure dentatus.*
ELYTRA *brevia, robusta, plerumque pube vestita.*
PEDES: *tibiis posticis longitudinaliter canaliculatis et calcaratis.*

Maxillary palpi (Tab. VIII. fig. 8 *m*) short, robust; the first joint minute; the second broader, and gradually dilated towards the apex; the third short, and broader than the second (the breadth being equal to the length); the terminal joint is broad, subglobose and flat.

Labial palpi (Tab. VIII. fig. 8 *n*) elongate, narrower than the maxillary palpi; the basal joint robust, the penultimate narrow and cylindrical, the ultimate joint attenuate.

Antennæ approximate, situated between the lower margins of the eyes, robust, filiform; the basal joint is dilated towards the apex; the second shorter and more minute.

Eyes lateral, situate at the base of the head.

Head short, transverse, depressed at almost right angles to the plane of the thorax, hardly produced in front; the surface is rugose, and for the most part impubescent.

Thorax transverse, in some species almost quadrate; the anterior angles are for the most part distinct; the sides are finely marginate and subsinuate, or produced medially into an obsolete tooth; the

* Derivatio incerta.

surface is rugose and deeply granulated, generally more or less impubescent.

Scutellum small, triangular.

Elytra robust, short, distinctly broader than the thorax; in most species clothed with a thick and very fine pubescence, punctate-striate.

Legs: the anterior sufficiently elongate. The *femora* are incurved, attenuate at their base, and gradually thickened towards the apex. The *tibiæ* are somewhat longer than the femora, straight, cylindrical, inflected at their immediate base. The *tarsi* are short; the first and second joints being flat and broad, in form triangular; the second joint being somewhat smaller than the first; the penultimate joint is considerably broader than the second, and deeply bilobed; the terminal joint is connected with the third at its base, and incurved; the apical claw is bifid, robust at the base. The *posterior femora* are short and broadly incrassated. The *tibiæ* (Tab. VIII. fig. 8 *h*) are short, incurved, and robust; the posterior surface is flattened and, near the apex, longitudinally hollowed out into a groove terminating in a socket for the reception of the tarsus; this groove is armed laterally with short and frequent comb-like teeth; immediately above the insertion of the tarsus its margin is produced into a broad and distinct tooth. The *tarsi* are short; the two basal joints are attenuate, the second being somewhat more minute than the first; the third joint is broader, subcircular, and somewhat longer than the second; the apical claw is entirely concealed from above by the globular inflation of the ultimate joint.

This genus is distinguished at once from *Cerichrestus* by its more robust and broader form. The distinct pubescence on the elytra, together with the form of the posterior tibiæ (which are robust, incurved, and armed above the insertion of the tarsus with a distinct spur), sufficiently separate it from other genera.

1. **Omototus morosus**. B.M.

Dej. MS. (Dej. Cat.).
Omototus carbonarius, *Chevr. (Dej. Cat.).*
—— tristis, *Lacordaire (auct. Dej. Cat.).*

O. *oblongo-ovatus, robustus, punctato-striatus, squamosus, niger; capite paulum producto, inter oculos bifoveolato, granulato; thorace quadrato, fortiter granulato, ad latera angulato; elytris punctato-striatis, æquatis, squamosis; antennis robustis, subfiliformibus, fuscis; pedibus fusco-nigris.*

Long. corp. $3\frac{1}{2}$ lin., lat. $1\frac{3}{4}$ lin.

Oblong-ovate, robust, punctate-striate, clothed with a very short and obsolete black squamose pubescence; in colour black. *Head*

P

short, transverse, slightly produced in front: above the labrum is a transverse triangular carination; immediately above the base of the antennæ are two distinct tubercular elevations, occupying almost the whole of the surface near the eyes (which in *O. quadripes* is represented by a depression): eyes situated at the base of the head, small; the line of the base is much less distinct than in *O. quadripes*: the surface is irregularly and deeply granulated; black. *Thorax* quadrate, decidedly broader in proportion to its length than in *O. quadripes*; the anterior angles are much depressed; the sides marginate, and produced medially into a lateral angle (almost as distinctly defined as the marginated angle in *Octogonotes*, and very different from the subsinuation of *O. quadripes*); the surface throughout is very coarsely and unevenly granulated. *Scutellum* obscure, triangular, impunctate. *Elytra* broader than the thorax, robust, punctate-striate, the punctures being quite concealed by a very thick and short squamose pubescence. *Antennæ* robust, filiform, subincrassated towards the apex; in colour fuscous-black. *Legs* robust, of a fuscous-black colour throughout (not partly flavous as in *O. quadripes*).

The form of the thorax (quadrate instead of transverse) and the colour of the legs seem to supply good specific distinctions between these closely allied forms; it is possible, however, that hereafter, by the inspection of a large series of examples, it may be shown that but one single species exists, subject to some considerable variation of form and colour.

Cayenne. In the collection of the British Museum, and in the cabinet of the Rev. H. Clark.

2. Omototus quadripes.
Chevr. MS.

O. *oblongo-ovatus, latus, robustus, impubescens, niger; capite brevi, granulato; thorace transverso, ad latera media subproducto, fortiter granulato; elytris punctato-striatis, subsquamosis; antennis filiformibus; pedibus piceis, femoribus et tibiis (ad basin) anterioribus flavis.*

Long. corp. 3½ lin., lat. 1¼ lin.

Oblong-ovate, broad, robust, impubescent, black. *Head* short, depressed at almost right angles to the thorax, and not produced in front; above the labrum is a transverse triangular plane (the colour of which is more distinctly rufous than the rest of the surface); above the base of the antennæ and between the eyes is a longitudinal irregular medial depression; the eyes are situated at the base of the head; the surface between the eyes and at the base irregularly and unevenly granulated, in colour darkly rufo-fuscous. *Thorax* transverse, broader than the head; the anterior angles are subdepressed; the sides marginate and, medially, obsoletely dilated or subsinuate in outline; the surface is uneven and irregular in form, broadly but slightly depressed at the base, and coarsely granulated throughout; the colour black. *Scutellum* small and triangular. *Elytra* broader than the thorax, robust, finely punctate-striate; when viewed under a high magnifying power, the surface between the striæ is finely punctate, and also towards the apex apparently clothed with thick, fine squamose pubescence. *Antennæ* filiform, short, robust, piceous. *Legs* piceous; the anterior femora and part of the tibiæ flavous.

Cayenne.

3. Omototus tuberculatus.

O. *ovatus, latus, robustus, pubescens, fuliginosus; capite brevi, inter oculos bituberculato; thorace quadrato, angulis anticis valde depressis, ad apicem bituberculato, ad basin transverse depresso; elytris latis, robustis, striato-punctatis, ad medium nigro- aut fusco-, ad apicem irregulariter testaceo-pubescentibus; antennis ad apicem subincrassatis, art. 1–6 fulvis, 7 et 8 testaceis, 9–11 fuscis; pedibus, tibiis posticis subincurvatis, piceis, tarsis posticis rufo-fuscis.*

Long. corp. 2½ lin., lat. 1½ lin.

Ovate, broad, robust, pubescent, fuliginous. *Head* short, transverse, depressed, slightly elongated in front; eyes moderately large, situate at the base of the head; above the labrum is a transverse triangular depression with a medial obsolete longitudinal carination: immediately above the insertion of the antennæ are two medial abrupt tubercles, while above them (at a somewhat greater distance from each other) are two others, *less prominent* (almost obsolete); these are separated from the basal line by a short medial transverse depression which is divided by a longitudinal carination: the surface is irregularly clothed with flavous pubescence. *Thorax* quadrate, rectangular; the anterior angles are much depressed; the sides marginate: two *broad* and *prominent* tubercles occupy the antemedial part of the disk; between them and the basal line is a transverse broad *shallow* depression: the surface is flavo-pubescent, especially near the base. *Scutellum* small, almost obsolete, triangular. *Elytra* broad, robust, covered with very coarse punctures arranged as striæ; near the scutellary angle the surface (when viewed laterally) is slightly raised, and covered throughout more or less with short scattered pubescence; at the shoulders this pubescence is hardly apparent; it assumes, medially (towards the margination and at the suture), a fuscous or dark ferrugineous hue, while *postmedially* are several unconnected small patches of yellowish-white pubescence.

Antennæ tolerably long, robust, slightly incrassated towards the apex; the first and second joints fulvous, the third and fourth rufo-fulvous, the fifth and sixth rufo-fuscous, the seventh and eighth (which are much shorter than any of the preceding) pale testaceous, the ninth to eleventh dark fuscous. *Legs* tolerably long and robust, the posterior tibiæ being somewhat incurved towards the apex, of a piceous colour throughout; the posterior tarsi (and the base of the tibiæ) are rufo-fuscous; the globular inflation above the apical claw dark rufous.

This species may be separated from its congeners by its greater size, and dark fuliginous colour; from *O. fuliginosus* (to which it is most nearly allied) it may be separated by the *prominent tubercles* on the thorax as well as its somewhat larger size, and by the irregular patches of white pubescence near the apex of the elytra.

Bogota. In the collection of Mr. Waterhouse.

4. Omototus braccatus.

O. ovatus, latus, robustus, subtiliter pubescens, rugosus, niger; capite depresso, ad basin bituberculato, granulato; thorace transverso, antice compresso, bituberculato, rugoso; elytris ad scutellum undique tuberculatis, quatuor, etiam aut quinque tuberculis inferioribus, subtiliter pubescentibus, sparsim punctatis; antennis fulvis; pedibus piceis, tibiis anterioribus fulvo vittatis, tibiis posticis (femoribusque extremis) fulvis.

Long. corp. 3 lin., lat. 1⅖ lin.

Ovate, broad, robust, apparently impubescent (except when viewed under a high power), black. *Head* short, transverse, depressed at right angles to the thorax, and slightly produced in front; immediately above the base of the antennæ is an obsolete transverse depression, which gives, at its upper margin, prominence to a raised transverse ridge, which does not extend laterally so far as the inner margin of the eyes; above, and unconnected with these, at the base of the head, are two distinct tubercles: eyes tolerably large, situated at the base of the head, not extending laterally so far as the anterior angles of the thorax; the surface throughout is coarsely and roughly granulated. *Thorax* considerably broader than the head, transverse (the breadth being not much greater than the length); the anterior angles are distinct, and depressed; the sides slightly marginate and anteriorly compressed; in front are two medial and longitudinal tubercles, on the outer sides of which are disposed other irregular carinations; the whole surface being coarsely and unevenly granulated. *Scutellum* large, triangular, clothed with short flavous pubescence. *Elytra* much broader than the thorax, robust, with deep and irregularly scattered punctures arranged throughout in the form of striæ; near the scutellary angles are two broad and prominent tubercles, while behind them, occupying the whole of the surface nearly as far as the apex of the elytra, are distributed five others, irregularly disposed, and in form slightly longitudinal; the humeral angles at their extremity are distinctly gibbous, so that the breadth across the shoulders is greater than the medial breadth; the whole surface is uneven and irregular, and clothed throughout (when viewed under a high power) with a short and thick piceous pubescence. *Antennæ*: the two basal joints fulvous (the rest, in the example before me, are wanting). *Legs* piceous; the posterior tibiæ and the extreme apex of the femora fulvous; the anterior tibiæ are banded with fulvo-fuscous.

Brazil. In the collection of M. Chevrolat.

5. Omototus nodosus. (Tab. VIII. fig. 8.)

O. *ovatus, brevis, robustus, griseo et fusco pilo omnino vestitus; capite brevi, inter oculos transverse tuberculato, ad basin granulato; thorace transverso, ad medium bituberculato, ad basin valde et transverse depresso, cinereo, et ad latera fulvo-pubescenti; elytris latis, ad scutellum bituberculatis, punctato-striatis, pilo cinereo, fulvo, et rufo-fusco vestitis; antennis art. 6–11 incrassatis, 1–8 testaceis, 9–11 pallide fuscis; pedibus rufo-fuscis, femoribus posticis fuscis.*

Long. corp. 2⅓ lin., lat. 1¼ lin.

Ovate, short, broad, clothed throughout with different shades of griseous and fuscous pubescence. *Head* short, depressed anteriorly, not produced; between the eyes (which are large and somewhat prominent) are two transverse tubercles (varying in direction and in prominence in different examples) of a more distinct rufous colour; the upper surface is finely granulated. *Thorax* transverse; the anterior angles are depressed and indistinctly subacute; at the base is a broad and deep transverse depression, while above this depression are two very prominent tubercles; the surface is clothed throughout with grey, ashy-grey, and (near the sides) fulvous pubescence. *Scutellum* small, triangular. *Elytra* broad, short, deeply punctate-striate, with two prominent tubercles near the scutellum, clothed throughout (like the thorax) with grey, fulvous, and rufo-fuscous pubescence. *Antennæ* short, gradually incrassated towards the apex (between the sixth and eleventh joints); in colour, the first joint to the eighth are testaceous, the ninth to the eleventh pale fuscous. *Legs* rufo-fuscous, the posterior femora being fuscous.

This insect is very nearly related to *O. tuberculatus*; it has the same prominent tubercles on the thorax and near the scutellum; it is also clothed like that species with different shades of pubescence: the thorax, however, is more transverse, less quadrate; the depression at the base of the thorax is more distinct, and (when viewed laterally) the tubercles are *more prominent* and *pyramidal*; the pubescence also is generally darker.

From the district of the Amazon River. In the collections of Mr. Baly, Mr. Bates, and the Rev. H. Clark.

6. Omototus Dohrnii.

O. oblongo-ovatus, robustus, punctato-striatus, pubescens, ferrugineus; capite brevi, inter oculos oblique foveolato; thorace transverso, antice elevato et bicarinato; elytris robustis, punctato-striatis, ante medium oblique depressis, fulvo- vel fusco-pubescentibus; antennis robustis, subtiliter dilatatis, art. 1–4 flavis, 5 et 6 rufoflavis, 6 et 7 testaceis, 8–11 flavo-fuscis; pedibus flavis, femoribus posticis infra fusco suffusis.

Long. corp. 2–2¼ lin., lat. 1–1¼ lin.

Oblong-ovate, robust, punctate-striate, pubescent, ferrugineous. *Head* transverse, slightly produced, depressed at right angles to the plane of the elytra; above the labrum is a transverse triangular plane; immediately above the insertion of the antennæ is a short longitudinal fovea (not extending to the basal line of the head), on either side of which is a minute oblique carination, made more apparent by depressions at the inner margins of the eyes; the eyes are large and prominent, situated at the base of the head, extending laterally beyond the anterior angles of the thorax; the surface at the base is finely punctate. *Thorax* transverse (almost quadrate), subcylindrical; the anterior angles depressed and obscure; the sides subsinuate and marginate; the posterior angles are considerably depressed, and the anterior medial disk elevated, and impressed with a broad longitudinal furrow, raising the surface *immediately* on either side of it into an oblong ridge or tubercle; the surface is very finely and thickly pubescent. *Scutellum* triangular. *Elytra* robust, considerably broader than the thorax; a broad antemedial depression extends obliquely upwards to the shoulders, giving an appearance of prominence to the scutellary angles; punctate-striate (the punctures being entirely concealed by a thick and short pubescence); the colour of this pubescence is for the most part ferrugineous, clouded (especially near the scutellum) with dark fuscous, and interspersed (especially at the oblique depression and near the suture) with irregular minute spots of pale cinereous. *Antennæ* robust, finely dilated towards the apex; the first to fourth joints flavous, fifth and sixth rufo-flavous, sixth and seventh testaceous, eighth to eleventh flavo-fuscous. *Legs* flavous, suffused with rufous; the posterior femora on their under surface being darkly fuscous.

This species differs from *O. nodosus* in its less transverse and narrower thorax; from *O. Cayensis* by its larger and more robust form, and by the more depressed basal angles of the thorax.

From Surinam (Paramaribo). In the collections of Herr Dohrn and the Rev. H. Clark.

7. Omototus nubilus.

Œdipodes nubilus, *Dej. Cat.* ed. 3. p. 408.
—— modestus, *Lacordaire (auct. Dej. Cat.).*

O. oblongo-ovatus, robustus, latus, punctato-striatus, fusco- et flavo-pubescens; capite brevi, haud producto, inter oculos transverse depresso, flavo, ad basin fusco; thorace transverso, antice bituberculato, ad basin transverse depresso, ferrugineo, ad latera fusco; elytris latis, robustis, punctato-striatis, ante medium obsolete depressis; antennis ad apicem subincrassatis, articulis 1–4 flavis, 5 et 6 rufo-fuscis, 7 et 8 testaceis, 9–11 fuscis; pedibus flavis, tarsis anterioribus femoribusque posticis fusco suffusis, tibiis tarsisque posticis rufo-fuscis.

Long. corp. 2 lin., lat. 1 lin.

Oblong-ovate, robust, broad, punctate-striate, clothed throughout with a fusco-flavous pubescence. *Head* short, transverse, slightly produced in front: between the labrum and the base of the antennæ is a transverse plane and glabrous depression; at the insertion of the antennæ is a medial longitudinal fovea, sharply defined and narrow, extending upwards and meeting a broad transverse depression which connects the inner margins of the eyes; the eyes are large and tolerably globose, situated at the base of the head; the surface is very finely clothed throughout with flavo-testaceous pubescence; in colour flavous, the base being margined with fuscous. *Thorax* transverse, rectangular; the anterior margin subemarginate; the sides distinctly marginate: at the antemedial centre of the disk are two oblong and distinctly prominent tubercles; behind these, a transverse depression at the base extends not quite so far as the basal angles, but subcircularly upwards; at the lateral margins (immediately above the margination) on either side are two smaller tubercles: the surface is clothed throughout with fine flavo-fulvous pubescence; the colour being ferrugineous, suffused at the sides with fuscous. *Scutellum* minute, triangular, impunctate, fuscous. *Elytra* considerably broader than the thorax, robust, short, punctate-striate, the striæ being shallow and almost concealed by a thick irregular pubescence, and the punctures being regular and *more distinct*; the surface is clothed with a thick flavo-fuscous pubescence, irregularly mottled with flavous and ashy-grey: an antemedial transverse obsolete depression extends obliquely upwards to the outer margins of the humeral angles, thus giving an appearance of prominence to the surface near the scutellary angles; the extreme apex of the humeral angles also is subprominent, causing the striæ near it to be slightly sinuate. *Antennæ* sufficiently fine, subincrassated towards the apex; the third joint is very considerably longer than any of the others, and the basal joints of the same breadth as the first; in colour, the joints first to fourth are flavous, fifth and sixth rufo-fuscous, seventh and eighth testaceous, and ninth to eleventh fuscous. *Legs* flavous, the anterior tarsi and posterior femora being suffused with fuscous, and the posterior tibiæ and tarsi rufo-fuscous.

This species approaches *O. Dohrnii* in form and general character; it is, however (besides the less piceous and more flavous colour of its pubescence), shorter and more robust, and the basal depression of the thorax is broader and more distinctly defined. From *O. nodosus* it differs also in its shorter form and in the different arrangement of markings on the head, and its less prominently bituberculated thoracic disk. From other species of the group (all of which resemble each other more or less in general appearance) it may be separated by its manifest difference in size.

Cayenne. In the collection of M. Chevrolat.

8. Omototus Cayensis.

O. oblongo-ovatus, latus, robustus, punctato-striatus, fusco- et fulvo-pubescens; capite brevi, inter oculos transverse depresso, ad basin rufo-flavo, flavo-pubescenti; thorace transverso, rectangulari, lateribus marginatis, antice globoso, bituberculato, ad angulos basales depresso; elytris latis, punctato-striatis, ad scutellum gibbosis, fulvo- aut fusco- irregulariter pubescentibus; antennis subincrassatis, art. 1–4 *et* 7 *et* 8 *flavo-testaceis,* 5, 6, 9–11 *fuscis; pedibus anterioribus flavis, tarsis tibiarumque apicibus fusco suffusis.*

Long. corp. 2 lin., lat. 1 lin.

Oblong-ovate, broad, robust, punctate-striate, clothed throughout with a fine but close fuscous or fulvous pubescence. *Head* short, transverse, depressed, not produced in front; above the labrum is a narrow transverse smooth depression, extending from which, as far as the base of the antennæ, is a minute medial carination: eyes prominent, globose, extending laterally as far as the anterior angles of the thorax; between the eyes is a medial longitudinal fovea, which reaches (at its upper extremity) an almost imperceptible transverse depression; at the base of the head the surface is rufo-flavous; clothed throughout with flavous pubescence. *Thorax* transverse (almost quadrate), rectangular; the sides are marginate, and the line of the base subsinuate; at the antemedial portion of the disk the surface is prominently raised, being divided into two oblong elevations by a broad longitudinal anterior depression; the base is comparatively depressed, more distinctly at the postical angles; the surface is clothed throughout with a rich fulvous pubescence. *Scutellum* triangular, pubescent. *Elytra* considerably broader than the thorax, subparallel, punctato-striate, the punctures being quite concealed by thick pubescence; the surface near the scutellum is distinctly gibbous; the colour of the pubescence is very varied: near the margination and at the base it is rufous, rufo-ferrugineous being the principal colour; near the suture (between the second and third striæ) there are three distinct but small markings of ashy-white colour; between these the surface is principally dark fuscous. *Antennæ* subincrassated gradually towards the apex; the first joint being broad, but elongated; the second short and ovate; the third and fourth attenuated, of equal length with the first; the fifth to eighth shorter and more dilated; the ninth to eleventh broader, and not longer, than the second; in colour, the joints first to fourth and seventh and eighth are flavo-testaceous, the fifth, sixth, and ninth to eleventh are darkly fuscous. *Legs* robust; the anterior flavous, the tarsi and apex of the tibiæ being suffused with fuscous (the posterior legs in the example before me are wanting).

This species differs from *O. fulvo-pubescens* in the colouring of its antennæ, in the less deeply-marked striæ on the elytra, and in its more close as well as differently marked pubescence.

Cayenne. In the collection of M. Deyrolle.

9. Omototus fulvo-pubescens.

O. oblongo-ovatus, latus, robustus, punctato-striatus, fulvo-pubescens; capite brevi, flavo-pubescenti, ad apicem rufo, ad basin fusco; thorace transverso, rectangulari, lateribus subsinuatis, antice elevato, bituberculato; elytris latis, robustis, subparallelis, punctato-striatis, ad basin elevatis, flavo-fusco, fulvo- et testaceo- (irregulariter) pubescentibus; antennis incrassatis, art. 1–8 fla-

vis, 9–11 *rufo-ferrugineis ; pedibus anticis flavis, mediis et posticis rufo-ferrugineis.*

Long. corp. 2 lin., lat. 2 lin.

Oblong-ovate, broad, robust, subparallel, deeply punctate-striate, clothed throughout with a fine fulvous (interspersed with fulvo-fuscous) pubescence. *Head* short, transverse, slightly produced in front; above the labrum is a transverse glabrous carination : eyes tolerably large, extending laterally as far as the anterior angles of the thorax; between the eyes is a transverse and obsolete (almost imperceptible) depression : the surface is flavous, clothed with a flavous pubescence; the colour near the labrum being rufous, and at the base fuscous. *Thorax* transverse, almost quadrate, rectangular ; the anterior angles subdepressed ; the sides obsoletely marginate and obscurely *sinuate* (not, as in *O. Cayensis*, rectilinear) ; the anterior medial disk is elevated, and is divided into two parts by a broad and tolerably deep longitudinal depression, thus forming two distinct antemedial tubercles; the base is transversely depressed, more deeply at the basal angles ; there is also a slight depression close to the subsinuation of the sides (which is not represented in *O. Cayensis*) ; the surface is in colour flavous, clothed throughout with flavous pubescence, medially more darkly flavous. *Scutellum* triangular, clothed with fusco-flavous pubescence. *Elytra* robust, considerably broader than the thorax, subparallel, punctate-striate, neither the punctures nor the striæ being concealed by the pubescence ; near the scutellary angles the surface is distinctly raised, and rendered more prominent by an antemedial depression, which does not exist in *O. Cayensis* ; the surface is clothed throughout with a flavous pubescence, irregularly mottled with flavo-fuscous and ashy-grey. *Antennæ* incrassated towards the apex; the joints first to eighth being flavous, and ninth to eleventh rufo-ferrugineous. *Legs*: the anterior flavous ; the medial and posterior rufo-ferrugineous.

Paramaribo, Dutch Guiana. From the collection of Herr Dohrn.

10. Omototus bituberculatus.

O. ovatus, robustus, subpubescens, fusco-ferrugineus ; capite brevi, super antennarum basin oblique foveolato, cinereo-pubescenti (ad basin piceo suffuso) ; thorace quadrato, antice bituberculato, pilo cinereo vestito ; elytris latis, punctato-striatis, pubescentibus, ad scutellum et suturam nigro-fuscis, ad latera nigro-flavis sparsimque cinereis ; antennis subincrassatis, art. 1–6 flavis, 7 et 8 testaceis, 9–11 fuscis ; pedibus pallide testaceis.

Long. corp. 2$\frac{1}{2}$–2$\frac{1}{2}$ lin., lat. 1$\frac{1}{3}$ lin.

Ovate, robust, subpubescent, in colour fusco-ferrugineous. *Head* depressed, slightly produced; eyes large and prominent, extending as far as the lateral margin of the thorax: below the base of the antennæ is a transverse triangular depression; immediately above it is an obsolete fovea in the form of the letter V; on either side of this fovea the eyes are margined by a longitudinal depression; the surface of the head is clothed entirely with an ashy-grey pubescence (at the base suffused with piceous). *Thorax* quadrate; the anterior angles depressed; the sides submarginate; the antemedial surface is raised, and forms two distinct and prominent tubercles; the whole surface clothed with an ashy-grey pubescence. *Scutellum* small, triangular, fuscous. *Elytra* broad, punctate-striate, completely covered with a thick short pubescence; the colour near the scutellary angles and along the suture is dark fuscous, at the sides dark flavous interspersed with ashy-grey. *Antennæ* slightly incrassated towards the apex; joints first to fourth flavous, fifth and sixth fusco-flavous, seventh and eighth testaceous, ninth to eleventh fuscous. *Legs* pale testaceous, suffused with fuscous.

Brazil. In the collection of the Rev. H. Clark.

11. Omototus artitus.

O. *ovatus, latus, subrobustus, pubescens, fuscus ; capite brevi, inter oculos transverse depresso ; thorace transverso, ad basin depresso, antice elevato et longitudinaliter foveolato ; elytris sat latis et robustis, punctato-striatis, irregulariter cœlatis, ante medium oblique depressis ; antennis subincrassatis, flavo-fuscis ; pedibus anterioribus flavis, posticis fuscis, tarsis flavis.*

Long. corp. $2\frac{1}{5}$ lin., lat. $1\frac{1}{4}$ lin.

Ovate, broad, subrobust, finely but irregularly pubescent, darkly rufo-fuscous. *Head* short, transverse, not produced; eyes tolerably large, situated at the base of the head, extending laterally as far as the anterior angles of the thorax; above the labrum is a transverse plane depression; between the eyes is a very minute longitudinal fovea, well-defined and thread-like, which reaches at its upper extremity a broad and shallow transverse depression extending between the inner and upper margins of the eyes: the surface (when viewed under a high power) is finely granulated and sparingly pubescent; in colour rufo-fuscous, at the base more darkly fuscous. *Thorax* transverse (nearly quadrate); the anterior angles are depressed; the sides marginate, and in outline subsinuate; the anterior margin is submarginate, the posterior slightly subsinuate: the base is occupied by a broad transverse depression, well-defined and deep; it extends obliquely upwards in the direction of (without reaching) the anterior angles, and gives a distinctly gibbous appearance to the anterior and medial portions of the disk; this prominent anterior eminence is sharply and deeply bisected by a broad longitudinal furrow: the surface is finely flavo- or rufo-pubescent throughout. *Scutellum* triangular, impunctate, fuscous. *Elytra* broader than the thorax, robust, punctate-striate, the punctures and almost the striæ being concealed by an irregular but thick pubescence; the surface is marked throughout by slight elevations and depressions: antemedially a broad shallow depression extends obliquely upwards towards the anterior angles; the anterior angles themselves are prominently gibbous; the scutellary surface is raised; and (when viewed from behind) two obsolete circular elevations are apparent postmedially, one on either side of the suture. *Antennæ* subincrassated towards the apex; the first joint broad, ovate; the second much shorter and narrower than the first; the third to the sixth fine, and of length equal to the first; the seventh to the eleventh dilated, broader than the first and hardly longer than the second; in colour, the first to the sixth flavous, the seventh and the eighth of a paler testaceous colour, the ninth to the eleventh pale fuscous. *Legs*: the anterior flavous throughout; the posterior fuscous, the tarsi being flavous, and the globular inflation of the posterior claw brightly rufo-fuscous.

From *O. bituberculatus* this species may be separated by the more piceous and differently distributed colouring on the elytra, and by its more prominently globose scutellary angles; from *O. fuscatus* it differs by its thick pubescence, and from *O. fulvo-pubescens* by the irregularly coloured (not concolorous) pubescence on the elytra.

Cayenne.

12. Omototus fuscatus.

O. *ovatus, latus, robustus, subpubescens, fusco-piceus; thorace quadrato, rectangulari, duobus antemediis tuberculis notato, ad latera et ad medium, longitudinaliter, flavo-pubescenti; elytris latis, robustis, valde punctato-striatis, subpubescentibus; antennis robustis, ad apicem incrassatis, flavis, art. 5, 6 et 9–11 fusco-ferrugineis; pedibus anticis flavis, posticis fuscis, tarsis tibiisque ad basin rufo-fuscis.*

Long. corp. 2 lin., lat. 1⅓ lin.

Ovate, broad, robust, subpubescent, fusco-piceous. *Head* short, slightly produced; below the base of the antennæ is a transverse ridge; eyes large and prominent; the surface of the head flavo-subpubescent. *Thorax* quadrate, rectangular; the anterior angles depressed; the sides slightly marginate; the antemedial surface is raised and longitudinally foveolated, thus forming two obsolete broad tubercles; the surface is clothed with pubescence, a medial longitudinal line and also the sides being flavo-pubescent. *Scutellum* triangular, impunctate. *Elytra* broad, robust, deeply punctate-striate, clothed (more sparingly than the thorax) with indistinct pubescence. *Antennæ* short, tolerably robust, incrassated at the apex; flavous, with the fifth, sixth, and ninth to eleventh joints fusco-ferrugineous. *Legs*: the anterior flavous; the posterior fuscous (the tarsi and the base of the tibiæ being rufo-fuscous); the globular inflation of the posterior claw bright rufous.

A single specimen was taken at Santarem (River Amazon) by Mr. Bates.

13. Omototus bimaculatus.

O. oblongo-ovalis, luridus, flavo pilo holosericeo omnino vestitus; capite subproducto, punctato; thorace transverso, marginato, ad basin paulo attenuato; elytris robustis, punctato-striatis, bimaculatis (maculæ nigræ rotundatæ parvæ); antennis robustis, art. 6–9 dilatatis, nigris, reliquis flavis; pedibus subpubescentibus, flavis.

Long. corp. 2¾ lin., lat. 1½ lin.

Oblong-oval, broad, robust, parallel, covered throughout with a short and thick yellow pubescence. *Head* short, transverse; below the insertion of the antennæ is a transverse triangular depression: eyes large, situated at the base of the head, not extending laterally so far as the angles of the thorax; between the eyes is an obsolete oblique fovea in the form of the letter V: the surface is finely punctate. *Thorax* transverse; the anterior angles depressed and slightly rounded; the sides marginate, more especially near the anterior angles; surface equate. *Scutellum* triangular, fuscous. *Elytra* broad, subparallel, robust, punctate-striate, with two slightly raised black pubescent spots (small and circular) placed medially between the third and fourth striæ. *Antennæ* short and robust; the first and second joints much dilated, the third to fifth slender, the sixth to ninth short and dilated; in colour, the first to fifth are flavous, the sixth to eighth black, the ninth to eleventh flavous. *Legs* flavous throughout, and slightly pubescent; the base of the posterior femora black.

This species may be separated from those of its congeners, to which it nearly approaches, by its larger size, and by the constriction of the sides at the base of the thorax.

Apparently a common insect in the Amazon district; from the neighbourhood of Ega, Santarem, Villa Nova and Para, and the Delta of the Amazon. In the collections of Messrs. Baly, Bates, and the Rev. H. Clark.

14. Omototus sexmaculatus. (TAB. IX. fig. 1.)

O. *ovatus, robustus, pubescens, flavo-fuscus; capite punctato; thorace transverso, lateribus parallelis (haud ad basin coarctatis); elytris punctatis, striatis, valde pubescentibus, maculis sex circularibus ornatis (maculis ad scutellum et ad apicem fuscis, ad medium nigris); antennis art. 6–8 valde dilatatis, nigris, reliquis fuscis.*

Long. corp. 2¾–3 lin., lat. 1½ lin.

Ovate, broad, subcylindrical, robust, pubescent, flavo-fuscous. *Head* short, slightly produced; above the labrum is a transverse triangular depression; the surface is thickly and coarsely punctate and impubescent (except at the inner margin of the eyes). *Thorax* transverse; the anterior angles subacute and depressed; the sides marginate and parallel; the surface is subcylindrical, more distinctly pubescent at the sides, finely punctate. *Scutellum* triangular, finely pubescent, impunctate, fuscous. *Elytra* robust, subparallel, punctate-striate (the striation being almost concealed by the pubescence); between the second and fourth striæ are placed on each elytron three circular spots, which are formed by a darker colour of the pubescence; those near the scutellum and also that near the apex are in colour fuscous, the central spots being more distinct and black. *Antennæ* short, robust, dilated towards the apex; the joints third to fifth elongated and slender, sixth to eighth abruptly dilated; in colour, the first to fifth are flavous, sixth to eighth black (the base of the sixth being fuscous), ninth to eleventh flavous. *Legs* flavous throughout.

This species differs from *O. bimaculatus* in the form of its thorax (the sides of which are *parallel*, and not constricted at the base), as well as in the six spots on the elytra.

From Ega (River Amazon).

15. Omototus binotatus.

O. *oblongo-ovatus, robustus, flavo-pubescens, fusco-flavus; capite elongato, antennis approximatis, inter oculos transverse foveolato; thorace quadrato, penitus subelongato, ad basin depresso et constricto; elytris punctato-striatis, maculis duabus, rotundatis, nigris, ad medium inter 2^{ndam} et 5^{tam} strias; antennis robustis,* *art.* 1–5 *flavo-testaceis,* 6–9 *dilatatis, nigris,* 10 *et* 11 *rufo-testaceis.*

Long. corp. 2⅓ lin., lat. 1 lin.

Oblong-ovate, robust, flavo-pubescent, fusco-flavous. *Head* elongate, somewhat produced in front; above the base of the antennæ (which are *approximate*), and between the eyes, is a transverse depression, which is partially concealed by the flavous pubescence at the inner margin of the eyes; surface punctate and rufo-flavous. *Thorax* quadrate (slightly elongated); the anterior angles slightly prominent and subacute (extending laterally considerably beyond the base of the head), much depressed; the sides are marginate, sensibly constricted at the base; a slight antemedial elevation gives to the base an apparent transverse depression. *Scutellum* triangular, pubescent, fusco-flavous. *Elytra* broader than the thorax, robust, subparallel, broadly but indistinctly punctate-striate (the striation being almost concealed by the pubescence); two circular black spots are situated medially between the second and fifth striæ and near the scutellum; the surface is slightly suffused with fuscous. *Antennæ* long, robust; the third to the fifth joints long and slender, sixth to ninth dilated; first to fifth flavo-testaceous, sixth to ninth black, tenth and eleventh rufo-testaceous. *Legs* tolerably robust.

O. binotatus differs from all the species (known to me) to which it seems nearly allied, by the *elongated* (instead of transverse) form of its *thorax.*

From the neighbourhood of Bahia. A single example is in the collection of the Rev. H. Clark.

16. Omototus humero-notatus.

O. oblongo-ovatus, testaceo-pubescens, flavus; capite inter oculos obsolete foveolato; thorace transverso, ad latera rectilineari; elytris latis, robustis, punctato-striatis, testaceo-pubescentibus, ad scutellum duæ maculæ circulares apparent, fusco suffusæ; antennis sat robustis, ad apicem subdilatatis, art. 1–5 *flavis,* 6–11 *fuscis; pedibus flavis, posticis subelongatis.*

Long. corp. 2 lin., lat. 1 lin.

Oblong-ovate, testaceo-pubescent, flavous. *Head* short, transverse, hardly elongated; above the labrum is a transverse triangular depression, and above the base of the antennæ between the eyes is an obsolete fovea in the form of the letter Y: the eyes are large, situated at the base of the head, and extending laterally as far as the anterior angles of the thorax. *Thorax* transverse, rectangular;

the anterior angles depressed; the sides submarginate and rectilinear; at the base is a broad transverse depression. *Scutellum* almost obsolete. *Elytra* broad, robust, punctate-striate, the punctures being broad and shallow, but for the most part concealed by a fine and thick testaceous pubescence, which is especially apparent along the line of the suture: two circular suffused fuscous spots occupy the space close to the scutellum, between the second and fifth striæ. *Antennæ* tolerably long and robust; the first and second joints dilated (the first being, as in the other neighbouring species, slightly reflected outwards, and the second short, ovate); the third to fifth joints attenuated and elongated; the sixth to eleventh joints shorter and slightly broader; the colour of the first to fifth being flavous, sixth to eleventh fuscous. *Legs*: the posterior pair subelongated; flavous throughout.

From St. Paul, Brazil. In the collection of M. Deyrolle.

17. Omototus sexnotatus. (Tab. IX. fig. 2.)

O. *oblongo-ovatus, parallelus, ferrugineus, flavo-pubescens; capite leviter producto, inter oculos in forma litteræ* T *foveolato; thorace transverso; elytris punctato-striatis, nigro-maculatis (maculæ duæ apud humeros, alteræ mediæ, alteræque ad basin disponuntur); antennis filiformibus, subincrassatis, ferrugineis, articulis 7mo-11mo nigris; pedibus flavis.*

Long. corp. 1¾ lin., lat. ¾ lin.

Oblong-ovate, parallel, ferrugineous, clothed throughout with a fine yellow pile. *Head* short, hardly produced, with an obscure transverse carination between the eyes, which joins at its centre a longitudinal ridge extending to the base of the antennæ (forming together the character of the letter T); the surface at the base of the head is levigate and finely punctate. *Thorax* transverse, marginate, at its anterior angles depressed; the antemedial surface is rounded; the base is transversely depressed. *Elytra* broad, robust, cylindrical, short, punctate-striate, very finely pubescent, with six irregular black spots, two at the scutellary angle (approaching, but not touching, the suture), two (which are oblong in form and obscure) postmedial, and two subapical and sutural. *Antennæ* somewhat robust, with a tendency to dilatation towards the apex; the five apical joints black, the rest ferrugineous. *Legs* flavous.

The size and arrangement of the six spots on the elytra (besides its parallel subcylindrical and short form) are quite sufficient to separate this species.

Brazil. In the cabinet of Mr. Baly.

18. Omototus sericeo-pubescens. B.M.

O. *oblongo-ovatus, sericeo-pubescens, flavo-fuscus; capite ad basin antennarum longitudinaliter foveolato; thorace ad medium transverse depresso; elytris parallelis, punctato-striatis, ante medium, post medium (ad marginem), et ad apicem irregulariter et obsolete depressis; antennis robustis, ad apicem subincrassatis, art. 1–6 flavis, 7 et 8 nigris, 9–11 flavis; pedibus flavotestaceis.*

Long. corp. $2\frac{1}{3}$ lin., lat. 1 lin.

Oblong-ovate, flavo-fuscous, covered throughout with a fine silky flavous pubescence. *Head* short, slightly produced; above the labrum is a transverse carination; immediately above the base of the antennæ is a short longitudinal fovea, while on either side of this, near to the inner margin of the eyes, is a broader and more distinct subcircular depression; eyes tolerably large, situated at the base of the head, extending laterally nearly as far as the anterior thoracic angles. *Thorax* transverse (almost quadrate), rectilinear; near its anterior margin is a central fovea, while at the sides (nearer to the base) are two other transverse medial depressions. *Scutellum* triangular, subpubescent. *Elytra* parallel, punctate-striate, with several broad distinct depressions; one, antemedially, near to the suture (which extends upwards and obliquely towards the shoulders), another, postmedial (near to the margin), and another near to the suture at the apex. *Antennæ* tolerably long and robust, slightly incrassated towards the apex; the first to sixth joints flavous, seventh and eighth black, ninth to eleventh flavous. *Legs* flavo-testaceous, the posterior tibiæ and inflation of the terminal claw being rufoflavous.

Columbia. A single example is in the collection of the British Museum.

19. Omototus transverso-notatus.

O. *oblongo-ovatus, subpubescens, flavo-ferrugineus; capite subpunctato; thorace quadrato, rectangulari, lateribus subsinuatis, ad apicem bituberculato, ad basin depresso; elytris latis, valde punctato-striatis, transverse et irregulariter costatis, oblique quoque fusco lineatis; antennis robustis, ad apicem incrassatis, art. 1–5 et 9–11 flavis, 6–8 piceis; pedibus flavis.*

Long. corp. $1\frac{1}{2}$ lin., lat. $\frac{2}{3}$ lin.

Oblong-ovate, sufficiently robust, sparingly pubescent, flavoferrugineous. *Head* short, abruptly deflected, slightly produced in front: eyes situated at the base of the head, extending laterally not so far as the anterior angles of the thorax; between the eyes and above the base of the antennæ is an obsolete oblique fovea in the shape of the letter Y: the surface is finely punctate, and at the inner margin of the eyes subpubescent. *Thorax* quadrate (slightly elongate) and rectangular; the sides are marginate and towards the base subsinuate; near the anterior margin are two oblong tubercles, distinctly and broadly prominent; the base is transversely depressed; the surface is punctate and subpubescent. *Scutellum* small, triangular. *Elytra* broad, deeply and coarsely punctate-striate, with several irregular ridges and depressions; a broad and deep, obliquely transverse depression (from the shoulders to the middle of the suture) is the most conspicuous; below this is another, transversely oblique, situated postmedially: the surface is flavo-pubescent; two irregular and suffused fuscous lines extend obliquely from the suture (slightly in the direction of the apex) to the margination. *Antennæ* robust, incrassated; the joints first to fifth flavous, sixth to eighth piceous, ninth to eleventh rufo-flavous. *Legs* flavous, the anterior tarsi and base of the tibiæ being piceous, the posterior tibiæ rufous, and the base of the posterior femora suffused with fuscous.

Tunantius, in the district of the River Amazon.

Genus 36. METRIOTES*.

PALPI MAXILLARES *sat robusti; art. 2^{ndo} latiori quam penultimo, incrassato; penultimo brevi, quadrato.*

PALPI LABIALES: *art. 2^{ndo} et 3^{tio} elongatulis, 2^{ndo} robustiori.*

ANTENNÆ *attenuatæ, filiformes.*

CAPUT *antice productum, depressum.*

THORAX *transversus, rectangularis, ad basin transverse lineato-foveolatus.*

ELYTRA *elongata, subparallela, depressa.*

PEDES anteriores *attenuati: tibiis posticis elongatis, a retro visis longitudinaliter excavatis; marginatione undique quinque aut sex calcaribus armata; unguicula ultima bifida, simplici, haud dentata.*

Labrum subcircular, narrow.

Maxillary palpi (Tab. III. fig. 8 *m*) sufficiently short, robust, distinguished in form from those of other genera by having the *second joint more broadly incrassated than the penultimate*; the basal joint

---

* μετριότης, modestia.

is minute, elongate, dilated towards the apex; the second is transverse, obliquely truncate at its base, its breadth being equal to nearly twice its length, and more than twice the breadth of the basal joint; the third is transverse, almost quadrate, cylindrical, about two-thirds the breadth of the second joint, and situated apparently (not, as in other genera, medially, but) *towards the side of* its apex; the terminal joint is short and acuminate, in breadth it is distinctly narrower than the third joint.

Labial palpi (Tab. III. fig. 8 *n*) somewhat smaller than the maxillary palpi; the second joint is elongate, and attenuate towards the base; the apical joint is almost as long as the second, more attenuate, and acuminate.

Antennæ situated on the line of the lower margin of the eyes, attenuate and filiform; the third and fourth joints are subequal, and nearly equal in length to the basal joint.

Eyes lateral, situated at the base of the head, large, in form sufficiently globose and suboval.

Head distinctly produced in front, in this character approaching closely to the form of the genus *Rhinotmetus*; above the labrum is an evident, but not abrupt or angulated, transverse depression; the anterior portion of the head is considerably depressed.

Thorax broader than the head, transverse, rectangular; the surface is equate; near the basal line is a transverse depression, not broad and shallow as in most other genera, but distinct and narrow, resembling somewhat the thoracic fovea in the genus *Monoplatus*.

Scutellum triangular, subelongate, situated in the plane of the elytra.

Elytra slightly broader than the thorax, *elongate*, subparallel, and *depressed*; the humeral and scutellary angles are very slightly raised.

Legs: the *anterior femora* and *tibiæ* subattenuate, the latter being straight, and hardly dilated towards the apex. The *tarsi* are short; the third joint is broader than the rest and slightly bilobed. The *posterior femora* (when seen transversely) are incrassated; in form ovate, attenuate towards the apex. The *tibiæ* are elongate, inflected at their immediate base, straight, and slightly thickened towards the apex; when viewed from behind, the posterior surface is longitudinally grooved; the margination of this groove is armed (from the middle to the apex) on either side with a row of five or six short and sharp spurs, thus closely resembling the tibia of the genus *Monoplatus*; the extreme apex of the tibiæ is terminated (as in other genera) below the insertion of the tarsus by two incurved claws. The *tarsus* is attenuate, and somewhat more elongate than in the adjoining groups; the first and second joints are long and narrow; the third is very short; the apical claw, which is completely concealed from above by the globular inflation of the last joint, is bifid, and unarmed at its inner surface by any basal tooth.

The form of this genus is very interesting, inasmuch as it presents several special peculiarities. In general facies it differs from all the species composing the genus *Hypolampsis* by its depressed form and subelongate posterior femora; and a careful microscopic examination shows still more interesting points of divergence, in its dilated *antepenultimate* joint of the maxillary palpi, and the series of spurs which arm the margination of the posterior tibiæ.

1. Metriotes Robinsonii. (TAB. III. fig. 8.)

M. *ovata, parallela, depressa, impubescens, punctato-striata, glabra, flava; capite transverso, antice producto, ad basin punctulato: thorace transverso, ad basin transverse foveolato; elytris elongatulis, punctato-striatis; antennis filiformibus.*

Long. corp. 1¾ lin., lat. ½ lin.

Ovate, parallel, depressed, impubescent, punctato-striate, glabrous; of a flavous colour throughout. *Head* transverse, depressed, and produced in front; below the base of the antennæ is a slight transverse depression; the surface is levigate, at the base punctate. *Thorax* broader than the head, transverse, anteriorly very slightly emarginate; the anterior angles are depressed and quite distinct; the sides are marginate and obsoletely sinuate; parallel to, and closely adjoining, the basal line is a transverse thread-like fovea, which (exactly corresponding in form to that in the genus *Monoplatus*) is not produced to the lateral margins, but is deflected to the line of the base; the surface is finely punctate. *Elytra* somewhat broader than the thorax, parallel, and depressed; the surface is punctate-striate, the punctures being distinct and the striæ almost obsolete; the scutellary angles are slightly raised. *Antennæ* attenuate and filiform. *Legs* attenuate, the postical femora and tibiæ being somewhat elongate.

I name this species after Mr. E. H. Robinson, to whom I am indebted for the care and diligence which he has shown as an artist and engraver in the preparation of the plates of this volume.

The single example upon which this genus is based (which is flavous throughout, and impubescent) was sent home by the late Mr. Squire from the neighbourhood of Rio Janeiro.

Genus 37. POËBATES*.

PALPI MAXILLARES *robusti, art. penultimo quadrato, cylindrico.*
PALPI LABIALES *elongati, minuti.*
ANTENNÆ *filiformes, haud robustæ.*
CAPUT *breve, pœne verticale, antice subproductum.*
THORAX *transversus, æquatus.*
ELYTRA *lata, robusta, subcylindrica, punctato-striata.*
PEDES *sat robusti; femoribus posticis brevibus, valde incrassatis; tibiis brevibus, inarmatis.*

Labrum subcircular.
Maxillary palpi (Front. fig. 7 m): the basal joint minute; the second abbreviated, and in form almost triangular; the third longer and considerably broader than the second; the fourth conical, in breadth equal to the apex of the third.
Labial palpi (Front. fig. 7 n) attenuate, elongate; the penultimate joint subcylindrical.
Antennæ approximate, situated below the inner margin of the eyes; short, filiform, the third, fourth and fifth joints being slightly more attenuate than the rest.
Eyes lateral, situated at the base of the head, globose.
Head short, depressed, almost vertical, somewhat produced in front; above the base of the antennæ transversely depressed.
Thorax broader than the head, transverse, rectangular, the basal angles being in some examples obsoletely obliquely truncate; the surface is æquate, and in *P. nigripes* subpubescent.
Elytra broad, much more robust than the thorax, short, subcylindrical, not antemedially transversely depressed, punctate-striate.
Legs: the *anterior femora* sufficiently robust, and slightly incurved. The *tibiæ* are slightly thickened towards the apex. The *tarsus* is *short*, the basal joint being somewhat dilated; the second joint is of the same form as the first, but considerably smaller; the third broader, subcircular, and distinctly bilobed: the apical claw is armed on either side at its under surface near the base with a short and robust inner tooth. The *posterior femora* are short and much incrassated. The *tibiæ* are short, slightly thickened towards the apex: when viewed from behind, a longitudinal groove is apparent, which forms a socket for the insertion of the tarsus; this socket is simple and unarmed. The *tarsi* are short and attenuated.

The species forming this genus separates itself at once from the

* ποίη, herba; βαίνω, incedo.

species of other adjoining genera by its short filiform antennæ, its robust, equate, and parallel elytra, and by its short posterior femora and tibiæ. Its facies (although generally similar to) is manifestly different from that of *Omototus*, from which it may be also at once distinguished by its filiform antennæ; from *Hypolampsis* it differs by the absence of any transverse depression on the elytra and by the form of its posterior tibiæ; from both groups it is distinguishable also by the form of its maxillary palpi.

1. Poëbates nigripes. (Front. fig. 7.) B.M.

P. *ovata, robusta, flavo-ferruginea, pubescens ; capite antice (super basin antennarum) oblique foveolato; thorace transverso, apud angulos posticos subdepresso; elytris punctato-striatis; antennis nigris; pedibus nigris, tarsis posticis piceo suffusis.*

Long. corp. 1¾ lin., lat. ¾ lin.

Ovate, robust, flavo-ferrugineous, pubescent. *Head* short, hardly elongated in front, punctate; between the eyes (above the base of the antennæ) is a Y-shaped depression. *Thorax* transverse; the anterior angles depressed, slightly compressed and rounded; two broad postmedial depressions are apparent near the humeral angles. *Scutellum* small, almost obsolete. *Elytra* robust, subparallel, punctate-striate. *Antennæ* filiform, with a slight tendency to dilatation towards the apex; the first joint is broad, dilated at the apex, and inflected outwards; the second short and ovate; the third, fourth and fifth of nearly equal length, but not so long as the first. *Legs* black, the posterior tarsi being suffused with piceous; the posterior apical inflated joint bright black; the anterior claws rufo-ferrugineous.

Apparently a common species in the Island of St. Paul's; found also in the neighbourhood of Rio Janeiro, and taken by my friend Mr. Gray and myself at Constancia during our visit to the Organ Mountains.

In the collection of the British Museum; also in those of Messrs. Baly, Gray, Miers, Waterhouse, and the Rev. H. Clark.

Genus 38. HYPOLAMPSIS*.

Palpi maxillares *elongati, art. penultimo robusto, quadrato, art. apicali conico.*
Palpi labiales *elongatuli, subcylindrici.*
Antennæ *robustæ, aut filiformes aut dilatatæ.*

* ὑπὸ, sub; λάμψις, fulgor.

Caput *breve, semper verticale aut penitus verticale, et antice obsolete productum, granulatum aut punctatum.*
Thorax *aut quadratus aut transversus.*
Elytra *lata; aliquando subglobosa, aliquando parallela; punctuto-striata, plerumque ante medium oblique depressa.*
Pedes *robusti; tibiis posticis inarmatis, simplicibus.*

Labrum subcircular, in some species medially sinuate.

Maxillary palpi (Tab. IX. fig. 3 *m*) incrassated; the first and second joints more or less attenuated; the third joint robust and transverse, the breadth being considerably greater than the length; sometimes in form globular.

Labial palpi (Tab. IX. fig. 3 *n*) elongate, cylindrical; the apical joint attenuate.

Antennæ approximate, situated below (or parallel with the inner margins of) the eyes; in some species of the group (as in *H. Lacordairii*) filiform and robust, in others (as in *H. albo-guttata*) subdilated or distinctly incrassated.

Eyes situated close to the base of the head, for the most part distinctly globular; their form is circular, or (in some few species, like *H. elegantula* and *H. nana*) with a distinct tendency to an oval form.

Head: at the base short and transverse; in all the species of the group vertical, the apex being for the most part more or less produced or subattenuate: in all the species there is, above the labrum, a transverse triangular plane; this plane is occasionally bounded by oblique carinations: the surface between the insertion of the antennæ and the base of the head is punctate, or more frequently granulated.

Thorax always somewhat broader than the head, and distinctly narrower than the elytra; in form it is either subelongate (as in *H. elegantula*), or in most species quadrate (as in *H. Balii*); it is occasionally, however, distinctly though not broadly transverse (as in *H. albo-guttata*); the form is always rectangular, the angles being always distinct or subacute; the sides are always marginate, frequently subconstricted (in some species, as in *H. elegantula*, distinctly constricted) at the base; occasionally the margin is in outline slightly sinuate; the surface is equate, generally flattened and depressed, rarely elevated or gibbous; at the base, for the most part, transversely depressed; more or less punctate, or granulated, and subpubescent.

Scutellum triangular, situated on (very rarely below) the plane of the elytra.

Elytra in all the species considerably broader than the thorax, sufficiently robust, elongate, parallel and subcylindrical or (in a few species, as in *H. æstivalis* and *H. porculus*) very broad, short and globose: the surface is for the most part antemedially transversely depressed, giving a prominence, more or less distinct, to the humeral or scutellary angles; in all the species punctate-striate, and pubescent or subpubescent: the colour in the different species has a degree of uniformity; it is always fuscous or flavo-fuscous; occasionally nigro-fuscous; never brightly coloured or variegated by distinct markings.

Legs robust; in general form a greater similarity is apparent than is the case with other parts of the body. The *anterior femora*, when viewed from in front, are cylindrical, generally attenuated towards the base, and sometimes towards the apex, where they are for the most part abruptly truncate. The *tibiæ* are (more or less distinctly) incurved at their immediate base, straight, slightly thickened towards the apex, and in some species distinctly flattened longitudinally when viewed from behind; that is, of a triangular rather than of a cylindrical form. The *tarsi* are in all the species short, frequently scarcely two-thirds the length of the tibiæ; the first and second joints are subequal, and in form triangular (the second being a trifle shorter and perhaps broader than the first); the third is much broader than the basal joints, transverse, and more or less distinctly bilobed; from the base of the third proceeds the terminal joint, which is, as usual, attenuated and subincurved; the terminal claw is bifid, and robust at the base: for the most part, certainly, the claw is simple and unarmed; in one or two species, however, there may be traced the *rudiments* of an inner basal tooth. *Posterior femora* broadly incrassated, and more evidently elongate than in the preceding genus, *Poëbates*. The *tibiæ* are short, incurved at their immediate base, straight, and dilated at the apex; the surface is longitudinally flattened (and also medially subcompressed when viewed directly from behind); this flattened surface is in some species slightly grooved, and terminates in a socket for the reception of the tarsus, which appears to be *more shallow* and *less excavated* than in other genera; in *H. elegantula* this socket is fringed with a few short and straight comb-like teeth. The *tarsus* is short and attenuate, the apical claw being quite concealed by the inflation of the last joint.

A very difficult group: it is composed entirely of minute species. After many weeks of careful microscopic investigation, I have ventured to bring all the species together under a single genus. It will have been obvious, from the preceding generic diagnosis, that there is very much dissimilarity in general form among the species included; nevertheless there are between these several divergent forms so many connecting links and intermediates, that I am quite unable to *satisfy* my own mind as to the exact limits of any subdivision that would suggest itself. In general facies there is a marked resemblance: the insects composing the group are never brightly coloured, never variegated by distinct markings; they are in colour fuscous, and for the most part pubescent. In the form of the *posterior tibia* also (which in this section of the Galerucidæ supplies such valuable generic characters), the different species present little, if any, dissimilarity: the tibia is longitudinally grooved (less apparently so than in other genera); the margination of this groove is simple, and unarmed by any even obsolete spur.

Subdivision A. *Elytris parallelis, plus minus robustis, plerumque ante medium oblique depressis.*

1. Hypolampsis melanotus.

H. *oblongo-ovata, parallela, subdepressa, nigra ; capite brevi, rufo ; thorace transverso, ad basin bidepresso, punctato, rufo ; elytris latis, parallelis, punctato-striatis, squamosis, ante medium oblique subdepressis, nigris, ad marginem undique rufis ; antennis dilatatis, fulvis, ad basin piceis ; pedibus rufis.*

Long. corp. $1\frac{2}{3}$ lin., lat. $\frac{3}{4}$ lin.

Oblong-ovate, parallel, subdepressed, black. *Head* short, transverse, not produced; eyes tolerably large, situated at the base of the head; the surface (when viewed under a high power) very finely punctate, of a dark rufous colour. *Thorax* transverse, rectilinear, rectangular; the anterior angles subdepressed; the sides obsoletely marginate; at the base (when viewed from in front) is a transverse obsolete depression, which does not extend to the posterior angles; the surface thickly and irregularly punctate (the punctures themselves being of uneven form, some circular, and some vermiculate), of a rufous colour throughout. *Scutellum* triangular, rufous. *Elytra* broader than the thorax, parallel, punctate-striate, the punctures being almost concealed by a thick and close squamose pile: a little before the middle is a broad, obliquely transverse depression, extending towards the shoulders and giving an appearance of prominence to the scutellary angles; the colour black, with margins (along the shoulders, the margination, and at the base) of a dark-red colour. *Antennæ* fine, dilated towards the apex; the joints one to six being elongate, narrower, and of a fulvous colour; the joints seven to eleven being shorter, distinctly dilated, and fuscous. *Legs* rufous throughout.

This handsome species is at once to be separated from its congeners by the colour of its elytra, which is pitchy-black, margined with rufo-flavous. It is a question whether it ought not to be separated generically: the elytra are more evenly parallel, and also somewhat more elongated; the posterior tibiæ also are shorter than is the case with most of the other species of the group.

Chili. In the collection of M. Chevrolat.

2. Hypolampsis Balii.

H. *oblongo-ovata, sat robusta, punctato-striata, ferruginea; capite brevi, haud producto, punctato; thorace quadrato, ad basin constricto, punctato, subpubescenti, piceo; elytris latis, oblique ante medium depressis, punctato-striatis, obsolete flavo-pubescentibus; antennis robustis, filiformibus, ferrugineis, art.* 7–11 *fusco-piceis; pedibus flavis.*

Long. corp. 2 lin., lat. 1 lin.

Oblong-ovate, sufficiently robust, deeply punctate-striate, obsoletely pubescent, ferrugineous. *Head* short, transverse, almost vertical, not produced in front; above the labrum is a transverse plane depression, which is bisected by a medial longitudinal carination (sometimes almost obsolete): the eyes are prominent and lateral; between the eyes the surface is deeply punctate. *Thorax* quadrate, constricted and transversely depressed at the base; the anterior angles are subacute and much depressed; the sides finely marginate; the surface is thickly punctate and finely pubescent (more distinctly at the base and sides); in colour piceous. *Scutellum* minute. *Elytra* broad, robust, subdepressed; an antemedial depression extends obliquely upwards towards the humeral angles, giving an appearance of prominence to the surface near the scutellum; deeply punctate-striate, clothed throughout (but more apparently at the apex) with obsolete flavous pubescence. *Antennæ* robust, filiform, with a tendency to dilatation towards the apex; the colour is ferrugineous, the joints seven to eleven being fusco-piceous. *Legs* flavous throughout, the posterior femora being suffused with ferrugineous.

H. Balii is distinguishable from all its congeners with which I am acquainted by its greater size; its deeply striated elytra, combined with its constricted thorax, also readily distinguish it.

Brazil. In the cabinets of Messrs. Baly, Deyrolle, and the Rev. H. Clark.

3. Hypolampsis elegantula.

H. *oblonga, ovata, robusta, subcylindrica, subpubescens, grisea; capite brevi, antice haud producto, punctato; thorace quadrato, ad basin constricto et transverse depresso, flavo-pubescenti; elytris sat latis, punctato-striatis, subtiliter oblique ante medium depressis;*

antennis robustis, filiformibus, rufo-flavis, ad basin piceo suffusis; pedibus rufo-flavis.

Long. corp. 1⅓ lin., lat. ⅔ lin.

Oblong, ovate, robust, subcylindrical, finely pubescent, of a griseous colour. *Head* short, not produced in front; eyes large, lateral, situated at the base of the head; between the eyes is a longitudinal medial fovea; the surface is finely punctate, and near the margin of the eyes subpubescent. *Thorax* quadrate, constricted at the base; the anterior angles are much depressed; the sides are marginate; at the base is a broad transverse depression, which is produced on either side obliquely to the humeral angles; the surface is finely flavo-pubescent. *Scutellum* triangular and minute. *Elytra* somewhat broader than the thorax, punctate-striate, the punctures being nearly concealed by a fine clothing of pale griseous pubescence; in some examples, where this pubescence is less apparent, a slight ante-medial transverse depression extends obliquely upwards towards the shoulders; near the scutellary angles are two suffused circular markings of piceous; two others somewhat larger, but equally suffused, are postmedial. *Antennæ* robust, filiform, the third joint being attenuated, and in colour rufo-flavous; the two basal joints are suffused with piceous. *Legs* rufo-flavous, the posterior femora and tibiæ being fusco-rufous.

This species may be recognized from *H. Balii* by its more distinct pubescence, and by the four suffused markings on the surface of its elytra; it differs from all its congeners by its greater size.

Taken by the late Mr. Squire in the neighbourhood of Rio Janeiro. In the collection of Mr. Baly.

4. Hypolampsis multicostata.

H. *oblongo-ovata, subelongata, subcylindrica, impubescens, nigra; capite brevi, inter oculos transverse depresso, granulato; thorace transverso, ad angulos basales depresso, subtiliter flavo-pubescenti, granulato; elytris subparallelis, punctato-striatis, ad apicem subtiliter flavo-pubescentibus; antennis tenuibus, ad apicem incrassatis, art. 1–6 flavis, 7–11 fuscis; pedibus flavis, femoribus posticis fuscis.*

Long. corp. 1⅖ lin., lat. 1 lin.

Oblong-ovate, subelongate, subcylindrical, impubescent, fuscous-black. *Head* short, transverse, subelongated; between the base of the antennæ and the labrum is a depressed plane, which is bounded on its upper surface by two oblique carinations; from the base of the antennæ extends a medial longitudinal minute fovea, which is terminated at its upper extremity by a broader and more obsolete transverse depression: eyes tolerably large, not extending laterally as far as the anterior angles of the thorax; the surface throughout is granulated, impubescent, and fuscous-black. *Thorax* transverse (almost quadrate), rectangular; the anterior angles depressed; the sides submarginate; at the base is a transverse *obsolete* depression, which is most apparent near the basal angles; the surface (when viewed under a high power) is very finely flavo-pubescent, and finely granulated throughout. *Scutellum* small, triangular, impunctate. *Elytra* somewhat broader than the thorax, subparallel, robust, deeply punctate-striate; a transverse antemedial depression extends obliquely upwards towards the humeral angles, giving an appearance of prominence to the surface near the scutellum; at the apex a fine flavous pubescence may be discerned with a high magnifying power. *Antennæ* fine, *slightly* incrassated at the apex, the joints one to six being flavous, seven to eleven (which are shorter and subdilated) fuscous. *Legs* flavous; the posterior femora being fuscous, and the globular inflation of the posterior claw rufo-fuscous.

Brazil. In the collection of M. Chevrolat.

5. Hypolampsis inæqualis.

H. *oblongo-ovata, subrobusta, subparallela, picea; capite ad apicem transverse carinato; thorace transverso, rectangulari, ad apicem et ad basin transverse depresso, ferrugineo-pubescenti; elytris punctato-striatis, ante medium transverse depressis, ad basin et ad latera ferrugineo-pubescentibus; antennis filiformibus, flavis, art. 7 et 8 ferrugineis; pedibus flavis, femoribus posticis piceis.*

Long. corp. 1¾ lin., lat. ¾ lin.

Oblong-ovate, tolerably robust, subparallel, of a piceous colour throughout. *Head* short, slightly elongated; immediately above the labrum is a transverse ridge, the ends of which are connected with the base of the antennæ by two other obliquely transverse carinations; eyes somewhat prominent, situated at the base of the head; the surface is finely punctate, subpubescent. *Thorax* transverse, rectangular, rectilinear; the sides submarginate; two distinct depressions extend transversely, one antemedially, and the other (which is broader) postmedially; the surface is clothed with a fine ferrugineous pubescence. *Scutellum* small and triangular. *Elytra* broadly punctate-striate, antemedially and transversely depressed; at the base and (sparingly) at the sides clothed with a ferrugineous pubescence. *Antennæ* filiform, attenuate; of a flavous colour, the seventh and eighth joints being ferrugineous. *Legs* flavous; the postical short; the femora being piceous, and the globular inflation of the posterior claw bright rufous.

This species is evidently abundant in the neighbourhood of Rio Janeiro, where it has been taken by Mr. Fry, as well as by Mr. Gray and myself. It is tolerably constant in colour and markings, and may be separated from most of its congeners by the irregular transverse markings on the elytra.

6. Hypolampsis Miersii.

H. *oblongo-ovalis, subcylindrica, punctato-striata, subtiliter pubescens, picea; capite brevi, vix producto, sparsim flavo-pubescenti: thorace transverso, ad basin constricto, punctulato, subpubescenti; elytris robustis, ante medium transverse depressis, punctatostriatis; antennis ad apicem dilatatis, art. 1–5 flavis, 6–8 piceis, 9–11 testaceis; pedibus flavis, femoribus posticis ad apicem piceo suffusis.*

Long. corp. 1½ lin., lat. ⅔ lin.

Oblong-ovate, sufficiently robust, subcylindrical, punctate-striate, finely pubescent, piceous. *Head* short, abruptly deflected at right angles to the elytra, hardly produced in front; below the base of the antennæ is a transverse triangular and depressed plane: eyes tolerably large, extending laterally as far as the anterior angles of the thorax; between the eyes is an obsolete medial carination; the surface is finely flavo-pubescent. *Thorax* transverse (almost quadrate), at the base *distinctly constricted* and transversely depressed; the sides faintly marginate; the surface is finely punctate and obsoletely pubescent. *Scutellum* triangular, impunctate. *Elytra* broader than the thorax, robust, antemedially transversely depressed; the scutellary angles are somewhat gibbous; punctate-striate (the punctures being shallow and the striæ broad and deep); the surface is irregularly clothed with obsolete pale pubescence. *Antennæ* attenuated, subdilated towards the apex; joints one to five flavous, six to eight piceous, nine to eleven testaceous. *Legs* flavous, the apex of the posterior femora being suffused with piceous.

This species differs from *H. inæqualis* in its concolorous elytra; it is more robust than *H. Dohrnii*, the markings of the antennæ are different, and the striæ on the elytra are deeper; it closely resembles in form *H. Murraii*, but is distinguishable from that species by its differently coloured and pubescent elytra; from all other allied species it may be separated either by the character of the markings on the antennæ, or by its greater size.

Surinam; Paramaribo. In the collection of M. Dohrn.

7. Hypolampsis Dohrnii.

H. *oblongo-ovata, subrobusta, obsolete pubescens, fusca; capite vix producto, punctato; thorace transverso, ad basin constricto et transverse depresso, punctato; elytris robustis, punctato-striatis, ante medium transverse depressis, fuscis, ad apicem et ad humeros rufo suffusis; antennis subdilatatis, art.* 1–6 *flavis,* 7 *et* 8 *fuscis,* 9–11 *testaceis; pedibus flavis, femoribus posticis fuscis.*

Long. corp. 1½ lin., lat. ¾ lin.

Oblong-ovate, subrobust and subparallel, obsoletely pubescent, fuscous. *Head* short, transverse, almost vertical, slightly produced in front; between the basal joints of the antennæ is an obsolete longitudinal carination; the surface is finely punctate and pubescent; eyes tolerably large, situated nearly at the base of the head. *Thorax* transverse (almost quadrate), constricted towards the base; the sides finely marginate; the base not so distinctly depressed as in the preceding species; the surface is thickly punctate and impubescent. *Scutellum* large, triangular. *Elytra* broader than the thorax, subcylindrical, punctate-striate, antemedially transversely depressed; the surface is very obsoletely pubescent, fuscous, suffused with paler rufous colour at the apex and near the humeral angles; this rufous colouring is more or less distinct in different examples. *Antennæ* slightly dilated towards the apex; joints one to six flavous (the first and sixth joints being in some specimens suffused with fuscous), seven and eight fuscous, nine to eleven testaceous. *Legs* flavous, the posterior femora being fuscous.

This species, closely allied to *H. Miersii*, may be separated from it by its less deep punctuation on the elytra.

Brazil and the Island of St. Paul's.

8. Hypolampsis albo-guttata. (Tab. IX. fig. 3.)

H. *ovata, lata, ferrugineo-picea; capite subproducto, ad apicem transverse carinato, inter oculos longitudinaliter foveolato; thorace transverso, ad medium subdilatato, subtiliter pubescenti; elytris latis, punctato-striatis, ante medium transverse depressis, maculis albis sparsim notatis; antennis ad apicem incrassatis, art.* 1–6 *rufo-fuscis,* 7 *et* 8 *pallide testaceis,* 9–11 *fuscis; pedibus flavis, tarsis anterioribus nigro-fuscatis, femoribus posticis piceis.*

Long. corp. 1½ lin., lat. ¾ lin.

Ovate, broad, impubescent, ferrugineo-piceous. *Head* short, transverse, subdepressed, elongated in front; above the labrum is a somewhat prominent transverse ridge, separated from the base of the antennæ by a smooth glabrous depression; immediately above the base of the antennæ (which are contiguous) is a short longitudinal fovea, above which (when viewed laterally or obliquely) a slight medial carination extends to the base; eyes large, somewhat prominent, extending laterally as far as the angles of the thorax; the surface finely punctate, and at the inner margin of the eyes subpubescent. *Thorax* transverse, rectangular; the anterior angles subacute and depressed; the sides marginate, the margination being medially subdilated, while immediately behind the anterior, and in front of the posterior angles, it is sensibly constricted: the surface (under a high magnifying power) very finely pubescent; two longitudinal irregular white lines extend on either side from the apex to the base, immediately within the line of margination. *Scutellum* distinct, triangular, very finely pubescent. *Elytra* broad, subdepressed, coarsely punctate-striate; an antemedial depression extends obliquely upwards towards the humeral angles: several small spots, formed of white pubescence (more or less distinct in the example before me), in number about fourteen, are scattered over the surface of the elytra, more frequently towards the apex; the surface (under a high magnifying power) shows traces of a very fine pubescence. *Antennæ* short, incrassated towards the apex; the first joint elongate and broad; second short, broad, ovate; third and fourth fine; fifth to eleventh gradually but distinctly incrassated: in colour, the first to sixth rufo-fuscous (the second and third being more palely rufous), seventh and eighth very pale testaceous, ninth to eleventh fuscous. *Legs*: anterior flavous, the base of the tibiæ and also the tarsi being fuscous; the posterior fuscous, the tibiæ being rufo-flavous.

Brazil. In the collection of Mr. Baly.

9. Hypolampsis Murraii.

H. *oblongo-ovata, robusta, subcylindrica, fortiter punctato-striata, impubescens, nigra; capite depresso, vix antice producto, granulato; thorace transverso, æquato, punctato; elytris robustis, punctato-striatis, nigris; antennis robustis, ad apicem subincrassatis, nigris, art. 10 et 11 testaceis; pedibus flavis, tarsis et tibiis (ad apicem) anterioribus fuscis, femoribusque posticis ad basin piceis.*

Long. corp. 1½ lin., lat. ¾ lin.

Oblong-ovate, robust, subcylindrical, deeply punctate-striate, impubescent, pitchy-black. *Head* transverse, vertically depressed, slightly produced in front; above the labrum is a transverse triangular plane depression; above the base of the antennæ are two obsolete tubercular elevations; eyes tolerably prominent, at the base of the head; the surface deeply granulated. *Thorax* transverse (almost quadrate); the anterior angles depressed; the *sides parallel* and marginate; the surface equate, and granulated, not so deeply as the head. *Scutellum* triangular, impunctate. *Elytra* robust, parallel, deeply and regularly punctate-striate, impubescent, except obsoletely at the apex. *Antennæ* robust, subdilated towards the apex, black, the two apical joints being testaceous. *Legs* flavous; the anterior tarsi and apex of the tibiæ suffused with fuscous, and the base of the posterior femora piceous.

This very distinct species may be separated from all others by its *uniformly pitchy-black* colour, its impubescence, and the arrangement of markings on the antennæ.

H. Murraii occurs not unfrequently in the suburbs of Rio Janeiro, where it was taken by Mr. Gray and myself, and also, in some abundance, by Mr. Fry during his visit to the Brazils in the spring of this year. Mr. Fry remarks respecting this species, " it congregates on the tops of some small shrub, one or two individuals frequently on each leaf; they are very difficult to secure, as they leap off with great force and activity on being approached."

10. Hypolampsis signaticornis.

H. *oblongo-ovata, parallela, subcylindrica, subtiliter pubescens, nigra; capite brevi, ad basin granulato; thorace transverso, ad basin constricto et transverse depresso, punctato; elytris punctato-striatis, ad medium oblique depressis, ad basin flavo-subpubescentibus; antennis incrassatis, ad apicem rufo-fuscis, articulis* 3, 4, *et* 8–11 *testaceis; pedibus flavis.*

Long. corp. $1\frac{1}{3}$ lin., lat. $\frac{2}{3}$ lin.

Oblong-ovate, parallel, subcylindrical, very finely pubescent, black. *Head* short, transverse, depressed at right angles to the plane of the thorax, produced in front; mandibles flavous, with the apex fuscous; above the labrum is a transversely triangular depression; eyes large, prominent, situated at the base of the head; the surface at the base (above the antennæ) is thickly granulated. *Thorax* transverse (the length being nearly equal to the breadth), constricted towards the base; the anterior angles are depressed; the sides are marginate; at the base is a broad and shallow transverse depression; the surface throughout is thickly and coarsely punctate. *Scutellum* minute. *Elytra* somewhat broader than the thorax, parallel, coarsely punctate-striate throughout, and at the apex clothed sparingly with obsolete flavous pubescence; a shallow transverse antemedial depression extends obliquely upwards towards the humeral angles, giving an appearance of prominence to the surface near the scutellum. *Antennæ* robust, incrassated towards the middle and apex; the third and fourth joints being of nearly equal length, longer than the others, and attenuated; the fifth to the eleventh short, and gradually dilated: in colour, the first and second are rufo-fuscous, the fifth to the seventh fuscous, the third, fourth, and eighth to eleventh testaceous. *Legs* flavous throughout, the globular inflation of the posterior claw being brightly rufous.

Para. In the collection of M. Chevrolat.

11. Hypolampsis nana.

H. *ovata, lata, robusta, impubescens, picea; capite brevi, granulato; thorace transverso (subquadrato), ad basin constricto, antice et ad basin transverse depresso, crebre punctulato; elytris robustis, valde punctato-striatis, transverse subdepressis, ad apicem et ad marginem rufo-ferrugineis; antennis filiformibus, rufo-ferrugineis, art. 7 et 8 rufo-piceis; pedibus rufo-ferrugineis, femoribus posticis suffuso-piceis.*

Long. corp. $1\frac{1}{4}$ lin., lat. $\frac{3}{5}$ lin.

Ovate, broad, robust, impubescent, piceous. *Head* short, slightly produced in front; below the base of the antennæ is a transverse, depressed, equate plane; the eyes are subprominent, extending laterally beyond the anterior angles of the thorax; the surface is granulated. *Thorax* transverse (somewhat quadrate), slightly constricted towards the base; the anterior angles subacute and depressed; the sides are marginate; near the anterior margin (and also more broadly at the base) is a transverse depression, most distinct near to the anterior angles; the surface is thickly and very finely punctate. *Scutellum* triangular. *Elytra* broad, robust, coarsely and deeply punctate-striate; a transverse antemedial depression extends obliquely upwards towards the humeral angles; the surface is piceous, at the apex broadly (and also at the margin) rufo-ferrugineous: a short transverse line extends from the sixth stria postmedially to the margination (in colour also rufo-ferrugineous); this line is sometimes interrupted and assumes the form of a spot. *Antennæ* filiform, rufo-ferrugineous, the seventh and eighth joints being rufo-piceous. *Legs* rufo-ferrugineous, the posterior femora being suffused with piceous.

This obscure little species is separated from most of its congeners by the transverse anterior depression of its thorax and the rufous apex of its elytra.

From the neighbourhood of Rio Janeiro. Taken by the late Mr. Squire.

12. Hypolampsis pumilio.

H. *ovata, lata, robusta, nigro-ferruginea; capite antice longitudinaliter obsolete carinato, punctato; thorace transverso, ad basin constricto et depresso, flavo-pubescenti, punctato; elytris robustis, punctato-striatis, ante medium transverse depressis, nigro-ferrugineis, ad scutellum piceo suffusis; antennis rufo-testaceis, art. 6–8 piceis; pedibus flavis, posticis rufis, ad femora piceo suffusis.*

Long. corp. 1½ lin., lat. ½ lin.

Ovate, broad, robust, of a nigro-ferrugineous colour, impubescent. *Head* short, slightly produced in front; below the base of the antennæ is a triangular plane depression; above the antennæ (when viewed obliquely) is a longitudinal medial ridge, almost obsolete, extending to the basal line; eyes tolerably large, situated at the base of the head; the surface is finely and thickly punctate. *Thorax* transverse (*almost quadrate*), constricted at the base; the anterior angles are depressed, the sides marginate; at the base is a broad and distinct transverse depression; the surface is very finely flavo-pubescent (when examined under a high power), and finely punctate. *Scutellum* triangular, piceous. *Elytra* broad, robust, deeply punctate-striate; from the antemedial suture a distinct depression extends obliquely upwards towards the shoulders; the surface is of a dark ferrugineous colour, suffused (near the scutellum, and irregularly throughout) with piceous. *Antennæ* rufo-testaceous, the sixth, seventh and eighth joints being piceous. *Legs*: the anterior flavous, the postical rufous, the femora being suffused with piceous.

This species (closely allied to *H. nana* in form and size) is separated from it not only by its distinct colouring, but by the form of its thorax, which is less transverse (almost quadrate); there is also an entire absence of any transverse depression near its anterior margin, which is so apparent in that species.

Rio Janeiro. In the cabinet of the Rev. H. Clark.

13. Hypolampsis ferrugineo-notata.

H. *oblongo-ovata, subcylindrica, impubescens, rufo-flava; capite inter oculos striato, punctato; thorace quadrato, ad basin constricto, ad basin distincte (et ad apicem tenue) transverse notato; elytris punctato-striatis, ad basin triangulari macula rufo-ferruginea notatis; antennis et pedibus rufo-flavis.*

Long. corp. 1⅓ lin., lat. ⅔ lin.

Oblong-ovate, subcylindrical, impubescent, rufo-flavous. *Head* short, transverse, not produced in front; above the base of the antennæ is a faint obsolete oblique ridge in the form of the letter V; the eyes are large, situated at the base of the head; the surface is thickly and finely punctate. *Thorax* quadrate, *somewhat constricted* at the base; the anterior angles are subacute and depressed, the sides marginate: at the base (when viewed laterally) is a broad and shallow transverse depression; a parallel depression (narrower and more distinctly defined) may be traced near to the anterior margin: the surface is finely and thickly punctate. *Scutellum* small, triangular. *Elytra* broader than the thorax, subparallel, punctate-striate; at the base, reaching from shoulder to shoulder, is a well-defined triangular marking of rufo-ferrugineous. *Antennæ* rufo-flavous. *Legs* rufo-flavous.

Brazil. In the cabinet of M. Deyrolle.

14. Hypolampsis parallela.

H. *oblongo-ovata, subparallela, elongata, sparsim subpubescens, nigro-picea ; capite brevi ; thorace elongato, angulis anticis oblique truncatis, ad basin transverse depresso, punctato ; elytris elongatulis, punctato-striatis, ad apicem et latera sparsim flavo-pubescentibus ; antennis ad apicem subincrassatis, art. 1–4 flavis, 5–11 flavo-ferrugineis ; pedibus anterioribus flavis, posticis piceo suffusis.*

Long. corp. 1½ lin., lat. ¾ lin.

Oblong-ovate, subparallel, somewhat elongated, under a high power sparingly pubescent; nigro-piceous. *Head* short, transverse, hardly produced in front; eyes large, extending laterally quite as far as the anterior angles of the thorax; the surface is finely granulated. *Thorax* elongated; the anterior angles are depressed and obsoletely truncate; the sides are marginate; at the base, and extending also along the sides, is a slight, obliquely transverse depression; the surface is finely punctate. *Scutellum* triangular, obsolete. *Elytra* subparallel, elongate, punctate-striate; at the sides and apex are slight traces of flavous pubescence. *Antennæ* slightly incrassated towards the apex; the joints one to four flavous, five to eleven flavo-ferrugineous. *Legs*: the anterior flavous, the posterior suffused with piceous.

The elongated thorax and more parallel form of this species distinguish it from other species in the group.

Brazil. In the cabinet of M. Deyrolle.

15. Hypolampsis campestris.

H. *oblongo-ovata, robusta, subtiliter pubescens, pallide ferruginea ; capite brevi, vix producto, punctulato ; thorace transverso, ad basin depresso; elytris robustis, punctato-striatis; antennis sat robustis, ad apicem obsolete dilatatis; pedibus ferrugineis.*

Long. corp. 1½ lin., lat. ⅔ lin.

Oblong-ovate, robust, parallel, *very finely* pubescent, punctate-striate, of a pale ferrugineous colour. *Head* short, vertical, hardly produced in front; immediately above the labrum is a transverse triangular depression; between the eyes (which are lateral, and situated at the base of the head) the surface is equate, unmarked by any carination or depression, and finely punctate. *Thorax transverse*, in front slightly emarginate; the sides parallel and finely marginate; at the base (when viewed laterally) is a transverse depression extending obliquely upwards towards the humeral angles; an obsolete transverse depression may also be traced immediately behind the anterior margin; the surface is finely punctate. *Scutellum* minute, triangular, pubescent, situated in the same plane as the elytra. *Elytra* robust, broader than the thorax, punctate-striate; an obsolete antemedial depression, extending obliquely upwards towards the shoulders, gives a slightly gibbous appearance to the scutellary angles. *Antennæ* robust, slightly thickened towards the apex. *Legs*, like the rest of the body, of a pale ferrugineous colour throughout.

H. campestris is well marked by the absence of any depression or carination between the eyes; its *pale* and *concolorous* surface, with its sufficiently robust elytra, also distinguish it from its congeners.

Brazil. In the collection of M. Deyrolle.

16. Hypolampsis fallax.

H. *oblongo-ovata, subparallela, attenuata, pallide ferruginea; capite inter oculos obsolete foveolato, punctulato; thorace quadrato, ad basin constricto, ad latera piceo suffuso; elytris attenuatis, punctato-striatis, fusco suffusis; antennis filiformibus, ad apicem subdilatatis, ferrugineis, art.* 7 *et* 8 *fuscis; pedibus ferrugineis, femoribus posticis rufo-ferrugineis.*

Long. corp. 1¼ lin., lat. ½ lin.

Oblong-ovate, subparallel, attenuated, finely punctate, subpubescent, of a pale ferrugineous colour. *Head* short, transverse, vertical, hardly produced in front; immediately above the base of the antennæ is a minute longitudinal fovea; the eyes are tolerably prominent, and situated laterally and near the base of the head; the surface between the eyes is finely punctate. *Thorax* quadrate, distinctly constricted, as well as transversely depressed at the base; the sides are finely marginate; the surface is obsoletely punctate, of a pale ferrugineous colour, suffused anteriorly, and more distinctly at the sides, with fuscous. *Scutellum* triangular, fuscous. *Elytra* somewhat broader than the thorax, parallel, elongate, finely punctate-striate; antemedially, an obsolete oblique depression towards the shoulders gives a gibbous appearance to the scutellary angles; the surface is finely pubescent; the colour is pale ferrugineous, suffused throughout with fuscous. *Antennæ* filiform, with a tendency to dilatation towards the apex, pale ferrugineous, the seventh and eighth joints being fuscous. *Legs* pale ferrugineous, the posterior femora being rufo-ferrugineous.

H. fallax is readily recognized by its *quadrate* and *constricted thorax* and by its *attenuated* elytra.

Brazil. In the collection of M. Deyrolle.

17. Hypolampsis nigrina.

H. *oblongo-ovata, subcylindrica, impubescens, picea; capite brevi, granulato; thorace subquadrato, ad basin leviter constricto, antice et ad basin transverse depresso, granulato; elytris subparallelis, punctato-striatis, tenuiter flavo-pubescentibus, piceis, ad basin et ad latera rufo suffusis; antennis piceis, ad basin rufis; pedibus rufo-ferrugineis, femoribus posticis fusco suffusis.*

Long. corp. 1½ lin., lat. ½ lin.

Oblong-ovate, subparallel, subcylindrical, impubescent, piceous. *Head* short, slightly produced; eyes tolerably large and prominent, situated at the base of the head; the surface is distinctly granulated. *Thorax* transverse (almost quadrate), slightly constricted near to (not immediately at) the base; the anterior angles are depressed, the sides marginate; near to the anterior margin, and also more distinctly and broadly at the base, is a transverse depression; the surface is finely granulated. *Scutellum* triangular. *Elytra* subparallel, punctate-striate, clothed (when viewed under a high magnifying power) very sparingly with flavous pubescence; piceous, obsoletely suffused near the apex and suture with rufous. *Antennæ* slightly incrassated towards the apex; piceous, with the basal joints rufous. *Legs* rufo-ferrugineous, the posterior femora being suffused with fuscous.

Island of St. Paul.

18. Hypolampsis minima.

H. *oblongo-ovata, parallela, fusco-picea, subpubescens; thorace quadrato, ad basin constricto; elytris subcylindricis, punctato-striatis; antennis longiusculis, ad apicem dilatatis, fusco-flavis; pedibus flavo-testaceis.*

Long. corp. 1 lin., lat. ⅔ lin.

Oblong-ovate, parallel, subcylindrical, fusco-piceous, clothed with a white hoary pubescence. *Head* short, somewhat depressed; eyes large, prominent, situated at the base of the head, and extending beyond the anterior angles of the thorax; the surface below the base of the antennæ is rufous; above thickly punctate, and in colour fusco-piceous. *Thorax* quadrate, distinctly constricted at the base; the anterior angles are depressed, the sides are marginate; the surface is transversely subdepressed at the base. *Scutellum* small, triangular. *Elytra* parallel, subcylindrical, broadly and distinctly punctate-striate; a slight antemedial depression extends obliquely upwards from the suture. *Antennæ* tolerably long, with a tendency to dilatation near the apex; in colour fusco-flavous. *Legs* flavo-testaceous.

From Santarem (district of the River Amazon). In the collection of Mr. Bates.

19. Hypolampsis atra.

H. *oblongo-ovata, subparallela, impubescens, picea; capite brevi, granulato; thorace transverso, rectilineari, ad basin leviter transverse depresso, punctato; elytris subparallelis, ante medium oblique depressis, punctato-striatis; antennis ad apicem subdilatatis, ferrugineis, ad apicem, etiamque art. 1 et 2, fuscis; pedibus rufo-ferrugineis, femoribus posticis fuscis.*

Long. corp. 1⅕ lin., lat. ½ lin.

Oblong-ovate, subparallel, impubescent, piceous. *Head* transverse, slightly produced; below the base of the antennæ are two obliquely transverse carinations; the eyes are situated at the base of the head; the surface is distinctly granulated. *Thorax* transverse, rectangular, rectilinear; the anterior angles are depressed and subacute; the sides are marginate; at the base is a slight and obsolete transverse depression (not broad and well-defined, as in *H. nigrina*); the surface is finely and thickly punctate. *Scutellum* triangular, obsolete. *Elytra* subparallel, antemedially depressed, and punctate-striate. *Antennæ* slightly dilated at the apex; in colour rufo-ferrugineous, the apical joints and also the first and second being fuscous. *Legs* rufo-ferrugineous, the posterior femora being fuscous.

This species differs from *H. nigrina* in the form of its thorax, of which the lateral margins are rectilinear and parallel; there is also an entire absence of any transverse depression near the anterior margin of the thorax.

From the Island of St. Paul. In the collection of Mr. Waterhouse.

20. Hypolampsis fragilis.

H. *oblongo-ovata, subcylindrica, attenuata, subtiliter flavo-pubescens, pallide ferruginea; capite brevi, transverso, haud producto, oblique inter oculos foveolato; thorace subquadrato aut quadrato, ad basin constricto, ad latera subtiliter piceo marginato; elytris subparallelis, aliquando ad medium suffuse nigro-submaculatis, punctato-striatis; antennis filiformibus, flavis; pedibus flavis, interdum fusco suffusis.*

Long. corp. 1⅓ lin., lat. ⅔ lin.

Oblong-ovate, attenuated, finely flavo-pubescent, deeply punctate-striate; of a pale ferruginous colour, which varies in shade in different examples. *Head* short, transverse, vertical, not produced in front; immediately above the base of the antennæ is an obsolete longitudinal medial and also (above this) two oblique foveæ (forming together the character of the letter Y); the longitudinal fovea is produced *obsoletely* to the line of the base: the eyes are large, globose, and lateral, situated at the base of the head; the surface is finely punctate and flavo-subpubescent. *Thorax* quadrate, constricted near the base; the anterior angles (when viewed laterally) are much depressed and obsolete; the sides are in outline sinuate and marginate; near the base the surface is transversely depressed, very finely punctate, clothed throughout (but more distinctly at the sides) with pale flavous pubescence; the colour is flavous, suffused medially with fuscous, and narrowly margined on either side with piceous (in different examples this coloration is subject to variation). *Scutellum* minute, subpubescent. *Elytra* subparallel, deeply and broadly punctate-striate, clothed throughout with pale flavous pubescence; in some examples there is a suffused faint circular or transverse postmedial marking of fuscous. *Antennæ* filiform, flavous. *Legs* flavous, occasionally suffused with fuscous.

This species appears to be very variable in shades of colour, though constant in form: it may be separated from most others of this difficult genus by the form and colour of its thorax, which is always distinctly constricted at the base, and also always more or less margined at the sides with fuscous: in some examples the elytra are almost concolorous, in others there is a rudimentary suffused circular spot placed postmedially, while in others, again, this spot is enlarged into a broader, but still obsolete and suffused band. I am indebted to the cabinet of my friend Mr. Fry for a definition of the species, which seems to be satisfactory; his collection contains a fine series of the insect, in its different gradations of colour, taken by himself on the outskirts of forests near Rio Janeiro. The species frequents some small shrub in considerable numbers; one or two individuals may occasionally be seen on almost every leaf; they are most difficult to secure, as they are very readily alarmed, and active.

Brazil; Rio Janeiro. In the cabinets of M. Deyrolle, Mr. Fry, and the Rev. H. Clark.

21. Hypolampsis Lacordairii.

H. *oblongo-ovata, subparallela, subpubescens, punctato-striata, pallide ferruginea; capite brevi, transverso, haud producto, punctato; thorace quadrato, ad basin constricto, punctato, flavo, ad medium et latera rufo-ferrugineo; elytris latis, subdepressis, flavo-pubescentibus; antennis filiformibus, flavis; pedibus flavis.*

Long. corp. $1\frac{1}{2}$ lin., lat. $\frac{2}{3}$ lin.

Oblong-ovate, subparallel, finely pubescent, punctate-striate, of a pale ferrugineous colour. *Head* short, transverse, vertical, not produced in front; immediately above the eyes is an obsolete longitudinal fovea, connected at its upper extremity with two others which are oblique, forming together the character of the letter Y; the surface is punctate; the eyes are large and prominent, situated at the base of the head, and extending laterally as far as the anterior angles of the thorax. *Thorax* quadrate, constricted at the base; the anterior angles are depressed, and broader than in *H. fragilis*; when viewed obliquely, an obsolete transverse depression (more distinct than in *H. fragilis*) is apparent, extending along the basal line: the surface is finely flavo-pubescent, punctate; in colour flavous; medially (in a longitudinal direction) rufo-ferrugineous; the margins also are suffused with fuscous. *Scutellum* minute. *Elytra* broad, subdepressed, subparallel, punctate-striate, the striæ being more shallow and the punctures deeper than in *H. fragilis*; finely flavo-pubescent, more regularly so than in *H. fragilis*; the surface is also covered with frequent long fine hairs (which are absent in the last species). *Antennæ* filiform and flavous. *Legs* flavous, the posterior femora and tarsi being suffused with rufous.

This species is closely allied to *H. fragilis*; it may, however, be distinguished by the broader anterior angle of its thorax, by its *broader* and more regularly pubescent elytra, and by the character of the striation.

Taken at Santarem and Villa Nova, in the Amazon district, by Mr. Bates.

22. Hypolampsis costulata.

H. *oblongo-ovata, parallela, robusta, subcylindrica, punctato-striata, subpubescens, nigro-ferruginea ; capite brevi, punctato ; thorace quadrato, ad latera marginato, ad basin transverse et oblique depresso, granulato ; elytris sat latis, parallelis, punctato-striatis ; antennis robustis, ad apicem subincrassatis, art. 1–5 ferrugineis, 6–11 fuscis ; pedibus anterioribus flavis, tibiis tarsisque fusco suffusis, posticis rufo-fuscis, tibiis tarsisque pallide rufis.*

Long. corp. $1\frac{1}{2}$ lin., lat. $\frac{2}{3}$ lin.

Oblong-ovate, parallel, robust, subcylindrical, deeply punctate-striate, sparingly pubescent, of a dark ferrugineous colour throughout. *Head* short, transverse, slightly elongated in front; below the base of the antennæ is a plane triangular depression ; immediately above the base is an obscure longitudinal line ; the eyes are somewhat small, situated at the base of the head, not extending so far as the anterior angles of the thorax ; the surface is punctate throughout, and sparingly clothed (more distinctly between the eyes) with ashy-grey pubescence. *Thorax* quadrate, rectangular ; the anterior angles depressed ; the sides are marginate ; at the base is a shallow transverse depression, which extends obliquely upwards along the sides to the humeral angles, and which gives a prominence to the anterior medial portion of the disk ; when viewed from in front, a longitudinal medial fovea is apparent, which is not extended to the base ; the surface is very finely and sparingly pubescent, and granulated. *Scutellum* small, triangular, impunctate. *Elytra* broader than the thorax, parallel, robust, rounded at the apex, deeply punctate-striate throughout ; an antemedial transverse shallow depression (when viewed laterally) gives an appearance of prominence to the anterior angles ; the surface is very sparingly clothed throughout with fine pubescence of an ashy-grey colour. *Antennæ* robust, slightly incrassated towards the apex, joints first to fifth being ferrugineous, and sixth to eleventh fuscous. *Legs* : the anterior flavous, the tibiæ and tarsi being suffused with fuscous ; the posterior femora are darkly rufo-fuscous, the tibiæ and tarsi being pale rufous.

Nova Granada, Bogota. From the collection of M. Chevrolat.

23. Hypolampsis meridionalis.

H. *oblongo-ovata, subcylindrica, tenue subpubescens, piceo-ferruginea ; capite inter oculos V-foveolato ; thorace transverso, ad basin subconstricto, ad apicem etiamque ad basin transverse depresso, flavo-subpubescenti ; elytris punctato-striatis, ad medium transverse depressis, tenue pubescentibus, piceo-ferrugineis, ad apicem et ad latera flavis et transverse ferrugineo-notatis; antennis testaceis; pedibus flavis.*

Long. corp. 1½ lin., lat. ⅔ lin.

Oblong-ovate, subcylindrical, very finely pubescent, piceo-ferrugineous. *Head* short, transverse, slightly depressed; above the base of the antennæ and between the eyes is an obsolete V-shaped fovea; the surface is finely granulated and rufo-ferrugineous. *Thorax* transverse, slightly constricted towards the base; the anterior angles are subtruncate and depressed; the sides are marginate; near the anterior margin is a distinct transverse depression, and at the base is another, broader and somewhat deep depression; the surface (when viewed under a high power) is clothed throughout with fine rufo-flavous pubescence. *Scutellum* small, fuscous. *Elytra* subparallel, antemedially transversely depressed; punctate-striate, the punctures being almost concealed by fine pubescence; in colour piceo-ferrugineous, with the apex, and also irregular longitudinal and transverse markings flavous. *Antennæ* fine, slightly incrassated towards the apex; the joints first and second are flavo-ferrugineous, third to sixth flavous, seventh and eighth flavo-piceous, ninth to eleventh flavo-testaceous. *Legs*: the anterior flavous; the posterior rufoflavous, the femora being suffused with piceous.

Brazil. In the cabinet of M. Deyrolle.

24. Hypolampsis squamata.

H. *oblonga, ovata, subparallela, fortiter punctato-striata, subpubescens, flavo-ferruginea; capite brevi, punctato, ad medium rufofusco; thorace quadrato, ad basin constricto et transverse depresso; elytris subparallelis, punctato-striatis, ante medium transverse depressis, flavo-pubescentibus, ferrugineis; antennis subincrassatis, flavis, art. 7 et 8 fuscis; pedibus flavis.*

Long. corp. 1½ lin., lat. ⅔ lin.

Oblong, ovate, subparallel, deeply and coarsely punctate-striate, subpubescent, flavo-ferrugineous. *Head* short, hardly produced in front, vertical; the eyes are globose and lateral, situated at the base of the head; the surface below and also above the base of the antennæ is deeply and coarsely punctate, unmarked however (as in some other species) by any tubercular elevations or depressions; clothed with obsolete pubescence, more apparently at the inner margin of the eyes; in colour rufo-ferrugineous, suffused medially with rufo-fuscous. *Thorax* quadrate, distinctly constricted at the base; the anterior angles are much depressed and obsolete; the sides are finely marginate, at the base transversely depressed; the surface is obsoletely flavo-pubescent throughout. *Scutellum* triangular. *Elytra* subparallel, deeply and coarsely punctate-striate; a transverse antemedial depression extends obliquely upwards to the shoulders; the surface is finely flavo-pubescent, in colour ferrugineous near the apex, and sides flavous. *Antennæ* fine, subincrassated near the apex, flavous, the seventh and eighth joints being fuscous. *Legs* flavous throughout.

This species may be distinguished from all others by the basal constriction of its thorax, *together with* the absence of carinations and depressions on the surface of the head. From *H. inæqualis* it may be separated by its concolorous thorax and elytra.

Brazil. In the collection of Mr. Miers.

25. Hypolampsis sylvatica.

H. oblongo-ovata, robusta, subcylindrica, brevis, flavo-pubescens, punctato-striata, flavo-ferruginea; capite inter oculos Y-foveolato; thorace transverso, ad basin constricto et depresso, punctato; elytris punctato-striatis, ante medium transverse depressis; antennis art. 1 et 2 flavis, reliqui desunt; pedibus testaceis, femoribus tibiisque posticis ferrugineo suffusis.

Long. corp. 1 lin., lat. ½ lin.

Oblong-ovate, robust, subcylindrical, short, finely but distinctly flavo-pubescent throughout, punctate-striate; in colour flavo-ferrugineous. *Head* short, transverse, hardly produced in front, above the labrum transversely depressed; immediately above the base of the antennæ is an obsolete longitudinal fovea, connected at its upper extremity with a more distinct and obliquely angulated depression, the two forming together the character of the letter Y; the surface is finely punctate and flavo-pubescent; the eyes are tolerably globose, and situated at the base of the head. *Thorax* transverse, constricted at the base; the anterior angles are depressed; near the anterior margin, as well as more distinctly at the base, the surface is transversely depressed, finely punctate, and pubescent. *Scutellum* small, pubescent. *Elytra* subcylindrical, punctate-striate, pubescent; a transverse antemedial depression gives a prominence to the surface near the scutellum. *Antennæ* (robust? and filiform?): the two basal joints are in colour flavous; the rest are unfortunately wanting. *Legs* pale testaceous, the posterior femora and tibiæ being suffused with ferrugineous.

Brazil. In the collection of the Rev. H. Clark.

26. Hypolampsis regia.

H. *oblonga, ovata, robusta, subtiliter pubescens, punctato-striata, rufo-ferruginea; capite depresso, punctato; thorace quadrato, ad basin valde constricto et punctato, flavo-pubescenti, rufo-ferrugineo, lateribus et linea media longitudinali piceis; elytris subcylindricis, ante medium depressis, punctato-striatis, rufo-ferrugineis, marginibus rufo-piceis, et ad apicem pubescentibus; antennis filiformibus, flavis; pedibus flavis, femoribus tibiisque posticis rufo-flavis.*

Long. corp. $1\frac{2}{3}$ lin., lat. $\frac{3}{4}$ lin.

Oblong, ovate, robust, finely pubescent, punctate-striate, of a rufo-ferrugineous colour. *Head* short, transverse, almost vertical, not produced in front; the eyes are large, lateral, and situated at the base of the head; the surface between the eyes is finely punctate. *Thorax* quadrate, very considerably constricted at the base; the anterior angles are depressed and subprominent; the sides are in form subsinuate and marginate; the surface near the base is transversely subdepressed, finely punctate, and sparingly clothed with flavous pubescence; the colour is rufo-ferrugineous, the sides (especially near the anterior angles) and a medial longitudinal line being piceous. *Scutellum* triangular, piceous. *Elytra* subcylindrical, antemedially transversely depressed, punctate-striate; in colour rufo-ferrugineous, the margins alone being suffused with piceous, and the apex being more distinctly pubescent. *Antennæ* filiform and flavous. *Legs* flavous, the posterior femora and tibiæ being rufo-flavous.

H. regia may be distinguished from its congeners by the absence of any carination or depression of the surface between the eyes, by its very decided constriction at the base of the thorax, and by the colour of its elytra.

From the neighbourhood of Ega, in the district of the River Amazon. Taken by Mr. Bates.

27. Hypolampsis flavo-notata.

H. *ovata, subparallela, sat robusta, tenuiter subpubescens, flavo-ferruginea; capite ad basin antennarum longitudinaliter subfoveolato; thorace quadrato, ad basin transverse depresso, ad angulos anteriores fovea obliqua notato, etiamque ad medium longitudinaliter impresso, flavo-pubescenti; elytris latis, punctato-striatis, ad apicem et ad latera flavo-pubescentibus et oblique fulvo-notatis; antennis testaceis; pedibus flavis.*

Long. corp. $1\frac{1}{3}$ lin., lat. $\frac{2}{3}$ lin.

Ovate, subparallel, tolerably robust; under a high power of the microscope very finely pubescent; in colour flavo-ferrugineous. *Head* short, transverse; above the base of the antennæ is an obsolete and short longitudinal fovea; the surface is finely pubescent. *Thorax* quadrate, rectilinear; the anterior angles are depressed, the sides marginate; at the base is a distinct and broad transverse channel; near the anterior angles are two slight oblique depressions, while a very faint longitudinal impression extends medially from the apex to the base; the surface is finely flavo-pubescent. *Scutellum* triangular, ferrugineous. *Elytra* broad, tolerably robust, punctate-striate, the striæ being subsinuate; a medial transverse depression gives an appearance of prominence to the base; the surface at the apex and near the margins is flavo-pubescent, and in colour nigro-ferrugineous, the margins and the apex being irregularly flavous, and marked in an obliquely transverse direction by short subsinuate bands of darker flavous. *Antennæ* filiform, in colour testaceous, the two basal joints being ferrugineous. *Legs* flavous throughout.

From the Island of St. Catherine, Brazil. In the collection of M. Deyrolle.

28. Hypolampsis vicina.

H. *oblongo-ovata, subcylindrica, subparallela, subtiliter pubescens, flavo-fusca; capite brevi, depresso, inter oculos oblique foveolato, granulato; thorace transverso, basin versus subconstricto; elytris sat latis, punctato-striatis; antennis ad apicem subincrassatis, flavis, art. 6–8 fuscis; pedibus flavis, femoribus posticis fuscis, tibiisque rufis.*

Long. corp. $1\frac{1}{3}$ lin., lat. $\frac{3}{4}$ lin.

Oblong-ovate, subcylindrical, subparallel, very finely pubescent, of a flavo-fuscous colour. *Head* short, depressed almost at right angles to the thorax, not produced in front; at the base of the antennæ are two minute oblique depressions extending to the upper and inner margins of the eyes, forming together the character of the letter V; the surface is finely granulated and subpubescent, more distinctly so at the base. *Thorax* transverse (almost quadrate), slightly constricted towards the base; the sides are submarginate, more broadly near the anterior angles; at the basal angles is a minute depression. *Scutellum* triangular, fuscous. *Elytra* distinctly broader than the thorax, tolerably robust, deeply punctate-striate, and when viewed under a high power covered with a short flavous or ashy-grey pubescence. *Antennæ* filiform, slightly incrassated at the apex; the joints one to five flavous, six to eight fuscous, nine to eleven flavo-testaceous, the apical joint being suffused with fuscous. *Legs* tolerably robust; the anterior flavous throughout; the posterior femora darkly fuscous, and the tibiæ rufous.

Columbia. In the collection of M. Chevrolat.

29. Hypolampsis Fryella.

H. *oblonga, ovata, flavo-pubescens, punctato-striata, pallide rufo-flava; capite brevi, inter oculos* Y*-foveolato, punctato, rufo-ferrugineo; thorace subquadrato, ad basin subtiliter constricto et transverse depresso, punctato, flavo-pubescenti, rufo-flavo; elytris subcylindricis, punctato-striatis, ante medium depressis, irregulariter flavo-pubescentibus; antennis subdilatatis, pallide flavis, art. 7 et 8 ferrugineis; pedibus pallide flavis.*

Long. corp. $1\frac{1}{2}$ lin., lat. $\frac{2}{3}$ lin.

Oblong, ovate, flavo-pubescent, punctate-striate, of a pale rufo-flavous colour. *Head* short, transverse, hardly produced in front; above the labrum is a transverse plane depression; immediately above the base of the antennæ is a small longitudinal medial fovea, which bisects at its upper extremity another transverse fovea, this latter extending obliquely to the upper and inner margin of the eyes; the eyes are in form globose, situated at the base of the head; the surface is finely punctate, and in colour rufo-ferrugineous. *Thorax* transverse (almost quadrate); the anterior margin slightly rounded; at the base the sides are subconstricted; near the basal line (and also less broadly near the anterior margin) the surface is transversely depressed; finely punctate, flavo-pubescent, and rufo-flavous, the sides being narrowly piceous. *Scutellum* triangular, impunctate, rufo-ferrugineous. *Elytra* subcylindrical, punctate-striate, antemedially depressed, clothed irregularly with thick pale flavous pubescence; this pubescence gives a pale flavous colour to the apex, to the margination, and also to an irregularly-formed medial oblique band, which extends from the margination to the fifth or sixth striæ; the antemedial depression also is similarly flavo-pubescent. *Antennæ* filiform, with a tendency to dilatation; in colour pale flavous, the seventh and eighth joints being ferrugineous. *Legs* pale flavous, the inflation above the apical claw being rufous.

The form of the thorax will identify this species from among most of its congeners; it is slightly constricted at the base, and transversely depressed at the anterior as well as the posterior margins; it may be distinguished still further by its pale flavous colour and the markings on the elytra.

Petropolis, Organ Mountains; Rio Janeiro. Taken by Mr. Fry, and in that gentleman's cabinet.

30. Hypolampsis fusca.

H. *oblongo-ovata, parallela, subcylindrica, subpubescens, nigro-fusca; capite inter oculos foveolato; thorace elongato, ad basin constricto et depresso; elytris punctato-striatis, transverse subdepressis; antennis robustis, subincrassatis, art. 1–4 flavis, 5–11 fuscis; pedibus anterioribus flavis, femoribus posticis nigro-fuscis, tibiisque rufis.*

Long. corp. $1\frac{1}{3}$ lin., lat. $\frac{1}{2}$ lin.

Oblong-ovate, parallel, subcylindrical, sparingly testaceo-pubescent, nigro-fuscous. *Head* short, very slightly produced; between the labrum and the base of the antennæ are two obliquely transverse carinations; immediately above the base and between the eyes is a slight but well-defined fovea in the form of the letter Y; the eyes are large, prominent, extending laterally as far as the anterior angles of the thorax; the surface is finely punctate. *Thorax* elongate, rectangular; the anterior angles are much depressed; the sides marginate, and constricted at the base; a broad transverse depression extends postmedially along the line of the base, which gives a distinct appearance of prominence to the antemedial surface; a faint longitudinal depression (apparent when viewed from behind) extends medially from the anterior margin nearly to the base. *Scutellum* triangular. *Elytra* subparallel, subcylindrical, punctate-striate, antemedially transversely subdepressed. *Antennæ* tolerably long, robust, subincrassated towards the apex; the joints one to four flavous, five to eleven (which are gradually dilated) fuscous. *Legs*: the anterior flavous; the posterior femora nigro-fuscous, and tibiæ rufous; the dilatation of the apical claw brightly rufo-piceous.

This species at first appearance closely resembles *H. minima*; both species are of nearly the same size, form, colour, and pubescence; *H. fusca* however is, on examination, obviously distinct; the Y-shaped fovea between the eyes, its elongated thorax, and the coloration of the posterior legs (as well as the difference in their relative *length*; the femora in *H. minuta* being short; in *H. fusca* more elongated, and extending nearly as far as the apex of the elytra) sufficiently distinguish it.

Petropolis (Organ Mountains); Rio Janeiro. In the collection of Mr. Fry.

31. Hypolampsis anceps.

H. *oblongo-ovata, subparállela, depressa, punctato-striata, impubescens, rufo-ferruginea, nitida; capite brevi, impunctato; thorace transverso, late marginato, ad basin foveolato, subtiliter punctato; elytris subparallelis, punctato-striatis, ad suturam rufo-notatis; antennis robustis, filiformibus, fuscis, ad basin rufis; pedibus rufo-ferrugineis.*

Long. corp. $1\frac{4}{5}$ lin., lat. $\frac{3}{4}$ lin.

Oblong-ovate, subparallel, somewhat depressed, punctate-striate, impubescent, shining, darkly rufo-ferrugineous. *Head* short, not produced in front; the eyes are large, in form globose, and somewhat prominent, situated at a little distance from the base of the head: the surface between the eyes (*immediately* adjoining the base of the antennæ) is slightly porrected in front, and coarsely and unevenly granulated; the rest of the surface is glabrous, with a few very minute spots grouped together medially. *Thorax* broader than the head, transverse, in front slightly emarginate; the anterior angles are depressed and subacute; the sides are broadly marginate, and in outline slightly rounded; at the base (when viewed laterally) is a transverse thread-like distinct fovea, extending parallel to, and closely adjoining the basal line; the surface (when viewed under a high power) is sparingly and very minutely punctate. *Scutellum* triangular, impunctate. *Elytra* broader than the thorax, subparallel, rounded at the apex, punctate-striate throughout (the punctures being most readily apparent near the margination, and becoming obsolete as they approach the apex); a faint transverse antemedial depression gives a slight appearance of prominence to the scutellary angles; the surface is of a rich dark rufo-ferrugineous colour, with suffused markings of rufous; a broad postmedial transverse band is well defined at its anterior margin (which is subcircular in form), but has no clearly-marked boundary towards the apex; medially, two circular spots (between the first and second striæ) closely adjoin (but are separated one from another by) the suture; while near the scutellum, the surface is, on either side of the suture, longitudinally marked with the same rufous colour. *Antennæ* robust, filiform; the first joint (as compared with that of adjoining species) is *relatively* much elongated; the three basal joints are in colour rufous, the rest are fuscous. *Legs* sufficiently elongated, rufo-ferrugineous throughout.

Brazil (St. Paul's). In the collection of M. Chevrolat.

Subdivision B. *Elytra robustiora, interdum subglobosa, brevia; lateribus plus minus rotundatis, haud parallelis.*

32. Hypolampsis robusta.

H. *ovata, lata, robusta, pubescens, pallide rufo-ferruginea; thorace quadrato, rectilineari, ad basin transverse depresso, linea longitudinali media, suffusa, picea; elytris latis, amplis, punctatostriatis, transverse subdepressis; antennis filiformibus, rufoflavis, ad apicem piceis; pedibus robustis, rufo-flavis.*

Long. corp. 1¼ lin., lat. ⅔ lin.

Ovate, broad, robust, of a rufo-ferrugineous colour, finely pubescent. *Head* short, depressed, slightly elongated in front; the eyes are subprominent, extending nearly as far as the anterior angles of the thorax; the surface is finely punctate, above the insertion of the antennæ very sparingly clothed with pubescence, ferrugineo-rufous. *Thorax* quadrate, rectilinear, rectangular; the anterior angles are depressed; the sides are marginate; the surface at the base is broadly and transversely subdepressed; subpubescent, and in colour rufo-ferrugineous, a longitudinal medial line being piceous, and the margination fuscous. *Scutellum* small, triangular. *Elytra* broad, robust, punctate-striate, broadly subdepressed from the antemedial suture towards the shoulders; finely pubescent throughout. *Antennæ* long, filiform (with a slight tendency to incrassation towards the apex), rufo-flavous, the apical joints being piceous. *Legs* robust, rufo-flavous; the anterior pair suffused at the base of the femora with piceous.

The pale colour and distinct pubescence of this species sufficiently separate it from the other species of the subsection.

Bahia. In the collection of the Rev. H. Clark.

33. Hypolampsis æstivalis.

H. ovata, robusta, impubescens, punctata, nigra ; capite brevi, subpunctato ; thorace transverso, rectangulari, flavo-pubescenti ; elytris robustis, punctato-striatis, ante medium transverse depressis ; antennis (? filiformibus) art. 1 et 2 flavis (ceteri desunt) ; pedibus flavis, femoribus posticis piceis.

Long. corp. 1¼ lin., lat. ½ lin.

Ovate, robust, impubescent, punctate, black. *Head* short, not produced in front; below the base of the antennæ is a transverse depression; the eyes are large, and in form globose, situated at the base of the head; the surface between the eyes is equate, and unmarked by any carination or depression; punctate. *Thorax* broader than the head, transverse, rectangular, rectilinear; the anterior angles are much depressed; the surface is equate, finely flavo-pubescent, obsoletely punctate, and of a dull black colour. *Scutellum* triangular, flavo-pubescent. *Elytra* much broader than the thorax, robust, subcylindrical, punctate-striate, the striæ being almost obsolete and the punctures distinct and deep; an antemedial transverse depression gives a prominence to the base; the surface is glabrous and black, tinged with rufous. *Antennæ*: the first two joints are flavous, the basal being suffused with ferrugineous (the rest are wanting). *Legs* flavous, the posterior femora being piceous, and the globular inflation of the postical claw rufo-flavous.

This species may be at once separated from *H. porculus*, to which it is nearly allied, by the absence of striæ as well as of pubescence on the elytra.

Brazil. In the collection of M. Deyrolle.

34. Hypolampsis pilosa.

Ill. (*auct. Mus. D. Chev.*).
Ill. Mag. v. p. 105.

H. *oblongo-ovata, robusta, lata, subcylindrica, pubescens, fusco-flava; capite brevi, granulato, flavo-ferrugineo; thorace transverso, antice subattenuato, æquato, flavo-pubescenti, fusco; elytris latis, globosis, punctato-striatis, flavo-pubescentibus; antennis subincrassatis, flavis; pedibus flavis.*

Long. corp. 1 lin., lat. ⅔ lin.

Oblong-ovate, very robust, subcylindrical, punctate-striate, clothed throughout with fusco-flavous pubescence. *Head* short, transverse, slightly produced in front, above the labrum transversely depressed; the upper surface between the eyes is apparently without fovea or depression; the surface is granulated, and in colour flavo-ferrugineous. *Thorax* transverse, subcylindrical; the sides much depressed, and in front subattenuated; the surface is equate and flavo-pubescent, the colour fuscous. *Scutellum* minute. *Elytra* very much broader than the thorax, globose, evenly punctate-striate; the striæ are distinct, but the punctures are entirely concealed by a thick flavous pubescence; the surface is equate and fuscous. *Antennæ* subincrassated towards the apex, flavous. *Legs* flavous throughout.

This species may be separated from its congeners by its broad and subglobular elytra, by the absence of any antemedial depression, and by its comparatively small and equate thorax.

Pennsylvania (N. America). From the collection of M. Chevrolat.

35. Hypolampsis porculus.

H. *ovata, lata, robusta, impubescens, nigro-picea; thorace transverso, ad basin et ad latera depresso, ad latera flavo-pubescenti, granulato; elytris latis, subglobosis, punctato-striatis, ante medium transverse subdepressis; antennis ad basin rufo-flavis (art. 3–11 desunt); pedibus anterioribus flavis, posticis femoribus piceis, tibiis subarcuatis, rufo-flavis.*

Long. corp. 1 lin., lat. ⅔ lin.

Ovate, broad, robust, impubescent, black. *Head* short, transverse, not produced; the eyes are tolerably large, and situated at the base of the head; the surface is granulated. *Thorax* transverse; the anterior angles depressed and obsoletely subacute; the sides marginate; near the anterior margin are two faint and obsolete prominences, which are caused by a broad subdepression at the base, and also more apparently at the sides; the surface is clothed at the sides very sparingly with flavous pubescence, and coarsely granulated. *Scutellum* triangular, impunctate. *Elytra* much broader than the thorax, subglobose, deeply and coarsely punctate-striate, antemedially transversely subdepressed. *Antennæ*: the basal joint rufoflavous (the rest are wanting). *Legs*: the anterior flavous; the posterior femora piceous, the tibiæ slightly arcuate near their base; short, rufo-flavous, the globular inflation of the posterior claw being bright rufous.

Brazil.

36. Hypolampsis gibba.

H. *ovalis, robusta, subpubescens, picea; capite brevi, subtiliter punctato, piceo; thorace transverso, oblique depresso; elytris latis, robustis, punctato-striatis, ad apicem et latera irregulariter rufo-pubescentibus; antennis brevibus, ad apicem subdilatatis, rufo-piceis, art. basalibus flavis; pedibus flavis, tibiis anterioribus femoribusque posticis piceo suffusis.*

Long. corp. 1¼ lin., lat. ¾ lin.

Oval, robust, finely pubescent, piceous. *Head* not produced in front, transverse; the eyes are large, lateral, and in form oval, situated near the base of the head; from the insertion of the antennæ to the basal line extends a medial longitudinal carination; the surface is finely punctate, and in colour piceous. *Thorax* transverse, rather broader than the head; the anterior angles depressed and subacute; the sides broadly marginate; the anterior angles are much depressed; from the basal line a broad depression extends obliquely upwards towards the humeral angles; the surface is finely punctate. *Scutellum* triangular, situated below the plane of the elytra. *Elytra* broad, robust, punctate-striate, clothed irregularly near the apex and also at the sides with rufo-flavous pubescence; this pubescence forms an obscure oblique band, which is more distinct near the margination; an antemedial transverse depression extends obliquely upwards towards the shoulders. *Antennæ* short, subdilated towards the apex, in colour rufo-piceous, the basal joints being flavous. *Legs* flavous, the anterior tibiæ and the postical femora being suffused with piceous.

This species is in general form nearly allied to *H. porculus*; it may, however, at once be separated from it by its more transverse thorax and the less deep punctuation on the elytra; from *H. æstivalis* it may be separated by its striation as well as by its pubescence.

Taken by the late Mr. Squire in the neighbourhood of Rio Janeiro. In the collection of Mr. Baly.

37. Hypolampsis suborbicularis.

H. *ovata, robusta, punctata, subpubescens, flavo-ferruginea; capite brevi, transverso, subtiliter granulato, impubescenti; thorace transverso, flavo-pubescenti, punctato; elytris latis, robustis, brevibus, ante medium transverse depressis, punctato-striatis; antennis subincrassatis, flavis, art. 5–8 fuscis; pedibus flavis, femoribus posticis rufo-flavis.*

Long. corp. 1 lin., lat. ½ lin.

Ovate, robust, punctate, finely pubescent, flavo-ferrugineous. *Head* short, transverse, not produced in front; the eyes are in form oval, situated at the base of the head, lateral; immediately above the base of the antennæ is a small medial longitudinal fovea; the surface is finely granulated and impubescent. *Thorax* transverse, slightly broader than the head; the anterior angles are depressed and almost obsolete; the sides subsinuate and finely flavo-pubescent; punctate. *Scutellum* minute, triangular. *Elytra* much broader and more robust than the thorax, short, antemedially transversely depressed; rows of punctures arranged in the form of striæ are distinctly apparent at the base and medially, but become obsolete near the apex. *Antennæ* short, subincrassated, the third joint being attenuate, the sixth to the ninth subincrassated (the rest are wanting); in colour flavous, the joints fifth to eighth being fuscous. *Legs* flavous, the anterior tarsi being suffused with fuscous, and the posterior femora rufo-flavous.

Brazil. In the collection of M. Deyrolle.

Genus 39. IMATIUM*.

PALPI MAXILLARES *robusti, subincrassati, art. ultimo haud elongato.*
PALPI LABIALES *attenuati, subcylindrici.*
ANTENNÆ *approximatæ, robustæ, incrassatæ, art. 5–10 brevibus.*
CAPUT *depressum, subverticale haud productum, granulatum, pubescens.*
THORAX *transversus, antice plus minus emarginatus, depressus, pubescens.*

* ἱμάτιον, vestis.

Elytra rotundata *vel subrotundata, late striato-punctata, pube dense vestita.*

Pedes: *tibiis anterioribus subincurvatis; posticis femoribus brevibus et incrassatissimis; tibiis pœne rectis, ad apicem extremum bicalcaratis.*

Labrum transverse, rounded at the margins.

Maxillary palpi (Front. fig. 8 *m*; Tab. IX. fig. 6 *m*) robust; the basal joint minute; the second somewhat broader at the apex and obliquely truncate; the third nearly twice the breadth of the second, in form globular; the apical joint is minute, not elongated.

Labial palpi (Front. fig. 8 *n*; Tab. IX. fig. 6 *n*) attenuate, subcylindrical, the penultimate joint being somewhat broader than the rest.

Antennæ approximate, situated between the lower margins of the eyes, robust, incrassated; the basal joint is long, thickened near the apex, and not inflected; the second is half the length of the first, much narrower, and in form ovate; the third and fourth are subequal in length, attenuate, and not broader than the second; the remaining joints are broadly dilated and abbreviated; near the apex of all the joints are four or five distinct or rigid hairs.

Eyes lateral, situated at the base of the head, in form subovate, not prominent.

Head depressed, almost vertical to the plane of the elytra, not produced in front; above the labrum is a transverse carination; the surface is clothed with coarse pubescence, and, below the pubescence, apparently punctate or granulated.

Thorax transverse, anteriorly emarginate; the sides are marginate; the basal line is produced medially (near the scutellum) into an obtuse angle; the surface is rounded, equate, and clothed throughout with coarse pubescence.

Scutellum triangular, situated slightly below the plane of the elytra, finely punctate, impubescent.

Elytra very broad and globose, rotundate, much broader and more robust than the thorax; the surface is unmarked by any antemedial transverse depression; punctate-striate; sometimes the striæ are nearly obsolete, and the punctures broad and shallow; the surface is clothed throughout more or less completely with coarse pubescence.

Legs: the anterior sufficiently long and robust. The *anterior femora* are cylindrical, slightly incurved. The *tibiæ* are straight, hardly dilated towards the apex. The *tarsi* (Front. fig. 8 *d*) are abbreviated, the two basal joints being triangular, and subequal in size not broader than the apex of the tibiæ; the third joint is almost twice the breadth of the basal joints, transverse, and subbilobed; the apical claw is bifid, and armed on either side at its base with a short robust spur. The posterior legs are short. The *femora* (Front. fig. 8*f*), when viewed laterally, are very broadly incrassated, the breadth being more than half the length. The *tibiæ* (Front. fig. 8*f*) are short and almost straight; when seen from behind, a longitudinal groove from the base to the apex is apparent; the margination of the groove is simple and straight; below the insertion of the tarsus the extreme apex is produced into two robust incurved claws. The *tarsi* (Front. fig. 8 *h*) are short and attenuate; the apical claw, which is minute, being almost entirely concealed by the globular inflation of the ultimate joint.

This genus is remarkable for its short and globular form and its covering of thick pubescence; it may be separated, *primâ facie*, by these two characters from all other genera in the group. The species composing it are apparently very rare, and found only in the neighbourhood of Rio de Janeiro.

1. Imatium tomentosum. (TAB. IX. fig. 6.)

I. *globosum, rotundatum, lævigatum, pube flava vestitum, rufo-ferrugineum; capite brevi, pæne verticali; thorace transverso, ad latera obsolete marginato, antice subcontracto; elytris subsphæricis, brevibus, striato-punctatis, ad apicem flavo-pubescentibus; antennis brevibus, incrassatis, art.* 1–4 *ferrugineis,* 5–11 *nigris; pedibus rufo-flavis, tarsorum anter. art.* 1–3 *nigris.*

Long. corp. 2½ lin., lat. 1¾ lin.

Subspherical, rotundate, broad, ferrugineous, clothed throughout (but especially at the margins) with a fine silken yellow pubescence. *Head* small, very depressed, almost entirely vertical; labrum dark ferrugineous: surface below the insertion of the antennæ subcomplanate; the antennæ are approximate; above the insertion of the antennæ and between the eyes is a medial longitudinal fovea: the eyes are small, situated at quite the base of the head, not extending laterally so far as the anterior angles of the thorax; the surface is coarsely granulated. *Thorax* transverse, depressed; the sides are *obsoletely* marginate and subcontracted towards the front; the basal line is angulated at the scutellum; the surface is rugose and granulated. *Scutellum* slightly elongate, subcordiform, impunctate. *Elytra* very broad, subspherical, short, with rows of coarse and shallow punctures arranged in the form of striæ, but almost concealed at the sides and near the apex by flavous pubescence. *Antennæ* much shorter than the elytra, incrassated, robust; the first joint long, broadly dilated at the apex; the second short, ovate; the third and fourth narrower than the first and second, and shorter than the first, slightly dilated towards their apex; the fifth to eleventh shorter (the terminal joints being shorter even than the second), broadly incrassated; in colour, the first to fourth ferrugineous, the fifth to eleventh black. *Legs* rufo-flavous throughout, the three basal joints of the anterior tarsi being distinctly black.

I. tomentosum differs from *I. rotundatum* in its non-concolorous antennæ, the black colour of the three basal joints of the anterior tarsi, and in the form of the punctures on the elytra, which are broader and less apparently deep than in the next species.

Brazil.

2. Imatium rotundatum.

I. *subsphæricum, valde flavo-pubescens, flavum vel fusco-flavum; capite abbreviato, depresso, ad basin antennarum obsolete bituberculato; thorace valde transverso, depresso; elytris latis, amplissimis, punctato-striatis; antennis brevibus, incrassatis, art. 1–8 fulvis, 9–11 flavis; pedibus flavis.*

Long. corp. $2\frac{3}{4}$ lin., lat. 2 lin.

Subspherical, thickly flavo-pubescent throughout, and in colour fusco-flavous. *Head* very short, much depressed (almost vertical); the eyes are small, not projecting laterally; between the eyes is an obsolete transverse depression; between this transverse depression and the base of the antennæ are two oblong tubercles (the channel between them forming, together with the transverse fovea, a depression in the form of the letter T); the surface of the head is flavous or fusco-flavous, and less distinctly granulated than in *I. tomentosum*. *Thorax* transverse (much more transverse than in *I. tomentosum*), considerably inclined or sloping towards the head; the sides are gradually compressed towards the apex and marginate, especially towards the anterior angles (which are much depressed); a broad and shallow transverse depression extends parallel to the basal line (most apparent when viewed in front). *Scutellum* triangular, flavous. *Elytra* much broader and more robust than the thorax, subspherical, punctate-striate, the punctures being deep and the striæ almost obsolete, clothed throughout with a thick pilose flavous pubescence. *Antennæ* short, robust, and incrassated; the first joint is long, and broadly dilated at the apex; the second is short and ovate; the third as long as the first, and rather longer than the fourth and fifth; the following joints are gradually dilated, especially the sixth to the eighth (but not so broadly as in *I. tomentosum*); in colour, first to eighth fulvous, ninth to eleventh flavous. *Legs* entirely flavous.

This species may be recognized (as compared with *I. tomentosum*) by its more pale flavous colouring (instead of ferrugineous), by the form of, and transverse depression at the base of, the thorax, by the less distinct dilatation of the antennæ, by the character of the punctuation on the elytra, and by the colouring of the antennæ and anterior tarsi.

Brazil.

3. Imatium velutinum. (FRONT. fig. 8.)

I. *ovatum, latum, subtiliter flavo-pubescens; thorace transverso, ad latera sinuato vel subrotundato, punctato; elytris robustis, brevibus, ante medium transverse depressis, punctato-striatis, ad basin distincte pubescentibus; antennis brevibus, art. 1–4 flavis, 5–9 dilatatis nigrisque, 10 et 11 flavo-testaceis; pedibus flavis.*

Long. corp. 2 lin., lat. 1¼ lin.

Ovate, broad, covered with a pale fulvo-flavous pubescence, of a flavous colour throughout. *Head* short, depressed, hardly produced; above the base of the antennæ and between the eyes is an obsoletely transverse, and another longitudinal depression, crossing each other at right angles; the eyes are tolerably large, situated close to the basal line; the surface is thickly punctate. *Thorax* transverse (almost quadrate), depressed; the anterior angles are subacute; the sides are marginate, and slightly constricted close to the anterior and posterior angles, and medially rounded; at the base is a slight transverse depression; the surface is slightly rotundate, thickly punctate, and finely pubescent. *Scutellum* triangular, impunctate, flavous. *Elytra* broad, robust, parallel, punctate-striate (the striæ being shallow, and the punctures broad); a transverse antemedial depression extends obliquely and upwards towards the humeral angles, giving an appearance of prominence to the surface adjoining the scutellum; the surface is almost glabrous (except under a high power, when it is seen to be finely pubescent), more distinctly pubescent at the apex. *Antennæ* robust, somewhat dilated towards the apex; the joints first to fourth flavous, fifth to ninth dilated, and in colour black, the tenth and eleventh flavo-testaceous. *Legs* tolerably robust; the terminal joint of the posterior tarsi strongly bilobed; the posterior robust and abbreviated; the colour is flavous throughout.

I feel some hesitation in placing this species in the same group as *I. tomentosum* and *I. rotundatum*; it is not quite so rotundate, the elytra (though broad and robust) are hardly hemispherical, and the form is not so globular; inasmuch, however, as there is little, except this general divergence of form, to separate it, I have determined to register it, provisionally at least, as an *Imatium.*

A single example of this species was taken by my friend Mr. Gray and myself near Petropolis, Organ Mountains, in February 1857.

Genus 40. SPARNUS*.

PALPI MAXILLARES *breves, dilatati, art. 3^{tio} subrotundato, art. 4to brevi, compresso.*

PALPI LABIALES *minuti, subcylindrici.*

ANTENNÆ *breves, incrassatæ.*

CAPUT *breve, depressum, lævigatum.*

THORAX *late transversus, angulis anticis depressis, lateribus antice subconstrictis.*

ELYTRA *depressa, lata, suborbiculata, punctata, impubescentia.*

PEDES *sat robusti, femoribus posticis* incrassatissimis, *apicibus* haud elytrorum apicem attingentibus.

Labrum short, subcircular, medially obsoletely sinuate.

Maxillary palpi (Tab. IX. fig. 4 *m*) short, dilated at the apex; the first joint minute, hardly more elongate than the second, and broad; the third transverse, the breadth being greater than the length, in form rotundate; the terminal joint is short, broad, and compressed.

Labial palpi (Tab. IX. fig. 4 *n*) minute, subcylindrical, robust.

Antennæ approximate, situated between the lower margins of the eyes, short, robust, and in form incrassated; the basal joint is elongate, subincurved, and dilated towards the apex; the second is short and ovate; the third of the same length as the first, attenuate; the fourth rather shorter than the third, and subdilated at the apex; the remaining joints are broadly incrassated and short.

Eyes lateral, situated at the base of the head, large, and globose.

Head short, considerably depressed, almost vertical, not produced in front; below the base of the antennæ is a deep triangular depression; between the eyes is a distinct and acutely depressed T-shaped fovea; the surface of the head is levigate.

Thorax broadly transverse; the anterior angles are much depressed and slightly rounded; the sides are marginate, diverging slightly one from another towards the elytra; the basal line is in form arcuate; the surface is equate and subglobose, the sides being broadly and distinctly depressed.

Scutellum triangular, punctate, levigate.

* σπαρνὸς, infrequens.

Elytra depressed, broad, the length being not much greater than the breadth; throughout the surface minute punctures are arranged, which become obsolete near the apex; the surface is equate, not antemedially depressed, and glabrous.

Legs robust. The *anterior femora* cylindrical, and dilated medially. The *tibiæ* are straight, incurved at their immediate base. The *tarsi* are short, the first joint being triangular, in breadth greater than the apex of the tibiæ; the second smaller and more transverse; the third considerably broader, transversely subcircular, and deeply bilobed; the apical claw is minute, bifid, and armed at its inner surface near the base with a short and robust claw. The *posterior femora* are (when seen transversely) very broadly incrassated, ovate, the length being equal to twice the breadth; distinctly shorter than in the genus *Cyrton*; the apex not reaching the apex of the elytra. The *tibiæ* are straight, and incurved at their immediate apex; when seen from behind, the posterior surface is longitudinally grooved and medially slightly compressed; the margination of this longitudinal groove is simple, not subsinuate; below the insertion of the tarsus, at the extreme apex, are two robust incurved claws. The *tarsi* are short and attenuate, the minute terminal claw being completely concealed from above by the globular inflation of the apical joint.

This genus may be easily recognized by its subrotundate and depressed form. Its glabrous surface, in which there is an entire absence of pubescence, separates it at once from *Imatium*, and its short posterior femora and tibiæ amply distinguish it from the genus *Cyrton*.

1. Sparnus globosus. (Tab. IX. fig. 4.)

S. ovatus, latus, globosus, subdepressus, fulvus, nitidus; capite brevi, transverse et longitudinaliter foveolato, impunctato, nigro, oculis magnis; thorace lato, transverso, impunctato, nigro; elytris subglobosis, brevibus, depressis, subtiliter striato-punctatis, fulvis; antennis brevibus, ad apicem dilatatis, nigris; pedibus robustis, nigris.

Long. corp. $2\frac{1}{4}$ lin., lat. $1\frac{1}{2}$ lin.

Ovate, broad, globose, subdepressed, impubescent, of a fulvous colour, shining. *Head* short, depressed (almost vertical), not produced in front; between the insertion of the antennæ are two minute carinations extending obliquely upwards to the inner surface of the eyes, rendered more prominent by a medial longitudinal fovea between them, and above them by a transverse fovea (which form together the character of the letter T); the eyes are large, and in form globose, lateral, situated at the base of the head; the surface is impunctate and glabrous, in colour black (the base of the antennæ, the labrum, and the maxillary palpi being suffused with rufo-fuscous). *Thorax* much broader than the head, transverse, in front emarginate; the sides are depressed, slightly constricted in front and marginate; the anterior angles are much depressed; the surface is impunctate, glabrous, black. *Scutellum* triangular, impunctate, and in colour rufo-fuscous. *Elytra* broader than the thorax, globose, subdepressed, with very fine punctures arranged in the form of striæ; of a fulvous colour. *Antennæ* robust, short, dilated at the apex, and black. *Legs* robust, and black.

Taken by Mr. Bates at Ega, in the district of the Amazon. In the collections of Messrs. Baly, Bates, and the Rev. H. Clark.

Genus 41. CYRTON*.

PALPI MAXILLARES *robusti, incrassati, art. penultimo dilatato.*
PALPI LABIALES *subcylindrici.*
ANTENNÆ *robustæ, breves,* subd*ilatatæ.*
OCULI *laterales, magni, ovales.*
CAPUT *haud antice productum, depressum.*
THORAX *late transversus, lævis, impubescens.*
ELYTRA *robusta, brevia, subrotundata, depressa, striato-punctata (punctis ad apicem penitus obsoletis), glabra.*
PEDES *sat robusti, femoribus tibiisque posticis leviter productis, femoribus apicem elytrorum attingentibus; tibiis posticis rectis, longitudinaliter marginatis, inarmatis.*

Labrum short, subrotundate, not medially subsinuate.

Maxillary palpi (Tab. IX. fig. 5 *m*) robust, incrassated; the first joint minute and quadrate; the second elongate and apically subdilated; the third as long as, and twice the breadth of the second, globose; the apical joint is broad and much depressed.

Labial palpi (Tab. IX. fig. 5 *n*) more attenuate than the maxillary, and subcylindrical, the second and third joints being nearly equal in length.

Antennæ robust, short, with a tendency to dilatation; approximate, situated between (not below) the eyes; the basal joint is shorter relatively than in the preceding genus, *Sparnus*, but more elongate than the second joint; the second is short and ovate; the third is attenuate, and of equal length with the first; the fourth is hardly longer than the second; the rest of the joints are robust and subequal in length.

* κυρτός, gibbus.

Eyes lateral, situated at the base of the head, large; in form globose and oval.

Head transverse, depressed at right angles to the plane of the elytra, short, hardly produced in front; between the eyes the surface is generally foveolate; the surface is smooth, glabrous, and impubescent.

Thorax considerably broader than the head, broadly transverse, in front slightly emarginate; the anterior angles are considerably depressed and rounded; the sides are marginate; the basal line is arcuate, that is, almost parallel to the anterior margin; the surface is equate, smooth, impunctate, and impubescent.

Scutellum large, triangular, impunctate, situated in the same plane as the elytra.

Elytra robust, *subcircular*, distinctly broader than the thorax, short, and depressed; throughout the surface are arranged rows of spots in the form of striæ; these spots are more obsolete as they approach the apex; the surface is smooth, equate, and glabrous.

Legs: the *anterior femora* tolerably robust, constricted towards the base, cylindrical. The *tibiæ* are short, constricted at their immediate base, and slightly thickened towards the apex. The *tarsi* are *short*; the first and second joints are transverse and triangular (the second being somewhat more minute than the first); the third joint is broader, and in form subcircular and slightly bilobed; the apical claw is bifid, at the base robust, and at its inner surface subsinuate, but unarmed by any inferior tooth. The *posterior femora* (when viewed transversely) are very broadly incrassated, in form ovate, and more broadly globose (less constricted) laterally than in the preceding genera; the apex extends *nearly to the apex of the elytra*. The *tibiæ* (Tab. IX. fig. 5 *g*) are robust, with a tendency to being incurved throughout their whole length; when viewed from behind, the posterior surface is longitudinally flattened and grooved, especially towards the apex, where it forms itself into a distinct socket for the insertion of the tarsus; the margination of this groove is straight, hardly subsinuate, produced at the upper part of the socket into a broad angle; the extreme apex (immediately below the insertion of the tarsus) is terminated by two robust and incurved spurs. The *tarsus* is short and attenuate, the third joint being shorter, and not broader, than the first and second joints; the globular inflation of the terminal joint conceals completely from above the apical claw.

This genus is remarkable for, and may be easily distinguished by, its *broadly ovate and depressed form*: its glabrous surface at once separates it from *Imatium*; it is less parallel, broader, and more ovate than the genus *Lithonoma*; while from both (as well as from the genus *Sparnus*) it may also be separated by the more elongated form of the posterior femora and tibiæ.

1. Cyrton anisotomoides. (Tab. IX. fig. 5.)

C. *rotundatum, depressum, rufo-flavum, impubescens; capite brevi, impunctato, flavo; thorace late transverso, punctato; elytris latis, subcircularibus, depressis, punctato-striatis; antennis incrassatis: pedibus, femoribus posticis subelongatis; flavis, femoribus posticis rufo-flavis.*

Long. corp. 2 lin., lat. 1¼ lin.

Rotundate, almost circular, depressed, rufo-flavous, impubescent, shining. *Head* short, not produced in front; the eyes are large and prominent; above the mouth is a transverse triangular depression; between the eyes and above the insertion of the antennæ is a cruciform fovea; the surface is obsoletely punctate, and in colour flavous. *Thorax* transverse, much broader than the head, rectangular; the anterior angles are depressed, the sides are marginate; the surface is equate, obsoletely punctate, glabrous, and in colour flavous. *Scutellum* large, triangular, impunctate. *Elytra* broader than the thorax, subcircular, depressed, punctate-striate, shining. *Antennæ* short, robust, incrassated towards the apex (from the fifth to the tenth joints); in colour, the first and second joints are flavous, the rest are black. *Legs*: the anterior slender; the posterior tolerably robust and elongated, the femora reaching as far as the apex of the elytra, and the tibiæ being tolerably long and *incurved*; the colour is flavous, the posterior femora and inflation of the hinder claw being rufo-flavous.

From the district of the River Amazon.

2. Cyrton sanguineum.

C. *ovatum, latum, subsphæricum, punctatum, glabrum, sanguineum; capite brevi, inter oculos transverse depresso, et ad medium longitudinaliter foveolato, impunctato; thorace lato, antice subemarginato, lateribus marginatis et sinuatis, ad latera longitudinaliter depresso; elytris latis, globosis, subtiliter striato-punctatis; antennis incrassatis, art. 6to longo, et quam 5to aut 7mo fere duplo major, art. 1mo–6to flavis, 7mo–10mo fuscis, 11mo flavo; pedibus anterioribus fulvo-flavis, femoribus posticis dilatatis, ad apicem in dente biproductis, rufis.*

Long. corp. 2 lin., lat. 1½ lin.

Ovate, broad, subspherical, punctate, glabrous, of a somewhat flavo-sanguineous colour throughout. *Head* small and short, transverse, *slightly* elongated in front; below the base of the antennæ are two oblique carinations extending downwards to the margins of the labrum; at the *sides* of the base of the antennæ are two broad and shallow depressions extending to the inner margins of the eyes, while immediately above the base is a medial longitudinal fovea, short and abrupt, which terminates in a broad and obliquely margined depression extending to the upper and inner margin of the eyes; thus the character of the letter T or of Y is formed (very distinct from the *cruciform* depression of *C. anisotomoides*): the eyes are large and globose, lateral, situated *near* to the base of the head; the surface (when viewed under a high power) is very finely punctate; the colour of the apex is flavous. *Thorax broad*, much broader than the head, transverse, narrow; the anterior margin is distinctly emarginate (more so than in *C. anisotomoides*); the anterior angles are obtuse and depressed; the sides are finely and evenly marginate, their outline being subsinuate, and in front subconstricted; parallel to, and at a short distance from the margination is a broad and distinct longitudinal depression; the surface throughout is impunctate and glabrous. *Scutellum* large, triangular, impunctate. *Elytra* considerably broader than the thorax, globose, and (when viewed under a high power) very minutely striate-punctate: in *C. anisotomoides* distinct striæ may be traced, and the punctures are considerably broader and deeper. *Antennæ* short, robust, clavate; the first joint long, attenuated at the base and incrassated at the apex; the second short and globular; the third longer than the first, attenuated at the base; the fourth and fifth broad, and almost as short as the second; the sixth *equal in length to the fourth and fifth united*; the rest short and dilated, the eleventh or terminal joint being attenuated at the apex: in colour, the joints one to six are flavous, seven to ten dark fuscous, and the eleventh flavous. *Legs*: the anterior flavous, suffused, especially on the upper margin, with rufous: the posterior femora are broadly dilated; at the apex, immediately below the insertion of the tibiæ, are two tooth-like spurs; in colour rufous.

This species is abundantly distinct from *C. anisotomoides*, not only in the distinct colouring (bright rufous (slightly flavous) instead of testaceous or testaceo-rufous), but in the form of the markings of the head, in its thoracic *longitudinal* marginal depression, and in the total absence of any striation on the elytra.

Taken by Mr. Bates in the neighbourhood of Ega, in the district of the River Amazon.

Genus 42. **LITHONOMA** *.

Rosenhauer (Thier. Andal. p. 335).
Chevrolat (Orbign. Dict. Univers. d'Hist. Nat.).
Foudras, Hist. Nat. des Altiçides (1860).
Allard, Annales de la Soc. Entom. de France, série 3. vol. viii. (1860) p. 44.

LABRUM *subsinuatum.*

PALPI MAXILLARES *elongati et robusti, art.* 3^{tio} *dilatato.*

PALPI LABIALES *attenuati, minuti.*

ANTENNÆ *robustæ, filiformes, art.* 3^{tio} *tenui.*

CAPUT *latum, subproductum, subverticale.*

THORAX *transversus, antice emarginatus, crebre et valde punctatus.*

ELYTRA *lata, robusta, subparallela, aliquando obsolete carinata, crebre et valde punctata.*

PEDES : *tibiis posticis ad marginationem calcaratis, robustis.*

Labrum transversely subcircular, broad.

Maxillary palpi (Tab. IX. fig. 7 m) elongate and robust; the basal joint minute; the second dilated at the apex; the third attenuate at the base and incrassated; the apical joint is attenuate and acuminate.

Labial palpi attenuate, elongate.

Antennæ approximate, situated below the lower margin of the eyes, robust, filiform; the third joint being more attenuate than any of the others, and, with the exception of the basal joint, longer than the others.

Eyes lateral, situated at the base of the head, in form circular and subglobose.

Head broad, almost vertical, subproduced in front; above the labrum is a transverse depressed plane; the base of the head is more or less coarsely granulated.

Thorax broadly transverse; the anterior margin is distinctly emarginate; the anterior angles are depressed and acute; the sides are marginate, and in outline rounded; the basal line is arcuate, that is, parallel to the anterior margin; the surface at the sides is broadly and evenly depressed, equate, and more or less coarsely punctured.

Scutellum triangular, impunctate, situated in the same plane as that of the elytra.

Elytra broad, robust, depressed, *sub*parallel, their greatest breadth being postmedial; the surface is equate, or, in one species (*L. Africana*), obsoletely and longitudinally bicarinated from the shoulders to

---

* λίθος, lapis ; νομή, cultus.

the apex; the surface is covered throughout (like the thorax) with deep and coarse thickly arranged punctures.

Legs sufficiently robust. The *anterior femora* subcylindrical, and attenuate near the apex; the surface being, like the elytra, coarsely punctate. The *tibiæ* are short, incurved at the immediate base, and slightly thickened towards the apex, which is armed at its extremity, below the insertion of the tarsus, with two minute spurs. The *tarsus* is short and robust; the basal joint is triangular, of the same breadth as the apex of the tibiæ; the second is *minute* and subcircular; the third is transversely oval and deeply bilobed; the apical claw is bifid, and armed at its inner surface with a minute, broad basal tooth. The *posterior femora* are short, and very broadly dilated. The *tibiæ* (Tab. IX. fig. 7 *g*) are short, incurved at their immediate base, and almost straight; when viewed from behind, the posterior surface is longitudinally grooved; the margination of this groove is in outline sinuate, or obsoletely toothed, and produced in front of the insertion of the tarsus into a distinct spur; the apex of the tibiæ is armed, below the insertion of the tarsus, with two robust incurved spurs; the tarsi are short and attenuate.

The genus *Lithonoma* is interesting as containing the only two species of the whole of this group which are to be found in Europe; it has a facies peculiarly its own: by its subparallel and depressed form it is evidently a connecting link between the preceding genera and the genus *Œdionychis*; it is distinguished at once by its parallel form, by the rounded sides of its transverse thorax, by the absence of striæ or stria-like punctures of its elytra, and by the excavated or (when viewed from behind) calcarate margination of the posterior tibiæ.

1. Lithonoma Africana. (Tab. IX. fig. 7.)

L. *ovata, subparallela, depressa, punctata, cyanea; capite brevi, granulato; thorace lato, transverso, lævigato, punctato, undique flavo-marginato; elytris latis, depressis, ad apicem rotundatis, punctatis, obsolete bicarinatis, longitudinaliter etiam vitta flava (post medium in marginationem deflexa) notatis, marginatione quoque flava; pedibus antennisque nigris.*

Long. corp. 2¾ lin., lat. 1⅔ lin.

Ovate, subparallel, depressed, thickly punctate, of a dark cyaneous colour. *Head* transverse, depressed, and slightly produced; the eyes are small, lateral, situated at the base of the head; the surface is irregularly granulated, more coarsely near the base of the antennæ. *Thorax* broad, transverse, broader than the head, in front distinctly but not deeply emarginate; the anterior angles are subdepressed; the sides slightly rounded and broadly marginate; the surface is levigate, and thickly and coarsely punctate; in front and at the base is a margin of fulvous colour, which extends nearly to the lateral angles; the margination also is broadly fulvous. *Scutellum* triangular, impunctate. *Elytra* broad, depressed, subparallel (the greatest breadth being postmedial), rounded at the apex; covered throughout with deep and closely arranged punctures: from the humeral angles extend longitudinally two slightly elevated but distinct ridges, becoming obsolete as they approach the apex; from the humeral angles also proceeds (in a line which inclines rather more towards the suture) a broad flavo-fulvous marking, which terminates abruptly before it reaches the apex by being deflected at an oblique angle to the margination; the margination itself also is broadly flavo-fulvous (more broadly at the apex). *Antennæ* robust, filiform, short, black. *Legs* robust, black.

This species appears to differ from its congeners, L. cincta and L. Andalusiaca, not only in the very distinct pattern of coloration, but also structurally. In none of the examples of either of these species before me can I detect a trace of any longitudinal carinations on the elytra.

Tangiers. In the collections of M. Chevrolat and the Rev. H. Clark.

2. Lithonoma cincta, *Fab.* (Tab. IX. fig. 8.)

Galleruca cincta, *Fab. Syst. Ent.* (1775), pars 2. p. 26. no. 62.
Chrysomela cincta, *Fab. Spec. Insect.* (1781), i. 132. 90.
  Fab. Mantissa (1787), i. 70. 119.
Altica cincta, *Oliv. Encycl. Méth.* (1789), iv. 106. no. 12.
Galeruca marginella, *Fab. Syst. Eleut.* (1801), i. 496. no. 90.
Haltica marginella, *Illiger, Mag.* (1807), vi. 55.
—— marginella, *Oliv. Ent.* (1808), vi. 688. 34. tab. 2. fig. 34.
Lithonoma marginella, *Foudras, Hist. des Altisides* (1860), 226.
  Allard, Ann. Soc. Ent. France (1860), p. 44.

L. ovata, lata, subdepressa, subparallela, punctata, nigro-cyanea, nitida; capite longitudinaliter foveolato, punctato; thorace transverso, lato, emarginato, punctato, antice et ad basin fulvo-notato, etiamque fulvo-marginato; elytris latis, depressis, subparallelis, ad apicem rotundatis, punctatis, maculis quatuor fulvo-flavis, ad marginemque flavis; antennis filiformibus, robustis, nigris; pedibus nigro-cyaneis, tarsis fusco suffusis.

Long. corp. 2½ lin., lat. 1⅓ lin.

Ovate, broad, subdepressed, subparallel, punctate, of a dark blue colour throughout, glabrous. *Head* short, transverse, slightly produced: at the base of the antennæ is a medial longitudinal groove extending upwards nearly to the base of the head; on either side of this is a short irregular depression, which form together with the medial fovea two slight longitudinal ridges: the eyes are small, situated at the base of the head; the surface of the head is coarsely and thickly punctate. *Thorax* broad, transverse; the anterior margin is slightly emarginate; the sides are rounded in outline, and distinctly marginate; the anterior angles are slightly depressed; the surface is smooth, levigate, and thickly punctate; at the anterior and posterior margins is a transverse flavous marking, which does not reach the lateral angles; the margination also of the sides is flavous. *Scutellum* triangular, impunctate. *Elytra* slightly broader than the thorax, subparallel, depressed, covered throughout with distinct and regularly distributed punctures; near to the suture are two irregularly shaped flavo-fulvous markings (the one, antemedial, being slightly the smaller of the two, and longitudinal or oblique in its direction; the other, postmedial, being somewhat larger, and circular or obliquely transverse); the margination also of the elytra is distinctly flavo-fulvous. *Antennæ* filiform, robust, short, the length of each of the joints from the fourth to the apex being hardly greater than its breadth; the colour is black. *Legs* robust, of a dark cyaneous colour throughout, the tarsi being somewhat suffused with fuscous.

With regard to the synonymy of this species there appears to have been considerable confusion. The insect itself is certainly well known as not infrequent in Portugal and Spain; and as certainly the *name* of the insect is well known, being established by unquestioned authorities as "*Lithonoma marginella*" of Fabricius and Illiger. The Stettin, Schaum's, and Marseul's Catalogues, as well as Dejean's, each give it under the name imposed by Fabricius; Marseul (as also Foudras, in his 'History of Halticidæ') appends to the name (*as a synonym*) "v. *cincta*, Oliv." And the fact that "*cincta*" of Olivier *belongs to this species* is also unquestionable; for the insect represented by this name is described accurately enough by Olivier in his 'Encyclopédie' (vol. iv. p. 106, species 12), "Altise bordée. Altica cincta, *Fab*. *Chrysomela saltatoria, nigra, elytris viridi-æneis, margine punctisque duobus albis.* Fab. Sp. Insect. i. 132. 90. *Elle se trouve en Portugal**."

The species is also most clearly defined by Fabricius in his 'Mantissa Insectorum' (1787), tom. i. p. 76:—

* I subjoin the detailed description from the 'Encyclopédie':—
"Altica cincta, *Fab*. Cette *Altise* est une des plus grandes. Sa tête est noire. Le corcelet est d'une couleur de bronze, un peu obscure, avec le bord antérieur et postérieur blanc. Les étuis sont d'un verd cuivreux; ils ont deux points et leurs bords blancs. Le corps est très-noir. Les cuisses postérieures sont très renflées. Elle se trouve en Portugal."

"**cincta,** 119. C. [Chrysomela] *saltatoria, nigra, elytris viridi-æneis, margine punctisque duobus albis.*"

The descriptions given by both these authors are not only accurate, but are quite inapplicable to any other species that we know of; by one of them the *locality* also is correctly given. And the works in which these descriptions were published, dating (Fab. Spec. Insec.) A.D. 1781, 1787, and 1789, have incontestably the priority to the sixth volume of Olivier's 'Entomologie,' which appeared in 1808, and to Fabricius's 'System. Eleut.,' which was published A.D. 1801.

One source, probably, of the confusion may be traced to an apparent mistake by Schönherr, in his 'Synon. Insect.' (1806 and subsequent years), who, although Fabricius speaks of his *Galeruca cincta* distinctly as "saltatoria," leaves this species in the genus proper of *Galeruca* (!) (*marginella* being transferred to Illiger's group of Halticas).

Another cause appears to be the fact that Olivier (as it seems) described the same insect twice under two different names,—as "*cincta*" in the 'Encycl. Méthod.' (following the proper Fabrician nomenclature), and also as "*marginella*" in his 'Entomologie.' This latter name, adopted also by Fabricius (System. Eleut., 1801), henceforth adopted by Illiger and subsequent writers,—the prior name "*cincta*" having been either lost sight of, or sunk as a synonym.

In seeking to form an opinion as to which of the two names has the greater claim, we have probably little difficulty in arriving at the following conclusions:—

1. That "*cincta*" (see above, extracts from the Encyclopédie, iv. p. 106; and from Fab. Mantissa Insec. i. 76) and "*marginella*" (see descriptions of insect under this name by Allard and others) have been both adopted with reference to the *same* insect.

2. That "*cincta*" has, in point of time, distinctly the priority, being published in 1781 and 1787,—"*marginella*" appearing for the first time in the 'Systema Eleut.' of Fabricius, published in 1801.

3. That since the publication of Illiger's work (1807) the name "*marginella*" has been universally adopted, and the name *cincta* universally ignored, or merely referred to (as by Marseul and Foudras) as a synonym.

The simple question then arises, Which has the greater claim? the universal consent of recent authors and catalogues, or the clear priority in point of time?

To such an inquiry, "universal consent" will clearly reply, that (the description of the species being sufficient and unmistakeable) *that* name that has the distinct priority in point of time ought to stand. "Quieta ne movere" doubtless is an excellent rule; but "order, nature's first law," suggests one that is still more excellent. Reluctantly, though without any doubt, we arrive at the conclusion that the present name of this species ought to give way to that of "*cincta*, Fab."

This insect appears to be frequently met with in Spain and Portugal. "Vigo" is given by M. Allard as a locality where it is not uncommon. I captured specimens at Barquero, a little village on the northern coast of Spain, when visiting that district with Mr. Gray in his yacht the 'Miranda,' on May 1, 1856.

3. Lithonoma Andalusiaca.

Rambur, in Dej. Cat. (1837).
Rosenhauer, Thiere Andalusiens (1856), p. 333, tab. 3. fig. e.
Foudras, Hist. N. des Altisides (1860), p. 228.
Allard, Ann. Soc. Ent. France (1860), viii. p. 45.

L. ovata, lata, depressa, subparallela, punctata, nigro-cyanea; capite granulato; thorace transverso, lævigato, ad latera, et margines ant. et post. fulvo-lineato; elytris latis, subparallelis, ad apicem rotundatis, fulvo-lineatis, fulvoque marginatis; antennis robustis, filiformibus, nigris; pedibus robustis, nigro-cyaneis.

Long. corp. $2\frac{4}{5}$ lin., lat. $1\frac{1}{2}$ lin.

Ovate, broad, depressed, subparallel, thickly punctate, dark cyaneous, shining. *Head* short, transverse, hardly produced, roughly granulated, more distinctly in front and less apparently at the base; above the base of the antennæ there is a total absence of any longitudinal depressions, which are apparent in *L. cincta*: the eyes are small, lateral, situated at the base of the head. *Thorax* broadly transverse, in front distinctly but not deeply emarginate; the anterior angles are subacute and slightly prominent; the sides are rounded and broadly emarginate; the surface is depressed, levigate, thickly and deeply punctate; at the anterior and posterior margins is a flavous line (not medial, as in *L. cincta*, but continued, although very finely, to the lateral angles); the margination also is broadly fulvous. *Scutellum* triangular, impunctate. *Elytra* broad, subparallel, depressed, slightly broader than the thorax, rounded at the apex, covered throughout with broad, deep and closely arranged punctures; a tolerably broad longitudinal fulvous band, commencing at the humeral angles, is terminated abruptly at a short distance from the apex; between this line and the margination are two very faint and minute longitudinal thread-like fulvous markings; the margination also is fulvous, more broadly and distinctly as it approaches the apex. *Antennæ* robust, filiform, black throughout. *Legs* robust, of a dark cyaneous colour.

L. Andalusiaca may be separated at once from *L. cincta*, not only by its somewhat larger size, and the different coloration of the elytra, but also by the absence of any frontal depressions.

This beautiful species is not uncommon at Malaga, and generally throughout Andalusia. Tangiers (*M. Allard*).

APPENDIX.

Page 10.—Add, after *Monoplatus apicatus*,

6 A. **Monoplatus Fryii.**

M. *oblongo-ovalis, robustus, subdepressus, niger, nitidus; capite brevi, subproducto, ad apicem transverse depresso, æquato, impunctato, nigro, inter oculos (juxta basin) fulvo bimaculato: thorace transverso, rectangulari, antice subtiliter emarginato, lateribus valde marginatis, antice depressis; æquato, ad basin transverse foveolato, impunctato, glabro: elytris latis, parallelis, ad apicem rotundatis, punctato-striatis, rufo-fuscis vel cervinis; ad basin macula undique subcirculari, ad medium fascia tenui, et ipso apice (late et omnino) nigris; antennis filiformibus, nigris; pedibus nigris.*

♀ Long. corp. 3 lin., lat. 1½ lin.

Oblong-ovate, subparallel; of the same form as the other species of *Monoplatus*. The *head* is very slightly produced in front; below the base of the antennæ is an obliquely transverse depression; the surface between the eyes is levigate, unmarked by any fovea; the colour is black, with two small circular fulvous markings at the upper and inner margins of the eyes; the eyes are large, in form globose, and situated laterally, at the base of the head. *Thorax* transverse; the anterior angles are distinct, and project laterally beyond the head; the anterior margin is subemarginate; the sides are straight, parallel, and broadly marginate; the surface is equate, impunctate, and glabrous; at the base, parallel to the basal line, is a transverse thread-like fovea, which is deflected to the line of the base before it reaches the lateral margins. *Scutellum* large, triangular, levigate. *Elytra* broader than the thorax, parallel, robust, distinctly punctate-striate, rounded at the apex; of a dark fawn-colour: at the base, on either elytron, is a broad, irregularly circular patch of black, which approaches closely to, but does not touch, the lateral margination or the suture; medially is a narrow transverse fascia of the same colour, which is broken at the suture by the distance of one stria, and extends in a slight bend to the commencement of the margination; the apex also is broadly and entirely black, the boundary-line being transverse and almost medial. *Antennæ* filiform, black. *Legs* black throughout.

I believe this to be quite a distinct species, and (although perhaps subject to some variation as to the coloration of the elytra) not a variety of any of the species of *Monoplatus* which I have had the opportunity of examining. It is connected by its peculiar fawn-colour with *M. bimaculatus*, and by the character of its markings with *M. apicatus*; its proper place would seem to be between those two species.

It may be readily recognized by its peculiar colour, together with the transverse black band (not circular spot, like *M. bimaculatus*) on the elytra.

Taken by Mr. Fry near Rio Janeiro.

Page 14.—11. Monoplatus quatuor-notatus.

Var. A. *Elytris ad apicem et basin haud maculatis, sed integriter et transverse, nigris.*

Var. B. *Elytris ad apicem et basin late nigris, vitta transversa ad medium elytrorum fusco suffusa.*

I have, from the collection of Mr. Fry, two varieties of this species, taken by him at Petropolis, Organ Mountains. In the one the apex of the elytra is entirely and continuously (though narrowly) black,— the marking at the base being also more continuous, though interrupted by a suffused fuscous coloration at the suture. In the other variety the black markings at the apex and base are produced, till they almost meet in the centre.

We may expect, from this inconstancy of the markings on the elytra, that a variety of this species may be met with with the elytra entirely black, or entirely black with the exception of the line of margination; such a variety would at first sight approach very closely to *Monoplatus distinguendus*, but might always be separated from it by the less distinct and *less broadly depressed* lines of striation on the elytra.

The sculpturing and the form of the examples before me do not vary at all from those of the specimens captured in the same locality in 1847 by Mr. Gray and myself.

Page 22.—Add, after *Monoplatus impunctatus*,

19. Monoplatus ephippium.

M. *oblongo-ovalis, parallelus, subdepressus, punctato-striatus, rufo-flavus, glaber; capite brevi, haud antice producto, impunctato, inter oculos longitudinaliter subtiliter foveolato, rufo-testaceo; thorace transverso (subquadrato), impunctato, ad basin transverse foveolato; elytris parallelis, punctato-striatis, ad basin nigris, ad apicem (quoad medium) rufo-flavis, ante medium maculis duabus magnis irregulariter circularibus rufo-flavis; antennis pedibusque flavis.*

Long. corp. 3 lin., lat. 1½ lin.

This beautiful species in form closely resembles the rest of its congeners; in pattern of colour (rufo-flavous and black) it bears a striking resemblance to *Physimerus ephippium*. The *head* is very obsoletely impressed between the eyes with a medial longitudinal fovea; the surface is impunctate. The *thorax* is transverse, almost quadrate; the sides are broadly marginate, and in outline somewhat *sinuate*; at the base is a transverse thread-like fovea, which is terminated by being inflected into the line of the base before it reaches the lateral margins; the surface is impunctate and glabrous; the colour is flavous, with an irregular suffused medial marking of fuscous. *Scutellum* large, triangular, impunctate, rufo-flavous. *Elytra* broad, robust, depressed, punctate-striate (less distinctly near the apex); the anterior part of the surface is black, the posterior rufo-flavous, the line of division being transverse in direction, and postmedial; a large flavous maculation, irregular in outline, occupies nearly the whole of the anterior and black portion of the surface (being separated from the suture and also from the margination by the breadth of a single stria); the surface also near the scutellum is *suffused* with rufous. *Antennæ* flavo-rufous. *Legs* flavo-rufous, faintly suffused with fuscous.

M. ephippium is a very distinct and beautiful species: it differs entirely from all other species that I have seen; the black antemedial portion of the elytra, which contains within it, on either elytron, a large irregular maculation of fulvous, abundantly separates it.

Page 52.—Add, after *Rhinotmetus canescens*,

19 A. Rhinotmetus neglectus.

R. *oblongo-ovalis, robustus, flavo-fuscus, flavo-pubescens; capite producto, longitudinaliter distincte canaliculato; thorace quadrato, antice valde constricto, ad basin transverse late depresso;*

elytris punctato-striatis, rufo-fuscis, flavo-pubescentibus, vittis duabus fusco suffusis, ad marginem et inter strias 3 *et* 5, *haud apicem attingentibus; antennis flavo-fuscis; pedibus flavis.*

Long. corp. 2½–2¾ lin., lat. 1 lin.

Oblong-ovate, somewhat more robust than the allied species; subparallel, clothed throughout with a fine flavous pubescence, in colour flavo-fuscous. *Head* broadly produced in front, the extreme apex being abruptly contracted; a well-defined carination extends medially from the base of the antennæ to the labrum; above the antennæ are two medial oblong tubercles, which are separated one from the other by a distinct fovea: the eyes are large and subglobose, in form oval, lateral; the base of the head is punctate, being clothed near the margins of the eyes with obsolete flavous pubescence; in colour the surface is in front pale flavous (the extreme apex being black), the base is rufo-flavous. *Thorax* not so elongate as in most of the species of this group, almost quadrate; the sides are finely but evenly marginate, broadly constricted at the apex, and parallel at the base; the surface is broadly transversely depressed at the base, and clothed throughout, but most distinctly at the base, with flavous pubescence. *Scutellum* obscure, triangular, clothed throughout with thick fusco-flavous pubescence. *Elytra* sufficiently robust, parallel, punctate-striate; the surface is in colour rufo-fuscous, and clothed for the most part with thick flavous pubescence: between the third and fifth striæ, near the margination (and also more narrowly at the suture), are two longitudinal markings of fuscous colour, caused by the absence of pubescence; these markings do not extend to the apex, and are irregular in outline. *Antennæ* robust, filiform, rufo-fuscous. *Legs* flavous throughout.

R. neglectus may be separated from its congeners by its *quadrate* (hardly elongate) thorax, in the form of which it approaches *R. nigricornis*, as well as in the rufo-flavous colour and thick flavous pubescence of its elytra.

Rio Janeiro. In the cabinet of the Rev. H. Clark.

Page 60.—Tetragonotes hexagona.

Var. A. *Flava, flavo-pubescens; pedibus flavis, tarsis nigris; elytrorum marginibus ad apicem tenuiter nigris.*

A beautiful variety of this species is in Mr. Fry's collection, taken by him in the neighbourhood of Rio Janeiro. It is smaller than the described species, being 2½ lines in length; it is more brightly flavous in colour, and covered throughout with a *very fine* flavous pubescence. The margination of the elytra is near the apex narrowly black; the colour of the legs is flavous, the tarsi only (and extreme apex of the tibiæ) being black.

Page 74.—Add, after *Physimerus virgatus*,

4 A. Physimerus vulgaris. B.M.

P. *oblongo-ovatus, robustus, flavus, flavo-pubescens; capite transverso, brevi, ad basin punctato; thorace transverso, rectangulari, lateribus subtiliter sinuatis, ad basin subdepresso; elytris robustis, punctato-striatis, pubescentibus, flavis, interdum longitudinaliter (inter strias 1 et 4) fusco suffusis; antennis filiformibus, robustis, flavis, ad apicem fuscis; pedibus flavis.*

Long. corp. 2½ lin., lat. 1 lin.

Oblong-ovate, robust, subcylindrical, of a flavous colour throughout, and clothed throughout with a fine pale-flavous pubescence. *Head* transverse, not produced in front; above the labrum are two obliquely transverse carinations; the eyes are large, circular, and lateral, situated at the base of the head; the surface between the eyes is finely punctate. *Thorax* transverse, rectangular; the anterior angles are much depressed; the sides are finely marginate and subsinuate; the surface (when viewed obliquely) is somewhat depressed at the base, and thus exhibits an obsolete medial transverse ridge. *Scutellum* situated in the same plane as the thorax, triangular, impunctate. *Elytra* sufficiently robust, subcylindrical, rounded at the apex; the surface is punctate-striate, the punctures being more or less concealed by pubescence: there is in some examples a manifest tendency to a darker coloration between the first and the fourth striæ; in some examples this longitudinal band is distinctly though suffusedly apparent (vanishing as it approaches the apex); in other examples it is entirely wanting. *Antennæ* robust, filiform; in colour flavous, the five apical joints being suffused with fuscous. *Legs* flavous or rufo-flavous throughout.

This species is closely allied to *P. virgatus* and also to *P. labialis*: from the former it differs in its concolorous thorax and elytra; from the latter it differs in the sculpture of its head and the form of its elytra, which are more robust and less attenuated at the apex. From both species it differs also by its larger size.

From the neighbourhood of Rio Janeiro. In the collection of the British Museum, and the cabinets of Mr. Fry and the Rev. H. Clark.

Page 81.—Add, after *Physimerus trivialis*,

14 A. Physimerus rusticus.

P. *oblongo-ovatus, latus, sat robustus, brevis, flavus et flavo-pubescens; capite brevi,* Y*-foveolato, ad basin punctato; thorace transverso, lateribus subsinuatis; elytris depressis, latis, ante medium transverse depressis, flavis, juxta scutellum macula suffusa triangulari communi, et ad medium macula circulari minuta fuscis; antennis filiformibus (ad apicem subdilatatis), rufo-flavis, art. 7 et 8 fusco suffusis; pedibus flavis.*

Long. corp. $1\frac{1}{3}$ lin., lat. $\frac{3}{4}$ lin.

Oblong-ovate, broad, sufficiently robust, short, of a flavous colour, and clothed throughout with a fine flavous pubescence. *Head* transverse, hardly produced in front; above the labrum is an oblique (nearly transverse) carination; above the base of the antennæ is a short longitudinal channel, which is terminated by another, transversely oblique, extending between the inner margins of the eyes, the two together forming the character of the letter Y; the surface at the base is finely punctate; the eyes are sufficiently globose, circular, lateral, and situated at the base of the head. *Thorax* transverse; the anterior angles are depressed; the sides are marginate and *sub*-sinuate; near the basal line is a well-defined transverse depression, which gives a slightly gibbous form to the antemedial disk. *Scutellum* small, triangular, of a fuscous colour. *Elytra* broad, robust, and depressed; when viewed laterally, a shallow antemedial transverse depression gives an appearance of prominence to the surface near the scutellary angles; the colour is flavous, a suffused triangular marking, common to both elytra, near the scutellum, and a minute circular medial spot between the sixth and the eighth striæ being fuscous. *Antennæ* filiform, long, with a tendency to dilatation towards the apex; in colour rufo-flavous, the seventh and eighth joints being suffused with fuscous. *Legs* flavous, the posterior tibiæ being suffused with rufous.

P. rusticus is a very distinct species; it is broad, and antemedially transversely depressed; its fuscous markings on the elytra also readily distinguish it.

A single specimen was taken by Mr. Fry, in the neighbourhood of Rio Janeiro.

Page 93.—Add, after *Physimerus griseostriatus*,

28. Physimerus Allardi.

P. *oblongo-ovatus, subdepressus, impubescens, glaber, rufo-ferrugineus; capite brevi, ad basin sparsim punctato; thorace transverso, impunctato, ad basin transverse foveolato, ferrugineo, ad latera et ad medium longitudinaliter fusco; elytris latis, punctato-striatis, ad medium transverse et juxta humeros longitudinaliter fusconotatis, marginatione etiam et sutura antemediis fuscis; antennis filiformibus, flavis; pedibus flavis, femoribus posticis ferrugineo suffusis.*

Long. corp. 1½ lin., lat. ¾ lin.

Oblong-ovate, sufficiently robust, depressed, impubescent, glabrous, of a bright rufo-ferrugineous colour. *Head* transverse, considerably depressed, not produced in front; above the labrum is an obsolete triangular depression; the surface of the base is levigate and sparingly punctate; the eyes are large and globose, in form oval. *Thorax* transverse, rectangular; the lateral margins are parallel (slightly subsinuate towards the apex); the surface is smooth and impunctate; parallel to the basal line is a minute transverse thread-like fovea, corresponding in form to the thoracic depression in the genus *Monoplatus*; in colour the thorax is rufo-ferrugineous, being broadly margined at the anterior angles with fuscous, a suffused medial longitudinal band is also fuscous. *Scutellum* triangular, impunctate, fuscous. *Elytra* distinctly broader than the thorax, finely punctate-striate, in colour rufo-ferrugineous; a suffused medial transverse fuscous marking extends from the suture to the margination, and thence upwards to the humeral angles; near the scutellum (between the fourth and sixth striæ) is a short suffused longitudinal marking of fuscous; the suture also is antemedially fuscous. *Antennæ* filiform, in colour flavous. *Legs* flavous, the posterior femora being suffused with ferrugineous.

P. Allardi is separated from its congeners by the form of its thoracic basal fovea; it is also readily distinguished by the broader and depressed form of its elytra, and by the transverse medial and scutellary longitudinal marking.

Taken by Mr. Fry in the neighbourhood of Rio Janeiro.

I name this species after my friend M. Allard of Paris, the excellent monographer of the Halticidæ of Europe.

Page 126.—Add, after *Homotyphus squalidus,*

5 A. Homotyphus cionoides.

H. *ovatus, robustus, latus, inæqualis, tuberculatus; pube nigra et fusca et sparsim rufo-fulva subtiliter vestitus, nigro-fuscus; capite brevi; thorace transverso, bituberculato, ad latera rugoso; scutello* flavo; *elytris latis, punctatis, rugosis, ad basin bituberculatis, nigris, ad latera et apicem fusco-flavis, vittis duabus transversis irregulariter nigris; antennis robustis, filiformibus, ad apicem subdilatatis; pedibus robustis, flavo-fuscis, nigro maculatis.*

Long. corp. 2 lin., lat. 1$\frac{1}{5}$ lin.

Ovate, broad, robust, irregularly and deeply sculptured, clothed throughout with a fine pubescence; in colour fuscous black. *Head* short, slightly produced in front; between the eyes the sculpturing is distinctly different from that of all other species of the group; the surface is transversely depressed, giving prominence to a transverse ridge immediately above the base of the antennæ; the surface is clothed throughout with fine pubescence, which is in colour black,— a medial longitudinal line, and the inner margins of the eyes, being flavous; the eyes are lateral, and situated nearly at the base of the head, in form oval. *Thorax* transverse, rectangular; the sides are marginate and slightly compressed in front; the whole surface is occupied by irregular and well-defined excavations and ridges; near the anterior margin are two contiguous and prominent tubercular elevations—on either side of these, and at the base, the surface is depressed, and yet corrugated with irregular ridges; the surface is clothed throughout with pubescence, rufo-fuscous suffused with fuscous,—the anterior tubercular elevations being more glabrous, and in colour distinctly rufous. *Scutellum* large, distinct, situated in the same plane as the elytra, in form subcordiform, and clothed with a dense pubescence of *pale flavous* colour. *Elytra* broad, short, robust, irregularly sculptured, deeply but sparingly punctate; the surface is, antemedially, slightly and broadly depressed, which gives a degree of prominence to the region near the scutellary angles, and also to two postmedial gibbous elevations; the whole surface is clothed with close and short pubescence, which (when viewed obliquely) is produced occasionally into irregular and rugged tufts of hair; the colour is, near the humeral angles, around the scutellum, and near the suture, black or fuscous black (the apex of the humeral angles itself being rufous); the sides are broadly flavo-fuscous (suffused occasionally with rufous), two irregular transverse markings from the margination towards the suture being fuscous black; the apex itself also is fuscous black. *Antennæ* robust, filiform, the apical joints having a distinct tendency to incrassation; in colour flavous, the seventh and eighth joints being flavo-fuscous. *Legs* robust, flavo-fuscous, the tibiæ being transversely barred with fuscous.

This beautiful species is at once distinguished from its congeners by the remarkably *deep* sculpturing of the thorax and the elytra, by its peculiar coloration and general appearance, which (as suggested by my friend Mr. Wollaston) closely resembles the species of the genus *Cionus*, especially perhaps *C. pulchellus*, and by the remarkable *pale flavous* colouring of the scutellum.

Rio Janeiro.

Page 149.—Genus 24. LOXOPROSOPUS.

For (THORAX) " *lateribus marginatis, et in angulum productis* " read " *lateribus marginatis et subsinuatis.*"

Page 150.

For (Thorax) " the sides are broadly marginate, the margination being generally produced into an angle," *read* " the margination being generally subsinuate."

Page 157.—Peribleptus lævigatus.

A single specimen of this species has been taken by Mr. Fry near Rio Janeiro, the colour of the body of which is, with the exception of the base of the head, entirely black, thus proving, as I had anticipated, that the specimen captured by Mr. Gray at Petropolis, and described at page 157, was in a state of immaturity.

Another example is in Mr. Fry's cabinet, captured by him on the same visit to Rio, which must be considered, I believe, to be a variety of this species: it is in size somewhat smaller, being in length $1\frac{3}{4}$ line, and in breadth $\frac{3}{4}$ of a line; in colour it is rufo-flavous, the apex of the elytra being suffused with fuscous.

Var. A. *Rufo-flavus, elytrorum apice fusco suffuso.*

Page 176.—Atyphus carbonarius.

I am enabled to ascertain the sexual characters of the genus *Atyphus* by an examination of a fine series of this insect brought home by Mr. Fry. The examples from which I drew up my description were all of them females; the males are smaller in size, being in length $2\frac{1}{2}$ lines and in breadth hardly more than 1 line; the head in the male is narrower and relatively smaller; the eyes are somewhat more globose; the thorax is not broadly transverse; the elytra are shorter and much less robust; the basal joints of the anterior tarsi are much broader; and the antennæ are somewhat more elongate and less robust. The examples captured at Rio Janeiro all belong to Var. C.

Page 177.—*After* **Atyphus** comes, *insert* (TAB. VII. fig. 5.)

SPECIES MIHI IGNOTÆ.

1. Œdionychis sericeus.

Perty (*Del. Anim. Artic.* p. 109. tab. 22. fig. 4).

Œ. *testaceo-pallidus; elytris obscuris, maculis sex pallidis.*
Long. 3′″, lat. hum. 1⅓′″.
[Long. corp. (secundum tabulam) 3½ lin.]
Habitat in montibus Prov. Minarum.

Caput fronte, labio superiore palpisque testaceis; mandibulis et vertice nigris. Thorax testaceus, subtilissime pubescens et punctulatus, antrorsum paulum angustatus. Scutellum fuscum. Elytra fusco-brunnescentia, tenuiter holosericea, maculis in quovis tribus pallidis, quarum una scutellaris, sub lente longitudinaliter punctata; subtus sordide testaceus. Mesostethium linea impressa. Antennæ corpore parum breviores, flavicantes, pilosulæ, articulis mediis obscurioribus. Pedes anteriores testacei; tibiis tarsisque fuscis. Pedes postici femoribus pubescentibus, testaceis, apice nigro; tibiis brunnescentibus, tarsorum articulo vesiculoso, brunneo.

2. Œdionychis porculus.

Perty (*Del. Anim.* p. 110. tab. 22. fig. 7).

Œ. *politus; capite, thorace et elytris antice badiis, his postice atris.*
Long. 3¼′″, lat. hum. 1⅓′″ vix.
[Long. corp. (secundum tabulam) 3½ lin.]
Habitat ad flumen Rio Negro dictum.

Caput breve, latiusculum, badium, oculis nigris. Thorax transversus, badius, angulis omnibus subacutis, puncto utrinque ad discum impresso. Scutellum badium, lævigatum. Elytra thorace latiora, polita, antice clare badia, sub lente longitudinaliter punctata, postice aterrima, lævia; subtus flavo-badius, nitidus. Antennæ ad basin valde approximatæ, corporis dimidio parum longiores, flavo-badii. Pedes flavo-badii, articulo tarsorum posticorum ultimo inflato obscuriore.

(Probably a *Pleurochroma*; and if so, nearly allied to *P. balteatum*.)

3. Œdionychis viridis.

Perty (Del. Anim. p. 110. tab. 22. fig. 6).

Œ. *subtus et femoribus posticis flavis, supra pallide viridis; elytris punctato-striatis.*

Long. 2½′′′, lat. hum. 1¼′′′.
[Long. corp. (secundum tabulam) 2 lin.]
Habitat in Brasilia æquatoriali.

Doubtless a *Phylacticus*, and closely allied to *P. olivaceus*. Perty's description of the insect is given in full at page 114.

It is not possible, with any degree of certainty, to refer any of the species described and figured by Olivier in the sixth volume of his 'Entomologie' to this group. The size of the insect is in no case given by him; and the globular inflation of the ultimate joint of the postical tarsus is unnoticed. In the absence, therefore, of type specimens, it would be useless to enumerate here such species as apparently might belong to the genera included in this volume. The same difficulty attaches to the elucidation of the species described by Germar and Fabricius.

CATALOGUS GEOGRAPHICUS

ET

GENERUM DIAGNOSES.

Tribus I. *Palpi maxillares filiformes.*

Genus 1. **Monoplatus** (pag. 2). Statura grandis; oblongus, *parallelus*, læte coloratus, glaber; thorace ad basin semper transverse foveolato; tibiis posticis calcaribus 6 aut 7 apud marginationem armatis, tarsis anterioribus art. basali dilatatis.

		Page
1. nigripes	Organ Mountains	5
2. Presidenciæ	Organ Mountains	6
3. distinguendus	Petropolis	7
4. Grayii	Organ Mountains	8
5. Miersii	Rio Janeiro	9
6. apicatus	Organ Mountains	10
6 A. Fryii	Petropolis	278
7. bimaculatus	Organ Mountains	11
8. croceus	Petropolis	11
9. jucundus	Rio Janeiro	13
10. sex-signatus	Brazil	14
11. quatuor-notatus	Organ Mountains	14, 279
12. semichalybeus	Brazil	15
13. semiviolaceus	Cayenne (?)	17
14. nigricans	Brazil	17
15. nigrimanus	Brazil	18
16. dimidiatipennis	Brazil	19
17. angulatus	Brazil	20
18. impunctatus	Brazil	21
19. ephippium	Rio Janeiro	280

Genus 2. **Roicus** (pag. 22). Statura grandis; subparallelus; thorace ad latera angulato (haud ut in *Monoplato* lateribus rectilinearibus); pedibus *longis*, tibiis distincte *incurvatis*.

| 1. sex-maculatus | Amazon | 24 |

Genus 3. **Euphenges** (pag. 25). Sat latus, robustus; antennis robustis; elytris ante medium valde oblique depressis; tibiis posticis ad apicem bicalcaratis.

                                                                                                   Page

    1. sericeus . . . . . Brazil 27
    2. Lemoeides . . . . Amazon 28

Genus 4. **Physonychis** (pag. 29). Subparallela, sat robusta; antennarum articulis 1mo, 8vo et ultimo dilatatis et productis; in ♂ tibiarum anticarum apicibus valde dilatatis, tibiis posticis rectis, ad marginationem inarmatis.

    1. smaragdina . . . . Senegal 31

Genus 5. **Rhinotmetus** (pag. 33). Elongato-ovalis; thorace elongato, *antice rotundato*; tibiis posticis juxta apicem ad marginationem unicalcaratis.

    1. leptocephalus (*Perty*)   Rio Janeiro 35
    2. marginatus . . . . Organ Mountains 37
    3. cruciatus . . . . . Organ Mountains 38
    4. spectabilis . . . . Organ Mountains 39
    5. crucifer . . . . . Brazil 40
    6. cyaneus . . . . . Organ Mountains 41
    7. assimilis . . . . . Brazil 42
    8. depressus . . . . Organ Mountains 43
    9. Waterhousii . . . Brazil 44
    10. ruficollis . . . . . Brazil 45
    11. cyanipennis . . . . Rio Janeiro 46
    12. sulcicollis . . . . Rio Janeiro 47
    13. elegantulus . . . . Island of St. Paul . . . 47
    14. inornatus . . . . Brazil 48
    15. Deyrollii . . . . . Brazil 49
    16. humilis . . . . . Rio Janeiro 50
    17. pallipes . . . . . Brazil 50
    18. flavidus . . . . . Brazil 51
    19. canescens . . . . Brazil 52
    19 A. neglectus . . . . . Rio Janeiro 280
    20. nigricornis . . . . Organ Mountains 52

Genus 6. **Tetragonotes** (pag. 53). Parallela; thorace elongato, rectangulari, ad latera distincte angulato; tibiis posticis apud marginationem sinuatis.

    1. elegans . . . . . Organ Mountains 55
    2. atra . . . . . . Organ Mountains 56
    3. calceata . . . . . Brazil 57
    4. subanchoralis . . . Venezuela 58
    5. angulicollis . . . . Brazil 59
    6. vittata . . . . . Organ Mountains 59
    7. hexagona . . . . . Brazil 60, 281

Genus 7. **Pachyonychis** (pag. 61). Sat robustus, depressus; thorace lateribus haud angulatis, sed coarctatis ad apicem et ad basin; tibiis posticis ad apicem calcaratis, tarsorum art. 2^{ndo} brevi.

    1. paradoxus . . . . Philadelphia 63

Genus 8. **Eutornus** (pag. 64). Statura et forma penitus ut in genere *Œdionyche*; robustus, latus, brevis; thorace lato; tibiis posticis rectis, inarmatis, brevibus.

                                                                                                       Page

    1. Africanus . . . . Sierra Leone 65

Genus 9. **Phædromus** (pag. 66). Parallelus, subattenuatus, *depressus*; thorace *transverso*, lateribus (ut in genere *Tetragonote*) angulatis; tibijs posticis ad marginationem *sub*sinuatis.

    1. Waterhousii . . . South Carolina 68

Genus 10. **Physimerus** (pag. 69). Sat latus, parallelus; antennis plerumque filiformibus (rarius *sub*incrassatis); thorace angulis anticis distinctis, haud ut in genere *Rhinotmeto* rotundatis, quadrato (rarissime transverso); tibiis posticis ad marginationem rectis, nunquam calcaratis.

    1. impressus . . . . Organ Mountains 71
    2. vittatus . . . . . Rio Janeiro 72
    3. quatuor-lineatus . . Brazil 72
    4. virgatus . . . . . Columbia 73
    4 A. vulgaris . . . . Rio Janeiro 282
    5. labialis . . . . . Mexico 74
    6. ambiguus . . . . Organ Mountains 75
    7. agilis . . . . . . Organ Mountains 76
    8. revisus . . . . . Brazil 77
    9. luteicollis . . . . Rio Janeiro 77
    10. inornatus . . . . Amazon 78
    11. minutus . . . . Amazon 79
    12. obscurus . . . . Brazil 79
    13. fascicularis . . . Organ Mountains 80
    14. trivialis . . . . Brazil 81
    14 A. rusticus . . . . Rio Janeiro 283
    15. juvencus . . . . Amazon 81
    16. ephippium . . . Amazon 83
    17. suboculatus . . . Para 83
    18. adumbratus . . . Amazon 84
    19. brevicollis . . . . Amazon 85
    20. angulo-fasciatus . Amazon 86
    21. bituberculatus . . Amazon 87
    22. bilineatus . . . . Amazon 88
    23. Batesii . . . . . Amazon 89
    24. irroratus . . . . Amazon 89
    25. nebulosus . . . . Rio Janeiro 90
    26. pruinosus . . . . Columbia 91
    27. griseostriatus . . Amazon 92
    28. Allardii . . . . . Rio Janeiro 284

Genus 11. **Glenidion** (pag. 93). Parallelum, elongatum; thorace transverso; pedibus posticis elongatis; tibiis *elongatis*, et rectis, inarmatis, ad apicem calcaratis, tarsorum articulo basali producto.

    1. rubronotatum . . . Brazil 95

Genus 12. **Hypantherus** (pag. 95). Latus, robustus, haud depressus; antennis plus minus incrassatis; thorace transverso; tibiis posticis juxta tarsorum insertionem apud marginationem calcaratis, ad apicem ipsum bicalcaratis.

                                                                  Page
1. concolor . . . . . Amazon 97
2. ambiguus . . . . Amazon 98
3. assimilis . . . . . Rio Janeiro 99
4. Batesii . . . . . Amazon 100
5. Deyrollii . . . . . Island of St. Paul 100
6. rufo-testaceus . . . Brazil 101

Genus 13. **Thrasygœus** (pag. 102). Latus, subdepressus; thorace lato; antennis filiformibus; tibiis posticis rectis, inarmatis.

1. eximius . . . . . Amazon 103
2. exaratus . . . . . Brazil 104
3. obscurus . . . . Brazil 105
4. undatus . . . . . Venezuela 106

Genus 14. **Eupeges** (pag. 107). *Robusta, subparallela*; antennis filiformibus; thorace *lato*, ad latera subrotundato; tibiis posticis simplicibus.

1. præclara . . . . . Amazon 108
2. scabrosa . . . . . Brazil 109
3. nigrifrons . . . . Brazil 109

Genus 15. **Phylacticus** (pag. 110). Sat robustus, parallelus; antennis filiformibus; thorace transverso; elytris subtiliter pubescentibus; tibiis posticis simplicibus, ad apicem ipsum bicalcaratis.

1. modestus . . . . . Amazon 112
2. ustulatus . . . . . Cayenne 113
3. olivaceus . . . . . Amazon 113
4. prasinus . . . . . Para 115
5. pollinosus . . . . Rio Janeiro 115
6. amabilis . . . . . Amazon 116

Genus 16. **Homammatus** (pag. 116). Robustus, latus, brevis; antennis subincrassatis; capite verticali; thorace subquadrato; elytris ante medium distincte transverso-depressis; tibiis posticis ad marginationem subsinuatis, haud calcaratis.

1. turgidus . . . . . Rio Janeiro 118
2. nitidus . . . . . Columbia 119

Genus 17. **Homotyphus** (pag. 120). Latus, subpubescens, plerumque subtiliter vel distincte tuberculatus; antennis plus minus dilatatis; thorace transverso; elytris ante medium plerumque transverse depressis; tibiis posticis rectis, ad marginationem ecalcaratis, ad apicem ipsum bicalcaratis.

		Page
1. lacunosus	Rio Janeiro	122
2. Vellereus	Minas Geraës	123
3. fuliginosus	Mexico	124
4. asper	S. America	125
5. squalidus	Mexico	126
6. holosericeus	Rio Janeiro	126
7. maculicornis	Mexico	127
8. Wollastonii	Bahia	128

Genus 18. **Ædmon** (pag. 129). Latum, robustum, ad latera rotundatum; antennis subincrassatis, robustis, hirsutis; thorace transverso, ad basin constricto; tibiis posticis ad marginationem unidentatis.

1. sericellum	Porto Rico	131

Genus 19. **Pleurochroma** (pag. 131). Latum, subdepressum, glabrum; antennis *subincrassatis*; thorace transverso; elytris brevibus, robustis; tibiis posticis ad marginationem simplicibus, subsinuatis.

1. balteatum	Amazon	133
2. nitidulum	Amazon	134
3. pallidum	Amazon	134

Genus 20. **Leptotrichus** (pag. 135). Robustus, brevis, subparallelus, sat convexus; palpis maxillaribus *elongatis* et *attenuatis*; antennis *distincte* incrassatis; capite verticali; thorace transverso, convexo; tibiis posticis ad marginationem rectis, ad apicem unicalcaratis.

1. castaneus	Amazon	136

Genus 21. **Panchrestus** (pag. 137). Robustus, brevis, parum convexus; antennis incrassatis (haud ut in genere *Leptotricho*); thorace transverso; lateribus interdum subtiliter angulatis; elytris ante medium transverse subdepressis; tibiis posticis simplicibus, brevibus.

1. pulcher	Amazon	139
2. rubicundus	Amazon	139
3. inconspicuus	Amazon	140
4. rufescens	Amazon	141

Genus 22. **Hylodromus** (pag. 142). Latus, robustus, *depressus*; antennis art. 3–6 incrassatis; thorace transverso, ad basin constricto; elytris depressis, sat latis; tibiis posticis apud marginationem simplicibus, ad apicem dilatatis et unicalcaratis.

1. dilaticornis	Amazon	143

Genus 23. **Cœlocephalus** (pag. 144). Subcylindricus, parallelus; antennis filiformibus, elongatis; capite brevi; thorace quadrato, ad basin constricto; tibiis posticis brevibus, simplicibus, ad apicem unicalcaratis.

                     Page
 1. pulchellus . . . . . Amazon 145
 2. amœnus . . . . . Amazon 146
 3. pygmæus . . . . . Amazon 147
 4. fusco-costatus . . . . Amazon 148

  Tribus II. *Palpi maxillares ad apicem incrassati.*

Genus 24. **Loxoprosopus** (*Guérin-Méneville*) (pag. 149 et 286). Subcylindricus, sat robustus; antennis longissimis, vel quam alia genera longioribus, filiformibus; capite verticali, antice subproducto; thorace transverso, rectangulari; tibiis posticis simplicibus, haud calcaratis.

  1. ceramboides (*Guér.-Mén.*) Rio Janeiro 151
  2. marginatus . . . . . Amazon 152
  3. humeralis . . . . . Amazon 153
  4. cœruleus . . . . . Amazon 154

Genus 25. **Peribleptus** (pag. 155). Latus, robustus, parallelus; antennis filiformibus, sat longis; capite brevi, haud antice producto; thorace transverso, ad latera subtiliter angulato, ad basin constricto; elytris ante medium oblique depressis; tibiis posticis brevibus, ad marginationem simplicibus, ad apicem unicalcaratis.

  1. lævigatus . . . . . Rio Janeiro 157, 286

Genus 26. **Octogonotes**, *Drap.* (pag. 158). Robustus, subparallelus; antennis filiformibus; capite brevi; thorace transverso, ad latera *distincte* angulato; elytris haud ante medium transverse depressis; tibiis posticis simplicibus, ad marginationem subsinuatis.

  1. brunneus . . . . . Amazon 160
  2. thoracicus (*Guér.-Mén.*) Cayenne 161
  3. Banoni (*Drap.*) . . . Cayenne 162
  4. binotatus . . . . . Cayenne 163
  5. sumptuosus . . . . Amazon 164
  6. bicinctus . . . . . Amazon 165

Genus 27. **Apalotrius** (pag. 166). Statura plerumque ut *Octogonote*; antennis filiformibus; thorace transverso, ad latera *rectilineari*; tibiis posticis calcare ad marginationem super tarsorum insertionem armatis.

  1. pubescens . . . . Amazon 168

Genus 28. **Exartematopus** (pag. 169). Latus, convexus, læte coloratus, impubescens; antennis robustis, apicem versus *subincrassatis*; capite verticali; thorace *lato*, rectilineari, angulis anticis *prominentibus*, depresso; elytris quam in genere *Octogonote* breviora, robustiora; tibiis posticis ad marginationem simplicibus, ad apicem distincte bicalcaratis.

		Page
1. nobilis	Espiritu Santo	170
2. scutellaris	Brazil	171

Genus 29. **Hydmosyne** (pag. 172). Subparallela, *depressa*; antennis filiformibus; capite *porrecto*; thorace ad apicem constricto; elytris parallelis; tibiis posticis juxta tarsorum insertionem calcaratis, haud (ut in genere *Atypho*) ad mediam marginationem.

1. inclyta	S. America	174

Genus 30. **Atyphus** (pag. 175). Parallelus, *cylindricus*; antennis filiformibus; thorace transverso, rectilineari; elytris parallelis; tibiis posticis ad mediam marginationem calcaratis.

1. carbonarius	Rio Janeiro	176, 286
2. flaviventris	Brazil	177
3. comes	Rio Janeiro	177, 287
4. furcipes	New Granada	178

Genus 31. **Gethosynus** (pag. 179). *Elongatus*, subcylindricus; antennis filiformibus; thorace transverso, ad latera subsinuato; tibiis posticis ad marginationem calcaratis.

1. sanguinicollis	Espiritu Santo	180

Genus 32. **Allochroma** (pag. 181). Latum, robustum, haud ut in genere *Gethosyno* subangustatum, plerumque ante medium transverse depressum, glabrum, coloratum (aliquando sed rarius pube tenui vestitum); antennis filiformibus, rarius incrassatis; thorace transverso, rectilineari; elytris latis, brevibus, robustis, rarius ante medium transverse depressis, plerumque glabris; tibiis posticis ad marginationem rectis aut sinuatis.

1. humerale	Amazon	183
2. coccineum	Rio Janeiro	184
3. sex-maculatum	Brazil, &c.	185
4. fasciatum	Guiana	186
5. piceum	Brazil	186
6. Balii	S. America (*loco haud citato*)	187
7. lunatum	Amazon	188
8. flavo-vittatum	Amazon	188
9. venustum	Brazil	189
10. nigro-marginatum	Rio Janeiro	190

11.	assimile	Rio Janeiro	191
12.	quatuor-pustulatum	Guatemala	191
13.	festivum	Brazil	192
14.	sex-signatum	Brazil	193
15.	generosum	Columbia	194

Genus 33. **Cerichrestus** (pag. 194). Parallelus, quam in genere *Allochromate* longior, plerumque subtiliter pubescens et punctato-striatus; antennis robustis, filiformibus, aut aliquando subtiliter incrassatis; thorace transverso, ad basin plus minus depresso; clytris parallelis, punctato-striatis, haud ante medium depressis; tibiis posticis simplicibus.

1.	Balii	Brazil	196
2.	apicalis	New Granada	197
3.	Deyrollii	Cayenne	198
4.	Batesii	Amazon	199
5.	tenuicornis	Amazon	200
6.	exiguus	Amazon	201
7.	Chevrolatii	S. America (*loco haud citato*)	202
8.	humilis	Amazon	203
9.	flavicans	Amazon	204
10.	marginicollis	Amazon	204

Genus 34. **Calipeges** (pag. 206). Robustus, subcylindricus (non ut in genere *Cerichresto* elongatus); antennis incrassatis (plus quam in genere *Cerichresto*); elytris latis, ante medium fortiter transverse excavatis; tibiis posticis simplicibus.

1.	crispus	Para	207

Genus 35. **Omototus** (pag. 208). Robustus, brevis, plerumque pubescens; antennis robustis, filiformibus, ad apicem interdum subdilatatis; thorace transverso (rarius subquadrato), ad latera aliquando sinuato; elytris brevibus; tibiis posticis ad marginationem plus minus calcaratis, rarius sinuatis.

1.	morosus	Cayenne	209
2.	quadripes	Cayenne	210
3.	tuberculatus	Bogota	211
4.	braccatus	Brazil	212
5.	nodosus	Amazon	213
6.	Dohrnii	Paramaribo	214
7.	nubilus	Cayenne	215
8.	Cayensis	Cayenne	216
9.	fulvo-pubescens	Paramaribo	217
10.	bituberculatus	Brazil	218
11.	artitus	Cayenne	219
12.	fuscatus	Amazon	220
13.	bimaculatus	Amazon	221
14.	sex-maculatus	Amazon	222
15.	binotatus	Bahia	222
16.	humero-notatus	Brazil	223

		Page
17. sex-notatus	Brazil	224
18. sericeo-pubescens	Columbia	225
19. transverso-notatus	Amazon	225

Genus 36. **Metriotes** (pag. 226). Elongata, subdepressa; palpis maxillaribus art. *secundo* lato et dilatato; antennis filiformibus, attenuatis; thorace transverso, rectangulari; elytris parallelis; tibiis posticis (ut in genere *Monoplato*) calcaribus quinque aut sex armatis.

1. Robinsonii	Rio Janeiro	228

Genus 37. **Poëbates** (pag. 229). Lata, robusta, subcylindrica; antennis brevibus, filiformibus; thorace transverso; elytris latis, brevibus, subcylindricis, haud ante medium transverse depressis; tibiis posticis ad marginationem simplicibus.

1. nigripes	Brazil	230

Genus 38. **Hypolampsis** (pag. 230). Statura brevis; sat lata, aut subglobosa aut parallela; thorace transverso (interdum quadrato); elytris brevibus aut elongatis, plerumque ante medium oblique depressis; tibiis posticis ad marginationem aut simplicibus aut sinuatis, rarissime calcaratis.

1. melanotus	Chili	233
2. Balii	Brazil	234
3. elegantula	Rio Janeiro	234
4. multicostata	Brazil	235
5. inæqualis	Rio Janeiro	236
6. Miersii	Paramaribo	237
7. Dohrnii	Brazil	238
8. albo-guttata	Brazil	238
9. Murraii	Rio Janeiro	239
10. signaticornis	Para	240
11. nana	Rio Janeiro	241
12. pumilio	Rio Janeiro	242
13. ferrugineo-notata	Brazil	242
14. parallela	Brazil	243
15. campestris	Brazil	243
16. fallax	Brazil	244
17. nigrina	Island of St. Paul	245
18. minima	Amazon	245
19. atra	Island of St. Paul	246
20. fragilis	Rio Janeiro	247
21. Lacordairii	Amazon	248
22. costulata	New Granada	249
23. meridionalis	Brazil	249
24. squamata	Brazil	250
25. sylvatica	Brazil	251
26. regia	Amazon	252
27. flavo-notata	St. Catherine	252
28. vicina	Columbia	253

		Page
29. Fryella	Rio Janeiro	254
30. fusca	Rio Janeiro	254
31. anceps	Island of St. Paul	255
32. robusta	Bahia	256
33. æstivalis	Brazil	257
34. pilosa, *Ill.*	Pennsylvania	258
35. porculus	Brazil	258
36. gibba	Rio Janeiro	259
37. suborbicularis	Brazil	260

Genus 39. **Imatium** (pag. 260). Rotundatum, pube dense vestitum; antennis incrassatis; tibiis rectis, simplicibus, haud ad marginationem calcaratis.

1. tomentosum	Brazil	262
2. rotundatum	Brazil	263
3. velutinum	Rio Janeiro	264

Genus 40. **Sparnus** (pag. 265). Rotundatus, suborbicularis, lævigatus; femoribus et tibiis posticis haud elongatis.

1. globosus	Amazon	266

Genus 41. **Cyrton** (pag. 267). Robustum, rotundatum, depressum, glabrum, striato-punctatum; femoribus tibiisque posticis elongatis.

1. anisotomoides	Amazon	269
2. sanguineum	Amazon	260

Genus 42. **Lithonoma** (pag. 271). Lata, subparallela, sat depressa; tibiis posticis calcare armatis.

1. Africana	Tangiers	272
2. cincta, *Fab.*	Spain	273
3. Andalusiaca, *Ramb.*	Spain	276

INDEX.

adumbratus, *Physim.*, 84.
ÆDMON, 129, 293.
æstivalis, *Hypol.*, 257.
Africana, *Lithon.*, 272.
Africanus, *Eutorn.*, 65.
agilis, *Physim.*, 76.
alboguttata, *Hypol.*, 238.
Allardi, *Physim.*, 284.
ALLOCHROMA, 181, 295.
amabilis, *Phyl.*, 116.
ambiguus, *Hypan.*, 98.
ambiguus, *Physim.*, 75.
amœnus, *Cœloceph.*, 146.
anceps, *Hypol.*, 255.
Andalusiaca, *Lithon.*, 276.
angulatus, *Monop.*, 20.
angulicollis, *Tetrag.*, 59.
angulo-fasciatus, *Physim.*, 86.
anisotomoides, *Cyrt.*, 269.
APALOTRIUS, 166, 294.
apicalis, *Cerich.*, 197.
apicatus, *Monop.*, 10.
artitus, *Omot.*, 219.
asper, *Homot.*, 125.
assimile, *Alloch.*, 191.
assimilis, *Hypan.*, 99.
assimilis, *Rhinot.*, 42.
atra, *Hypol.*, 246.
atra, *Tetrag.*, 56.
ATYPHUS, 175, 295.
Balii, *Alloch.*, 187.
Balii, *Cerich.*, 196.
Balii, *Hypol.*, 234.
balteatum, *Pleur.*, 133.
Banoni, *Octog.*, 162.
Batesii, *Cerich.*, 199.
Batesii, *Hypan.*, 100.
Batesii, *Physim.*, 80.
bicinctus, *Octog.*, 165.

bilineatus, *Physim.*, 88.
bimaculatus, *Monop.*, 11.
bimaculatus, *Omot.*, 221.
binotatus, *Octog.*, 163.
binotatus, *Omot.*, 222.
bituberculatus, *Omot.*, 218.
bituberculatus, *Physim.*, 87.
braccatus, *Omot.*, 212.
brevicollis, *Physim.*, 85.
brunneus, *Octog.*, 160.
cæruleus, *Loxop.*, 154.
calceata, *Tetrag.*, 57.
CALIPEGES, 206, 296.
campestris, *Hypol.*, 243.
canescens, *Rhinot.*, 52.
carbonarius, *Atyp.*, 176, 286.
castaneus, *Lept.*, 136.
Cayensis, *Omot.*, 216.
ceramboides, *Loxop.*, 151.
CERICHRESTUS, 194, 296.
Chevrolatii, *Cerich.*, 202.
cincta, *Lithon.*, 273.
cionoides, *Homot.*, 285.
coccineum, *Alloch.*, 184.
CŒLOCEPHALUS, 144, 294.
comes, *Atyp.*, 177, 287.
concolor, *Hypan.*, 97.
costulata, *Hypol.*, 249.
crispus, *Calip.*, 207.
croceus, *Monop.*, 11.
cruciatus, *Rhinot.*, 38.
crucifer, *Rhinot.*, 40.
cyaneus, *Rhinot.*, 41.
cyanipennis, *Rhinot.*, 46.
CYRTON, 267, 298.
depressus, *Rhinot.*, 43.
Deyrollii, *Cerich.*, 198.
Deyrollii, *Hypan.*, 100.
Deyrollii, *Rhinot.*, 49.

dilaticornis, *Hylod.*, 143.
dimidiatipennis, *Monop.*, 19.
distinguendus, *Monop.*, 7.
Dohrnii, *Hypol.*, 238.
Dohrnii, *Omot.*, 214.
elegans, *Tetrag.*, 55.
elegantula, *Hypol.*, 234.
elegantulus, *Rhinot.*, 47.
ephippium, *Monop.*, 280.
ephippium, *Physim.*, 83.
EUPEGES, 107, 292.
EUPHENGES, 25, 290.
EUTORNUS, 64, 291.
exaratus, *Thras.*, 104.
EXARTEMATOPUS, 169, 295.
exiguus, *Cerich.*, 201.
eximius, *Thras.*, 103.
fallax, *Hypol.*, 244.
fasciatum, *Alloch.*, 186.
fascicularis, *Physim.*, 80.
ferrugineo-notata, *Hypol.*, 242.
festivum, *Alloch.*, 192.
flavicans, *Cerich.*, 204.
flavidus, *Rhinot.*, 51.
flaviventris, *Atyp.*, 177.
flavo-notata, *Hypol.*, 252.
flavo-vittatum, *Alloch.*, 188.
fragilis, *Hypol.*, 247.
Fryella, *Hypol.*, 254.
Fryii, *Monop.*, 278.
fuliginosus, *Homot.*, 124.
fulvo-pubescens, *Omot.*, 217.
furcipes, *Atyp.*, 178.
fusca, *Hypol.*, 254.
fuscatus, *Omot.*, 220.
fusco-costatus, *Cœloceph.*, 148.
generosum, *Alloch.*, 194.
GETHOSYNUS, 179, 295.
gibba, *Hypol.*, 259.
GLENIDION, 93, 291.
globosus, *Sparn.*, 266.
Grayii, *Monop.*, 8.
griseostriatus, *Physim.*, 92.
hexagona, *Tetrag.*, 60, 281.
holosericeus, *Homot.*, 126.
HOMAMMATUS, 116, 292.
HOMOTYPHUS, 120, 292.
humerale, *Alloch.*, 183.
humeralis, *Loxop.*, 153.
humero-notatus, *Omot.*, 223.
humilis, *Cerich.*, 203.
humilis, *Rhinot.*, 50.
HYDMOSYNE, 172, 295.
HYLODROMUS, 142, 293.
HYPANTHERUS, 95, 292.
HYPOLAMPSIS, 230, 297.
IMATIUM, 260, 298.

impressus, *Physim.*, 71.
impunctipennis, *Monop.*, 21.
inæqualis, *Hypol.*, 236.
inclyta, *Hydm.*, 174.
inconspicuus, *Panch.*, 140.
inornatus, *Physim.*, 78.
inornatus, *Rhinot.*, 48.
irroratus, *Physim.*, 89.
jucundus, *Monop.*, 13.
juvencus, *Physim.*, 81.
labialis, *Physim.*, 74.
Lacordairii, *Hypol.*, 248.
lacunosus, *Homot.*, 122.
lævigatus, *Perib.*, 157, 286.
Lemoeides, *Euphen.*, 28.
leptocephalus, *Rhinot.*, 35.
LEPTOTRICHUS, 135, 293.
LITHONOMA, 271, 298.
LOXOPROSOPUS, 149, 286, 294.
lunatum, *Alloch.*, 188.
luteicollis, *Physim.*, 77.
maculicornis, *Homot.*, 127.
marginatus, *Loxop.*, 152.
marginatus, *Rhinot.*, 37.
marginella, *Lithon.*, 273.
marginicollis, *Cerich.*, 204.
melanotus, *Hypol.*, 233.
meridionalis, *Hypol.*, 249.
METRIOTES, 226, 297.
Miersii, *Hypol.*, 237.
Miersii, *Monop.*, 9.
minima, *Hypol.*, 245.
minutus, *Physim.*, 79.
modestus, *Phyl.*, 112.
MONOPLATUS, 2, 289.
morosus, *Omot.*, 209.
multicostata, *Hypol.*, 235.
Murraii, *Hypol.*, 239.
nana, *Hypol.*, 241.
nebulosus, *Physim.*, 90.
neglectus, *Rhinot.*, 280.
nigricans, *Monop.*, 17.
nigricornis, *Rhinot.*, 52.
nigrifrons, *Eupeg.*, 109.
nigrimanus, *Monop.*, 18.
nigrina, *Hypol.*, 245.
nigripes, *Monop.*, 5.
nigripes, *Poëb.*, 230.
nigro-marginatum, *Alloch.*, 190.
nitidulum, *Pleur.*, 134.
nitidus, *Homam.*, 119.
nobilis, *Exart.*, 170.
nodosus, *Omot.*, 213.
nubilus, *Omot.*, 215.
obscurus, *Physim.*, 80.
obscurus, *Thras.*, 105.
OCTOGONOTES, 158, 294.

ŒDIPODES, 1.
olivaceus, *Phyl.*, 113.
OMOTOTUS, 208, 296.
PACHYONYCHIS, 61, 290.
pallidum, *Pleur.*, 134.
pallipes, *Rhinot.*, 50.
PANCHRESTUS, 137, 293.
paradoxus, *Pachyon.*, 63.
parallela, *Hypol.*, 243.
PERIBLEPTUS, 155, 294.
PHÆDROMUS, 66, 291.
PHYLACTICUS, 110, 292.
PHYSAPODES, 1.
PHYSIMERUS, 69, 291.
PHYSONYCHIS, 29, 290.
piceum, *Alloch.*, 186.
pilosa, *Hypol.*, 258.
PLEUROCHROMA, 131, 293.
POËBATES, 228, 297.
pollinosus, *Phyl.*, 115.
porculus, *Hypol.*, 258.
porculus, *Œdionychis*, 287.
præclara, *Eupeg.*, 108.
prasinus, *Phyl.*, 115.
Presidenciæ, *Monop.*, 6.
pruinosus, *Physim.*, 91.
pubescens, *Apalot.*, 168.
pulchellus, *Cœloceph.*, 145.
pulcher, *Panch.*, 139.
pumilio, *Hypol.*, 242.
pygmæus, *Cœloceph.*, 147.
quadripes, *Omot.*, 210.
quatuor-lineatus, *Physim.*, 72.
quatuor-notatus, *Monop.*, 14, 279.
quatuor-pustulatum, *Alloch.*, 191.
regia, *Hypol.*, 252.
revisus, *Physim.*, 77.
RHINOTMETUS, 33, 290.
Robinsonii, *Metriot.*, 228.
robusta, *Hypol.*, 256.
ROICUS, 22, 289.
rotundatum, *Imat.*, 263.
rubicundus, *Panch.*, 139.
rubronotatum, *Glen.*, 95.
rufescens, *Panch.*, 141.
ruficollis, *Rhinot.*, 45.
rufo-testaceus, *Hypan.*, 101.
rusticus, *Physim.*, 283.
sanguineum, *Cyrt.*, 269.
sanguinicollis, *Gethos.*, 180.

scabrosa, *Eupeg.*, 109.
scutellaris, *Exart.*, 171.
semichalybeus, *Monop.*, 15.
semiviolaceus, *Monop.*, 17.
sericellum, *Ædm.*, 131.
sericeo-pubescens, *Omot.*, 225.
sericeus, *Euphen.*, 27.
sericeus, *Œdionychis*, 287.
sex-maculatum, *Alloch.*, 185.
sex-maculatus, *Omot.*, 222.
sex-maculatus, *Roicus*, 24.
sex-notatus, *Omot.*, 224.
sex-signatum, *Alloch.*, 193.
sex-signatus, *Monop.*, 14.
signaticornis, *Hypol.*, 240.
smaragdina, *Physon.*, 29.
SPARNUS, 205, 298.
spectabilis, *Rhinot.*, 30.
squalidus, *Homot.*, 126.
squamata, *Hypol.*, 250.
subanchoralis, *Tetrag.*, 58.
suboculatus, *Physim.*, 83.
suborbicularis, *Hypol.*, 260.
sulcicollis, *Rhinot.*, 47.
sumptuosus, *Octog.*, 164.
sylvatica, *Hypol.*, 251.
tenuicornis, *Ccrich.*, 200.
TETRAGONOTES, 53, 290.
thoracicus, *Octog.*, 161.
THRASYGŒUS, 102, 292.
tomentosum, *Imat.*, 262.
transverso-notatus, *Omot.*, 225.
trivialis, *Physim.*, 81.
tuberculatus, *Omot.*, 211.
turgidus, *Homam.*, 118.
undatus, *Thras.*, 106.
ustulatus, *Phyl.*, 113.
Vellereus, *Homot.*, 123.
velutinum, *Imat.*, 264.
venustum, *Alloch.*, 189.
vicina, *Hypol.*, 253.
virgatus, *Physim.*, 73.
viridis, *Œdionychis*, 288.
vittata, *Tetrag.*, 59.
vittatus, *Physim.*, 72.
vulgaris, *Physim.*, 282.
Waterhousii, *Phæd.*, 68.
Waterhousii, *Rhinot.*, 44.
Wollastonii, *Homot.*, 128.

THE END.

EXPLANATION OF FRONTISPIECE.

	Page
Fig. 1. MONOPLATUS GRAYII	8

  m. Maxillary palpus.   *k.* Front view of head.
  n. Labial palpus.

Fig. 2. MONOPLATUS QUATUOR-NOTATUS 14

  b. Anterior femur and tibia.   *m.* Maxillary palpus.
  d. Anterior tarsus.   *n.* Labial palpus.
  e. Anterior claw.

Fig. 3. RHINOTMETUS MARGINATUS 37

  m. Maxillary palpus.   *k.* Front view of head.
  n. Labial palpus.

Fig. 4. RHINOTMETUS CRUCIATUS 38

  f. Posterior femur and tibia.   *m.* Maxillary palpus.
  h. Posterior tarsus.   *n.* Labial palpus.
  i. Posterior claw.

Fig. 5. RHINOTMETUS DEPRESSUS 43

  b. Anterior femur and tibia.   *m.* Maxillary palpus.
  d. Anterior tarsus.   *n.* Labial palpus.
  e. Anterior claw.

Fig. 6. HOMOTYPHUS LACUNOSUS. 122

  m. Maxillary palpus.   *s v.* Side view of body.
  n. Labial palpus.

Fig. 7. POËBATES NIGRIPES 230

  d. Anterior tarsus   *m.* Maxillary palpus.
  f. Posterior femur and tibia.   *n.* Labial palpus.
  h. Posterior tarsus.

Fig. 8. IMATIUM VELUTINUM 264

  d. Anterior tarsus.   *m.* Maxillary palpus.
  f. Posterior femur and tibia.   *n.* Labial palpus.
  h. Posterior tarsus.

EXPLANATION OF PLATE I.

	Page
Fig. 1. MONOPLATUS NIGRIPES	5
f. Posterior femur.	
Fig. 2. MONOPLATUS DISTINGUENDUS	7
h. Posterior tarsus. *i.* Posterior claw.	
Fig. 3. MONOPLATUS BIMACULATUS	11
g. Posterior tibia.	
Fig. 4. MONOPLATUS SEXSIGNATUS	14
Fig. 5. ROICUS SEXMACULATUS	24
d. Anterior tarsus. *i.* Posterior tarsus.	
e. Anterior claw. *m.* Maxillary palpus.	
f. Posterior femur and tibia. *n.* Labial palpus.	
Fig. 6. EUPHENGES SERICEUS	27
Fig. 7. EUPHENGES LEMOEIDES	28
d. Anterior tarsus. *m.* Maxillary palpus.	
g. Posterior tibia. *n.* Labial palpus.	
Fig. 8. PHYSONYCHIS SMARAGDINA	31
a. Antennæ. *m.* Maxillary palpus.	
g. Posterior tibia.	

EXPLANATION OF PLATE II.

	Page
Fig. 1. RHINOTMETUS SPECTABILIS	39
Fig. 2. RHINOTMETUS CYANEUS	41
Fig. 3. TETRAGONOTES ELEGANS	55
m. Maxillary palpus. *n*. Labial palpus.	
Fig. 4. TETRAGONOTES ANGULICOLLIS	59
d. Anterior tarsus. *g*. Posterior tibia.	
Fig. 5. TETRAGONOTES SUBANCHORALIS	58
h. Posterior tarsus.	
Fig. 6. TETRAGONOTES VITTATA	59
Fig. 7. PACHYONYCHIS PARADOXUS	63
a. Antenna. *m*. Maxillary palpus.	
d. Anterior tarsus. *n*. Labial palpus	
f. Posterior femur.	
Fig. 8. EUTORNUS AFRICANUS	65
m. Maxillary palpus. *a*. Antenna.	
n. Labial palpus.	

EXPLANATION OF PLATE III.

	Page
Fig. 1. PHÆDROMUS WATERHOUSII	68
m. Maxillary palpus. *g.* Posterior tibia.	
n. Labial palpus.	
Fig. 2. PHYSIMERUS AMBIGUUS	75
Fig. 3. PHYSIMERUS JUVENCUS	81
m. Maxillary palpus. *n.* Labial palpus.	
Fig. 4. PHYSIMERUS EPHIPPIUM	83
m. Maxillary palpus. *n.* Labial palpus.	
Fig. 5. PHYSIMERUS BILINEATUS	88
Fig. 6. PHYSIMERUS BATESII	89
Fig. 7. PHYSIMERUS IRRORATUS	89
Fig. 8. METRIOTES ROBINSONII	228
m. Maxillary palpus. *f.* Posterior femur and tibia.	
n. Labial palpus.	

EXPLANATION OF PLATE IV.

		Page
Fig. 1. Hypantherus concolor		97

    c. Anterior tibia.   *h.* Posterior tarsus.
    d. Anterior tarsus.   *m.* Maxillary palpus.
    g. Posterior tibia.   *n.* Labial palpus.

Fig. 2. Hypantherus Deyrollii 100

Fig. 3. Thrasygœus eximius 103

    d. Anterior tarsus.   *m.* Maxillary palpus.
    g. Posterior tibia.   *n.* Labial palpus.

Fig. 4. Eupeges præclara 108

    g. Posterior tibia.   *m.* Maxillary palpus.
    h. Posterior tarsus.   *n.* Labial palpus.

Fig. 5. Phylacticus modestus 112

    m. Maxillary palpus.   *d.* Anterior tarsus.
    n. Labial palpus.

Fig. 6. Phylacticus olivaceus 113

    m. Maxillary palpus.   *g.* Posterior tibia.
    n. Labial palpus.

Fig. 7. Homammatus turgidus 118

    c. Anterior tibia.   *m.* Maxillary palpus.
    d. Anterior tarsus.

Fig. 8. Homammatus nitidus 119

    a. Antenna.   *m.* Maxillary palpus.
    g. Posterior tibia.   *n.* Labial palpus.
    h. Posterior tarsus.

EXPLANATION OF PLATE V.

	Page
Fig. 1. HOMOTYPHUS HOLOSERICEUS	126

Fig. 2. ÆDMON SERICELLUM 131
        g. Posterior tibia.   *m.* Maxillary palpus.

Fig. 3. PLEUROCHROMA BALTEATUM 133
        m. Maxillary palpus.   *g.* Posterior tibia.
        n. Labial palpus.

Fig. 4 LEPTOTRICHUS CASTANEUS 136
        m. Maxillary palpus.   *n.* Labial palpus.

Fig. 5. PANCHRESTUS INCONSPICUUS 140
        m. Maxillary palpus.   *n.* Labial palpus.

Fig. 6. PANCHRESTUS RUFESCENS 141

Fig. 7. HYLODROMUS DILATICORNIS 143
        m. Maxillary palpus.   *n.* Labial palpus.

Fig. 8. CŒLOCEPHALUS PYGMÆUS 147
        h. Posterior tarsus.   *m.* Maxillary palpus.

EXPLANATION OF PLATE VI.

	Page
Fig. 1. LOXOPROSOPUS CERAMBOIDES (*Guér.-Mén.*)	151

    m. Maxillary palpus.   *k.* Front view of head.
    n. Labial palpus.

Fig. 2. LOXOPROSOPUS MARGINATUS 152

Fig. 3. PERIBLEPTUS LÆVIGATUS 157

    m. Maxillary palpus.   *n.* Labial palpus.

Fig. 4. CŒLOCEPHALUS PULCHELLUS 145

Fig. 5. OCTOGONOTES BRUNNEUS 160

    m. Maxillary palpus.   *d.* Anterior tarsus.
    n. Labial palpus.

Fig. 6. OCTOGONOTES BANONI (*Drap.*) 162

Fig. 7. OCTOGONOTES BINOTATUS 163

    g. Posterior tibia.

Fig. 8. OCTOGONOTES SUMPTUOSUS 164

EXPLANATION OF PLATE VII.

	Page
Fig. 1. APALOTRIUS PUBESCENS	167

    m. Maxillary palpus.   *g.* Posterior tibia.
    n. Labial palpus.

Fig. 2. EXARTEMATOPUS NOBILIS 170

    m. Maxillary palpus.   *n.* Labial palpus.

Fig. 3. EXARTEMATOPUS SCUTELLARIS 171

Fig. 4. HYDMOSYNE INCLYTA 174

    m. Maxillary palpus.   *o.* Mandibles.
    n. Labial palpus.

Fig. 5. ATYPHUS COMES 177

    m. Maxillary palpus.   *g.* Posterior tibia.
    n. Labial palpus.

Fig. 6. GETHOSYNUS SANGUINICOLLIS 180

    m. Maxillary palpus.   *g.* Posterior tibia.
    n. Labial palpus.

Fig. 7. ALLOCHROMA SEXMACULATUM 185

    m. Maxillary palpus   *n.* Labial palpus.

Fig. 8. ALLOCHROMA FASCIATUM 186

EXPLANATION OF PLATE VIII.

	Page
Fig. 1. ALLOCHROMA LUNATUM	188
Fig. 2. ALLOCHROMA SEX-SIGNATUM	193
Fig. 3. ALLOCHROMA GENEROSUM	194
Fig. 4. CERICHRESTUS BATESII	199

    m. Maxillary palpus.   *g.* Posterior tibia.
    n. Labial palpus.

Fig. 5. CERICHRESTUS FLAVICANS	204
Fig. 6. CERICHRESTUS MARGINICOLLIS	204
Fig. 7. CALIPEGES CRISPUS	207

    a. Antenna.   *m.* Maxillary palpus.

Fig. 8. OMOTOTUS NODOSUS	213

    m. Maxillary palpus.   *h.* Posterior tarsus.
    n. Labial palpus.

EXPLANATION OF PLATE IX.

	Page
Fig. 1. OMOTOTUS SEX-MACULATUS	222
Fig. 2. OMOTOTUS SEX-NOTATUS	224
Fig. 3. HYPOLAMPSIS ALBO-GUTTATA	238

    m. Maxillary palpus.   *n.* Labial palpus.

Fig. 4. SPARNUS GLOBOSUS	266

    m. Maxillary palpus.   *n.* Labial palpus.

Fig. 5. CYRTON ANISOTOMOIDES	269

    m. Maxillary palpus.   *g.* Posterior tibia.
    n. Labial palpus.

Fig. 6. IMATIUM TOMENTOSUM	262

    m. Maxillary palpus.   *n.* Labial palpus.

Fig. 7. LITHONOMA AFRICANA	272

    m. Maxillary palpus.   *g.* Posterior tibia.
    n. Labial palpus.

Fig. 8. LITHONOMA CINCTA, *Fab.*	273

CATALOGUES
OF
THE ZOOLOGICAL COLLECTION
IN
THE BRITISH MUSEUM.

I. VERTEBRATA.

List of Mammalia. By Dr. J. E. GRAY, F.R.S., F.L.S. &c. 1843. 2s. 6d.

Catalogue of the Mammalia. By Dr. J. E. GRAY, F.R.S. &c.
    Part 1. Cetacea. 12mo, 1850. 4s., with Plates.
    Part 2. Seals. 12mo, 1850. 1s. 6d., with Woodcuts.
    Part 3. Hoofed Quadrupeds. Section I. (Ungulata furcipeda). 12mo. 1852, with Plates of Genera, 12s.
This work contains the description of the genera and species, and figures of the chief characters of the genera.

List of Mammalia and Birds of Nepaul, presented by B. H. Hodgson, Esq., to the British Museum. By Dr. J. E. GRAY and G. R. GRAY. 12mo. 1846. 2s.

Catalogue of Mammalia and Birds of New Guinea. By Dr. J. E. GRAY, F.R.S., and G. R. GRAY, F.L.S. 8vo. 1858. 1s. 6d. With Figures.

List of Genera and Subgenera of Birds. By G. R. GRAY, F.L.S. 12mo, 1855. 4s.

List of Birds. By G. R. GRAY, F.L.S., F.Z.S. &c.
    Part 1. Raptorial. Edition 1, 1844; edition 2, 1848. 3s.
    Part 2. Passeres. Section I. Fissirostres. 1848. 2s.
    Part 3. Gallinæ, Grallæ and Anseres. 1844. 2s. (Out of print.)
    Part 3. Section I. Ramphastidæ. 1855. 6d.
    Part 4. Columbæ. 1856. 1s. 9d.

List of British Birds. By G. R. GRAY, F.L.S. &c. 12mo. 1850. 4s.

List of the Eggs of British Birds. By G. R. GRAY, F.L.S. &c. 12mo. 1852. 2s. 6d.

Catalogue of Shield Reptiles. By Dr. J. E. GRAY, F.R.S. &c.
    Part 1. Testudinata. 4to. 1855. £1 : 10s. With figures of all the new species, and of the skulls of the different genera.

Catalogue of Reptiles. By Dr. J. E. GRAY, F.R.S., V.P.Z.S. &c.
    Part 1. Tortoises, Crocodiles and Amphisbænians. 1844. 1s.
    Part 2. Lizards. 1845. 3s. 6d.
    Part 3. Snakes (Crotalidæ, Viperidæ, Hydridæ and Boidæ). 12mo. 1849. 2s. 6d.

Catalogue of Colubrine Snakes, and Appendix to Part 1. By Dr. ALBERT GUNTHER. 12mo. 1858. 4s.

Catalogue of Amphibia. By Dr. J. E. GRAY, F.R.S., V.P.Z.S. Part 2. Batrachia Gradientia. 12mo, 1850. 2s. 6d. With Plates of the Skulls and Teeth.

Catalogue of Amphibia. By Dr. A. GUNTHER. Part 2. Batrachia Gradientia. 8vo. 1858. 6s. With Plates.

Catalogue of Fish. By Dr. J. E. GRAY, F.R.S.,F.L.S.,V.P.Z.S. Part 1. Cartilaginous Fish. 12mo, 1851. 3s. With two Plates.

These Catalogues of *Reptiles*, *Amphibia*, and *Fish*, contain the characters of all the genera and species at present known; the latter are illustrated with figures of the genera.

Catalogue of Fish, collected and described by L. T. GRONOW. 12mo. 1854. 3s. 6d.

Catalogue of Lophobranchiate Fish. By Dr. J. J. KAUP. 12mo. 1856. 2s. With Plates.

Catalogue of Fish. By Dr. J. J. KAUP. 8vo. With many Plates. Part 1. Apodes, &c. 1856. 10s.

List of British Fish; with Synonyma. By A. WHITE, F.L.S. &c. 12mo. 1851. 3s.

List of Osteological Specimens. By Dr. J. E. GRAY, F.R.S. &c. and G. R. GRAY, F.L.S. 12mo. 1847. 2s.

II. ANNULOSA.

Catalogue of Lepidoptera. By G. R. GRAY, F.L.S., F.Z.S. Part 1. Papilionidæ, with coloured figures of the new species. 4to. 1852. £1 : 5s.

List of Lepidopterous Insects.
Part 1. Papilionidæ, &c. 12mo. 2nd edit. 1856. By G. R. GRAY, F.L.S.
Part 2. Erycinidæ, &c. 12mo. 1847. 9d. By E. DOUBLEDAY, F.L.S.
Part 3. Appendix to Papilionidæ, Erycinidæ, &c. 1848. 9d.

List of Lepidopterous Insects, with descriptions of new species. By FRANCIS WALKER, F.L.S.

Part 1. Lepidoptera Heterocera. 12mo. 1854. 4s.
Part 2. 1854. 4s. 6d.
Part 3. 1855. 3s.
Part 4. 1855. 3s.
Part 5. 1855. 4s.
Part 6. 1855. 3s. 6d.
Part 7. 1856. 4s. 6d.
Part 8. 1856. 3s. 6d.
Part 9. 1856. 4s.
Part 10. 1857. 3s. 6d.
Part 11. 1857. 3s. 6d.
Part 12. 1857. 3s. 6d.
Part 13. 1858. 3s. 6d.
Part 14. 1858. 4s. 6d.
Part 15. 1858. 4s. 6d.

List of British Lepidoptera; with Synonyma. By J. F. STE-
PHENS, F.L.S., and H. T. STAINTON, M.E.S.
    Part 1. 12mo. Ed. 2. 1856. 2s.   Part 3. 1853. 9d.
    Part 2. 1852. 2s.   Part 4. 1854. 3s.

List of Hymenopterous Insects. By F. WALKER, F.L.S.
    Part 1. Chalcididæ. 12mo. 1846. 1s. 6d.
    Part 2. Additions to Chalcididæ. 1848. 2s.

Catalogue of Hymenopterous Insects. By F. SMITH, M.E.S.
    Part 1. Andrenidæ, &c. 12mo. 1853. 6s., with Plates.
    Part 2. Apidæ. 1854. 6s., with Plates.
    Part 3. Mutillidæ and Pompilidæ. 1855. 6s., with Plates.
    Part 4. Crabronidæ, &c. 1856. 6s., with Plates.
    Part 5. Vespidæ. 1857. 6s., with Plates.
    Part 6. Formicidæ. 1858. 6s., with Plates.

Catalogue of British Hymenoptera. By F. SMITH, M.E.S.
    Part 1. Apidæ. 12mo. 1855. 6s.

Catalogue of British Formicidæ, Sphegidæ, and Vespidæ. By F. SMITH, V.P.E.S.

Catalogue of British Ichneumonidæ. By THOMAS DESVIGNES, M.E.S. 12mo. 1856. 1s. 9d.

List of British Aculeate Hymenoptera; with Synonyma, and the description of some new species. By F. SMITH. 1851. 2s.

Catalogue of Dipterous Insects. By F. WALKER, F.L.S.
    Part 1. 12mo. 1848.   Part 4. 1849. 6s.
        3s. 6d.   Part 5. Supplement I. 1854. 4s. 6d.
    Part 2. 1849. 3s. 6d.   Part 6. Supplement II. 1854. 3s.
    Part 3. 1849. 3s.   Part 7. Supplement III. 1855. 3s. 6d.

Catalogue of Homopterous Insects. By F. WALKER, F.L.S. With Plates.
    Part 1. 12mo. 1850. 3s. 6d.   Part 4. 1852. 4s.
    Part 2. 1850. 5s.   Supplement. 1858. 4s.,
    Part 3. 1851. 3s. 6d.   with Plates.

Catalogue of Neuropterous Insects. By F. WALKER, F.L.S.
    Part 1. 12mo. 1852. 2s. 6d.   Part 3. 1853. 1s. 6d.
    Part 2. 1853. 3s. 6d.   Part 4. 1853. 1s.

Catalogue of Neuropterous Insects. By Dr. HAGEN.
    Part 1. Termitina. 12mo. 1858. 6d.

Catalogue of Hispidæ. By J. S. BALY, M.E.S. 8vo. 1858. 6s. With Plates.

Catalogue of Hemipterous Insects. By W. S. DALLAS, F.L.S. &c. With Plates, Part 1. 12mo. 1851. 7s.   Part 2. 1852. 4s.

    The Catalogues of *Hymenopterous, Dipterous, Homopterous* and *Hemipterous* Insects contain the description of the species in the Museum which appeared to be undescribed.

Catalogue of British Bruchidæ, Curculionidæ, &c. By JOHN WALTON, F.L.S. 12mo. 1856.

Catalogue of Cassididæ. By Professor BOHEMAN. 12mo. 1856. 3s.

Catalogue of Coleopterous Insects of Madeira. By T. V. WOLLASTON, F.L.S. 8vo. 1857. 3s.

Nomenclature of Coleopterous Insects (with characters of new species).
    Part 1. Cetoniadæ. 12mo. 1847. 1s. By A. WHITE, F.L.S.
    Part 2. Hydrocanthari. 1847. 1s. 3d. By A. WHITE, F.L.S.
    Part 3. Buprestidæ. 1848. 1s. By A. WHITE, F.L.S.
    Part 4. Cleridæ. 1849. 1s. 8d. By A. WHITE, F.L.S.
    Part 5. Cucujidæ. 1851. 6d. By F. SMITH, M.E.S.
    Part 6. Passalidæ. 1852. 8d. By F. SMITH, M.E.S.
    Part 7. Longicornia. By A. WHITE, F.L.S. With Plates.
        Part 1. 1853. 2s. 6d. Part 2. 1855. 3s. 6d.
    Part 8. Cassididæ. By A. WHITE. 1856. 3s.

List of Myriapoda. By G. NEWPORT, F.R.S. &c. 12mo. 1844. 4d.

Catalogue of Myriapoda. By G. NEWPORT, F.R.S. &c.
    Part 1. Chilopoda. 12mo. 1856. 1s. 9d.

List of British Anoplura, or Parasitic Insects; with Synonyma. By H. DENNY. 12mo. 1s.

List of Crustacea; with Synonyma. By A. WHITE. 1847. 2s.

List of British Crustacea; with Synonyma. By A. WHITE, F.L.S. 12mo. 1850. 2s. 6d.

Catalogue of Entozoa; with Plates. By W. BAIRD, M.D., F.L.S. 12mo. 1853. 2s.

Catalogue of British Worms. By G. JOHNSTON, M.D. 8vo. With Plates.

III. MOLLUSCA.

Guide to the Collection of Mollusca. By Dr. J. E. GRAY, F.R.S. &c. 8vo. Part 1. 1856. 5s.

Catalogue of the Mollusca. By Dr. J. E. GRAY, F.R.S. &c.
    Part 1. Cephalopoda Antepedia. 12mo. 1849. 4s.
    Part 2. Pteropoda. 1850. 1s.

Catalogue of Bivalve Mollusca. By Dr. J. E. GRAY, F.R.S. &c.
    Part 1. Placuniadæ and Anomiadæ. 12mo. 1850. 4d.
    Part 2. Brachiopoda Ancylopoda. 1853. 3s. Figures of genera.

Containing the characters of the recent and fossil genera, and the descriptions of all the recent species at present known.

Catalogue of Phaneropneumona or Operculated Terrestrial Mollusca. By Dr. LOUIS PFEIFFER and Dr. J. E. GRAY. 1852. 5s.

Catalogue of Conchifera. By M. DESHAYES.
    Part 1. Veneridæ, &c. 12mo. 1853. 3s.
    Part 2. Petricolidæ. 6d.

List of British Mollusca and Shells; with Synonyma. By Dr. J. E. GRAY, F.R.S.
Part 1. Acephala and Brachiopoda. 12mo. 1851. 3s. 6d.

Catalogue of Pulmonata. By Dr. LOUIS PFEIFFER and Dr. J. E. GRAY, F.R.S.
Part 1. 12mo. 1855. 2s. 6d.

Catalogue of Auriculidæ, &c. By Dr. J. E. GRAY, F.R.S. 12mo. 1857. 1s. 9d.

List of the Shells of the Canaries, described by M. D'ORBIGNY. 12mo. 1854. 1s.

List of the Shells of Cuba, described by M. D'ORBIGNY. 12mo. 1854. 1s.

List of the Shells of South America, described by M. D'ORBIGNY. 12mo. 1854. 2s.

List of the Mollusca and Shells collected and described by MM. EYDOUX and SOULEYET. 12mo. 1855. 8d.

Catalogue of the Collection of Mazatlan Shells. By P. P. CARPENTER. 12mo. 1857. 8s.

List of Mollusca. By Dr. J. E. GRAY, F.R.S.
Part 1. Volutidæ. 12mo. 1858. 6d.

Nomenclature of Mollusca. By Dr. W. BAIRD, F.L.S. &c.
Part 1. Cyclophoridæ. 12mo. 1851. 1s. 6d.

IV. RADIATA.

Catalogue of Marine Polyzoa. By G. BUSK, F.R.S.
Part 1. Chilostoma. 12mo. 1852. 17s. With Plates.
Part 2. Chilostoma. 12mo. 1854. 15s. With Plates.

List of British Radiata; with Synonyma. By Dr. J. E. GRAY, F.R.S. 12mo. 1848. 4s.

List of British Sponges; with Synonyma. By Dr. J. E. GRAY, F.R.S. 12mo. 1848. 10d.

Catalogue of the Recent Echinida. By Dr. J. E. GRAY, F.R.S.
Part 1. Echinida irregularia. 12mo. 3s. 6d., with Plates.

V. BRITISH ZOOLOGY.

List of the British Animals; with Synonyma and references to figures.
Part 1. Radiata. By Dr. J. E. GRAY. 1848. 4s.
Part 2. Sponges. By Dr. J. E. GRAY. 1848. 10d.
Part 3. Birds. By G. R. GRAY. 1850. 4s.
Part 4. Crustacea. By A. WHITE. 1850. 2s. 6d.
Part 5. Lepidoptera. By J. F. STEPHENS. 1850. Ed. 2, 1856. 1s. 9d.

Part 6. Hymenoptera. By F. SMITH. 1851. 2s.
Part 7. Mollusca Acephala and Brachiopoda. By Dr. J. E. GRAY. 1851. 3s. 6d.
Part 8. Fish. By A. WHITE. 1851. 3s.
Part 9. Eggs of British Birds. By G. R. GRAY. 1852. 2s. 6d.
Part 10. Lepidoptera (continued). By J. F. STEPHENS. 1852. 2s.
Part 11. Anoplura or Parasitic Insects. By H. DENNY. 1s.
Part 12. Lepidoptera (continued). By J. F. STEPHENS. 1852. 9d.
Part 13. Nomenclature of Hymenoptera. By F. SMITH. 1853. 1s. 4d.
Part 14. Nomenclature of Neuroptera. By A. WHITE. 1853. 6d.
Part 15. Nomenclature of Diptera. By A. WHITE. 1853. 1s.
Part 16. Lepidoptera (completed). By H. T. STAINTON, M.E.S. 1854. 3s.

Catalogue of British Hymenoptera (Bees). By F. SMITH. 1855. 6s., with Plates.

Catalogue of British Ichneumonidæ. By THOMAS DESVIGNES, M.E.S. 12mo. 1856. 1s. 9d.

Catalogue of British Bruchidæ, Curculionidæ, &c. By JOHN WALTON, F.L.S. 12mo. 1856.

N.B.—These Catalogues can be obtained at the Secretary's Office in the BRITISH MUSEUM; or through any Bookseller.

VI. BOOKS ILLUSTRATING OR DESCRIBING PARTS OF THE ZOOLOGICAL COLLECTIONS.

The Illustrated Natural History. By the Rev. J. G. WOOD, M.A., F.L.S. &c. New edition. 12mo. 1855.

Illustrations of Indian Zoology, from the Collection of Major-General Thomas Hardwicke. By Dr. J. E. GRAY, F.R.S. Folio. 2 vols. 1830–1835.

Zoology of the Voyage of H.M.S. Beagle. Edited by CHARLES DARWIN, F.R.S. 4to. 1840–1844.

Zoology of the Voyage of H.M.SS. Erebus and Terror. Edited by Sir JOHN RICHARDSON, M.D., F.R.S. &c., and Dr. J. E. GRAY, F.R.S. 4to. 1844–1845.

British Museum—Historical and Descriptive. 12mo. 1855.

Natural History of the Animal Kingdom. By W. S. DALLAS, F.L.S. &c. Post 8vo. 1855.

Zoological Miscellany. By W. E. LEACH, M.D., F.R.S. 8vo. 3 vols.

Spicilegia Zoologica. By Dr. J. E. GRAY, F.R.S. 4to. 1829–1830.

Zoological Miscellany. By Dr. J. E. GRAY, F.R.S. 8vo. 1831.
Knowsley Menagerie. Part 2. Hoofed Animals. By Dr. J. E. GRAY, F.R.S. Folio. 1850.
A Monograph of the Macropodidæ. By JOHN GOULD, F.R.S. Folio. 1841-1844.
Mammals of Australia. By JOHN GOULD, F.R.S. Folio. 1845.
Popular History of Mammalia. By A. WHITE, F.L.S.
Popular History of Birds. By A. WHITE, F.L.S.
Genera of Birds. By G. R. GRAY, F.L.S. Illustrated by plates by D. W. MITCHELL, Sec. Z.S. Folio. 3 vols. 1844-1849.
The Birds of Jamaica. By P. H. GOSSE, F.R.S. 8vo. 1847.
Illustrations of the Birds of Jamaica. By P. H. GOSSE, F.R.S. 8vo. 1849.
Monograph of Ramphastidæ. By JOHN GOULD, F.R.S. Folio.
Birds of Australia. By JOHN GOULD, F.R.S. Folio. 1848.
Report on the Ichthyology of the Seas of China and Japan. By Sir JOHN RICHARDSON, M.D., F.R.S. 8vo. 1846.
Fauna Boreali-Americana. The Fish. By Sir JOHN RICHARDSON, M.D., F.R.S. &c. 4to. 1836. With Plates.
Synopsis Reptilium. Part 1. Cataphracta. By Dr. J. E. GRAY, F.R.S. 8vo. 1831.
Illustrations of British Entomology. By JAMES F. STEPHENS, F.L.S. 10 vols. 8vo. 1827-1835.
A Systematic Catalogue of British Insects. By J. F. STEPHENS, F.L.S. 8vo. 1829.
The Nomenclature of British Insects. By J. F. STEPHENS, F.L.S. 8vo. 1829 & 1833.
A Manual of British Coleoptera. By J. F. STEPHENS, F.L.S. 12mo. 1839.
Insecta Britannica. Diptera. By F. WALKER, F.L.S. 8vo. 1851-1856.
Monographia Chalciditum. By F. WALKER, F.L.S. 8vo. 1839.
Entomology of Australia. Part 1. Phasmidæ. By G. R. GRAY, F.L.S. 4to.
Synopsis of species of Phasmidæ. By G. R. Gray, F.L.S. 8vo. 1835.
Genera of Diurnal Lepidoptera. By EDWARD DOUBLEDAY, F.L.S., and J. O. WESTWOOD, F.L.S. Illustrated by W. C. Hewitson. 4to. 2 vols. 1846-1850.
Monographia Anoplurorum Britanniæ, or British species of Parasitic Insects. By HENRY DENNY, F.L.S. 8vo. With Plates.

Fauna Boreali-Americana. The Insects. By W. KIRBY, F.R.S. 4to. 1837. With Coloured Plates.

Insecta Maderensia. By T. VERNON WOLLASTON, M.A., F.L.S. 4to. 1854. With Plates.

Malacostraca Podophthalmia Britanniæ. By W. E. LEACH, M.D., F.R.S. 4to. 1817–1821.

A Monograph of the Subclass Cirripedia. By CHARLES DARWIN, F.R.S. 8vo. 2 vols. 1854.

Natural History of the British Entomostraca. By W. BAIRD, M.D., F.L.S. &c. 8vo. 1850.

Figures of Molluscous Animals, for the use of Students. By MARIA EMMA GRAY. 5 vols. 8vo. 1850–1857.

A Synopsis of the Mollusca of Great Britain. By W. E. LEACH, M.D., F.R.S. 8vo. 1852.

Catalogue of the Land Shells of Jamaica. By C. B. ADAMS. 8vo. 1851.

Catalogue of Testaceous Mollusca of the North-east Atlantic and neighbouring Seas. By R. MACANDREW, F.R.S. 8vo. 1850.

Illustrations of the Geology of Yorkshire. By JOHN PHILLIPS, F.R.S. 4to. 1836.

A Monograph of the Crag Mollusca. By SEARLES V. WOOD, F.G.S. 4to. 1850.

A History of British Starfishes. By EDWARD FORBES, F.R.S. 8vo.

A History of the British Zoophytes. By GEORGE JOHNSTON, M.D. 8vo. 1838.—Ed. 2. 8vo. 1847.

A History of British Sponges and Lithophytes. By GEORGE JOHNSTON, M.D. 8vo. 1842.

A Synopsis of the British Diatomaceæ. By W. SMITH, F.L.S. 8vo. 2 vols. 1854–1856. The Plates by T. West.

Proceedings of the Zoological Society. Series 1 and 2.

Transactions of the Entomological Society.

January 1859.

www.ingramcontent.com/pod-product-compliance
Lightning Source LLC
Chambersburg PA
CBHW021151230426
43667CB00006B/343